Living at the Edges of Capitalism

Living at the Edges of Capitalism

ADVENTURES IN EXILE
AND MUTUAL AID

Andrej Grubačić and Denis O'Hearn

UNIVERSITY OF CALIFORNIA PRESS

University of California Press, one of the most distinguished university presses in the United States, enriches lives around the world by advancing scholarship in the humanities, social sciences, and natural sciences. Its activities are supported by the UC Press Foundation and by philanthropic contributions from individuals and institutions. For more information, visit www.ucpress.edu.

University of California Press
Oakland, California

Library of Congress Cataloging-in-Publication Data

Names: Grubaéciâc, Andrej, author. | O'Hearn, Denis, 1953- author.
Title: Living at the edges of capitalism : adventures in exile and mutual aid / Andrej Grubaéciâc And Denis O'Hearn.
Description: Oakland, California : University of California Press, [2016] | Includes bibliographical references and index.
Identifiers: LCCN 2015036704| ISBN 9780520287297 (cloth : alk. paper) | ISBN 9780520287303 (pbk. : alk. paper) | ISBN 9780520962484 (ebook)
Subjects: LCSH: Exiles—Social networks—Case studies. | Ejâercito Zapatista de Liberaciâon Nacional (Mexico) | Indians of Mexico—Social networks—Mexico—Chiapas. | Don Cossacks—Social networks—Russia (Federation)—Don River Region. | Prisoners—Social networks. | Capitalism—Moral and ethical aspects—Case studies.
Classification: LCC HM741 .G78 2016 | DDC 305.9/06914097275—dc23
LC record available at http://lccn.loc.gov/2015036704Manufactured in the United States of America

25   24   23   22   21   20   19   18   17   16
10   9   8   7   6   5   4   3   2   1

In keeping with a commitment to support environmentally responsible and sustainable printing practices, UC Press has printed this book on Natures Natural, a fiber that contains 30% post-consumer waste and meets the minimum requirements of ANSI/NISO Z39.48-1992 (R 1997) (*Permanence of Paper*).

For Alice and Staughton Lynd
A life well lived.

CONTENTS

ILLUSTRATIONS

MAPS

FIGURES

PREFACE

The subject of this book is exile. Not in the sense it is usually expressed: as a longing for something lost or a hope to return to what one once had. For us exilic life is not Victor Hugo's "long dream of home," a nostalgic longing to *return* to something, but rather a journey of hope for a future that has not yet been. The instances of hope we have chosen to research for this book are provided by people who left or were banished from places of discontent and sought something better.

Both of us hold an interest in exilic community that comes from our own experiences. We have both lived in places that attempted something akin to exilic community, one of us in a war zone where people had to practice mutual aid in order to exist, the other in a historic experiment in self-management. Both experiments ended, one in a peace process and a return to "normal" electoral politics, the other in a tragic war and split-up of the transethnic political community. Along the way, both of us became exiles in the usual political sense, unable to return to our communities because we were hunted by corrupt state police forces.

Our journey together began around the topic of exile, although one of us did not know it at the time, and neither of us called it that yet. Andrej participated in a study group that was organized by Staughton Lynd and a group of prisoners including Mumia Abu Jamal and Bomani Shakur. Their first readings were *Nothing but an Unfinished Song*, Denis's biography of the Irish hunger striker Bobby Sands, and an interview that Andrej conducted with Denis about Irish exilic experiences.[1] That interview was life-changing. Not only did it bring us together as compañeros and scholars but it revealed something that Denis had not yet put into words: that the Irish movement, while self-identified as socialist and sometimes Marxist, was also anarchist in a critical way. Like many other revolutionaries, Irish guerrillas thought that they were in the process of overthrowing an oppressive state; but they were also practicing prefigurative politics. They were trying to build *today* the community that they wanted to have in the future. When Bobby Sands got out of prison for a few months in 1976, he began to build institutions and practices of mutual aid in his occupied and war-torn community on the outskirts of Belfast. As we will show in chapter 5 of this volume, he and his comrades took that practice and intensified it in the H-Blocks of Long Kesh Prison. They worked hard at building exilic community.

Andrej and Staughton continued that theme in their book *Wobblies and Zapatistas*, which was an attempt to seriously probe the affinities of Marxism and anarchism and to rethink how a movement that we now would think of as exilic could combine the best of those two traditions ... and ditch the worst of them.[2]

By December 2012, when we were invited to speak to a conference in celebration of the 170th anniversary of Peter Kropotkin's birth in his home town of Dmitrov, we were well along the way to developing a shared vision of exilic community based on the great man's principles of *mutual aid*. Visiting Dmitrov, Volgograd, and the Cossack *stanitsa* Ust'-Medveditskaya with our friends Slava Yashchenko and Olga Rvachiova was both a homecoming and a new beginning. Denis had begun his academic career as a student of the Soviet economy, and his earliest publications are about the Soviet *second economy*, a sort of inverted version of this book's subject that one might call "living at the edge of socialism."[3] His self-imposed exile in the war zone of West Belfast was an escape from an oppressive US economics profession and his research on Soviet economic reform in Moscow and Novosibirsk. For his part, Andrej had grown up in a Yugoslavia that was in many ways a mirror-image of the Soviet regime, another "edge" of socialism-as-it-actually-existed.[4]

Visiting with Cossacks in 2012 and seeing how their once-exilic community had been transformed convinced us that they were indeed an appropriate focus for our research questions about exilic life. A major reason for this was our insistence that we could not whitewash the problems of exilic community-building; it was and is important to be realistic about the pressures that states and world-capitalism apply to such communities and the traps into which they can easily fall. In understanding this, we were strongly influenced by Dale Tomich's suggestion to use Albert Hirschman's concepts of exit, voice, and loyalty.[5] We believe this has been one of the most fruitful developments of our work: all exilic communities, it seems, are forced to make loyalty bargains, and such bargains are among the most dangerous moments in exilic community development. As we will show in chapter 3, the Cossacks' loyalty bargain with Muscovy precipitated the disintegration of the exilic space and its transformation largely into a cultural showpiece. But our meetings, conversations, and observations of Cossack life *today* also provided a more hopeful lesson that echoes Kropotkin's observations: one can still observe practices of mutual aid and solidarity even in a community that has been ravaged by centuries of oppression by various states and by the economic pressures of the capitalist world-system.

Inclusion of the Zapatistas in this study was a no-brainer. Both authors spent periods living among them and admired their insistence on practicing principles of mutual aid while eschewing the "attractions" of capitalist consumerism. Both of us feared for the vulnerability of their project. We saw exilic life in action, for example, in the unwaged boot factory, the health clinics, and especially in the *secondaria* in Oventic, where a different education is shown not only to be possible but also to be clearly preferable to the institutionalized schools and universities where we have spent so much of our lives. After observing Zapatista education, Denis returned to his job at Queens University in Belfast, where he was forced to give a "professorial lecture," a horrible tradition of the British university system where the newly ordained Professor appears in robes while the audience listens quietly without even an opportunity to ask questions. It was the opposite of what he had experienced with the *promotores* and *alumni* in Oventic. His professorial lecture was entitled "Why Is the University Such a Bad Place for Learning?" There were no robes. But community activists and ex-prisoners were planted in the audience to interrupt, make comments, and generally democratize the pomp and circumstance. It was a *structural exilic practice* in the heart of capitalist education and one that befitted the exilic tradition of Bobby Sands and his comrades.

Andrej's struggle was decisively influenced by the breakup of Yugoslavia. For him, Yugoslavia was never a country, nor simply a nation-state; it represented an ideal and an approximation of a trans-ethnic, pluricultural space. Yugoslavia was an expression of a much older dream, of Balkan federation, imagined as a stateless, horizontally organized regional association. His grandparents were political prisoners—partisans and communists who spent their lives fighting fascism and ethnic nationalism. The breakup of Yugoslavia into miniature ethnic states was the beginning of his first exile. Now a man without a country, state, or nationality, he discovered Zapatismo, an example of exilic life that would exercise an important influence on his politics thereafter. The most important question he continued to struggle with, in terms of both his politics and his research, was the possibility of *another* politics: inter-ethnic politics of care and mutual aid, free of ethnicity and nation-state. The "insurgent ethnicity" of the Zapatistas, an ethnicity that, paradoxically, refuses to be an ethnicity, provided a glimpse of a solution. Further, Andrej's scholarly interest in anarchist ideas, in particular those of Peter Kropotkin, brought him in touch first with Noam Chomsky and later with Immanuel Wallerstein, both of whom had made it possible for him to emigrate to the United States. In this second exile, Andrej's encounters with Staughton Lynd and Denis O'Hearn provided a new sense of political and inter-ethnic possibility, primarily through their collective encounter with a very different group of exiles: men in supermax prisons.

Both of us have probably learned more from prisoners and ex-prisoners than any other social group. We have known them in and out of prison and on several continents. In 2009, after long discussions in Ohio State Penitentiary, Denis and Bomani Shakur began a course at Binghamton University in which prisoners from supermaxes and SHUs in different states participated along with the students. Everyone read books by "experts" about prison life but this was a course with a difference: the *real* experts were the prisoners. The students corresponded with them, asking questions about the descriptions and theories of prison life presented by Michel Foucault and others. The prisoners, including Todd Ashker and Danny Troxell, housed in the "short corridor" of Pelican Bay's notorious security housing unit (SHU) in California, also read about and learned from experiences of other prisoners around the world. Their remarkable initiatives, which emerged from this time in the form of the birth of the Short Corridor Collective, are discussed in chapter 5. Soon, Andrej initiated a similar course at the California Institute of Integral Studies, and similar courses followed at Youngstown State, Shawnee State, Boğaziçi University in Istanbul, and elsewhere.

One of the most significant outcomes of the US prison movement that emerged during and after 2009 is not just that the prisoners adopted forms of nonviolent resistance, including mass hunger strikes, but that they developed trans-ethnic, pluricultural spaces that transcended the racialized gang divisions that the state has promoted in its prisons since at least the 1960s. Prisoners' insistence that they are not black, white, or Chicano, but comprise a *prisoner class*, has parallels with Yugoslavia . . . and the Don and Chiapas. As will be apparent from chapter 5, the result was partial and sporadic. What more could be expected from people who are locked for decades in 24/7 solitary, in cells the size of a parking space?

Todd Ashker, who wrote many of the remarkable documents that came out of Pelican Bay's Short Corridor Collective, told us that he thought many times about the communities that the Irish prisoners developed in the H-Blocks during the late 1970s. He and his comrades hoped to develop something similar, but it was difficult; they came from very different ethnic and social backgrounds, from different social groups on the streets and in prisons, rather than from a single social movement with members often from the same neighborhoods, as in Northern Ireland. The men of the Short Corridor Collective never quite achieved the intense solidary community and oral culture that the Irish prisoners achieved. But, then, as Ashker says, what the Short Corridor Collective achieved was even *more* remarkable given the disparate origins of its members and the particular hostilities of the SHU environment.

In many ways, therefore, our descriptions of exilic communities in prisons are less complete, less satisfying, and rougher than the other two instances we present: Cossacks and Zapatistas. They are perhaps less intentional, but more profound for that reason. We insisted on including this example in our study precisely because it shows the power of Kropotkin's most essential insight: no matter how much states and capital impose institutions and practices of possessive individualism, no matter how their institutions work toward the separation of individuals from community and from each other, the people themselves will re-create their own institutions and practices of mutual aid. Our highest value is mutuality, sociability, solidarity.

This is what informs our research and our method in this study. As much as possible we sought not to analyze our subjects but to hear their voices.[6] As opposed to research based on possessive individualism, our own approach to scholarship is based on mutual aid in research. Our friendship and intellectual companionship played an important part in this. Our decision to work together was also political. In a university environment that is increasingly based on the struggle for tenure, individual distinction, and competition, we have tried, in the making of this book, to show another way of practicing scholarship: prefigurative in relating to each other and to the exiles with whom we worked. Incorporating mutual aid in research does not imply loss of objectivity. While we sought out instances of mutual aid and community-building, we tried also to be acutely aware of the limitations and dangers inherent in what we have called exilic life. Ironically, this may be easiest to do when we talk about prisons—where exilic community is often least developed and the barriers to its creation are so high—because we have more direct contact with prisoners and ex-prisoners than with Zapatistas or, obviously, Don Cossacks of the sixteenth century. We know prisoners, talk to them, and accompany them. To an extent, we have been able to achieve an important degree of mutual aid in research with exiles in Chiapas, as well, either in our direct contacts and ethnographic observations in Zapatista communities or through great friends like Ramor Ryan, Michael McCaughan, Emma Shaw Crane, Charlotte Saenz, and Father Henry, who have accompanied Zapatistas for many years. It is much more difficult to achieve a research practice based on mutual aid in a historical study like that of the Don Cossacks because we rely so much on secondary sources by historians who so often write history "from above." We hope our short time among them has helped us to gain empathy. But, more importantly, our empathy comes from our commitment to the practice of mutual aid and the project of exilic community. Thus, we hope we have successfully recognized practices of mutual aid even through the haze of mainstream historical accounts.

ONE

Introduction

MATERIAL LIFE AND EXILIC SPACES AND PRACTICES

SINCE THE DEVELOPMENT OF STATES, and even under clan society, groups of people have either escaped or been exiled from their places of living. Some joined other clans or moved into other state jurisdictions, but many established or joined self-governed communities outside of state jurisdiction and regulation. As nation-states and capitalism developed, and particularly as new regions were incorporated into the emerging capitalist world-system beginning in the sixteenth century, the problem was not simply how to escape states but also how to escape capitalist relations and processes of accumulation that were bundled up with state control. But people still did it. Well-known historical examples of escape include Russian Cossacks, pirates, and escaped slaves, or maroons.[1] Contemporary examples of territorial escape include the Zapatistas in Mexico, land occupations, and even political prisoners.[2] Structural escape has been identified in urban communities in the heart of Jamaica, in the shack-dwelling areas of African cities, and on the outskirts of large South American cities.[3] Numerous studies exist on each of these examples of exilic spaces and practices, but no study has brought them together in a single analysis. In this book, we examine exilic experiences comparatively, asking what we can learn from them both historically and in contemporary society, and what they can tell us about possible futures.

We build on the recent scholarly attention given to the notion of nonstate spaces, which we chose to call *exilic spaces* because they are populated by communities that attempt escape from both state regulation (the focus of much anarchist analysis) and capitalist accumulation (the focus of Marxism). Exilic spaces can be defined as those areas of social and economic life where people and groups attempt to escape from capitalist economic processes, whether by territorial escape or by the attempt to build structures that are autonomous of capitalist processes of accumulation and social control.

We will address the following questions: How do people leave the spaces, structures, and/or processes of world-capitalism? Whom do they identify as "the enemy"? Do they practice mutual aid and solidarity in communities or organize mainly on a household basis? Are there rules of entry and exit? How are their practices located geographically and structurally with respect to states, the interstate system, and economic structures, including markets, farms, and corporations? How do their decisions and hierarchies about how they will expend human efforts—for example, between leisure, collective joy, subsistence, and accumulation—differ from spaces that are dominated by capital? What kinds of bargains do exiles make and with whom, and how do such bargains affect their ability to sustain political and economic autonomy? And, finally, how are the outcomes of these questions affected by changes in global capitalism, including economic cycles, the rise of new leading sectors and worldwide divisions of labor, and the changing presence and experiences of antisystemic movements?

We follow Fernand Braudel's proposal that capitalist life consists of three parts or "sectors": the market economy; the anti-market, or monopoly capitalism ("where the great predators roam and the law of the jungle operates"); and material life ("that lowest stratum of the non-economy, the soil into which capitalism thrusts its roots but which it can never really penetrate").[4] While the market economy and monopoly capital have been exhaustively researched and analyzed, the lowest (and largest) sector of material life is still undertheorized, especially with respect to groups and societies that attempt to "refuse" capitalism, either completely or in certain parts of their lives. After laying out our conceptual approach for studying and understanding exilic spaces and practices, we will closely examine several historical and contemporary examples of exile that we believe provide some characteristic lessons: Cossacks, Zapatistas, and prisoners in solitary confinement. We end by summarizing what we have learned from these cases and give our assessment of what remains to be done in future research.

BACKGROUND

To analyze the historical development of world-capitalism, we can follow a well-worn path from Marx to Wallerstein, with diversions through Joseph

Schumpeter, Alfred Chandler, Karl Polanyi, and others. Marx is still unsurpassed in his laying out of the processes of accumulation, the hidden abode of labor, class struggle, and the inherent tendencies of crisis and recovery within capitalism. Schumpeter, Chandler, and others explain processes whereby innovations in technology, technique, and organization of capitalism, particularly large corporate capitalism, or monopoly capital, drive outward shifts of productivity and periodic contractions. Finally, approaches to the uneven development of world-capitalism lay out the processes whereby different forms of production and labor are integrated into a singular global division of labor; they seek to identify regularities and variation in how the system changes over time.

Yet these cannot help us much in thinking about cooperation and self-organization from below, either by escape from capitalism or within its interstices. This shouldn't be a surprise. Marx's energy went into his main intellectual project of understanding the organization and development of capitalist commodity production. In *Capital*, the only real attention to cooperation is an examination of cooperative activities as forms and consequences of factory production, where workers "merely form a particular mode of existence of capital."[5] Here, we want to know how people cooperate in the process of providing their material subsistence *but also* such very human necessities as shared communications, collective joy, and the formation of solidarity within communal spaces.

Moving forward in time, contemporary analyses of world-capitalism, from Luxemburg and Lenin to Baran and Sweezy to world-systems analysis, have emphasized an unevenly developed world-economy, including the behavior of giant monopolies in the core of the system as well as zones that are not dominated by proletarian commodity production.[6] While the forms of organizing capital and labor relations in these latter zones are not classically capitalist, they are nonetheless capitalist economies insofar as their predominant ways of producing things and the things that they produce are determined by their relationship to world-capitalism. Yet again, however, these approaches have little to say about how cooperation and self-organization emerge either beside or in the interstices of capitalism.

The political economies of place-based exit, of the spaces where cooperation may occur, are usually regarded as exotic but irrelevant to the workings of capitalism. Nonstate territories are spaces of refuge for bandits, criminals, outcasts, and "villains of all nations," where "the worst of the worst" hide from the law. Therefore, much of the real historical experience of these spaces has been lost, often replaced and even debased by the romantic images of Hollywood. Despite the pioneering work of scholars like Linebaugh, Rediker, and Boeck,[7] few people know much about Cossack or pirate life beyond Yul Brynner, Errol Flynn, or Johnny Depp.

Recovering this "waste of experience" requires what de Sousa Santos calls a *sociology of absences and emergences*. The sociology of absences is research into actually-existing social practices and institutions that have been actively made nonexistent, that is to say, treated as unbelievable alternatives to the status quo. Real historical and contemporary existences are made absent by labeling them ignorant, backward, inferior, local (or particular), and unproductive. The sociology of emergences consists in constructing a future of concrete, utopian, and realist possibilities. The two sociologies are linked because the recovery of what has been made absent provides the raw materials for possible alternative futures to capitalism. "Whereas the sociology of absences amplifies the present by adding to the existing reality what was subtracted from it . . . the sociology of emergences enlarges the present by adding to the existing reality the possibilities and future expectations it contains."[8]

In the present volume, we journey to swamps, forests, mountains, and deserts; but also into places within capitalism where people practice cooperation, direct democracy, and mutual aid. The latter includes households, shack dwellings, tenant yards, churches, and prisons. The goal of our journey is to understand the political and economic practices and institutions that develop within *exilic spaces*, that is, places where groups of people gather in escape or forced exile from state control and the processes of capitalist accumulation in its various forms.[9] By comparing experiences, we hope to locate patterns and regularities about when and under what conditions escape societies develop characteristics that have recently become a popular theme of social sciences in work on "real utopias" and the science of altruism.[10] We explore the dynamics of communities that engage in such social practices in the face of world-systemic processes that militate against them and active attempts to render them nonexistent. And we inquire into the conditions under which hidden everyday practices of real utopias become a vocal, antisystemic protest against the dominant transcript of capitalist modernity. The modern-day Zapatistas are an excellent illustration of a moment when a hidden transcript of exilic politics and economy shoulders its way onto the public stage of the capitalist world-economy.

Such a place-based sociology of state-breaking and self-organization would avoid some of the more rigidly functionalist interpretations of uneven development or world-systems analysis and, at the same time, give a historical and political-economic framework and structure to recent "anarchist" (anti-state) interventions in social theory. We propose that neoliberal globalization makes the study of these spaces and regions not less relevant, but more so. They are system-evading spaces that are inseparable from the system in the sense that they represent a "dark twin" of the world-system, defined by Wallerstein as an "integrated network of economic, political and cultural processes the sum of which hold the system together."[11] They are the parts of Braudel's "material life" into which capitalism has not been able to sink its roots . . . at least for now.

WHERE WE STAND, WHERE WE PROPOSE TO GO

Previous calls to study spaces and practices of escape have taken two major forms. First, scholars in the Marxist-feminist tradition pointed to the centrality of reproduction and reproductive labor in the constitution of society. They argue that transformation from capitalism requires not a fundamental change in technological innovation but in social relations, whereby the reproduction of our lives is organized as a collective process and no longer subordinated to the valorization of capital.[12]

Second, scholars influenced by Kropotkin's[13] writing on cooperation and voluntary association have recently offered arguments for inventing a new field of study: comparative research of nonstate spaces as geographical expressions of cooperation and concentrated mutual aid that may stand in contradiction to the development of capitalism (or that, in certain cases or to certain degrees, may be subsumed within it). Contemporary scholars such as Scott and Zibechi put forth the possibility of escape zones, or "shatter zones," that either survive capitalist incorporation or develop because of failures of capitalism to meet human needs.[14]

These approaches often assume that nonstate spaces are outside of the capitalist world-system. This produces assumptions (1) that the rules of development of nonstate spaces are independent of world-capitalism and (2) that the actors who populate nonstate spaces are totally outside of capitalism. In our approach, this is at most a hypothesis that requires empirical proof; our working hypothesis (our expectation) is that exilic spaces and actors do interact with world-systemic processes, institutions, and actors and that the interesting research question is how and to what degree this interaction limits their self-activity and how these limits change over time. To return to Braudel's analogy, if utopian groups succeed in fertilizing the soil of material life, they may also attract and nourish the roots of capital and give it reasons and ways to penetrate.

We distinguish between spatial and structural withdrawal. Most of the overt literature on nonstate spaces assumes that they lie geographically outside of capitalism and, for a time at least, live an existence that is largely external to regional- and world-capitalism. Yet nonstate spaces may be structural: although people work, produce, and trade in the capitalist economy, they spend parts of their lives doing activities that are not fully incorporated into the structures of capitalist accumulation. This could include things done in the household, the community, or elsewhere, for self-benefit, for the benefit of others, or simply for enjoyment. Rather than assuming that one lives either within or outside of states or capitalist economies, we propose that it may be more useful to follow the lead of Wright's class theory and assume that most people have *contradictory locations* with regard to states and formal labor.[15] Some things draw them into world-systemic and state-centered processes and others lead them to withdraw or seek withdrawal from those processes. Some of the things they do for reasons of altruism or mutual aid may be contradictory in the sense that they strengthen aspects of community while they simultaneously cheapen the cost of reproducing labor and thus contribute positively to capitalist accumulation.

We propose, therefore, that the unit of analysis of any understanding of nonstate spaces must be a unitary capitalist world-economy and that the analysis of nonstate spaces or activities must be carried out within that context. If so, the first question that must be posed is how these spaces or activities relate to different levels of the world-economy (local, regional, global) and, in the extreme case that they do not, what the dynamic forces are that may threaten the autonomy of spaces and activities.

Other key strands of analysis may help illuminate organization and activities in exilic spaces and their relationships to capitalism. In chapter 2 we suggest several beginning points, and we will work out their implications in the empirical cases of this book. One is the distinction that Polanyi and Hopkins make between substantive and formal conceptions of economy and economic activities. An initial working hypothesis is that the world of the formal (market) economy is that of capitalism, while nonstate spaces or activities are organized by substantive economic relations like reciprocity and redistribution, householding, and even gifting.[16] Yet this is complicated by the fact that many reciprocal and redistributive activities take place "within" capitalism and may even act to support it (household activities that cheapen the reproduction of labor, state welfare activities that are countercyclical).

Another frame of analysis that may help capture the dynamic interactions between those who seek cooperation and self-organization and those authorities and organizations that represent the interests of capital is Hirschman's work on exit, voice, and loyalty.[17] Those who seek to achieve exit by entering into nonstate or exilic spaces may have to pay a price to keep the wolf from baying at the door, and that may mean exhibiting one or another form of loyalty to the states from which they seek autonomy. As we shall see in the case of Cossacks, the demands of loyalty may weaken the institutions and practices of autonomy.

INITIAL ATTEMPTS TO CONCEPTUALIZE NONSTATE SPACES

The first systematic attempt to analyze cooperation and self-organization, both historically and anthropologically, was Kropotkin's *Mutual Aid: A Factor of Evolution.* Darwin's theory of natural selection, especially as popularized by his "bulldog," Thomas Huxley, and the English naturalist Alfred Russel Wallace, emphasized a "gladiatorial view" of survival of the fittest: "the war of all against all." Kropotkin developed another view, using some of the best biological, anthropological, archaeological, and historical knowledge of his time, including his own research and observations in Siberia. He emphasized how mutual aid rather than combat is the chief criterion of success in the struggle for existence. In doing so, he followed an important Russian school of humanist critique of competitive Darwinism from fields like zoology and biology, most notably the so-called *law of mutual aid* developed by the ichthyologist Kessler. In 1909 Kropotkin noted: "Kessler, Severtsov, Menzbir, Brandt—four great Russian zoologists, and a 5th lesser one, Poliakov, and finally myself, a simple traveler, stand against the Darwinist exaggeration of struggle within a species. We see a great deal of mutual aid where Darwin and Wallace see only struggle."[18]

This Russian School's ultimate conclusion, as summarized by Kropotkin, is as follows:

> If we ... ask Nature: "who are the fittest: those who are continually at war with each other, or those who support one another?" we at once see that those

animals which acquire habits of mutual aid are undoubtedly the fittest. They have more chances to survive, and they attain, in their respective classes, the highest development of intelligence and bodily organization.[19]

Kropotkin's great innovation is that he added his own historical/anthropological analysis to the bio/zoological critiques of gladiatorial Darwinism, moving the discussion of mutual aid from biology to human society. Kropotkin argues that in each stage of human development—from clan to family to village to town to medieval city to the early modernity of his own time—new forms of social organization and regulation arose that tended to drive people apart. Yet in each stage, mutual aid reappeared as a common way of organizing social relations from below, acting as a sort of antidote that communities used to protect themselves not just against the cruelties of nature but primarily against proto-state, then state, then capitalist forms of regulation and oppression. While some of Kropotkin's more sanguine generalizations about "primitive" societies have been modified by subsequent ethnographic studies, his central principle of the conflict between institutions of mutual aid and possessive individualism seems as relevant today as when he wrote it, as evidenced by a number of studies that repeat his central thesis, although often without giving him credit.[20]

The most ambitious contemporary attempt to understand nonstate spaces from this tradition is Scott's analysis of the "art of not being governed." Expanding on the work of his mentor, Clastres,[21] Scott made a forceful argument for what he calls a history of those who "got away," a history of people's "struggle against the state." Although the study of the Southeast Asian region that he calls "Zomia" is the central concern of Scott's book, the production of nonstate geographies has not been confined to Southeast Asia. Living without a state was, according to Scott, not a sociohistorical anomaly but a common human project:

The encounter between expansionary states and self-governing peoples is hardly confined to Southeast Asia. It is echoed in the cultural and administrative process of "internal colonialism" that characterizes the formation of most modern Western nation-states; in the imperial projects of the Romans, the Hapsburgs, the Ottomans, the Han, and the British; in the subjugation of indigenous peoples in "white-settler" colonies such as the United States, Canada, South Africa, Australia, and Algeria; in the dialectic between sedentary, town-dwelling Arabs and nomadic pastoralists that have characterized much of Middle Eastern history. The precise shape of the encounters is, to be sure, unique to each case. Nevertheless, the ubiquity of the encounter between self-governing and state-governed peoples—variously styled as the raw and the cooked, the wild and the tamed, the hill/forest people and the valley/cleared-land people, upstream and downstream, the barbarian and the civilized, the backward and the modern, the free and the bound, the people without history and the people with history—provides us with many possibilities for comparative triangulation.[22]

Scott proceeds to identify a pattern of state-making and -unmaking that produced, over time, a periphery composed as much (or more) of refugees as of people who had never been state subjects: a zone of refuge, or shatter zone, "where the human shreds of state formation and rivalry accumulated willy-nilly, creating regions of bewildering ethnic and linguistic complexity." We can find nonstate spaces

> wherever the expansion of states, empires, slave-trading, and wars, as well as natural disasters, have driven large numbers of people to seek refuge in out-of-the-way places: in Amazonia, in highland Latin America, in that corridor of highland Africa safe from slave-raiding, in the Balkans and the Caucasus. The diagnostic characteristics of shatter zones are their relative geographical inaccessibility and the enormous diversity of tongues and cultures.[23]

A project of "alternative area studies" of nonstate (or shatter) zones would require comparative research on diagnostic characteristics, as well as the repertoires of state-repelling or state-preventing strategies, or strategies of escape. But, as we shall argue below, such a project would also require an analysis of protective strategies that might include bargain-making with the very states from which a group seeks escape—possibly involving forms of "escape" that are not primarily geographical but that take place within the centers of state territories. In other words, a key research question is whether there are non-geographic routes of escape.

If for Scott the first principle of evasion is geographical, the second principle is economic: the agriculture of escape. Shifting cultivation from one crop to another was, according to Scott, the most common agro-political strategy against state-making and state appropriation. Particular crops are better suited to escape: in particular, they are crops that are inaccessible to the state, either because they can be grown in difficult terrains or because they are hard to count/measure and therefore to tax. The escape grain of choice in Southeast Asia was maize, which could be grown in areas that were too high, too steep, too dry, and too infertile for hill rice. The New World favorite escape crop was cassava. But hill people also moved from crop to crop. Scott's main point is that some crops allow people to disperse more widely than others; and wider dispersal encourages a social structure more resistant to incorporation, hierarchy, and subordination because it introduces a "friction of space" that exhausts the attempts of the state to extend its power.

If the agriculture of escape is a strategic choice, argues Scott, so is social organization. Somewhat controversially, and very much in the spirit of arguments first offered by Clastres, Scott sees illiteracy, which he chooses to call nonliteracy or orality, as a strategic choice designed to impede appropriation. The world of writing is, for stateless people, indelibly associated with states. People without (written) history are choosing not to have history, at least as fixed history, in order to maximize their room for cultural maneuver. Some phenomenologists take the advantages of orality even further, arguing that the development of abstract writing was associated with a loss of a wide array of perceptive abilities and technologies, the retention or recovery of which could even give cooperating communities important technological advantages that would enhance their resistance to incorporation.[24] In a contemporary example of a forced exilic space, O'Hearn relates isolated prisoners' ability to develop solidary cultures of resistance to the removal of written materials and the active development of an oral culture.[25]

In most cases, escape social structures are relatively egalitarian and "flexible." In the absence of surplus-absorbing religious or political establishments, the "sociological pyramid" of Zomia is rather flat and local. There are distinctions of status and wealth, but they are local and unstable, partly because hill farmers move so regularly to new farmlands. Thus, Scott observes an equality that is built from dispersal, movement, and fierce individualism rather than cooperation, from the insistence not to be governed rather than from self-governance. If there is cooperation and mutual aid among hill peoples, it is undertheorized and underdescribed by Scott, who mostly refers to communities made up of bewilderingly complex cultural amalgams, veritable patchworks of identities and ethnicities, where marriages across ethnic groups and across space (across several valleys) are the norm and reproduce an identity among hill dwellers. Nonstate spaces served as "cracks" in the status quo, functioning as "magnets, attracting individuals, small groups, and whole communities seeking sanctuary outside the reach of colonial power."[26] Thus, Scott speaks of "innumerable small units, seemingly in constant movement," of societies where the elementary unit is the household and where "villages, tribes, and confederations [are] provisional and shaky alliances."[27]

The exceptions, for self-protection against imminent state threats, are occasional millenarian and Holy-man revolts, together with rebellious cosmologies, which Scott views as escape structures of a high order.

Today, according to Scott, talk of nonstate spaces makes no sense. We have moved from encounter to the effective end of a great enclosure, from a world that is all periphery and almost no center to the all-encompassing architecture of a modern state that has been able to enclose these nonstate spaces. We have moved from "little nodes of power" to a modern state that has effectively brought nonstate spaces and people "to heel" and where "the headlong pursuit of this end by regimes otherwise starkly different suggests that such projects of administrative, economic, and cultural standardization are hard-wired into the architecture of the modern state itself."[28]

In other words, after an era of "small-scale states" characterized by the "expansion of state power," we are now entering "an era in which virtually the entire globe is 'administered space' and the periphery has been enclosed." Here, by making an explicit comparison with the English enclosure movement, Scott returns to the language and thesis of his earlier work on seeing like a state: the aim of enclosure—in the name of progress, literacy, and social integration—is to make sure that people's activity was "legible, taxable, assessable, and confiscatable."[29] About this long-run trend there can be not a shred of doubt: not just Zomia, but other nonstate regions from Africa to Latin America, are now essentially "statified."

Does this mean that nonstate spaces and activities are defunct, and that the project we stated at the outset is merely a historical anomaly? We propose not. We point to several key deficiencies in Scott's method of analysis that limit his conception of "nonstate" and "escape." For one thing, it is entirely geographical. People escape the state by moving into spaces that are beyond its reach. Thus, for Scott, once the "modern state" develops "distance-demolishing technologies" that encompass the globe and "so diminish the friction of terrain," there are no more places to which people can escape.[30]

Moreover, Scott's political economy is limited to his "agriculture of escape," that is, to people's ability to produce crops that the state can neither assess nor tax. There is no significant description of self-governance or direct democracy, or of production beyond escape agriculture. The hill people's sole strategy is to create friction that the state finds too expensive to cross; thus autonomy ends for hill people when the state develops friction-dissolving technologies of space. Once one introduces a broader conception of political economy and recognizes that different kinds of economic activities may be beyond the control of the state and market, not necessarily geographically but in social-structural terms, one opens up the possibility that "distance-demolishing technologies" of the state are insufficient to snuff out all possibilities of escape. We propose, as a research hypothesis, the possibility of structural cracks in the capitalist world-system—and in nation-states, localized states, and the interstate system—where people practice escape production, or mutual aid.[31] We also propose, from our understanding of contemporary movements like the Zapatistas in southeastern Mexico or the Movimento dos Trabadhores sem Terra (MST) in Brazil, that geographical escape may not be as anomalous as Scott suggests, even though it may require more intricate strategies and face greater threats than those developed or faced by the people of Zomia.

In certain social contexts, such as urban neighborhoods, one might expect that proximity rather than dispersal is more conducive to cooperation. Scott's main argument in favor of the advantages of dispersal is mostly about the difficulties a state faces in managing dispersed populations; state control "runs of out of breath" when it faces distance and dispersion, altitude, rugged terrain, or mixed cultivation. Yet he may underestimate the difficulties of engaging in mutual aid and direct democracy in such areas as well. Identification of the conditions in which dispersal and/or concentration are related to cooperation and mutual aid is one important object of the comparative analysis we suggest here.

One approach to the study of nonstate spaces that opens up possibilities beyond Scott's geographical escape has been elaborated by Zibechi. Unlike Scott, Zibechi is interested in contemporary urban nonstate spaces, especially in Latin America. As a consequence of neoliberal shock therapy and a crisis of the state, he argues, a new relationship between people and spaces has arisen. Neoliberal forces have caused greater internal migration in the last two·decades and widened rifts and fissures in which the poor have been able to create "new forms of sociability and resistance."[32] People are moving toward spaces at the outskirts of major cities (*asentamientos*) and in the countryside, outside of the control of capital or where capital has a limited and distant presence. New settlements have new characteristics as a consequence of what Zibechi calls dispersed space. The urban new space comes with a new autonomous urban economy:

> Production of livelihood in the territories signals a second radical break from the industrial past. The popular sectors have erected for the first time in an

urban space a set of independently controlled forms of production. Although these remain connected to and dependent on the market, vast sectors now control their forms and rhythms of production, and are no longer dominated by the rhythms of capital and its division of labor.[33]

Zibechi explicitly relates these new urban spaces and popular survival networks with recent revolutionary events in Latin America. Dispersed spaces are home to an underground politics that makes more visible manifestations possible:

> In the daily life of divided societies, public time dominates the scene; the only audible voices are those of the economic, political and union elites. For this reason the Argentine insurrection was both "unexpected" and "spontaneous" to those elites, who could not hear the underground sounds, despite the fact that for more than a decade the voices had been echoing from below anticipating the approaching event.[34]

Zibechi regards this as evidence of a new dynamic movement of people away from capitalism and toward increasingly autonomous self-activity, both politically and economically.

> We are witnessing the creation of new situations marked by the deepening of differences. The unemployed from the popular sectors who live in asentamientos affirm their difference by turning themselves into picketers and later into autonomous producers. The route is very similar among other groups in the region that combine the flight from capitalist relations with the simultaneous creation of relations within the dispersion, as a way of affirming difference.[35]

He further identifies a relationship between the breakup of territories (in terms of loss of state legitimacy in some regions or among certain classes) and economies, with a profound crisis of the existing forms of representative government. During a crisis, the flight of capital is accompanied by a loss of legitimacy of elected representatives connected to certain territories or communities. In Bolivia, for instance, anti-state movements that were forged in nonstate urban spaces like El Alto or certain neighborhoods in Cochabamba, practice a directly democratic style of politics that is often called "backseat driving." In this case, communities or groups engage in politics by designating representatives to go before them (*ante ellos*) and relate to them in a politically transformed way. Notice, however, that despite Zibechi's transformative claims, these are not complete withdrawals from representative politics; by sending delegates "to go before them," communities seek to ensure that representative politicians at the regional or national levels actually represent their will, while simultaneously practicing alternative forms of direct democracy in their communities. This fragile and often contradictory relationship between "exit" and "voice" is an issue that we will address at length in subsequent sections of this analysis.

MISSING FACTORS

Taken together, the works of Scott and Zibechi indicate that comparative research on extra-state geographies could tell a story of considerable importance. It is a story of state evasion, self-barbarization, and pluricultural encounter that constitutes a counternarrative to the state-centric, civilizationist, and nationalist one that has dominated Western social sciences. The comparative study of state-breaking projects is an important contribution to historical social science. It is the obverse of state formation, without which state formation cannot be understood properly. In order to accomplish this goal, however, we need to both challenge prevailing concepts and introduce some aspects that Scott and Zibechi have missed.

While Scott's thesis of nonstate spaces is compelling, there is almost no mention of capitalism, no mention whatsoever of the capitalist world-economy, and, surprisingly, very little mention of self-governance or mutual aid, which are activities around which an "exit economy" can be built and sustained (if Kropotkin is right about the survival advantages of cooperation). Without an adequate analysis of the political economy of nonstate spaces *in the context of historical capitalism*, we are left with several problems. First, the modern state is not adequately theorized because it is not recognized as part of an interstate system but is rather seen as an unchanging entity that has remained more or less the same since early agrarian societies, only with greater capacity and technologies of power. Second, enclosure is conceptually divorced from the regionally specific processes of incorporation into the capitalist world-economy. As a result, while this process appears to Scott as universal, complete, and finished, it is actually variable, contested, partial, and ongoing. This is why we propose to study the continuing existence of cracks, or exilic spaces, *within* the capitalist world-economy. Finally, a conventional comparison of nonstate attributes like geography or agriculture is mechanistic and formal, eclipsing a more nuanced and dynamic understanding of the specific nature of individual local histories as parts of unified historical processes of capitalist development on a world scale.

Zibechi, unlike Scott, incorporates political economy; but he ignores history. From a historical perspective (for example, Kropotkin's analysis of mutual aid), there is nothing new about the emergence of nonstate spaces and nonmarket activities. Zibechi detects a "new relationship between people and territories,"[36] yet this relationship is anything but new. It may be specific and original in any given manifestation, but it is also a predictable response to the logic of exit inscribed in the *longue durée* of historical capitalism. Instead of ruptures and breaks, we see a long-term, large-scale historical process of state-making and state-breaking, of state formation and state de-formation, of ongoing and uneven incorporation and exilic reappropriation and recovery. Thus, there may be more historical continuity between Scott and Zibechi than either would concede.

We propose that nonstate spaces are products of specific forms of incorporation in the capitalist world-economy. In laying out his own understanding of the capitalist world-system, Braudel briefly proposes the ongoing existence of "black holes in the world-economy." Because they defy world-systemic processes of incorporation and are thus (almost or partially) outside of commercial exchange and contact, these black holes are "outside of the world time." They are "backward islands" in the mountains or other inaccessible places and while "there can be no doubt whatsoever of the[ir] existence," they are a fleeting presence.[37] Researching them is like undertaking "underwater expeditions"; one is bound to swim up to the surface disappointed with the paucity of evidence.[38]

Braudel's "black holes" are self-organized spaces, structured outside the realm of the interstate system and capitalist accumulation. They may be left aside by the encroaching process whereby core powers incorporate external arenas into the capitalist world-economy, or (we suggest here) they may be responses to that encroachment, a form of defense by populations who, for one reason or another, refuse to be incorporated. In Scott's terminology, "black holes" are a manifestation of what he calls *infrapolitics*: "an unobtrusive realm of political struggle" that includes a "wide variety of low-profile forms of resistance that dare not speak in their own name."[39] Infrapolitics is essentially a strategic form of resistance that subjects must assume under conditions of great peril. It provides a "structural underpinning for more visible political action, not as a substitute, but as its condition."[40]

We refer to the production of such forms of place-based politics within the cracks of the global capitalist system as the *infrapolitics of the capitalist world-economy.* Infrapolitics describes the very process of breaking from systemic processes of state and capital. It is a process of (self)organization of relatively autonomous and only partially incorporated spaces and the subsequent antagonistic relationship between exilic spaces and the hierarchical organizations of a capitalist world-economy.

Once we place our subject of research in the context of world-capitalism, the term "nonstate spaces" no longer seems to capture its historical complexity. It is clearer to speak of instances and spaces of exit, and exilic spaces and territories. Gray speaks of *exilic spaces* as physical and psychological spaces of refuge for the urban poor in Jamaica.[41] Although Gray defines the spaces and what takes place within them almost entirely in cultural terms, as spaces where a humiliated population seeks recovery and social honor, the concept is useful for our project because it combines a sense of spatial exile with one of structural exit from "acceptable society" (in this case, capitalism) even though one is technically still "in" that society and at times participating in its institutions and even working in its formal economies. Exilic spaces are not beyond the intrusion and surveillance of the state, especially during heightened times of activity such as elections, but they are largely places of refuge from the state and from "civilized" society. In Jamaica, they are inferior urban spaces: street corners, tenement yards, streets, ghetto neighborhoods. They are spaces of cultural hybridity, both "black power" and borrowings from dominating cultures, including British colonialism and US consumerism. Politically, says Gray, "inclinations to self-governance and autonomy" in such spaces move "from restraint to indiscipline."[42] The actions of the groups that form are often aggressive, rude, and even harmful to the poor populations in the spaces. Yet they may have subversive and even popular effects, especially when common crime becomes a matter of official concern and anti-crime campaigns take on political overtones. In these cases, "ideological rule-breaking" is engaged by youth gangs, the unskilled unemployed who are deprived of work by political victimization, street vendors who have turned their backs on wage labor, the minimum-wage lumpen proletariat, and jobless school dropouts.

Although Gray avoids analyzing the economy of exilic spaces, he does speak of the ecology of the street and the tenement yard, which people share as resource but also sometimes experience as an invasion. It is a space of public performances, theater, music, and sport. Much of its economy is informal, and there is much public sharing and cooperation, just as there is much theft and squabbling. Using exilic space as a broader concept offers the possibility of connecting such disparate experiences as the Cossack territory with urban slums in postcolonial Jamaica. Exilic spaces represent not only an escape from the state but also attempted exit from the totality of hierarchical relations that form the capitalist world-economy, of which the state is only a part.

Is it improbable to think that the history of the capitalist world-system is, to a degree, a history of struggle against self-activity in exilic spaces? From a long historical view, attempts to incorporate and integrate local economic actions and institutions into regional and global divisions of labor may be viewed, among other things, as a struggle against autonomous, or external, economy. State formation as part of capitalist incorporation could be seen, among other things, as a struggle against processes of state *de*-formation. The history of the interstate system is a history of struggle against nonstate spaces. Incorporation is a process not only of integration of new territories into a systemwide division of labor but also of integration of self-organized, extra-state spaces.

The politics of exilic spaces is usually not regarded as relevant to our understanding of capitalist development and change (thus, the need for de Sousa Santos's *sociology of absences*). Braudel describes "black holes" as fleeting; we suggest they are more ubiquitous and resilient than that and that we *can* research them given the right methods and theoretical foundations.

THE STRUCTURE OF THIS BOOK

What follows is an in-depth study of several kinds of exilic spaces that we think are characteristic in certain ways and that pose patterns and possible generalities for future studies of exilic spaces and practice. The Cossacks, a historical case of exile, provides an example of how exile was possible before state formation and capitalism predominated; Cossack autonomy persisted across long periods of state formation and phases of expansion and contraction of the capitalist world-system. Cossack longevity provides an initial set of patterns of dynamic change: changing bargains between the autonomous space and a state that consolidated its power to the point of regional hegemony. Then we shift to a contemporary case of territorial exile: the Zapatistas of southeastern Mexico, who burst into world prominence with their occupation of urban centers in the state of Chiapas in 1994 but whose more important contribution to this study comprises a series of nearly invisible efforts to create and re-create a new kind of society within the interstices of Mexican capitalism. Efforts by the Zapatistas to reform their modes of governance to become more directly democratic and resistant to corruption go together with continuing difficulties in maintaining economies of exit, a delicate balance that is held together by forms of external economic dependence and loyalty that continue to threaten exilic autonomy. Finally, we observe an extreme example of an exilic space that practically amounts to laboratory conditions: the creation and development of solidary communities among prisoners. Prisoners in open prison camps have developed remarkable communities based on mutual aid, in part to compensate for the lack of material provisions; this solidarity and mutual aid intensified even more after states attempted to undermine these practices by isolating captives in cellular prisons. We see this primarily among northern Irish political prisoners in the late 1970s but also among Kurdish and Turkish prisoners in post-2000 Turkey, as well as among inmates in US supermax prisons.

We conclude this volume by combining and comparing some of our findings on this journey to exilic spaces across time. We speculate about the future of exilic spaces, their promise and limitations. As long as that stratum of society that Braudel calls *material life* continues to resist the roots of capital, such attempts at exit and autonomy can be expected to persist.

TWO

Thinking about and Researching Exit and Recapture

INCORPORATION, CYCLES, DIVISIONS OF LABOR, AND CONTROL

IN THE FIRST CHAPTER we set out some basic questions that we want to ask about what we have termed *exilic spaces and practices*. The dynamic questions we propose have much to do with what Braudel calls "world time." As we understand it, world time refers to the rhythms and patterns of organization and change of the world-economy—cycles of accumulation and their associated divisions of labor and technologies of production and control; hegemonic regimes and their geographic priorities, leading sectors, and global reach; general world development and how it impacts the abilities and desires of local authorities to impose control over populations and labor. The broad patterns and forms of change are associated, imperfectly, with local regimes of control and forms of incorporation. When Braudel refers to "black holes" that are "outside of world time," he refers to the ability of certain communities to withstand the processes of incorporation associated with it.

As Hopkins and Wallerstein[1] present it, the world-economy consists of a system of multiple states of unequal power linked in an interstate system; this is not a mere assemblage of states but an ordered structure. The structure's order, its rules and mechanisms, are predominantly about the law of value; that is, to one degree or another they ensure that conditions prevail whereby capital, especially that which is organized in the core of the system, can be invested profitably and therefore accumulate over time. As accumulation proceeds and the system expands, capital is constantly in search of new labor, resources, and markets. Thus, capitalism intensifies in areas where it is already established as it incorporates new areas with fresh labor into the system.

Areas that were external, in the sense that their economic relations with the capitalist world-system were limited mainly to trade in luxury goods,[2] are increasingly brought into the world-system so that what they produce and trade is influenced or determined more and more by the world-systemic law of value.

Yet there are constant pressures against the law of value, especially from direct producers who struggle to reduce exploitation and alienation in the workplace, who try to gain more value in the marketplace, and "perhaps above all" struggle for greater rights in the political arena. The main function of states and of the interstate system is to protect the law of value against these threats by "(a) creating states strong enough to limit the political pressures of the direct producers; (b) creating an interstate system too weak to permit the imposition of true world market monopolies; and (c) creating states strong enough to assist entrepreneurs to overcome obstacles to the spread of the law of value."[3]

Together with the phased nature of innovations in the techniques and technologies of production, these conditions produce uneven or phased economic growth that, nonetheless, has enabled expanded accumulation over time. More and more production relations have been commodified, that is, brought within (imperfect) markets, where they are valued and distributed. During downturns, especially, there are pressures for restructuring the world-economy and its constituent regions, or zones. Restructuring includes attempts to deepen the capitalist process, which, in turn, means an uneven process of renewing and deepening connections between zones of the world-economy, as well as drawing in new regions that were previously external or largely external to the world-economy. Restructuring is often associated with the rise of a new *hegemony*, that is, a single power that has world dominance economically, politically, and militarily. And each such rise is usually associated with a new global production regime, which can be identified by one or a small group of leading economic sectors (for Holland, entrepôt trade; for Britain, cotton and then railroads and iron; for the US, consumer durables and then computers), and by a different characteristic form of rule (British territorially based colonial empire vs. US direct-investment-based imperialism). Yet within these defining regime types there is significant local variation.

What does incorporation mean for a zone that has been external to the system? Or, how does restructuring affect a region that has already been incorporated but that becomes "reincorporated" or transformed due to changing production priorities of the world-system (in Jamaica, for example, the transition from British colonialism to US imperialism, and the associated transition from slave sugar to corporate bauxite)? At its simplest, incorporation means making what was external internal, or restructuring activities in the region so that they conform with and participate in the priorities of the capitalist world-economy (as much as possible), especially in terms of a region's integration into the worldwide division of labor. According to Wallerstein, this has two main parts: (1) transforming production so that the activities that take place in an area are "essential" to the worldwide division of labor and (2) transforming governance so that state structures become members of and operate within the rules of the interstate system. In practice, however, this means four major structural transformations of a region: setting up new and bigger economic units of production and/or distribution; establishing new ways of acquiring cheap and disciplined labor; creating or transforming governance that "relate[s] to the requirements of the political superstructure of the capitalist world-economy"; and building new institutional and physical infrastructures "or rather the extension of that which already exists in the capitalist world-economy to cover the zone being incorporated."[4]

Yet these changes are not simply determined by the requirements of the whole system and particularly by the aims of core states and capitals. This brings us to the same conclusion that some world-systems analysts have already reached. In response to functionalist top-down interpretations of world-systemic processes, McMichael proposes a system of *incorporating comparison* where incorporation and subsequent changes in any given part of the system are contingent on historically specific relations between the incorporating powers and the region that is being incorporated, on the specific aims that the core has in incorporating a region, and on the bargaining powers that the region itself may have to place conditions on its incorporation.[5] In this formulation, the system is created and re-created by the histories of incorporation and peripheralization of its parts. Of course, within this context the desires and actions of core states and capitals are particularly influential although not determinant, and local forces have more or less ability to influence the outcome of the way world-systemic processes are applied in their given cases.

This relational approach to understanding systemic change is important in understanding the development of production, including labor relations within regional or local economies as they are incorporated or peripheralized. Important inroads in this area have already been made by those who approach the capitalist world-economy as a concrete historical entity, not an abstraction, as in Marx's *Capital*.[6] It is constructed and reproduced through the mediation of various interrelated and interconnected processes, always historically specific, mutually constituted, and integrated as a sociohistorical whole. As a concrete articulation of diverse relations of production, exchange, and power, the world-economy is a "unified, structured, contradictorily evolving totality" that is defined by the interrelated nature of its parts.[7] More than a mere sum of economic processes, it is a unified network of political power, social domination, and economic activities that presupposes the unity of the global and the local. Because of this, the complex relations within it are both necessary and contingent: "necessary because of the systemic unity imposed by the interdependence of the forms of production, exchange, and political power; and contingent because the particular character of those forms is always the product of specific, complex, uneven historical processes within the relational network."[8]

Within this framework, capital as a wage relation is different from world-capitalism, which is a combination of diverse forms of labor in which capital acts as an axis for the integration of the whole. During the long sixteenth century, capital in its wage form ("core capital" in world-system terminology) became structurally articulated with other forms of organization and control of labor through the process of incorporation. Waged labor became an integrative axis around which other forms of labor, including slavery and other forms of unfree labor, were articulated. Historical capitalism is a system that links all forms of labor control with capital as its central axis.

Incorporation, therefore, was and is an impartial and contradictory process whereby historical labor forms—serfdom, slavery, small mercantile production, reciprocity, and so on—were brought into the service of capital and integrated into a worldwide division of labor that had the wage form at its core. In addition, new labor forms were created or old ones revived in new form. A critical and illustrative part of this process is Tomich's concept of a *second slavery*, where unfree labor relations reemerged in world-capitalism at a time when slavery was supposedly on the wane, but in a new form that was created by the incorporation of new regions into the world-economy and the reperipheralization of regions like the US South, parts of the Caribbean, and Brazil.[9] It was distinguished from colonial slavery "by new commodities, produced in unprecedented quantities, in regions formerly marginal to the Atlantic economy [and] in reconfigured polities."[10]

Along with the combination of different labor forms, the nation-state is a modern form that combines other historical forms of control over the distribution of collective authority. Relationships between different societal power relations within capitalist modernity are neither unilinear nor unidirectional. They are not all moving toward a single regime of government. World-capitalism is a historically negotiated and structurally heterogeneous whole, where one or more components have primacy, but not as determinants or as a basis for determinations.

This is especially true with the development and consolidation of the interstate system. Tilly calls modern states "protection rackets," increasingly powerful and effective units that not only demand a monopoly over the legitimate use of force but also use it to create threats and then charge social units for protection. To the degree that exilic spaces are considered threats to the state's and then the interstate system's monopoly, not just over the use of force but over the protection of an expanding world-economy, we would expect states to use their power vis à vis exilic spaces as a protection racket. As Tilly puts it, early in the state-making process, different entities shared the right to use violence "in a continuum from bandits and pirates to kings, via tax collectors, regional power holders, and professional soldiers." But as nation-states and the interstate system "purveyed violence on a larger scale, more effectively, more efficiently, with wider assent from their subject populations, and with readier collaboration from neighboring authorities," they first controlled and then attempted to remove the rights of others to use violence and force.[11] This does not mean, however, that contention and challenges to state power "from below" disappeared. Rather, they continued to appear in new forms and with different chances of success, depending on local conditions and the situation of incorporation in the world-economy.

If the capitalist world-economy is conceived as a complex and structured totality, full of contradictions, then the role of comparative historical sociology is to theoretically reconstruct the historical development of specific local experiences that have been produced by it and that together make it up. We need to construct and reconstruct fundamental categories of analysis from historically specific processes. This method allows us to connect local processes and histories to diverse processes of politics and the economy of historical capitalism. This casts a very different light on the process of incorporation in the capitalist world-economy than a functionalist and system-centered method. For our purposes, it provides a concrete, locally and historically grounded way of analyzing the impacts of world-systemic processes like incorporation on the development or survival of exilic spaces.

Local specificities, we suggest, will be particularly important in the way that authorities and exilic communities bargain and interact, and in the outcome of those interactions at any given time. Such local specificities will be foremost in determining the availability of different strategies of exit and voice, and the chances of successfully maintaining autonomy, including the nature of exilic production possibilities and of loyalty bargains between exilic communities and local authorities. These are not just local bargains between the exilic community and the regional power, but must be considered in the context of the world-economy—increasingly so as the region within which exilic communities exist is integrated more closely into world-systemic institutions and processes.

For the purposes of a project on exilic spaces, there are two key and related parts of this process: the impacts on states and their capacity to exert control over exiles or potential exiles, and the impacts that new economic activities and units have on the demand for labor. With regard to states, existing political structures have to be greatly reorganized or even eliminated and replaced by new structures. Wallerstein says that this involves a delicate balancing act: "If they were too strong they could obstruct flows of commodities, capital, and labor; if they were too weak they could not prevent others (particularly those within their jurisdiction) from obstructing them."[12] The need to keep this balancing act is a major reason why some states were allowed to develop as independent states while others took the form of colonies. In any case, since a main objective of incorporation is the successive elimination of alternatives to the capitalist world-economy, one would expect that regional states would exert more and more control over exilic peoples, communities, and spaces. This would entail (1) forcing, cajoling, or enticing them to produce bulk goods for export; and (2) exerting greater external control over local government, possibly by transforming direct democracy and its charges/delegates into representatives that are appointed from above or outside. Whether and how this happens would be a major question for research on exilic spaces.

Put another way, the question is how the possibilities and realities of exilic spaces differ during the periods when the regional state is external to the world-economy, during and after incorporation, and in successive stages of reintegration into the restructured world-economy, with new hegemonic power hierarchies, leading economic sectors, and global and regional divisions of labor. One hypothesis, which Scott seems to put forward although not in a world-systemic context, is that exilic spaces belong to a previous world time and that they become increasingly anomalous as world development, accumulation, and state formation proceed. Alternatively, however, we propose the possibility that the characteristic forms of exilic spaces change across world time. In particular, where the nature of escape was once spatial, and exilic spaces were geographically separate from the states and productive systems from which certain people exited (i.e., into remote regions such as mountains or steppes), today's exilic spaces may be structurally separate, involving niches or cracks within capitalism where groups or communities can practice mutual aid and direct democracy. We further propose that this kind of separation or escape may be less complete or comprehensive than before. In the next two sections, we examine the kinds of economic activities that take place in exilic spaces, how they relate to capitalism, and how they may emerge within its interstices; and whether today's escapee, rather than becoming a complete exile from capitalism, is more likely to have a contradictory location with respect to capitalism, living partly within it (perhaps working as wage laborer) and partly outside of it (creating prefigurative spaces characterized by mutual aid and direct democracy).

EXIT, VOICE, AND LOYALTY

What are the strategic choices of actors who are either discontents within the capitalist world-economy or who reluctantly face incorporation within it? In a short but useful analysis, Hirschman lays out the options ("responses to decline") faced by discontented actors in "firms, organizations, and states." In short, when such institutions fail to satisfy their expectations, actors or groups face the choices of leaving them (exit) or trying to change them by making their opinions heard (voice). Those who inhabit the exilic spaces we propose to research have clearly chosen the exit option, either by moving geographically or by trying to organize activities outside of the structures of capitalism. But there are caveats. First, while choices concerning exit and voice may be contradictory in many ways, they are neither mutually exclusive nor are they independent of each other. Second, although economists view exit as primarily "economic" and frictionless (the market choice "not to deal" with a seller, employer, or state) and voice as primarily "political" and cumbersome (trying to change the conditions under which one "buys" or "sells"), institutions including states and corporations manipulate societies and institutions in ways that can make exit (or entry) difficult. In addition, as Hirschman insists, the only way to come to a complete understanding of social forces is through a close look at the interplay of market and nonmarket forces, which "will reveal the usefulness of certain tools of economic analysis for the understanding of political phenomena, and vice versa."[13]

While the two main responses to discontent with something (including citizenship, workplace, and residence) are exit and voice, a third factor, loyalty, impacts the availability of the other two. Although Hirschman never fully analyzes it, loyalty may be a choice (an important case, as we shall see, for maintaining exilic spaces) or it may be relatively fixed, for example, by practice, culture, or ideology. Hirschman's main consideration is the interrelation of exit and voice. At the simplest level, the presence of an exit option makes voice less likely to be used and, conversely, when exit is closed off discontents are more likely to try to effect change by making their voices heard. But there are other interesting interrelations between the two choices.

First, the likelihood that one can express voice effectively is considerably higher if voice is backed up by the threat of exit. Therefore, it stands to reason that if states can close off the real possibility of exit by making its consequences unpalatable, they may also close off the effectiveness of voice. Yet states and firms may have other, greater reasons to block exit, especially to retain labor. If so, the consequences for residents or workers can be much greater than mere loss of voice if cutting off exit means that they must remain in unfree labor. This is a basis for the emergence of maroon communities and also explains why states put such huge effort into stopping the flow of new escapees into them.

For both of these reasons states may stifle exit and thereby stifle effective voice. "If the organization has the ability to exact a high price for exit, it acquires a powerful defense against one of the members' most potent weapons: the threat of exit. Obviously, if exit is followed by severe sanctions the very idea of exit is going to be repressed And, "since the high price of exit does away, on the other hand, with the threat of exit as an effective instrument of voice," states can simultaneously repress both voice and exit.[14]

It is no surprise, then, that rather than being characterized as "merely ineffective or 'cumbrous,' exit has often been branded as criminal, for it has been labeled desertion, defection, and treason."[15] Nor are states the only agents who use this strategy. Employees who threaten to leave the firm are called "disloyal," people who refuse the world of paid work are "bums" and "hoboes"; nomads are "gypsies"; citizens who threaten to or make exit are "traitors" or even suspected "terrorists."

This is where loyalty comes in. Expressing voice may invite threats of forced exit: those who complain at work are labeled disloyal; in society, unpatriotic ("Love it or leave it"). Provision is even generally made to expel or imprison disloyal members or groups: "an instrument—one of many—which 'management' uses . . . to restrict voice by members."[16] As a rule, loyalty holds exit at bay and activates only reasonable and acceptable voices, if any.

These strategies are important considerations for the research of exilic spaces, since exit is necessary to establish substantive autonomy, whether in the geographic or structural sense. Because of a penchant among critical scholars to see states as all-encompassing—and increasingly so over time, as proto-states are succeeded by nation-states and by hegemonic states in the interstate system—perhaps the first instinct is to see escape/exit or capture/recapture as distinct alternatives. Yet historically the outcome appears to be less distinct. The state's initial response to exit may be to attempt recapture. Failing this, it will try to manage exit. It will bargain with those who remain external to its direct control.

Here is where we can extend Hirschman to an area that he does not explore. Those who exit may have to pay a price to maintain their autonomy. One possibility is that the state (or a hegemonic state in the interstate system) will attempt to "starve them out" (the Cuban option) so that the result of exit is bad enough to dissuade others from following suit. Another option is that a local state will allow continued autonomy through a bargain, on the condition that the exile pays a price of "loyalty" through one or another mechanism. For example, Cossacks to the south of Muscovy and Maroons in the "cockpit" of Jamaica agreed to police the frontier for the state, even to send back new escapees in order to quell further attempts.[17] Pirates in the emerging Atlantic economy made bargains to attack enemy ships for a sponsoring state that turned a blind eye to their raids.[18] In the North American West, the Comanche policed the frontier against other first nations as a price of loyalty to maintain autonomy in face of pioneer encroachment.[19] Exiles may also police frontiers against contending states so that the exilic space becomes a "buffer zone" that may actually cheapen the cost of defending the state's borders and maintaining regional hegemony.

But are such bargains stable? A most important research question is not only the nature of loyalty bargains and their impacts on the internal organization of exilic societies, but also their dynamics. As state boundaries expand and the "friction" of control (in Scott's terms) is overcome, exilic communities may be overrun. Or, the changing world-economy can have a determining impact on exilic spaces and exilic regimes. For example, the hegemonic shift from Holland to Britain and the accompanying industrial revolution created strong pressures for peripheral and previously external regions to produce inputs for the industrial economy, including grain. As Russia became a "breadbasket" for the West, how did pressure to introduce farming and produce for the world market impact exilic regimes such as the Cossacks? One hypothesis is that such pressures compelled the transition of Cossack production from herding to farming, which in turn applied incorporative pressure that encroached on Cossack political autonomy. As the Russian state became stronger and was itself incorporated into world-economic structures, the terms of the loyalty bargains that it made with Cossacks turned progressively in its favor and eroded the exilic nature of Cossack territories.

In a broader context, the research questions are (1) are such dynamics generally in favor of states and against exilic communities? and (2) what are the combinations of regional and global, infrastructural and technical factors that either strengthen or erode exilic autonomy over cycles of world-system accumulation? Is it inevitable that exilic communities will be lured into activities where the technologies of incorporation and capture are greater?

VOLUNTARY OR FORCED EXIT: BARE LIFE
AND EXILIC LIFE

Of course, all of this assumes that exiles have made a voluntary choice to exit and that authorities at different levels of the world-system want to reincorporate them. In some cases, however, exile may be forced, and certain populations are excluded from aspects of "normal" social life. In a sense, all exit has elements of force and voluntarism. At one extreme, exiles choose to move to achieve autonomy and meaning, yet the fact that they feel they must move to achieve these goals introduces an element of compulsion. At the other extreme, states expel people who have chosen to act in ways that contradict the logic of state and capitalist regulation. There are different combinations of force and choice. The earliest Cossacks we observe in chapter 3 largely *chose* to move into geographical territories that they identified as places of autonomy and liberty, although they were also escaping compulsion in Muscovy and beyond. The earliest Zapatistas of chapter 4 were expelled into the remote jungle from better lands of Chiapas, where they built an exilic society. Later exiles chose to move into autonomous Zapatista territories. The prisoners we observe in chapter 5 were forcibly expelled from "normal" society into prisons and from "normal" prison societies into long-term solitary confinement.

What do people lose or gain when a state expels them?

Goffman says that those who are expelled are *stripped* of the identities they formed within their former communities.[20] Yet, of what are they stripped? Are they stripped of essential rights, or simply of the accoutrements of modern individualism and consumerism that even discontents accumulate in capitalist society? Does the stripping of a possessive-individualist identity enable or even compel one to practice mutual aid and solidarity (*exilic identity*)? Is it even possible that attempts to "strip" exiles of individual "rights" might leave them open, possibly for the first time, to collective identities and practices? Under what conditions might the actions of the authorities have the perverse effect of driving exiles closer together in mutual aid and solidarity?

The most popular postmodern theorists of expulsion, Foucault and Agamben (whose ideas, unlike those of Goffman, are largely produced through logical/philosophical constructions rather than real observations), answer such questions pessimistically. What they call *biopower* and *bare life* are unlikely to provoke or enable emancipatory practices, including those that we have termed exilic practices, partly because both assume that the state wants to simultaneously expel *and* control the exile.

For Foucault, forced expulsion to the prison involves the exercise of *biopower,* the defining characteristic of modern state power and strategy. Whereas classical societies kept a strict division between biological life (*zoe*) and political life (*bios*), in modern societies "the basic biological features of the human species became the object of a political strategy."[21] States punish intention and not just action; imprisonment (a new form of exile) is designed to change renegade intention by introducing discipline into the very actions and perceptions of the captive's body. This is achieved primarily by "the gaze," through which the authorities make captives believe that they are under constant threat of surveillance. Over time, captives internalize discipline by imposing restrictions on themselves *as if* they were being watched and subject to punishment. This self-discipline is reinforced in the prison through constant regulation of activities so that a captive's day is normalized through natural bodily performance rather than through reflection and thoughtful action.[22] Without possibility of thought, intersubjective communication, and collective action (either as mutual aid or resistance), there is little possibility that prisoners will develop exilic practices and solidarity. Yet, as we shall see in chapter 5, the testimonies and observations of prisoners themselves indicate that Foucault's *panopticon*—the fully surveilled prison—is a fiction of his method. In real prisons, the pragmatic objectives of authorities are more likely to be to place prisoners in an architecture where they cannot do harm and then to ignore them as much as possible, at least whenever guards or other authorities are not practicing violence against them.

This is more akin to Agamben's adaptations of Foucault's concepts to describe forced expulsion in camps. Agamben contrasts *bare life* with "good" life, as Arendt (supposedly following Aristotle) contrasted biological existence (*zoe*) with political life (*bios*).[23] According to Agamben, bare life existed in antiquity, yet its form changed with modernity. Classical societies such as the Greeks had categories of humans who were excluded from the polis *and* exposed to violence that was not counted as crime. Ancient Roman law included the category of *homo sacer*, humans banished by the sovereign who could be killed with impunity but were unworthy of juridical trial or sacrifice. Outside of human or divine law, *homo sacer* thus lived a bare existence. But such societies also distinguished sites of bare life from those of sovereign power, or political life. The threshold of the home constituted a distinct barrier between bare life and "good" life (in the arena of political voice and participation, in the city); "simple natural life is excluded from the polis in the strict sense, and remains confined—as merely reproductive life—to the sphere of the *oikos*, 'home.'"[24]

For Agamben, "A society's 'threshold of biological modernity' is situated at the point at which the species and the individual as a simple living body become what is at stake in a society's political strategies . . . the entry of *zoē* into the sphere of *the polis*—the politicization of bare life as such—constitutes the decisive event of modernity."[25] In modernity, then, *bare life* is not a separate or natural process of reproduction of life in the home but rather a product of national sovereignty, of the decision by the sovereign to create a "state of exception" wherein certain people (and, potentially, any of us) are exiled or banished from political life. The state places these people in a given space, or "camp," where residents face a sort of civil death and are stripped of those things that make them human (that is, in Agamben's reckoning, the ability to speak and the right to engage in political life). There, they may be subject to violence by authorities (*a la homo sacer*) and such violence is not even considered a crime.

Yet such sites of the exercise of power over bare life are not external to "society" (as was the home or exile in antiquity) but are kept within society by the decision of the sovereign to create a *state of exception*. Exile is no longer outside of the community as in antiquity but instead becomes hidden within it. In "camps," bare life becomes part of a hidden norm within society, essentially a voiceless existence that is part of and *within* the political. "Insofar as its inhabitants were stripped of every political status and wholly reduced to bare life, the camp was also the most absolute biopolitical space ever to have been realized, in which power confronts nothing but pure life, without any mediation."[26]

Much of this is hardly new. Goffman's observations about "stripping" presage Agamben although without direct reference by the latter. The camp, however, is only the blunt end of the subsumption of bare life into the realm of politics. While Agamben questions why Foucault concentrated on prisons but never on camps, he concedes that

> the decisive fact is that, together with the process by which the exception everywhere becomes the rule, the realm of bare life—which is originally situated at the margins of the political order—gradually begins to coincide with the political realm, and exclusion and inclusion, outside and inside, bios and zoē, right and fact, enter into a zone of irreducible indistinction. At once excluding bare life from and capturing it within the political order, the state of exception actually constituted, in its very separateness, the hidden foundation on which the entire political system rested.[27]

By now, "the great State structures have entered into a process of dissolution and the emergency has . . . become the rule."[28] "For millennia," Foucault observed, "man remained what he was for Aristotle: a living animal with the additional capacity for political existence; modern man is an animal whose politics places his existence as a living being in question."[29] Thus, as Foucault argues, the modern Western state has "integrated techniques of subjective individualization with procedures of objective totalization to an unprecedented degree"; Foucault refers to a "political 'double bind,' constituted by individualization and the simultaneous totalization of structures of modern power."[30] In other words, we live in a *carceral society* or, as Agamben would put it, the "camp" has become a regularized part of society at large.

In an age of Abu Ghraib and Guantanamo—not to mention long-term solitary confinement in many countries throughout the world—Agamben's analysis seems revealing. Are not large groups of (mostly) men who are deemed to be the "worst of the worst" and thus, essentially, *homo sacer*, excluded from good life and subjected to horrific extrajudicial violence whether by waterboarding or by long-term isolation? Is it not true in the age of mass incarceration in the United States that the state of exception has now become the norm, and a norm that bleeds its way into society at large as millions of people of color and poor whites are segregated into ghettoes where they are excluded from public voice and from meaningful political life— what one US observer calls the *new Jim Crow*?[31]

So what is the problem, then, with Agamben and, by extension, Foucault? Several critics have argued that Agamben and Foucault lack a theory of "emancipatory possibilities."[32] They, correctly, ask whether the state of bare life could create common grounds for a movement against state power, biopower, or economic subjugation. Yet even these critiques dissatisfy. Ziarek, for example, puts forth hunger strikes as an example of how prisoners can use their "bare life" conditions as a weapon of voice and emancipation (we shall return to hunger strikes in chapter 5, although in a different context). Yet her case, suffragettes attempting to get the vote, narrows the definition of emancipation to inclusion within the *polis*. She thus, like Foucault and Agamben, accepts a narrow definition of the "good life" as participation in the *polis* and fails to recognize alternatives that are not only about democracy but also about other forms of "life," including contemplation, leisure, and, importantly, the production of collective joy. To use the terminology of Hirschman, this critique of Agamben and, by implication, Foucault, only recognizes the alternatives of voice and loyalty and *not of exit*. Exilic societies, as we have defined them, consist of parallel practices and institutions of life that do not mimic those of mainstream societies. Not only do exilic communities practice the "art of not being governed"; more precisely, they govern themselves and practice mutual aid.

Once we return to mutual aid as definitive of exilic practice, we are left with the question of exilic economy: how do communities subsist if not through their work in the formal economy? To answer this question, we turn first to the distinction between substantive and formal economy.

FROM EXILE TO AUTONOMY: SUBSTANTIVE AND FORMAL ECONOMY

At this point it will be useful to distinguish the kinds of economic activities that may take place in exilic spaces from those that are integrated into the world-capitalist (including local) economy, and the relationship between the two. In the course of this paper we have referred to things like "cooperation," "mutual aid," "self-activation," and "escape agriculture," but at this point we want to be more specific and more systematic. When we introduce the concept of economy, several questions arise. What kinds of economic activities are characteristic of exilic spaces? Are they likely to be communal, do they support mutual aid and equality, or are they fragmented at individual or household levels? What are their dynamic properties—are they sustainable, do they tend to reintroduce hierarchies and inequalities? How, if at all, can we distinguish economic activities that enable the production and reproduction of exilic spaces from those that, even if not commodified, are integrated into the processes that enable and ensure world-capitalist accumulation?

An initial distinction is between what Hopkins and Polanyi call *substantive* and *formal* economy. Formal economy is the economy of classical and neoclassical economics, a system whereby scarce resources are distributed among unlimited wants through a (supposedly self-regulating) price-setting market. The problem is one of "efficiency," "economizing," or getting the most out of what has been endowed. We can add dynamics to the system and allow for growth, but there is still a problem of economizing at each output level and at any given time. Those economic activities that will succeed in such a system are the ones that produce more output (of higher exchange value) at a lower cost (fewer or cheaper labor and resource inputs). Notice, however, that these are also activities that produce an economic surplus that, in capitalism, is associated with the accumulation of wealth.

In the real world, as Polanyi points out at length, "self-regulating markets" are imperfect social creations that are manipulated by states and corporate actors. The idea of "economizing" can include many things that are not recognized in neoclassical economics, including the integration of unfree labor into the global division of labor and the plunder of resources by force.[33] These are important sources of accumulation as well as uneven development in the world economy.

The "substantive view" of economy looks at the myriad ways in which people provide for themselves and for each other. Many activities take place outside of market exchange. This includes nonformal economic and social relationships, many of which are considered to be "traditional" and outmoded but which, nonetheless, persist and even thrive in so-called advanced capitalist economies. Polanyi and Hopkins refer to several kinds of substantive activities that are unrecognized by the formal definition of economy, including reciprocity (doing things for each other), redistribution (transfer of resources from one person or group to another), and householding (direct production for own or household use).[34] A further category, gifting, is not directly treated by Polanyi or Hopkins, although the social meanings and consequences of gifting can be varied and profound.[35] Indeed, all of these substantive economic activities have hidden meanings and contexts, depending on the culture in which they occur. Rather than being "free" or "voluntary" they may be required by cultural norms, and wrong participation may invite social punishments.

Once we take these things into account, we can see that "economic" and "non-economic" actions and institutions are combined in many different ways throughout a given society. Social roles may have non-economic bases and thus carry a primarily non-economic logic for how they are carried out, yet people in them will undertake actions that have clear economic impact. Hopkins speaks of a priest who gives food to the poor or a purchasing agent in a school or university, but we could as easily speak of parents "gifting" their children's teachers, a community presenting food to a stranger upon entry to the village, or families exchanging "home visits" that involve, by expectation, certain combinations of food and drink. In other words, economic roles and actions may be embedded in social institutions, including cultural practices.

On the other hand, a (not-so-) new "science of altruism"[36] proposes that we may actually be hardwired to help others, without regard even for reciprocity, leaving Polanyi's and Hopkins's categories of substantive economic practices still too restricted by their expectations of eventual repayment. When we see someone in need or want, our tendency is to help them, regardless of whether we may someday need someone to return the favor. To take things a step further, insofar as we are sociable beings, we value doing things *together*, a tendency that is also elided in concepts like altruism and reciprocity. Our old friend Kropotkin makes this quite clear: *mutual aid* is not merely about reciprocity or helping each other, but *doing things together as a community*. This is not just necessary for survival in the face of adversity or threat, but also a key to living an enjoyable and fulfilling life.

Thus, the Polanyian concepts of embeddedness or even substantive economy may not go far enough. In exilic spaces as in precapitalism, the conceptions "economic" and "non-economic" may even be redundant. Turner suggests that one " would do better to start from Marx's and Engels' programmatic 'anthropological' definition of production in *The German Ideology*, in which production is said to comprehend, not merely the production of the means of subsistence, but of human beings and families, social relations of cooperation, and new needs as well."[37] And, as Graeber notes, "economy" in many precapitalist societies included all of those things that were "valued" in the sense that people were willing to expend their energies and time obtaining or making them. Often, they were not merely self-provisioned but actually given away![38] Perhaps more importantly, in nonmarket societies it is apparent that the things on which people expend most of their energies are not even the subsistence activities that one might define as economic according to a substantive view of economy, but rather activities of socialization (*producing* children, people, and social relations as well as things).

Clearly, economy in its broader definition involves time, effort, and commitment. Effort is connected to commitment since intensity, creativity, attention to detail, and quality are all impacted by alienation and force as well as solidarity, empathy, and hope. When one brings time into the equation, an interesting result emerges: workers struggle to reduce the working day when effort is regulated by a boss or manager and is tied to wages; yet effort is intensified and time lengthened when it is regulated by interest, creativity, and solidarity. "Development" has a vast impact on the allocation of time during the day and, combined with the degree to which work and life are separated, it fundamentally changes not just how we spend our "working day" but how we spend our whole day.

Komlosy argues from a world-historical perspective that the meaning of "work" has changed since the thirteenth century so that it now refers only to those things that produce exchange values or, at best, directly support the production of exchange values through reproducing labor. The exertion of energies in ways that do not directly support the production of exchange values, by being redefined as *not* work, are thus devalued, not simply made worthless or even invisible, but even *negatively valued* as "time wasting." Moreover, it was only under capitalism and colonialism that work became associated with pain (disutility). According to the *work ethic*, expenditures of energy in ways that are fun cannot be work.[39] By contrast, indigenous people have specific terms for each activity they engage in but no general term to denote work and differentiate it from *non*work.

To the extent that it is based on mutual aid, the *work* of making exilic society is not just the household chore of producing children but the joint chore of producing community. This involves a great deal of cultural work. As Ehrenreich notes, long before people had a written language or settled into villages they saw dancing as important enough to record on stone.[40]

Neurological sciences indicate that "music together with dance have co-evolved biologically and culturally to serve as a technology of social bonding. Findings of anthropologists and psychiatrists ... show how the rhythmic behavioral activities that are induced by drum beats and music can lead to altered states of consciousness, through which mutual trust among members of societies is engendered."[41]

Yet, "civilized" people stereotyped indigenous people as "lazy" and were incensed by "easy" crops that enabled natives to expend efforts on cultural rituals rather than "work." They launched a "global campaign against festivities and ecstatic rituals":

> At some point, in town after town throughout the northern Christian world, the music stops. Carnival costumes are put away or sold; dramas that once engaged a town's entire population are cancelled; festive rituals are forgotten or preserved only in tame and truncated form. The ecstatic possibility, which had first been driven from the sacred precincts of the church, was now harried from the streets and public squares.[42]

After that, festivals were "occupied" by the lower classes and the dispossessed as a way of exercising discontent and making voice. At the upper end, behavior was governed by the "civilizing" requirements of court manners.[43] Along with the end of public joy came an "epidemic of melancholy," first in seventeenth-century England, then eighteenth-century Germany, and then, by the nineteenth century, throughout the Western world.[44]

There appears to be a contradiction. The natives are "lazy" when it comes to physical labor yet they have "vitality" in the practice of customs such as dancing. This should not surprise us: it takes us right back to "value" as the regulator that determines where people exert their physical, emotional, and spiritual efforts, at least in the absence of capitalist labor regulation and consumerist alienation. Outside of capitalism, once subsistence is achieved, the center of economy/value is the production of people and community, often through collective joy. "Development" may be seen as the attempted replacement of public joy by commodity production. Is there a dialectic, parallel to Kropotkin's struggle between mutual aid and possessive individualism, where exilic actors invest great time and effort into expressions of collective joy and to the work of building community, while capital and state institutions support the development of what Crary[45] calls "24/7 capitalism," a regime where leisure and joy are increasingly subsumed by capitalist work relations?

SUBSISTENCE: THE MARGIN BETWEEN EXILIC AND CAPITALIST LIFE?

Regardless of the value a society places on nonmaterial things such as the production of community, it must still provide basic subsistence: food, clothing, shelter. With regard to material subsistence, one might propose that the formal market economy is the world of capitalism and the substantive extramarket economy is the "outside" world, including that of exilic spaces, where things are provided according to usefulness and need rather than the law of value, and resource-uses and distributional questions are decided by individual agreements, direct democracy, or representative systems rather than by market price and ability to pay. This distinction may hold in the limiting case, where exilic communities, or shatter zones, are completely external to the capitalist world-system, perhaps before incorporation. But Scott concedes that that is a marginal and nearly impossible world, of limited interest to us today.

Rather, in the modern world-system even substantive activities that are not allocated by the market must be considered, in the first instance, by their relationship to capitalist accumulation and the law of value within the world-economy. From the earliest stages of the formation and expansion of the modern world-system, householding and extramarket activities were at the center of strategies of incorporation. According to Hopkins and Wallerstein, an important way to make newly incorporated units more profitable was to subsidize export-oriented activities by using labor that had other sources of income, including from substantive activities:

> The crucial change was to bring about some form of economic activity which would be responsive to the pressures emanating from the "market" of the world-economy. In order to be responsive, this economic activity had to have a work-force that was both available and dispensable, and was relatively well-disciplined when working. This was no small task, and often required force or force majeure (the removal of plausible alternatives).
>
> In order to keep this workforce at a relatively low level of pay (by the existing standards of the world-economy), they had to be located in household structures in which the work on this new "export-oriented activity" formed only a small part of the lifetime revenues of the households of which the workers were members. In this case, other household activities which brought in revenues in multiple forms could "subsidize" the remuneration for the "export-oriented activity," thereby keeping the labor costs very low. To the extent that a workforce was absorbed in an "export-oriented activity," it had less time than previously to engage in food-cultivating activities. The implication of

this was that behind the organization of the "export-oriented activity" there must have existed, or have come to be organized, a group providing food that was somehow sold to this workforce. And to the extent that there were both new export-oriented areas and new (or expanded) food-producing areas, there may have to have been a "people-producing" area which supplied the additional labor force (in multiple forms, from slavery to temporary migration).[46]

Actually, the foregoing quote is somewhat misleading because the food- and service-producing groups in incorporated societies did not necessarily sell to the newly incorporated workforce but often provided food and services directly, for example, through households. Reproductive labor continues to be an important way that the nonmarket substantive economy subsidizes the formal economy by cheapening the cost of labor. Many services and products that could be marketized and paid for out of the wage bill, thus raising pressure to increase wages, are provided mostly by women within the household but also by people generally throughout communities. As Federici writes,

> In capitalist society reproductive work is not the free reproduction of ourselves or others according to our and their desires. To the extent that directly or indirectly it is exchanged for a wage, reproduction work is, at all points, subjected to the conditions imposed on it by the capitalist organization and relations of production. In other words, housework is not a free activity. It is "the production and reproduction of the capitalist's most indispensable means of production: the worker."[47]

But Federici also claims that this part of the substantive economy is under continuous and vicious attack by the formal economy, a clear indication of our claim that incorporation is an ongoing and incomplete process. The recent phase of neoliberal globalization, for instance,

> has produced a historic leap in the size of the world proletariat, through a global process of enclosures that has separated millions from their lands, their jobs, their "customary rights" and through the increased employment of women ... By destroying subsistence economies, by separating producers from the means of subsistence, by making millions dependent on monetary incomes, even when unable to access waged employment, once again, the capitalist class has through the world labor market, regained the initiative, re-launched the accumulation process, cut the cost of labor-production. Two billion people have been added to the labor market.[48]

At the same time, through structural adjustment and other conservative macroeconomic policies, states have disinvested in pensions, health-care services, public transport, and so on, reducing (at least during the current period of accumulation) the redistributive side of the substantive economy. As a result of this withdrawal of states from subsidizing the reproduction of labor, many activities that were redistributive are now either marketized (especially in wealthier zones of world-capitalism) or, for the masses who cannot afford to buy reproductive services, are provided more intensively in the home or the community.

Nor is "homework" equivalent to householding. This, of course, was already true of early capitalism, where activities like spinning and weaving were carried out in homes to supplement farming incomes or to provide money when farming and grazing were largely for self-consumption. Today, there has been a considerable deconcentration of industrial production into homes, often as informal work, and not just in the formal economy.[49]

In the southern cone of South America, for example, Zibechi argues that the "flight of capital, that is, the victory of the workers' insubordination, reflected the workers' flight from capitalist relations of production and subordination." The residents of new exilic spaces, communities of tens of thousands on the outskirts of existing cities, set up "independently controlled forms of production," and although they remained connected to and dependent on the market, "vast sectors now control their forms and rhythms of production, and are no longer dominated by the rhythms of capital and its division of labor."[50] The new poor survived by providing services, recycling materials discarded by consumerist society, and setting up micro-enterprises and family retail operations of all kinds. Some began basic manufacturing. And the demand for products and services often seems to come from self-governance. People in these spaces have tended to build their own habitat, from houses to public spaces, streets, marketplaces, and even sewage and water.

In El Alto, for instance, 70 percent of the working population is engaged in family or small semi-entrepreneurial activities, including restaurants, construction, and manufacturing. There and elsewhere, Zibechi describes a "new social and labor culture ... marked by nomadism, instability and changed work relations."[51] In family production units nonrenumerated family work predominates, with family members teaching each other how to do the work. How quickly and sometimes even how the task is done is left up to the producer as long as deadlines for orders are met. In other cases, microbusinesses combine several or many family units, where the "owner" pays wages and also gives families assistance, in a kind of moral economy.[52] García Linera observes "a greater autonomy of work management" since production "is not directly supervised by the owner," and he argues that production is "non-capitalist" and sustainable at least in "the historic and medium-term form of expanded reproduction of capital in Bolivia."[53]

There is an argument that autonomy from the state is positively associated with economic autonomy in exilic spaces. If the most important problems of the locality—the construction and maintenance of environment (housing, water, sewage, streets), education, and health—are managed through different and more directly democratic processes, this creates significant demand for local enterprise and services. Research is needed on how these are provided. In Zapatista communities, for instance, infrastructural work as well as education and health work is unpaid, although there is reciprocity, as housing, food, and other basic needs are met by the community (authors' observations).

So far, most descriptions of economies in these exilic spaces are optimistic in terms of their assumptions that the economy is somewhat autonomous from the existing regional and world-capitalist economy. Yet Zibechi also refers to exilic activities being connected to and even dependent on the market. It is unclear how these activities vary with respect to their relationships to the market economy, even to mainstream manufacturing sectors, for which these new enterprises with new work forms may act as subcontractors. Nor do we know much about the degree to which the reproduction of labor in these areas subsidizes labor costs in the capitalist economy. In Guatemala, for instance, there are ex-guerrilla communities that are autonomous from municipal or regional government in most respects, and who organize and self-provide village infrastructures, including health and education. Yet most households are still dependent on money incomes from casual day labor in the nearest city or municipality. The cost of labor in these day-markets is without doubt cheapened by a combination of an overabundance of casual labor supply and the fact that much of the workers' subsistence is self-provided within the community. Even in the Zapatista communities there is concern about the degree to which young people migrate to regional labor markets to supplement family incomes; sometimes they do not return (authors' observations).

All of these are examples of the difficulties of defining and researching exilic economic activities, particularly in the case of structural exit. Once we recognize the points about reproductive labor made by Federici and others, as well as the difficulties autonomous communities have in meeting all of their needs through nonwaged economic sectors, a key question is whether freely provided and mutually beneficial, often *communal*, exilic labor *can* constitute free activity—"the free reproduction of ourselves or others according to our and their desires." Do the dynamics of exilic life, as Zibechi and others optimistically suggest, enable communities to move further toward economic autonomy? Or do world-systemic processes and pressure force them to revert more and more to dependence on wage labor, money incomes, and market purchases rather than self-provisioning? These issues will arise in each of our case studies in this volume.

A central question about exilic activities, then, is their impact on capitalist accumulation and their relationship to processes of accumulation. This raises a further point that is indirectly made in the distinction between substantive and formal economics. Formal economists continually talk about scarcity and the importance of economizing and efficiency to the success of an economic system. Yet the emphasis in substantive economy is on provisioning, or the supply of the things that people need. The substantive view of economy this emphasizes not economizing, but rather social surplus and its disposition. Many exilic activities may even be "non-economic," as the term is currently understood, insofar as people choose to exert much time and effort in building social relations in their communities.

Here, one must reintroduce the connections between political and economic organization. For some time, approaches to alternative decentralized economic organization have emphasized different forms and models of self-management, including the right of associated producers, consumers groups, or other decentralized associations to decide how a surplus would be distributed. The question then arises how exilic communities will decide among alternatives, and that raises questions regarding forms of governance and powers that they have over the surplus (both material surplus but also labor time) and the distribution of economic resources and activities. A basic question is whether there is private property and, if not, how land and other forms of property will be allocated and reallocated. Even decentralized economic models emphasize the role of some governing body to protect the economic and legal rights of members of the community.[54] The following research questions arise: Do exilic communities produce a surplus from autonomous self-provisioning activities? If so, how is the surplus used and by whom? Does or can disposition of the surplus in the community strengthen economic autonomy and enable the exilic zone to delink from world-capitalism?

Finally, there is a question of whether certain kinds of economic organization are more sustainable than others. One of Kropotkin's central hypotheses is that the communities that are most likely to survive in a hostile environment are the ones who practice cooperation, or mutual aid, rather than competitive rivalry. Although Kropotkin dealt mainly with natural threats, one could extend his reasoning to the ability of exilic spaces to resist attempts by states to reincorporate them into capitalist economic processes. An important test of this hypothesis is whether exilic communities are more likely to practice forms of mutual aid on a regular basis or whether they turn to such mechanisms only when threatened (e.g., the case of millenarian movements). What are the rights and obligations of households as opposed to associations of households? Moreover, are those communities that practice cooperation across different kinds of economic activities more likely to survive pressures from the world-economy than those that have other ways of organizing their economies, whether hierarchical or extremely decentralized to the household level?

CONCLUSIONS AND DANGERS

In this chapter, we have laid out a series of issues that are central to the study of exilic spaces, defined as those areas of social and economic life where people and groups attempt to escape from capitalist economic processes, whether by territorial escape or by attempts to build structures that are autonomous of capitalist processes of accumulation and social control. We propose that this is necessary for the complete study of world-capitalism, that the creation and re-creation of exilic spaces constitute a common world-systemic process. Formation and re-formation also invite *de*-formation. We propose a comparative study of exilic spaces—from mountains, swamps, and pirate ships to ghettos, tenement yards, and experimental self-managed workplaces. We have introduced quite a few concepts to cover strategies of exit, politics of exilic spaces, exilic economic activities, and the relationships of exilic social economy to world-capitalism. At the risk of oversimplifying, it is useful to present a typology of exilic positions and related research questions we are proposing in this book. We invite others to add to, amend, and otherwise engage this summative representation.

Type of escape: Geographical, structural, mixed. Geographical exilic spaces depend on spatial features for their protection and separation from regional state control or world economic processes. They may be in remote or hard-to-get places like mountains, swamps, jungles, steppes, and deserts. They are protected, for a time, by the processes Scott calls "friction," whereby the state's costs of establishing authority increase as distance increases. Protection breaks down as new technologies enable states and capitals to overcome this friction. *Structural escape* attempts to create barriers between controls of state and capital, for example, by squatting or occupying instead of paying rents, and by self-provisioning rather than working in the formal economy. The point is to escape control of decisions by market signals, the international law of value, or state power and to increase individual or group control over decision making. Many exilic spaces may combine the two strategies, or types of escape.

World time—by incorporation and by hegemonic regime (Holland, Britain, US). Each time period (pre-incorporation, incorporation, peripheralization) may be associated with likely types of exilic escape. Pre-incorporation escape is likely to be geographical and may conform to the idea of "nonstate spaces" with associated "escape agricultures," as in the case of Zomia. Early Cossacks may be another example, although their herding/raiding economy leads us to prefer "escape economies" to "escape agriculture." Incorporation is a period of capturing new spaces by bringing them into global divisions of labor and associated trading regimes. It includes the imposition of new economic units of production and trade, new ways of acquiring and controlling labor, new state institutions of control, and new infrastructures. We expect that the incorporation of an area will impose pressures against geographic escapers, who will make political bargains to extend their periods of escape, go further into the hinterlands beyond incorporation, or try to find new forms of structural escape as they are "captured" geographically. Under peripheralization, world-systemic processes that are associated with protecting the law of value will be deepened, including the four typical processes that are associated with incorporation. This is not a singular or finished process, however, and each period of restructuring that is associated with the rise of a new hegemonic regime will provide new threats and opportunities for escape as forms of hegemonic control change (Dutch arms-length control over trade routes, British direct territorial colonial control, US anticolonialism mixed with preferential trade and direct investment, Japanese "new forms of investment")[55] and as the international division of labor changes according to new leading world economic sectors (cotton, iron and steel, cars and consumer durables, computers and other high-tech instruments; the outsourcing of textile and clothing production).

Governance: Household, direct democracy (delegation/charge), representation1 (internal selection), representation2 (external selection), authoritarian.[56] Although there may be a temptation to see these forms of governance as mutually exclusive, our initial researches indicate that this may be variable and even mixed. Scott, for example, describes forms of governance in Zomia that move from highly decentralized and household based to (one might surmise) some combination of direct democracy and authoritarian leadership in the form of millenarian movements.[57] Cossack governance seems to differ according to different social milieu; herding and commons were managed through a combination of households and direct democracy while governance of military service varied between direct democracy, the two kinds of representation (atamans were locally chosen and then appointed by the state), and authoritarian leadership. Contemporary exilic spaces including attempts at "real utopias" appear to use many varieties of governance, from direct democracy and delegation (*mandar obedeciendo*) in Zapatista communities to authoritarianism by certain African armed insurgencies. In new urban spaces in Latin America, it appears that there are forms of direct selection of delegates among small groups of households (e.g., by "city block") as well as direct assembly decision making for key decisions. In El Alto in Bolivia there are reportedly between 400 and 550 neighborhood juntas, with one for every thousand inhabitants over the age of ten.[58] People in the new urban spaces appear to directly decide and manage questions about construction, infrastructure (sewage, water, roads, etc.), and other matters. But much more research is required about the varieties of decision-making processes in new urban spaces (under "structural escape") and about the causes of variation in governance.

Economy. If Scott and others are correct, the economies of pre-incorporation "shatter zones" are built on local-level subsistence production, the organization of which varies from household to community levels. Early exilic communities appear to practice "escape agriculture" in some cases, but in others they build economies based on herding and raiding. Structural escape, on the other hand, is based on self-provisioning at household and community levels but may also be dependent on the market for some material needs, including money. Obvious questions: What is produced or which services rendered in exilic spaces? How are economic units organized and at what level (e.g., household, associations of households, micro-enterprises, etc.)? What are their relations of production, and who has power over how things are produced, when, and at what rate? Are these activities, as some propose, "new" and "anticapitalist" forms of free provision of effort? Do exilic economic activities produce a surplus? In what form does such a surplus appear and how it is disposed and distributed? How are decisions made about disposal of the surplus? What are the relationships between local governance, material and social infrastructures, and exilic activities? How is human effort distributed between material provisioning and communal activities, including collective joy and leisure? Does production of a surplus create pressures for new inequalities, or does it strengthen cooperative activities?

Economy/capitalism relation. Very difficult research questions must be asked about the relationships between exilic economic activities and regional and world-capitalist institutions and processes. Even the most autonomous communities with developed structures and institutions for self-provisioning, at household to community levels, may continue to depend on regional labor markets for money incomes and world trade networks for bought commodities that supplement their own produce. They may also depend on markets for what they produce. Insofar as the exilic economic structures are centered on provisioning, do they cheapen the labor that moves to regional labor markets, in the sense that day or casual workers can work for less money? What processes draw exilic communities back into regional and world markets? What might enable them to strengthen their position of autonomy from regional and world-capitalism?

Space/state mediation. What, if any, is the relationship between the exilic space and the regional state? What combinations are there of autonomy and loyalty? And if the local state can demand some loyalty bargain, are exilic communities able to keep that relationship at arm's length, or do loyalty obligations create dependent relationships? If the latter, is there an inevitable process, possibly connected with world-systemic cycles, that pulls exilic communities "back into" the interstate system?

Exilic membership. Who are the members of exilic communities? Are they full exiles, in the sense that their lives—their social, political, and economic activities—are overwhelmingly "within" the exilic space or governed by exilic processes? Or to what extent and how are they in contradictory locations, with part of their lifework governed by exilic processes and ties, and part by relationships to the world-economy? Do they pay taxes, work, and shop in the formal economy? If so, under what circumstances and to what degree does this affect their standing in the exilic community and their ties to the exilic space?

There is a temptation to view exilic spaces as utopian reverse images of world-capitalism, whose processes they are attempting to escape. They are potentially utopian but they are not always islands of desirable economy and politics. First, they might enable a considerable degree of egalitarian and cooperative economy and participative political practices, but these are not their defining characteristics, nor will they necessarily happen. Cossack and pirate economies, although relatively egalitarian, cooperative, and democratic, carried out horrific raids and practiced violence not only against enemies but against their own. They could be macho at best and terribly misogynistic at their worst, as evidenced by the story of the great Cossack hero Stenka Razin drowning his Persian bride to satisfy his shipmates. Gray's description of Jamaican exilic spaces today is a bleak one, of extreme poverty, intracommunal violence, aggression, and "rude otherness."[59] Even if exilic communities are based on egalitarian principles and avoid these shortcomings, they are often frustrated and incomplete, marked by contradictory elements, and sometimes paid for by complicit involvement with states and hierarchical processes of the world-economy.

Nor should the autonomy of these spaces and territories be exaggerated. World-capitalism does not allow a complete outside. As such, exilic spaces are paradoxical: they are simultaneously inside and outside of the system, extra-state, but intrasystemic. As Braudel reminds us, capital is never able to commodify everything; there is always an active, dialectical process of contestation and negotiation. We have already referred to exilic economic activities as contradictory substantive practices, which are anti-capital in certain respects or at certain times but supportive of capital in others, even simultaneously.

Thus, the question about the dynamics of exilic spaces is the following: can they develop those activities or aspects of activities that limit the reproduction of state and capital, while keeping at bay those that reinforce capitalist accumulation and valorization?

Finally, we should be leary of functionalist analyses of world-capitalism. Only a history that is sensitive to the interrelation and unity of diverse processes can help us understand the paradoxical location and production of exilic spaces and territories in the capitalist world-economy. To understand exilic reality, we must develop a heuristic strategy at two distinct levels: first, we should conceptualize exilic spaces as specific configurations in relation to the immediate state-spaces; and second, we need to address their simultaneous embeddedness in spatiotemporal frameworks of the world-economy as a whole. One way to look at it is to imagine a complex movement of global pressures and local responses conditioned by a variety of contexts. Systemic regularities produce distinctive local spaces within a unifying global framework of "world time." Seen in this way, exilic spaces are part of the making and remaking, the economic structuring and restructuring, of the capitalist world-economy and political power. Exilic spaces are always in process; they are always being made and remade, composed and decomposed. But like Kropotkin's institutions and practices of mutual aid, they never go away. There is nothing spontaneous or surprising, for instance, about the emergence of the Mexican Zapatistas as an example of an exilic reappropriation. Nor is it surprising when semi-autonomous groups such as the Bolivian *cocaleros* make bargains with and even participate in representative government. In the world-system, many things are possible. The research we propose will examine the limits of those possibilities, in their full variation and regularity.

We begin with Cossacks, a long history of exile and autonomy, and a fascinating case of the interactions of exit and loyalty.

THREE

Cossacks

RUSSIA, THE CAPITALIST WORLD-SYSTEM, AND COSSACK EXIT

THE COSSACKS ARE A LEGENDARY PEOPLE. To understand them as an exilic society we must separate legend from historical reality even though, as with another group we will analyze (Zapatistas), the legends reflect their power as exiles, rebels, even renegades. The dynamics of their escape and exilic development should be understood not only relative to the consolidation of Russian state power, with which they had to negotiate and renegotiate escape, but also in the context of both sides' changing place in the capitalist world-system.

Immanuel Wallerstein places Russia outside of the emerging European economic system.[1] For him, sixteenth-century Russia was a separate world-economy, only incorporated into the structures of the modern world-system in the late eighteenth century. His argument hinges on several differences between Russia and the rest of eastern Europe: (1) the nature of trade; (2) the strength and role of state machinery; and, as a consequence of the two prior points, (3) a difference in the strength and role of the Russian urban bourgeoisie. Wallerstein constructs his perspective in constant dialogue with sociospatial forces and changes at smaller scales. Unlike Polish trade, the direction, nature, and volume of Russian trade tended to create an independent economy with Moscow at its center. Russian trade with the East and South was as important as with the West, and the latter was not critical for the functioning of its economy, despite the fact that the export of raw materials predominated. The attempt to establish Russia as a Baltic power during the Livonian War (1558–83) was paradoxically both a failure and a success: it prevented the incorporation of Russia into the capitalist world-economy led by Holland, allowing the Russian state to pursue its goal of imperial independence.[2] The "delayed incorporation thesis" is implicit in Wallerstein's contention that Ivan's defeat delayed the absorption of Russia into the European world-system.[3]

An early objection to Wallerstein's account of Russian incorporation was raised by Nolte, who concluded that Russia (and eastern Europe as a whole) was indeed part of the Dutch-led world-system and that those regions should be considered semi-peripheral.[4] According to Nolte, the history of Russian foreign trade in the sixteenth century provides no support for placing it outside of capitalism. If Russian incorporation was somewhat delayed, this was due to political factors rather than economic structure or relations.

A more serious challenge to Wallerstein locates Russia in the periphery of the capitalist world-system from its beginnings. Kagarlitsky, building on the work of the Russian historian Mikhail Pokrovsky,[5] argues that Russia was incorporated into world-capitalism in the sixteenth century.[6] After the Livonian War, Russia could have become an external zone, outside of the boundaries of the world-system. However, Ivan IV (1530–84) was desperate to insert Russia into the emerging capitalist hierarchy. For Kagarlitsky, the history of Russia reveals contradictions that are typical of peripheral capitalism: "on one hand, it cannot continue without the center; that is, foreign influence provides it with the stimulus necessary for development. But, on the other hand, the more that peripheral capital develops, the greater its need to protect its own interests, or at least to obtain better conditions for itself."[7] In a tragic dilemma for the Russian state, the only real alternative to peripheral development through incorporation into European trade networks was isolation and stagnation.

Interestingly, Kagarlitsky does not rely on the concept of the semiperiphery to explain the ambiguity of the Russian position as both a "great power" and an underdeveloped region with a serf economy. Russia was indeed an empire, but a peripheral one, both an independent state and an object of colonization with imperial people who were, in essence, colonized. The period after the Livonian War was one of forced and rapid reintegration of Russia into world trade as a supplier of raw materials for the expanding world-economy. This was a process of "self-colonization" in which the powerful state was active on two fronts: enserfing its population while simultaneously securing trade routes for the export of raw materials, which were extracted by bonded labor, to the West. The so-called peculiarities of Russian history were created by this dual and conflicted role, which is best understood by situating Russia within the framework of the capitalist world-economy and away from the host of sociopsychological explanations that still dominate much of the thinking about "Russian despotism." Russia was underdeveloped because of its closeness and innumerable links to Europe, not by its isolation and remoteness. The proximity of Europe made it impossible for Russia to escape the processes of modernization that defined its backwardness. "The more backward the Russian Empire, the more successfully it was integrated into the world system."[8] Peter the Great's (Peter I) revolution, more than anything else, was a cultural revolution from above and a continuation and acceleration of these trends. The politics of the Muscovite state in the sixteenth century made the Petrine reforms inevitable: they were a culmination of Russia's trajectory of (under)development, not an aberration.

Russia's peripheral status created a "lag" behind the West: its ever advancing incorporation into the capitalist world-system required a reorganization of state and cultural structures, which assumed a "European facade" under Peter I. Russian backwardness was a product of serfdom, which was itself a result of capitalist modernity. In other words, "steadily growing incorporation into the world system required the modernizing of Russian capitalism."[9] The expanding world-economy required a Russian state that could answer its demands by intensifying labor exploitation and instituting bonded labor, making it competitive on the world market.

While these insights provide fertile ground for a historicized conception of Russia's incorporation into the world-system, specificities of Russian political, social, and economic development have yet to be resolved. We join the discussion from a somewhat unusual vantage point: by taking an "exilic view" from the space of the Don Cossacks, we illustrate and illuminate not only the history of Russian state formation but also the nature of Russia's incorporation into the capitalist world-system. The Cossacks were an answer to world-systemic incorporation, as a movement to escape the increasingly oppressive relations of the emerging Russian class structure by setting up a parallel *exilic* society; moreover, the historical development and eventual reincorporation of Cossack spaces under Russian state control are an important part of any explanation of Russia's changing place in the capitalist world-system.

The historical relationship between the exilic space, the Russian state, and the world market was one of mutual formation. From the standpoint of the rise of capitalism, these three instances represent distinct angles of vision onto a singular world-historical process. Framing these moments as separation-in-unity allows us to add concrete details to what is still perhaps a vague notion of the exilic space. The following analysis is framed by two principal questions: how did Russia's changing place in world-capitalism affect the exilic space of the Don Cossacks, and how did that exilic space in turn influence Russia-in-world-capitalism?

Standard accounts of early Russian history focus on its backwardness, commonly perceived as a defining peculiarity of Russian development. Students in East and Central Europe before 1989 were forced to memorize "Karamazin's thesis":

> The cloak of barbarism that darkened the Russian horizon hid Europe from us at the very time when beneficial knowledge and skills were increasingly multiplying there, when people were freeing themselves from servitude, and when close bonds were forged between cities for their mutual defense in troubled times; when the invention of the compass had widened navigation and trade; when governments were encouraging artisans, artists, and scholars; when the universities were arising for the pursuit of higher learning; when minds were growing used to contemplation, to correctness of thought; when manners were becoming more mild; when wars were losing their earlier ferocity; when the well-born grew ashamed of slaughters, and when noble heroes were famed for their mercy to the weak, for their magnanimity and honor; when urbanity, humanness, and courtesy had become known and admired.[10]

This statement had influential adherents. Marx was not immune to its charm, and the vision of both liberal and Soviet historians was colored by the "darkened horizon" wrought by the Tatar-Mongol invasion.

In recent decades, this explanation for Russian peculiarities has fallen into disrepute.[11] Still, one could argue that the Tatar-Mongol invasion was responsible for the gathering of Russian lands around Moscow. Not only did Muscovy restore commercial relationships with Greece, it also arrested the process of fragmentation and destruction of Russian economic space that had been at work since the ninth century. More essentially, Tatar influence modernized the nascent state of Muscovy. An active relationship with the Tatars not only prevented the loss of Novgorod to Lithuania but also presented an "important step in the direction of creating a modern state."[12] Muscovite grand princes, confirmed by the khan, had more than enough maneuvering space to build a relatively stable political system, a broad financial base that rested on taxation, trade, and a "joint alliance between the princes and Tatars, aimed at joint exploitation of Russian masses."[13]

How was Moscow, by no means the most impressive candidate for such a task, able to unite the lands of the Rus? Lieberman argues that Ivan III (1440–1505) and his immediate successors, skillfully exploiting internecine Tatar disputes, were successful in "a) enhancing their security by seizing zones intermediate between their own territorial core and those of rival states like Lithuania; b) obtaining prized northeastern furs for export, while improving access to Baltic, Caspian, and Arctic Ocean ports; and c) opening the steppe to eventual Russian settlement."[14] The year 1450 was the watershed moment and, according to Hellie, the first half of the sixteenth century was "probably the most peaceful and most prosperous period in Russian history prior to [1945–85]."[15]

The key development in Ivan's administration was the creation of a new form of tenure: conditional land grants (*pomestia*) held on condition of service and the institution of a new "middle service class" of loyal officers who received them. *Pomest'e* estates, situated largely in the frontier areas, numbered as many as 17,500 in 1570. This efficient system of promoting royal authority in the countryside—compounded by agrarian transformation, the spread of commerce, urban growth, and territorial expansion—was advanced enough to impress Western travelers. "The country betwixt [Moscow and Iaroslavl]," wrote one such traveler in 1553, "is very well replenished with small villages, which are so well filled with people, that it is wonder to see them: the ground is well stored with corn which they carrie to the cities of Moscow in such abundance that it is wonder to see it."[16] What the traveler did not see was that this system was held together by government regulations that made peasant work and residence obligations increasingly compulsory, "beginning with the Code of 1497 and culminating in the Assembly Code of 1649."[17]

An important factor in the formation of the state of Muscovy was trade, in particular, control over transit routes, and especially the Volga trade route. Kagarlitsky argues that the need to maintain order along trade routes impelled the state to impose its control through new institutions. The history of state formation for Kagarlitsky is the history of conquest of the Volga route. Both local and international capital required a state that would become a modernizing force.[18]

Most historians agree that the reign of Ivan IV (1547–84) was a critical period in Russian history, in terms of both internal social structure and external policy.[19] Two factors were fundamental to Ivan's power: the growth of a patrimonial state machinery and a central bureaucracy with a tax base. Ivan's reign is marked by his decision not to expropriate the feudal aristocracy but to place an emphasis on expansion instead. In 1556, *pomestia* became a "loyal standing army," linked to the central authority and ready to fight for supremacy on the Baltic. After the end of the Livonian War (even if this end was inconclusive), Ivan was left without money and land.

Ivan's politics eventually led to *oprichnina,* an administrative arrangement that many historians continue to see as a "terrorist" operation. It was nothing of the sort. Rather, *oprichnina* was a successful attempt to check the disintegration of the state-space.[20] Essential to the new arrangement was the division between lands belonging to the Boyars (*zemshchina*) and those belonging to the Tsar (*oprichnina*). The latter comprised mostly trade routes and trade towns. This spelled the end to the delicate class alliance that had been established by Ivan's decision not to expropriate the feudal aristocracy, but to seek an alternative in expansion. This "internal war" spelled the end of the fragile compromise, much to the satisfaction of mercantile capitalists and English merchants. The latter received the first privilege extended to the foreign capital in Russian history, as they were allowed to become subjects to administrative reform.

After the death of Ivan, Russia found itself in a vulnerable position. The last Russian tsar of the Rurik Dynasty, Feodor Ivanovich, died in 1598. The period of Russian history between then and the establishment of the Romanov Dynasty in 1613, known as the Time of Troubles, was a time of intense, internal struggles characterized by the flight of peasants from affected areas and state attempts to prevent and control their flight. The fact that Poland and Sweden were divided as a result of the Thirty Years War, the war "that blended all European wars into one," was probably responsible for the survival of Moscow. Regardless, these were cataclysmic years, culminating in a series of famines in 1601–3 and the steppe uprising of Bolotnikov in 1606–7.[21] The flight of the population from the European regions of Russia was massive. The election of Michael Romanov in 1613[22] was not enough to prevent peasants from leaving. Most joined either the Cossacks or the *pomeshchiki* (local representatives of the tsar who were chronically short of labor in the "newly opened lands" in the south).

The process of enserfment, an essential ingredient of state formation, was also catalyzed during the reign of Ivan IV. The state's resolve to restrict peasant movement can be traced to 1580, when it was prohibited under an institution called the "forbidden years."

> The enserfment of the Russian peasantry was a drawn-out process spanning some three hundred years and developing in three basic stages, the first and third of which were long and the second of which was relatively short. During the second half of the fifteenth and most of the sixteenth centuries the

peasants' freedom was gradually limited; then, during the last two decades of the sixteenth century and the first decade of the seventeenth, a sudden and complete prohibition of their right to move occurred.[23]

After a brief interlude during the reign of Boris Godunov, restrictions were fully restored in 1603. Kolchin describes this as the third stage of enserfment when, in the seventeenth and first half of the eighteenth century, restrictions were solidified and codified and Russian serfdom "came increasingly to resemble chattel slavery."[24] Authorities were seeking to make peasants "legible" by registering them in local cadasters and subjecting the rural population to the control of the police. Every year after 1603 was a forbidden year, until the first full, legal codification of serfdom in the legislative code (*ulozhenie*) of 1649.[25]

Between the mid-fifteenth and mid-sixteenth centuries, then, Muscovy grew from one of several Russian principalities (and a small one, at that) to the center of a real empire. From 1462 to 1533 the area controlled by the state of Muscovy increased sevenfold, and during the remainder of the sixteenth century it doubled again.[26] Externally, the realm expanded from a tiny area in 1280 to almost four hundred thousand square kilometers by 1462.

With state formation came serfdom. The most prized possession in Russia at this time was people, not land. The growth of Muscovy and the rise of serfdom that accompanied it was directly linked with the opening of exilic space on the Don. Kolchin refers to the "extraordinary depopulation of central Russia," quoting British ambassador Gilles Fletcher, who wrote in 1588 that "many villages and towns [were] . . . uninhabited, the people being fled all into other places by reason of the extreme usage and exactions done upon them."[27] Increasing numbers of peasants were fleeing to the Cossack territory on the Don. Before the eighteenth century, when Moscow was only one of a few emerging power centers, its territorial sovereignty was limited by other "fragments" of limited sovereignty. The most important "fragment" was the exilic space in the south: the Don Cossack Host (see map 1).

RULE AND EXIT

In the same way that the Russian state was trying to protect its autonomy from the emerging world-economy, the Cossacks of the Don were struggling to preserve (and develop) their autonomy. Most Russian historians have neglected this mutually formative and symbiotic relationship.

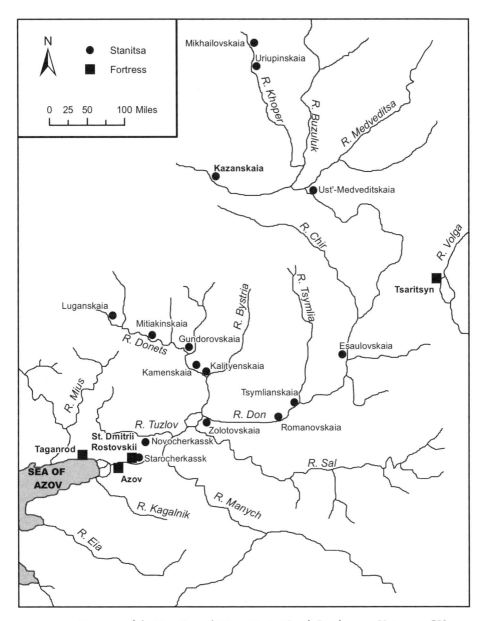

MAP 1. Territory of the Don Cossack Host. Kevin Heard, Binghamton University GIS Core Facility.

The Host came into being in the sixteenth century through its formalized relationship with the state. This relationship rested on an *exilic bargain*, an agreement according to which the Cossacks offered strategic loyalty to the state, including military services against the enemies of the state, and were allowed in return to run their territory as they saw fit. They organized a version of what we now call "autonomy" (see next chapter, on Zapatista exiles), a sophisticated system of decentralized, direct democracy and a communal, substantive economy. Russian state sovereignty developed in tandem with exilic sovereignty: the territorialization of rule was intimately linked to the territorialization of exit.

For Muscovy, the bargain with the Don was important in several respects. The "loyalty" of the Host—itself a pragmatic, strategic choice—provided the vulnerable Muscovite state-space with relative territorial safety from Tatars by inserting a "buffer zone" between the empire and potential invaders. In addition, the bargain facilitated a complex and ultimately successful diplomatic struggle against Turkey, furnished the state with the strength to resist the incorporative pressures of the European world-economy, and initiated the development of modern territorial sovereignty with the establishment of the so-called Belgorod line along the southern border (see map 2).

The mutual character of this relationship was profound but perhaps unstable in the long run. The exilic formation of the Don Cossacks was a result of peasant flight from central Russia, a direct result of Moscow's state formation. Both the formation and the eventual de-formation of the Host's exilic sovereignty were a consequence of the erection of the Belgorod line. This imperial boundary was built between the 1620s and 1653 in response to the threat of Tatar invasions *and* new waves of peasant flight triggered by the intensification of serfdom in central Russia. It was a collection of fortress cities and improvised obstacles, sheltering the state-space from Tatar invasions. Yet, as Boeck observes, like the Chinese wall, they served not only to keep the outsiders out but also to keep the insiders in.[28] The Don Cossacks used the relative stability afforded by the "exilic" bargain to form an autonomous, decentralized polity (a veritable "gathering of Don Cossack lands") around the Cossack capitol of Cherkassk and to define an "exilic constitution" based on "liberties" that included state-resisting and cooperative practices of politics, economy, and exilic membership. Yet, eventually, the Belgorod line also served its other function, to staunch the flow of escapees from Russian lands, thus limiting the lifeblood of Cossack society.

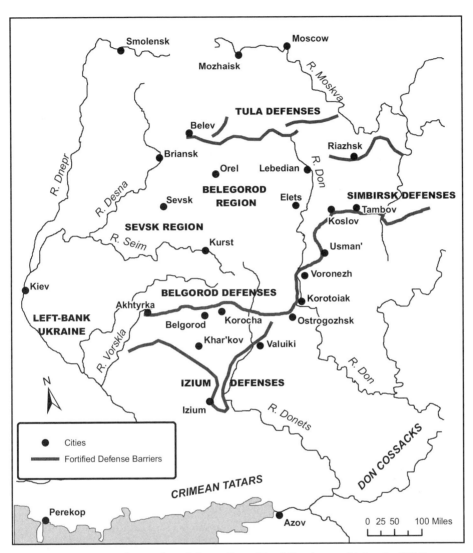

MAP 2. Moscow and its southern defenses. Kevin Heard, Binghamton University GIS Core Facility.

THE EXILIC BARGAIN

The first mention of the Don Cossacks' territory dates from 1549. Correspondence between Tsar Ivan and Nogai Tatar prince Iusuf acknowledges the existence of the Cossacks on the banks of the Don River. Another letter from Ivan to the Nogai Tatars hints at its mixed ethnic composition:

"There are many Cossacks roaming in the steppe, Kazanis, Crimeans, Azovites, and other insolent [*balovni*] Cossacks."[29]

In his discussion of the origins of the Don Cossacks, Menning speaks of several early designations and warns that Cossack ethnic history was lost "in the cloud of hazy and contradictory rhetorics."[30] Recent historiographic work removes some of the fog. The word "*kazak*" is almost definitely of Turkish or Arab origin, and the Don Cossacks themselves are the result of an encounter between Slavic and Turkic peoples. The name of the first *ataman* (leader), Sary Azman, is indisputably Turkic. In Boeck's description, the Don Cossacks were a "socio-cultural fusion comprised of diverse elements, but committed to an anti-bureaucratic and egalitarian political system . . . Early Cossack identity was not defined by common language or common origins, but by common interest."[31] An original fusion of heterogeneous elements, histories, and cultural experiences, the Don Cossacks were not just another group of horseman warriors, but a non–state-space—an *exilic territory*.[32]

This exilic space of the Don represented "the largest, and most powerful, and perhaps most typical of all pre-revolutionary Cossack hosts." Exilic membership was inclusive, open to exiles from professions as varied as pirates, fugitives, bandits, and petty criminals, all of whom came together to form a society with no masters and "beyond the reach of any law."[33] The Don Cossack Host was a free territory, a place where the Cossacks resisted Ottomans, Crimeans, Kalmyks, Nogai Tatars, and of course, Muscovites. This was a world without borders or state-like forms of governance—a "huge, un-policed no-man's land."[34]

The immediate neighbors of the Host were Tatars, nomadic subjects of the Crimean khanate, a client polity of the Ottoman Empire. A constant trickle of settlers, particularly Russian and Ukrainian peasant-fugitives, augmented the number of Cossacks living in the Don until they united to form a single host, or *voisko*, sometime in the first quarter of the sixteenth century.[35]

The importance to exilic formation of relationships with the state in Moscow is recognized by Hrushevsky, who suggested that imperial subsidies were crucial in organizing and structuring the Host.[36] The Don Host did not exist, at least not in coherent form, until interaction between Cossacks and the Russian state was transformed from an episodic to a long-term relationship. Together with the majority of Cossack historians, however, Hrushevsky underemphasized the mutual character of this relationship and the fact that both polities were formed in relationship to each other. The nonstate was the "dark twin" of the state. In other words, two forms of polity formation, and two forms of territorialization, constituted each other. It was not Moscow that created the Don Host; it was the relationship between the exilic space and the state, almost symbiotic in nature, that made each of their formations and subsequent territorializations possible.

The Don Cossacks, under the ataman Misha Cherkashenin, struck a deal with the Russian imperial court in the mid-sixteenth century: in exchange for armed accompaniment of the tsar's forces from Rylsk to Azov, Cossacks would receive an annual subsidy in the form of money, gunpowder, and clothes, as well as the authorization to conduct trade in Russian towns. There is no doubt that the imperial subsidy facilitated the process of exilic formation, the gathering of scattered Cossack communities around the Host. Concurrently, Cossack protection of Moscow's southern frontier undoubtedly influenced the contours of the state.

The paucity of documents precludes accurate reconstruction of the bargain. However, sources scrutinized by Russian historians supply valuable information. We know that Don Cossacks participated in the campaigns of Ivan the IV (1530–84) and in 1659 they were a trusted ally in the struggle around Astrakhan. Relationships with Boris Godunov were more strained and led to a temporary suspension of the subsidy, which resumed only after the new Romanov dynasty took the throne in 1613. Boeck outlines the exilic bargains as follows:

> The tsars' alliance with the Don Cossacks was in many important ways fundamentally different from their relations with the Kalmyks and other nomadic groups of the steppe frontier. The tsars did not demand diplomatic hostages (*amanaty*) from the Don Cossacks, they did not succeed in early attempts to make Cossacks swear oaths of allegiance and they permitted the transfer of both firearms and gunpowder, which were denied to the nomads, to the Don Host. The Don Cossacks acknowledged an allegiance to the tsar and performed services for him in the steppe in exchange for an annual subsidy and the right to tax exemptions while trading in Russia. At the same time they lived outside of the Muscovite state, governed themselves without outside interference, and conducted independent relations with other frontier communities ... In addition to several small delegations (*legkie stanitsy*) sent each year to Moscow with reports, each fall the Don Host sent a large delegation (*zimovaia stanitsa*) to winter in the capital. While being wined and dined at court, these Cossacks were generously rewarded with diplomatic gifts consisting of luxury goods such as clothes, furs, devotional objects, and weapons. The government compensated Cossacks for travel expenses and

assigned each Cossack a subsistence allowance consisting of money and liquor. Every Spring these recipients of the tsar's benevolence were sent back to the Don to renew the reciprocal cycle of service, reporting news, and reward.[37]

The Don exiles agreed to guard the borders of Muscovy in return for "the waters and grasses, but not for estates."[38] Their military service was not mandatory, but voluntary.

From the state's point of view, there were advantages and disadvantages to this bargain. The Don Cossacks provided invaluable help in defense against the Tatars and were part of a strategic alliance against the Ottomans and the Crimean territories. The Russian push to the south would have been impossible without collaboration between the state and the exilic space. In the early seventeenth century, however, the steppe also presented a danger to the sovereignty claims of the tsar. Tatar raids regularly devastated southern districts, disregarding the tsar's monopoly on violence and undermining his claims of exclusive jurisdiction over his subjects. As Boeck points out, the steppe also existed as a "juridical void beyond the grasp of bureaucrats."[39] Russians who were willing to endure the dangers of steppe life could easily emancipate themselves from government control by migrating there. In addition, the Don was an "exilic model" that could, and did, inspire peasant unrest in central Russia. The subtle (and not so subtle) threat of the Cossacks manifested itself clearly.

It is fair to assume, at least before the eighteenth century, that the state did its best to undermine the exilic sovereignty of the Host despite being too weak to impose its will on the steppe. Indeed, the original intention and purpose of the state subsidy was to exert influence over the Cossacks and undermine their institutions.[40] A more effective move, after the conquest of Ukraine, was the construction of the Belgorod line—the fortress system that surrounded the Don Host on three sides with territory under Muscovite control.[41] Other attempts to curb the Cossack autonomy included state trading sanctions aimed at coercing the Cossacks to return peasant-fugitives. A grain embargo in 1660 had serious consequences as the Cossacks were not agriculturally self-sufficient. Their response to the shortage of grain was to undertake more raids and plundering expeditions in the lower Volga.

Since the reign of Ivan IV (1530–84), Don Cossack exiles had been considered vassals of the tsar. Yet the Russian tsars were unable to seriously influence Cossack affairs. Moscow's efforts were limited to "persuasion, rebuke, threats, and financial inducements."[42] As we will show below, this policy of non-intervention changed with Mikhail Romanov (1613–45) and Aleksei Mikhailovich (1646–76), marking the (modest) beginning of Moscow's "long climb to ascendancy in the south steppe" and the effective end of exit-with-autonomy.[43]

For the Don Cossacks, the exilic bargain had benefits. It bought time and space to institutionalize autonomous structures of governance and economy. And it enabled them to protect their exilic sovereignty and jurisdiction. The fugitive community was undoubtedly aware of the downsides of the bargain; the subsidy allowed the Russian state to exert economic pressures on the Cossacks, who had no other source of gunpowder or grain.

TERRITORIALIZATION OF RULE AND EXIT

In the sixteenth century, the frontier protecting the isolated "islands of Russian settlement" was uncertain and undefined.[44] The last line of control, according to documents from 1630, was the town of Voronezh. Territorial boundaries and sovereignty were in continual flux. Several movements of exilic migration shaped the form the Russian "territorial state" would take. The era of the open frontier corresponded to the first exilic movement.

In the seventeenth century, the "dynastic realm" of the Romanovs had already been transformed into a new political organization: the "territorial state."[45] The *territorialization of rule* is commonly defined as the symbolic fusion of political authority and geographical area.[46] Boeck has convincingly argued that imperial borders represent "the single most neglected aspect of Russian empire-building."[47] In their focus on "dramatic moments of imperial expansion," historians have failed to see important attempts to "stop, control, consolidate, and patrol rather than endlessly advance."[48] This is surprising, as the Belgorod line in the south was the first borderline (in the modern sense) built in early modern Europe.[49] A mechanism of control that significantly increased Russia's military capabilities, the Belgorod fortress line also became a boundary of territorial sovereignty. The fortification contributed to the conception of the state as demarcated space. This was the beginning of the territorialization of rule that culminated with Peter's "territorial culture" and Catherine's territorial organization.[50] Through these processes, a new kind of (Russian) state came into being.[51]

While it is crucial to highlight the territorialization of rule as an important facet of state formation, it is equally important to acknowledge the obverse process: concurrent with attempts to "put the state on the map" and define the space of the state, a state-*breaking* process created a political geography of its own. The common statement that territory is the natural ground of the state conceals how the territory is, at the same time, a natural ground of *exit*.[52] Through the process of the territorialization of exit, a sovereign, exilic space was established away from Moscow's surveyors as they tried to impose state authority on the ground. A mapless, exilic community emerged, with a claim to the territory they called "the River."

The exilic formation of the Don Cossacks was a result of peasant flight from central Russia; it was also a direct result of Moscow state formation. The Belgorod line, an imperial boundary, was built between the 1620s and 1653 in response to new waves of peasant flight that had been triggered by increased exploitation in central Russia. Territorialization of rule and territorialization of exit developed in tandem through a process we might call "co-territorialization." The Don Cossacks used the relative stability afforded by the "exilic bargain" to form an autonomous exilic space and to define an "exilic constitution" around a set of liberties that ran through the polity and economy and consolidated the inclusive nature of exilic membership.

THE EXILIC SPACE

If Cossacks were not given their liberty (*volia*), they would not serve on the Don and they would not obey.

GRIGORII KOTOSHIKHIN

Before the eighteenth century, the organization of the Don Cossacks can be described as exit-with-autonomy. The exilic space exhibited the "diagnostic characteristics" of nonstate spaces described by Scott: friction of space, agriculture of escape, decentralization, an egalitarian and flexible social structure, escape-based cultural identities, and a rebellious cosmology. The security of the Don Cossack exilic space rested on a number of state-resisting practices and on autonomous practices of cooperation. Its exilic constitution, referred to by the Cossacks as "liberties," prevented the recapture of exiles, thereby thwarting the systemic pressures pulling exiles back into the space of the state. Elements of the exilic constitution—the decentralized organization of territory; the directly democratic structure of the self-governing assembly; the system of "right to refuge" and inclusive exilic membership; systemic resistance against professionalized knowledges that would depend on experts; and egalitarian structures of production, distribution, and provisioning—all served to prevent recapture and to keep threatening state relationships beyond the exilic bargain from forming. It is worth discussing these issues in depth.

Exilic Territory

The first structure of escape is geography. The land along the Don, the land that "liberated from all kinds of misfortunes," was the territory of exit. Its remoteness was crucial to the process of exilic formation. The Land of the Don Host, or Zemlia Voiska Donskogo, was concentrated in the lower reaches of the Don River (map 1), separated from Russia by many miles of uninhabited and uncultivated steppe. Here, Cossacks were safe from control by Moscow: far from the state, but not too far to welcome those on the run from it; "the Don has always been a haven for runaways."[53]

Three topographical features dominated the landscape of exilic territory. First, the "life-giving Don," a river that "never runs dry," and its tributaries formed a life-sustaining web in a region where water and wildlife were otherwise scarce. Second, the steppe was a fertile, almost unbroken expanse of grassland around the Don, a "treeless, gently undulating land whose regularity was broken only by an occasional stream, river, drywash, or gully."[54] Third, the city of Azov had been an important transit point since the Middle Ages and a focal point of relationship between the Ottomans, Russians, Tatars, and Cossacks. Azov was a "critical node of interface between the economies of the Eurasian steppe and the Black Sea" and a main theater of Ottoman-Russian interaction until the mid-eighteenth century.[55] The Cossacks' relationship with Azov was symbiotic and existed in the larger context of imperial competition at the margins of the capitalist system.

An additional feature of the territory would become a key factor in later exilic development: the distinction between the north (land around the Khoper, Medveditsa, and Donets Rivers), which was inhabited after 1650 and later contained by the Belgorod line, and the earlier inhabited south, removed from the Belgorod line and in active communication with the Black Sea, Azov, and the Kuban' steppes.

Replenished by streams of new arrivals escaping serfdom, the Don Cossack Host organized its territory as a decentralized system of communities under the territorial jurisdiction of the Host in Cherkassk. The first wave of migration from central Russia included runaway serfs, criminals, freebooters, and all other outcasts and outlaws: "bold ones" (*smel'chaki*) who wanted to reinvent themselves in a society that knew nothing of "class, permanent hierarchy, or inherited status."[56] Both push and pull factors encouraged population flows: serfdom as a sufficiently strong stimulus to encourage resettlement from Russia and the attractions of liberty on the Don.[57]

During this first wave, the state was weak and uninterested in extradition. In the words of the Moscow bureaucrat and later defector to Lithuania Grigorii Kotoshikhin, "Those who were sentenced to punishment for banditry or thievery and other crimes, stealing from and plundering their boyars, they leave for the Don. If they happen to for some reason come to Moscow, after spending just a week or a month on the Don, no one has any recourse against them for any [past] affair."[58] The government made a distinction between the documented and undocumented, between those who were traveling "*po otpusku*" (with permission) and those who were moving "*samovol'stvom*" (without permission). Nonetheless, Moscow's Ambassadorial Chancery did not require the extradition of exiles at this time, although frontier towns could arrest those who had not yet reached the Don. As late as 1653, when the construction of the Belgorod line was completed, Cossack territory was free of investigators looking for fugitives.[59] The territory in this part of the steppe was inhabited by *pomeshchiki* (local representatives of the tsar), who encouraged a "rapid spread of serfdom in the south steppe." [60] The state policy of non-extradition alienated support among Russian landowners, who were adversely affected by the flight of their serfs.[61]

The second wave of serf flight triggered genuine concern for the authorities in Moscow and a rather dramatic change in their previously relaxed policy. The open frontier was replaced by the Belgorod line, a fortification system built on the northern boundary of Cossack territory in 1635 to protect the southern flank of Russia against Tatar invasions. If the line was built to contain Tatar raids (to keep people out), its purpose soon turned to limiting the movement of the tsars' Russian subjects (to keep people in).[62] The regulation of 1649 (*Ulozhenie*) introduced serfdom as a form of migration control and permanently bound peasants to their residences as recorded in the tax rolls. In 1666, the state sent its first general decree to the Don Host demanding that it stop harboring refugees. The choice before the state was simple: either enter into a confrontation with the exiles, disturbing the strategic balance in the south at the precise moment when the support of the Don Host in Ukrainian affairs was very much needed, or prevent peasant flight in other ways (i.e., a system of fortifications). With the Belgorod line, an administrative boundary emerged as a response to the flight of serfs attracted to the exilic model of the Cossack space. It would be hard to find a more decisive example of the influence of exilic space on state formation and the territorialization of sovereignty in central Russia.

While the Belgorod line was moderately successful in limiting flight, the prohibition of peasant movement remained an elusive goal. The intensification of serfdom provoked a massive movement of peasants into the Don. In 1648, in the aftermath of the Azov siege and devastating Turkish raids, the Don Host reported that seventeen hundred Cossacks received the annual subsidy from the Russian government. Around 1668 the subsidy was divided among three thousand Cossacks. In 1675 the number was estimated at six thousand, and by 1696 the number of Cossacks enrolled for service was about eight thousand. The number of Cossack settlements tripled between 1650 and 1700.[63] This exilic wave created tension between new migrants in the north and older migrants in the south of the exilic space, a tension that would eventually undermine the solidarity and exilic sovereignty of the Host.

The Russian-Don boundary entered a third phrase in May 1670 in the wake of Stenka Razin's revolt,[64] when Muscovy attempted an economic blockade of the exilic space. The new policy is outlined in a memo quoted by Boeck: "Additionally, no traders whatsoever are to travel to the Don, with any goods, or grain or food supplies, or with anything else, until the Don is purified of Sten'ka's banditry. And ... if any traders attempt to go to him with any goods or [food] supplies or anything else ... those outlaws are to be put to death without any mercy in the towns of the Belgorod regiment."[65] In 1671, the imperial boundary between Russia and the Don acquired all the trappings of "modern" international boundaries when the state introduced travel documents and border patrols.

Nonetheless, independent exilic waves continued to flow into the Don, including peasants without documents (including Old Believers[66]), adventurers fleeing the Russian penal system, and conscripts avoiding the mobilizations of Peter the Great (1672–1725). Russians from the nearby Black Earth Region—towns like Voronezh, Tambov, and Sartov—dominated the exilic movement that peaked around 1740, which was followed by a period of decline.[67] In the last quarter of the eighteenth century, the living conditions of recent exiles were reduced from tenant-like living to a serf-like existence on the large estates of a newly formed Cossack nobility.[68] Ukrainian fugitives started arriving as early as the 1620s and 1630s, during the Cossack Azov campaign. These Ukrainian escapees joined the Russian exilic tide to the Don steppe and the "legendary Cossack way of life."[69] The Ukrainian exilic wave received a new impetus a century later, in the 1720s, with exiles arriving from regions east of the Dnieper River, and subsided only in the first decade of the nineteenth century.[70]

Politics

We have come to claim our freedom
With our ataman Stenka Razin,
From wicked judges and officials.

Rebel hymn

Even before the Cossack social structure solidified in the mid-seventeenth century, says Menning, "the members of the Don Host prided themselves on the equality of all their brethren."[71] Boeck concurs, arguing that the political system of the Don "functioned fairly well as long as most residents of the region were satisfied with the levels of political liberties and economic opportunities available to them."[72] As late as 1638, when the Muscovite government requested the dispatch of the Host's "best people" to Moscow, the Cossacks haughtily replied that there were no "best people"; all Cossacks were equal.[73]

The language historians generally use to describe Cossack democracy reveals a statist bias. Menning speaks of a "rudely egalitarian polity," "egalitarian camaraderie," and "rudimentary democracy."[74] In reality, Cossack society was a consensus-based, direct democracy—an open political system based upon group consensus that stood "in marked contrast to the increasingly centralized and bureaucratic despotism of Muscovy."[75] Far from primitive, Cossack exilic space developed more democratically than the autocratic organization of Muscovy.

The Cossack political system was a decentralized regime of local assemblies and elected officials. Its principal institution was the *krug* (local assembly, or "circle"), where the whole community resolved conflicts through public debate. The krug was an institution endowed with complete sovereignty and all-encompassing power; it decided "all major legislative questions, conducted Cossack foreign policy, and resolved important judicial disputes involving the interpretation or violation of Host law."[76] Later relegated to a largely ceremonial role as exilic autonomy was lost to Russian state authority,[77] the krug was both the symbol and the real center of Cossack democracy, with wide-ranging authority. It decided declarations of war and peace, the division of spoils from raids, diplomatic matters, legal matters, and questions involving relationships with the Russian state (what we have termed the *loyalty bargain*). Convened in the *maidan* (Turkish for "square" or "large open space"), the krug was held in plain view of the population and was open to all Cossacks.[78] The main krug was held in the Cossack capital of Cherkassk, on a fortified island in the lower Don, where the populace received Muscovite officials. According to Patrick Gordon, Scottish military expert and advisor to Prince Golitsyn, issues were decided by acclamation, where the "greatest part of them [the people] approve ... by throwing up their caps and crying out lubo, lubo, [*sic*] which is as much as, it pleaseth."[79]

The krug acted simultaneously as judge and jury, without any experts or professionals trained in written law. Its executive power was embodied in the institution of the *ataman* (local leader), who was elected by universal consent (*vseobshchim sovetom*). While he had several duties, the ataman's main role seems to have been to preside over the sometimes rowdy meetings of the krug and to submit proposals for its approval. He was expected to carefully use persuasion without exercising dictatorial powers. Even in times of war, his decisions were subject to popular challenge in the assembly.[80] He would facilitate meetings, sometimes "pleading with tears in his eyes" or speaking with "intense passion," other times himself participating in "brawls and fist fights."[81] The ataman was aided by three deputies, one *esaul* (head clerk), and three *d'iaki* (clerks). He held office for two years with no limit on reelection. Popular atamans, like Frol Minaev, were elected up to twenty times.

Boeck provides a splendid description of one krug that "demonstrates several important features of the Cossack view of justice." Involving a certain Moscow bureaucrat by the name of Andrei Lazarev, the incident is worth quoting in full:

> In 1649 Lazarev was called to the krug to testify about letters he wrote to the tsar complaining that Cossacks were not complying with government orders. Fearing for his life and claiming—perhaps feigning—illness, he declined to appear, stating that if guilty of any offense he would answer only to the tsar, not to the Cossacks. Outraged, the Cossacks assembled in the krug and "all shouted that for those words it would be pleasing (*liubo*) to them to execute [Lazarev]." The "sword of the Host" (*sablia voiskovaia*)—its very name indicative of a collective ritual element—was brought out in preparation for an execution, and a group of Cossacks was sent to drag Lazarev by the feet to the krug. Luckily for him, the quick intervention of the men under his command

prevented an immediate execution. Not long thereafter, however, Lazarev was seized after praying in a chapel—not even Orthodox religious obligations provided an exemption from answering to the assembly—and was dragged in front of the krug "like a prisoner." There he was upbraided by Ataman Naum Vasiliev for secretly writing to the tsar. Lazarev's explanation that "as from God, so from the tsar nothing can be kept concealed" failed to satisfy the crowd. A witness who was called to testify that Cossacks in Moscow had faced censure in the Ambassadorial Chancery for Lazarev's actions, failed to corroborate the ataman's accusation. According to Lazarev, "seeing Naum's obvious falsehood, that he agitates for my death even though I am innocent, [the crowd] vociferously shouted at him [Vasiliev], and . . . no more speeches after that were addressed to me."[82]

Lazarev was a subject of Cossack laws; he could be sentenced or exonerated only by the Cossack Assembly. This, in fact, is what happened. The objections of the ataman notwithstanding, Lazarev was given no "diplomatic immunity" but he received a fair hearing.

Avrich describes a similar process in his narrative about Stenka Razin's exploits. In 1671, the Cossack rebel leader inaugurated self-government "in the Cossack manner" in the Russian town of Tsaritsyn. In the assembled krug, he and his army decided together where to go next. Later, after victory in Astrakhan, in accordance with Cossack tradition, he divided up the loot in equal shares and proceeded to establish a "Cossack-style regime" on the model of the Don Host. The population of Astrakhan was divided into "thousands, hundreds, and tens, with a town krug and elected officials." He did the same in Saratov in June 1670, following "the Cossack way there, so that all men could be equal."[83] The same pattern of replacing the existing administration with a krug, ataman, and elected elders was repeated in Kazan.

These examples reflect a decentralized exilic territory.[84] The directly democratic form of government in Cherkassk was "repeated in every settlement or stanitsa [village] where an elected ataman managed daily Cossack affairs for a local assembly that met only periodically or in the event of emergency."[85] The elected officials "implemented the collective will of all Cossacks living in stanitsa."[86] Smaller stanitsas had smaller krugs, where the local ataman and *esaul* (clerk) facilitated the making of all important decisions affecting local affairs. Only the decision about war and peace was exclusively the jurisdiction of the Host in Cherkassk. All Cossack communities were expected to comply with orders for mobilization sent from the Host, and occasionally they sent representatives to a *s'ezd* (convocation) of the whole Host. Among the mechanisms meant to ensure the participation of various

FIGURE 1. Don Cossacks in Tsaritsyn, festival of historical reconstruction (May 3, 2015). Viacheslav Yaschenko.

Cossack communities were probation, control over the government subsidy, and the issuing of threats. In 1673, for instance, a message from the Host warned that anyone failing to comply with an order "would be eternally subject to violence and plunder from fellow Cossacks."[87]

The Don Cossacks lived by their own free will and not by decree—the marked absence of codified law or written history indicates an egalitarian, state-avoiding mentality, institutionalized to prevent the emergence of experts who could challenge the participatory form of exilic politics. In 1691, the Host reported that it could not determine how many Cossacks had defected to join a group of renegades because "our population is free, not recorded (*liud u nas ne zapisnoi vol'noi*)."[88] This "illegibility" was an essential part of their exilic sovereignty, at the same time serving as a mechanism that prohibited the development of state-like practices. "One of the chief preoccupations of the Cherkassk leadership," Avrich remarked, "was to keep the Muscovite system, which was drawing nearer and nearer with the advance of colonization and the fortified frontier, from penetrating their domain."[89] The absence of written law is emblematic of the broader pattern.

The exilic space was a society without a state, but not a society without power. Power, as Clastres argues, is not purely a coercive force. "Political power is universal," he claims, "immanent to social reality," inherent in human nature and thus to social life. Clastres distinguishes between "coercive" power and "noncoercive" power. To the extent that an exilic space is free from control and domination, it "never allows technical superiority to change into a political authority."[90] Internal social relations may prevent the transformation of noncoercive *power-to* to *power-over* (coercive power). The example of the Don Cossacks supports Clastres's proposition that "nonstate," or nondominant, power relations are possible in any society. Lefebvre refers to this form of social organization as *autogestion*. For the Don Cossacks, the rejection of alien determination also implies the rejection of any state as an organization of space that places itself above society. Thus, "each time a social group . . . refuses to accept passively its conditions of existence, of life, or of survival, each time such a group forces itself not only to understand but to master its conditions of existence, autogestion is occurring."[91] For Lefebvre, *autogestion* aims at the creation of a genuinely differential space, "which represents for capitalism an antagonistic and ruinous tendency."[92] The Don Cossacks understood that in order to change life, "we must first change space."[93]

Economy

Not withe the plough is our dear, glorious earth furrowed,
Our earth is furrowed with the hooves of horses;
And our dear, glorious earth is sown with the heads of
    Cossacks

Seventeenth-century Cossack rebel song

What kinds of economic activities were characteristic of the Don exilic space? Were they communal, with mutual aid and equality? Or were they fragmented at the individual or household levels, as in Scott's description of Zomia? What were their dynamic properties? Were they sustainable, and did they tend to reintroduce hierarchies and inequalities? What would the substantive view of Cossack economy look like? And, how do the Cossacks relate to economies and economic activities, including trade that exists "outside" the exilic space? Is there a relationship between the formal market economy and the substantive extramarket economy in the "exilic" world? More broadly, how—if at all—can we distinguish economic activities that enable the production and reproduction of exilic spaces from those that set limits on it?

Cossack exilic economy rested on two main pillars: raiding and the government subsidy. Agriculture played a relatively insignificant role. Stock raising existed in the early days but was limited to cattle, horses, and sheep (mostly stolen from nomadic neighbors), which provided hides, wool, milk, and meat.[94] Only in the eighteenth century did grain farming become a major economic activity, not as a factor enabling the exilic space to reproduce itself but through the creation of an export-oriented landed class among established Cossacks in conflict with new exiles. This signaled the beginning of the end of the Cossacks as exiles-with-autonomy.[95]

Historians do not agree about the exact nature of Cossack dislike for agriculture before the end of the seventeenth century. According to some, agriculture was inscribed in the collective mentality as a synonym for serfdom. The law of 1690 forbade Cossacks to till the land under penalty of death.[96] The Scottish military expert Patrick Gordon observed that "on the Don it is strictly prohibited to sow or reap any corns."[97] Yet many historians propose that the lack of agriculture was the result of a class conspiracy of better-off Cossacks to preserve their monopoly on plundering expeditions.[98] This became part of a Soviet historiographical tendency to expose inequality in Cossack society. An alternative reading is that agriculture was forbidden because it was inextricably identified with serfdom, inequality, and the loss of exilic liberty, especially in the context of the demographic pressures and scarcity of resources resulting from the exilic wave of fugitives in the 1660s and 1670s. This interpretation also corresponds to the simultaneous efforts of the state to increase the number of border guards on the Belgorod line. At any rate, a Cossack economy dominated by grain growing and stock raising emerged only in the eighteenth century.[99]

The old Russian proverb "Without the tsar the land is a widow, without the tsar the people is an orphan" was not popular in the Don, where land was collectively owned and fell into two categories. First, land allocated to a local *stanitsa* (village) was known as *stanichnaia*. According to custom, the local assembly divided this land among members of the *stanitsa*. The krug also divided land among families according to need. The individual portion of the *stanichnaia* land, called the *pai*, or portion, was either cultivated by the family or rented to itinerant peasants (later, to wealthier Cossacks with access to a large workforce). Another portion of *stanichnaia* land was retained for common use, as pastureland, meadowland, or for timber reserves (in 1821, common-use land amounted to over 16 million acres of Don territory). The second type of land was *voiskovaia*, or free land, under central control. *Voiskovaia* land was available to Cossacks who desired to homestead but not own land, and it was commonly granted by decree. Empty land with *voiskovaia* status was immense, probably over six and a half million acres by the end of eighteenth century.[100]

In the absence of substantial agriculture, raiding was the center of the economy. Both Tatars and Cossacks participated in the raiding economy between the Black Sea and the northern Don, deriving their subsistence "from the shifting boundaries between the Islamic and Christian worlds."[101] The adventures of these "steppe-based bandits" brought them as far as the outskirts of Constantinople. They swept across the steppe "as wild geese fly, invading and retiring where they see the advantage."[102] Cossacks outfitted small fleets of shallow-draft longboats (*strugi*) for hit-and-run raids against Tatar settlements or Turkish and Persian towns on the coast of the Black and Caspian Seas. According to Avrich, "They showed extraordinary courage and ingenuity striking with lightning speed at the coastal settlements of the Turks and Crimean Tatars, then escaping in their light and maneuverable *strugi* before any effective force could be collected against them."[103] Lest one should get overly romantic about the exilic or utopian nature of early Cossack society, it is important to remember that raiding was an extremely violent activity. An official from Nizhni Novgorod who witnessed many raids described the Cossacks as "barbarous and inhumane people . . . more cruel than lions."[104]

Dangerous as it was, raiding was exceptionally lucrative. As long as the number of Cossacks remained relatively small and the surrounding states were not strong enough to impose effective power on the Northern Black Sea littoral, raiding remained a profitable source of income. After each successful raid the spoils were divided up equally among the participants, guaranteeing the cohesion of Don Cossack society.[105] The party leader received a somewhat larger share, and the ataman and other Cossack officials also received part of the spoils. Raiding was a substantive exilic activity that provided material stability and solidarity, thus contributing to the autonomy of the Host.

The practice of ransom was part of raiding. A document from 1686 reveals that the ransom value of two hundred Tatars in 1686 may have exceeded that year's government cash subsidy to the Cossacks (five thousand rubles) by a ratio of more than three to one.[106] Many ransom deals involved credit. A document from 1701 details the claims of a dozen Cossacks regarding outstanding ransom debts owed to them by Tatars. Some involved money, but the majority consisted of hundreds of pieces of cloth and textiles, as well as paper, archery equipment, and boots. Those captives not prominent enough for ransom were sold as slaves. A ransom broker, Boeck argues, served as a "cultural ambassador," an expert in obscure economic practices such as *baranta* (literally, "that which is due to me") and *razdelka* (settlement). The lower Don "was a place of fierce contestation, as well as cross-cultural face-to-face transactions, oaths, and trust—all part of the lively economic life of the steppe."[107]

Apart from raiding, the other pillar of the Don Host's exilic economy before the eighteenth century was the *zhalovan'e*—the annual government subsidy in money and kind, dispensed regularly after 1632 in return for Cossack services to the state.[108] This was a cornerstone of the exilic bargain established with Moscow. The subsidy consisted of gold, grain, gunpowder, lead, and cloth. The grain supply, comprising several tons, was the most precious part of the subsidy. Second in importance were the two tons of lead and gunpowder. The subsidy also included money, textiles, and liquor (although Cossacks also distilled their own liquor). The ataman who led the delegation received the *bashlovka* (reward), as well as diplomatic gifts and tax-free goods. In this way some atamans accumulated considerable wealth, although this was not common before the eighteenth century. In a much celebrated event, the spring release of the Cossack subsidy was greeted with fanfare and prayers known as the *Donskoi otpusk*.

Trading was not as important as raiding or the subsidy, yet it reveals a significant economic connection to the state space. The exilic territory depended on Russian goods and markets. From Russia, the Don Cossacks imported grain, liquor, clothes, and textiles. Russian traders then returned from the territory with traditional Don exports: furs, skins, salted fish, and caviar. And, according to Avrich, "traders from Cherkassk carried, along with their goods, a message of liberty and self-rule."[109]

The structure of trade with Ottoman territories is obscured by fragmentary evidence; this was, after all, a world without customs posts or commercial taxes. One lone document from 1699 suggests that three boats from Crimea carried several hundred pieces of cloth and clothing (made from materials ranging from camel hair to silk), over three tons of dried fruit, hundreds of pounds of soap and rice, pieces of porcelain ware, and over forty gallons of *narbek*, a popular alcoholic beverage. In 1704, a Turkish trader coming from Cherkassk paid customs duties on more than two tons of caviar.[110] The main locus of trade was the ancient Cossack capital of Cherkassk. Menning provides a vivid description of trade in the town:

> A large settlement with many handsome one-story houses, Cherkassk had hosted, since the days of its founding in the seventeenth century, a lively year-round trade in livestock, grain, and other goods useful in the Don economy. At the height of its fame as the seat of Cossack government, Cherkassk's crooked and crowded streets were the scene of numerous trade booths, where local and visiting merchants displayed their wares, bargained with Cossacks from outlying stanitsas and farmsteads, and lent, by their presence, a cosmopolitan flavor to life in an outlying frontier post. As residents and visitors to the town were well aware, the Cossack capital had at least one important drawback. Every spring the waters of the Don, which bordered the settlement on three sides, rose high enough to inundate many streets and houses. Because of this annual nuisance and its associated health problems, Cherkassk's future was limited.[111]

The capital was relocated in the nineteenth century to the confluence of the Aksai and Tuzlov Rivers. This was to become Novocherkassk, or New Cherkassk, an "architectural show place of the Don."[112] Hosting trading booths, annual trade fairs, and the religious feast of the Holy Trinity, Novocherkassk became a main commercial and administrative center by the second half of the nineteenth century.

Salt extraction and beekeeping were important exilic occupations, but hunting and fishing were especially widespread. Only the residents of a given stanitsa had the right to fish its waters; in addition, Cossacks fished the Azov Sea and lower Don. The majority of the catch was consumed by Cossacks and the rest exported to Russia. As late as the eighteenth century, fishing occupied third or fourth place in terms of value of commodities in the Don economy. Only in the late eighteenth and nineteenth century did the Cossacks, together with Ukrainian laborers, transform fishing into a major Don industry.

Exilic economic practices on the Don, before incorporation, were external to the capitalist world-system, but very much dependent on the state in Moscow. The Cossack exilic autonomy was rife with the nonmarket, substantive economic activities that Polanyi calls *provisioning*. In the early parts of their exilic history, this substantive economy based on raiding occurred outside of the formal economy to the extent that most things were provided according to usefulness and opportunity rather than exchange value. Resource-uses and distributional questions were decided by individual agreements, direct democracy, or representative systems rather than by market price and ability to pay. However, this autonomy from the state was only partial, and was bought with violence. The major economic activity of the steppe, raiding, was parasitic. The second pillar, government subsidy, was also obtained at the cost of committing extreme violence on behalf of the state.

Three critical factors that influenced the nature of economic life in the Don also demonstrate the degree to which Cossacks became caught up in the Russian state's protracted and uneven incorporation into the capitalist world-economy: an environmental crisis (especially, depletion of the forests); organized Russian attempts to recapture exiles; and the agrarianization of exilic life.

The ecology of escape can be destructive. The constant need for raiding ships depleted old-growth forests in the Don. This, combined with more aggressive imperial politics, left Cossack sea adventures at the mercy of empire. Both the Russian and Ottoman states would later exploit the environmental crisis to end Cossack raids, which were gradually replaced by settled ranching, agriculture, and commercial fishing. The process of incorporation into the capitalist world-economy (which began in the eighteenth century) had several decisive implications on the exilic economy. The Petrine state constrained Cossack raiding, which was further constrained by ecological crisis and scarce resources. At the same time, pressure to produce grain for the world market created social divisions among Cossacks, between the ever-increasing number of fugitives moving to the Don (new migrants) and the steadily bureaucratizing and class-forming older migrants. A class system emerged, with strong pressure to turn new migrants into serfs.

Autonomy and the Right to Refuge

The Don Cossacks were not a peculiar group of Russians, or a Russian equivalent to frontiersmen in the United States. Rather, they were a voluntary association forged in opposition to the emerging state and class structure within Russia. Insurgency and exile was a state-refusing strategy. Apart from their polity and economy, the question arises about the sources of solidarity that one expects to associate with direct democracy and substantive economy. One might expect ethnicity to be a source of such solidarity, but could other voluntary forms of association and common identity have a stronger impact on the formation of solidary community, including shared sacrifices and hopes?

Boeck insists that "early Cossack identity was not defined by common language or common origins, but by common interest."[113] Aleksandr Rigel'man encountered the Don Cossacks in the 1770s, remarking that "they cannot say anything certain about their origins. They believe that they descend from some free (*vol'nykh*) peoples, and most probably come from the Circassians and mountain peoples. Therefore they do not consider themselves Muscovites by nature (*prirodoiu*). They think that they have Russified, while living with Russia, but not that they are Russians."[114]

The Cossacks were ethnically heterogeneous. Kotoshikhin again offers the perspective of an observing witness: "Don Cossacks," he wrote, "are by birth and stock (*porodoiu*) Muscovites and of other towns, newly baptized Tatars, Zaporozhian Cossacks, and Poles." In 1659, the Don Cossacks reminded the tsar that "in our Host live many foreigners who have crossed over, Turks and Tatars, and also Greeks, and people from various other lands ... who serve together with us." "On the Don," the Host explained in another document, "live people of many lands. Even those who are Russian people they live with *basurmanki* (Muslim women) and others were begotten from *basurmanki*."[115] Don Cossacks spoke many languages, including Russian, Turkish, and Ukrainian. Russians who arrived at the Don hailed from three principal directions: central Russia, Ukraine, and Tatar lands.

The exilic space was a form of voluntary association with a common interest in building and protecting the autonomy of the territory. Its multi-ethnic character was not a historical accident but a strategy that kept the state (and state-like practices) at a distance by forging a *non-ethnic* identity.[116] "The River" was not only defined by non-ethnicity, or multi-ethnicity—it was defended by it. A Cossack could not be Russian, as a Russian was a subject of the state. Even though many Cossacks were of Slavic background, their exilic membership was based on agreement to forget those origins and to create new, non-assimilable identities.[117] In the eighteenth century, faced with the problem of fugitives and limited resources, the strategic decision to switch from one exilic mechanism (inclusive membership) to another (exclusive membership based on ascriptive identity) would transform the society and, we argue, break down the solidary community undergirding autonomy.[118]

The right to refuge was a central organizing principle of the exilic membership that was explicitly non-ethnic (later, in chapter 5, we will see how prisoners may cross racial boundaries to form a "convict race"). Stenka Razin famously told a state official that "among the Cossacks it has never been the custom to hand over fugitives." Patrick Gordon, Razin's contemporary, observes: "The greatest rogues and evildoers are most acceptable when they come and best trusted because they are assured that they will not return for fear of punishment, yet being once admitted and settled here, they must live under strict laws as to theft, robbery, and other misbehavior, and are according to their wisdom, courage, and activity esteemed."[119]

This right to refuge was not so much a manifestation of heroic defiance as an exilic practice designed to protect the autonomy of the Host. The Cossacks understood that they presented a serious danger to the state. In order to force the state to respect the terms of the exilic bargain, the Don Host welcomed fugitives who replenished their ranks while making the state weaker.

The Cossacks consciously worked to create what we are calling an exilic model. Their strategic choice to welcome those who decided to "go Cossack" and to disseminate news and legends about life in the exilic space—"the message of liberty and self-rule"—pressured the state to define its relations with the Cossacks very cautiously. The south was indeed "where all the peasant wars had begun," and the Cossacks provided not only "military leadership, but a spirit of equality and justice and a model of independence, of a free and untrammeled life, that posed a serious challenge to the centralized aristocracy."[120]

For Avrich, the exilic space was a haven for the dispossessed; "by setting an example of autonomy and self-determination, imperfect though it might be, the Cossack 'republic' on the Don presented a challenge the Romanovs could not long afford to ignore."[121] The influence of the exilic model was particularly evident during Razin's rebellion in 1670, when the Siberian town of Tomsk declared its intention to "start a Don" on the upper Oblast. Arguably, the real danger that the exilic space posed was not so much Cossack swords, but the demonstration effect of autonomous mechanisms of cooperation enacted in the Don. The liberated Don represented a promise of land and liberty, of cooperation, self-provisioning, and mutual aid instead of serfdom. This promise came not only from their weapons but also (rather) from the cooperative exilic practices of decentralized communities, as well as their decision to defend and strengthen these material and symbolic practices. Cossack swords and sabers had no meaning without the political and economic life that existed in the exilic space.

LOYALTY, VOICE, AND THE REPRODUCTION
OF EXILIC SOLIDARITY

The fundamental tension confronted by any exilic space is scarcity and material self-sufficiency. We have proposed that in order to avoid an exit-without-resources trap, exilic peoples use the complementary strategies of voice and loyalty. Voice for the Cossacks meant armed rebellion and the threat of armed rebellion. Loyalty was expressed as a strategic dependence on extra-space actors, in this case primarily the Russian state. As noted, the Don Cossacks developed an exilic bargain that was initially beneficial to them. They could obtain subsistence resources beyond what was possible through raiding; and, at first, the loyalty bargain even facilitated sovereignty-building by solidifying the legitimacy of the Cossack Host. This legitimacy was increased by the popularity of cooperative practices and structures that were defined as "liberty," just as Zapatistas some centuries later would define them as "autonomy" (see chapter 4).

The cost of the bargain, however, was significant. In the medium-to-long-run, it set in train processes of negotiation and renegotiation that would reduce autonomy, resulting in the transformation from *exit-with-autonomy* (cooperative exilic practices) to *exit-without-autonomy* (hierarchical exilic practices), and, even later (until today), to *autonomy-without-exit* (distinct ethno-cultural practices within the Russian polity and economy).

We can see the forces for change in the exilic loyalty bargain by observing chronic Cossack uprisings. The most important were led by Ivan Bolotnikov (1606–7), Stepan (Stenka) Razin (1670–71), Kondratii Bulavin (1707–8), and Emilian Pugachev (1773–74). Through them, we see the tensions that were developing in the relationship between an increasingly powerful Russian state and an increasingly weak Don Host. Historians disagree about how to characterize the uprisings. Most Soviet historians call them peasant wars. Others argue that each uprising had distinctive features and that the composition of rebel forces included different combinations of peasants, Cossacks, townspeople, and even, in the case of Bolotnikov, landlords (*pomeshchiki*). Most non-Soviet historians regard the rebellions as civil wars between the border and the center, or frontier uprisings against the forces of centralization. In other words, they were conservative responses to processes of modernization and state formation. Finally, a few historians propose that the rebellions were Cossack uprisings and the Don River the most fertile breeding ground for "peasant" rebellions. We largely agree with the last position, although why this should be the case is clear only if one places the uprisings in the context of the historical change of exilic society and, especially, the tensions caused by the exilic bargain as it became increasingly unfavorable to autonomy on the Don.

What of the revolutionaries' goals? Some Soviet historians celebrate the uprisings as revolutionary attempts to "liquidate the serfholding system."

Others are more skeptical of their ideological content, pointing to the lack of revolutionary consciousness and "naïve monarchism." The so-called "pretender" phenomenon and the return-deliverer myth of a noble tsar—in Pugachev's case, a *true* tsar—were recognized as evidence of the limited worldview of the peasant.[122]

In reality, the rebellions do not lend themselves to simple explanation. Bolotnikov's peasant rebellion brought together rather disparate class elements. Its goal was a double restoration: of the true tsar and free peasants, liberated from unjust exactions. Razin's rebellion was quite different. It was an idealist attempt to institute more liberated zones: local self-governing enclaves with elected atamans. In this respect, there are interesting comparisons to be made with the "Other Campaign" of the Zapatistas at the beginning of the twenty-first century (see the next chapter). On the other end of the ideological spectrum, Pugachev's rebellion was a carefully organized military operation with an elaborate ideology. His movement's 1774 manifesto, aimed at the abolition of serfdom and institution of "Cossack democracy," proclaims,

> By this decree ... we grant to all hitherto in serfdom and subjection to pomeshchiki the right to be faithful slaves [i.e., subjects] of our crown, and we award them the old cross and prayer, heads and beards, liberty and freedom always to be cossacks, without demanding recruit levies, soul taxes or other monetary obligations, possession of the lands, the woods, the hay meadows, the fisheries, and the salt lakes, without payment or obrok, and we free all those formerly oppressed by the villainous nobles and bribe-takers and judges, all peasants and all the people oppressed by obligations and burdens ... [As for] those who hitherto were nobles, with their estates, those opponents of our power and disruptors of the empire and ruiners of the peasants, catch, kill, and hang them, and treat them just as they, having no Christianity, treated you, the peasants. With the annihilation of these enemies and miscreant-nobles, all may feel peace and a tranquil life, which will last through the ages.[123]

What of the relationship between the Russian state and the Don? While most historians share Menning's conviction that the ever-changing relationship between the Don Cossack Host and the tsarist state was a "single underlying theme," there is significant disagreement about the nature of that change. Most Don Cossack historians regard the politics of the Russian state as a coherent project aimed at subjugating the Don.[124] Subjugation was dictated by the need to resolve an inherently contradictory relationship. "[As the] Don Host as an independent entity posed at least a latent threat to Imperial Russia, Peter the Great and his successors employed every instrument at their disposal, including diplomacy, coercion, military force, and administrative subordination to curb the Cossacks and bring them under full control." This conscious assault on Cossack autonomy resulted in the "transformation of the Don Cossacks into a special class whose sole purpose was to serve the military needs of the Tsarist State."[125] According to Riabov,[126] the fate of the Don Host was sealed by the end of the eighteenth century, while Svatikov[127] dates the loss of Don statehood to 1723. The explanation for this sudden exilic decadence usually resides in the decline of Cossack military power. The Don Host might have been a "formidable force" in the sixteenth and seventeenth centuries, but in the eighteenth century both Moscow and the Ottoman state were able to maintain large armies in the steppe. The Cossacks were not agriculturally self-sufficient, instead depending on the state for sustenance. So the outcome was inevitable; it was just a matter of when.

Boeck takes a different approach, premised on a dynamic model that recognizes the benefits both sides derived from cooperation. He denies that Peter's policies toward the region lacked coordination or coherence. Rather, as the great enemy of the Cossacks, Peter was in fact an ambivalent empire-builder who "left no clear decree on the degree to which Cossacks would be made to conform to imperial norms." Peter's politics gave rise to "a series of piecemeal decisions that could, as a result of bureaucratic compromise, incognizance, or give and take, chip away at Cossack autonomy." There is no evidence that Peter ever envisioned, let alone attempted, direct administrative subjugation of the Don. The Cossacks' own decision to recognize the border and to claim rewards for patrolling it—in other words, their willingness to adapt to the new rules of the steppe and the world of borders—transformed the Don Host and (for a time) prevented their political extinction.[128]

The Cossacks' three protective strategies—exit, voice, and loyalty—were complementary. Voice, a protective strategy aimed against Russian suppression, took several major forms: (1) the threat of dispersal, leaving the Russian frontier exposed to Tatar raids; (2) "silent" refusal of imperial impositions and directives; (3) exilic communication; and (4) open rebellions like those of Razin, Bulavin, and Nekrasov. Exilic communication requires further comment. Propaganda coming from the Don could influence peasant populations in central Russia. The exilic space was presented as a refuge for all who craved land, freedom, and the promise of economic self-sufficiency. This form of communication assumed special significance during times of rebellion, so different forms of voice were used simultaneously.

An important element of exilic communication was *transvaluation*. Historians were long puzzled by the Cossack practice of presenting their rebel leaders as deceased emperors who were resurrected (from death or from captivity) to defend the rights of the Russian peasantry. According to the anthropologist Tambiah, *transvaluation* is "the process of assimilating particulars to a larger, collective, more enduring, and therefore less context-bound, cause or interest."[129] This explains the "resurrection" of Russian tsars (the pretender phenomenon) in messages sent from the Don to central Russia. By reimagining "honest and true" tsars, the Cossacks became protagonists of the struggle for tradition and peasant rights, linking with and galvanizing rebellious serfs and townsmen between the Don and Moscow. False emperors served as a way to give Cossack voice a corporeal form with which serfs and peasants "outside" of the exilic space could identify. This process of exilic commmunication has also been used by exiles in Chiapas, as we will show in our analysis of the Zapatistas.

Loyalty, on the other hand, meant a relationship of strategic dependence on the state in Moscow. Rather than unquestioning loyalty, this was an interdependent and strategic relationship in which both sides benefited from what the other had to offer. Thus, in a sense, the Russian state was also "loyal" to the Cossacks, though in time this would change. The initial exilic loyalty bargain between the Don Host and the state was established in the sixteenth century as a mutually beneficial agreement between two polities that allowed for parallel processes of state and exilic formation, for the simultaneous territorialization of rule and exit. Moscow was able to "gather the Russian lands," while the Cossacks organized the Host and established jurisdiction on "the River." The agreement rested on reciprocal obligations, and it did not imply any substantive enforcing agreement—the Cossacks' military service was voluntary. Menning provides confirmation of this from 1630, when the Don Cossacks refused to help Michael Romanov in his action against Lithuania because they objected to "blood-letting among Christians."[130]

What troubled many historians (and obscured the strategic quality of the relationship) was the content—often submissive in nature—of the communications issued by the Host. Letters from the exilic space described the River as the tsar's hereditary possession (*otchina*) and addressed their reports to the emperor from his slaves/bondsmen (*kholopy*). In 1632, the Host sent a letter to the tsar stating that "you, Great Sovereign, are at liberty to take our heads." In the early 1700s, the Host petitioned the tsar as follows:

> We, the whole Host, your bondsmen, tearfully beg your Great Sovereign's mercy, because in your Great Sovereign's decree an order has been issued to build a fort between the Don and Ilavly on the lower bank, between our, your bondsmen's, above-mentioned Cossack stanitsas. Also forests have been declared protected/off limits and in those gorodki, both northern and lower, our Cossacks have great apprehension about the construction of forts, believing that this is the result of the Great Sovereign's anger with them. It will be impossible for them to live in those aforementioned gorodki because of encroachment. In those yurts there will no longer be ample expanse and liberty (volia) in fisheries, forests, lands, hay fields, and other resources and the Cossacks in those gorodki will have nothing to subsist on . . . This is why many of the Cossacks from those four gorodki are experiencing apprehension and desire to disperse in different directions . . . We have from ancient times owned, along both sides of the Don and other rivers, the yurts, waters, fisheries, lands, forests, and various other resources that are situated between our, your bondsmen's, Cossack gorodki. Never before have we been subject to encroachment or ejection (izgoni).[131]

This seemingly submissive petition usefully combined both loyalty (to the Great Sovereign) and voice (the threat of dispersal "in different directions"). A similar tone was used in a petition from 1675:

> If you now, Great Sovereign, order that such newly arrived people be seized from the Don and that Sen'ka Buianka and the Cossacks be taken, let it be as you will (v tom tvoia volia). For you are free to impose your sovereign will on all of us, your bondsmen. In order that we, your bondsmen, seeing such an order by the Great Sovereign do not disperse in different directions from your sovereign hereditary possession, the river Don, and hand over your sovereign's hereditary possession to your eternal enemies, Great Sovereign have mercy on us.[132]

This letter was a clear warning to the "Great Sovereign" that any politics going against the terms of the exilic bargain would have serious consequences. The Cossacks were exiles, not vassals, and both loyalty and voice were interrelated strategic options cautioning the state that it would be more prudent to keep its distance.

Surely, the state saw the true nature of these messages. Menning notes that "from the Tsarist point of view, Razin's rising and the subsequent revolt of Kondratii Bulavin (1707–08), effectively demonstrated that the Cossack military sword possessed two cutting edges, one useful and the other potentially lethal to the existence of the Russian State."[133] The obverse might be said for the Cossack right to refuge, which was useful to the exiles in the short term, as it made the Russian state weaker, yet also presented a challenge to Cossack sustainability, as the resources of the Don were limited.

An important feature of the Don before Razin's rebellion was scarcity. A basic contradiction of the Don Cossack exilic space was between (scarce) resources and (promised) autonomy. We have referred to this as an *exit-without-resources* trap and propose it as a common predicament of exilic spaces. Although the first recorded evidence of conflict over resources between Cossack communities dates from the 1680s, it is safe to assume that competition for economic resources began in the late 1660s, when the Host in Cherkassk began to adjudicate local boundary disputes between the *domovitye* (householders) of the southern Don and the *golutvennye* (naked ones) of the north. The former were "wealthier Cossacks of long-standing residency" who made their fortune through raiding and then began to lead a more settled way of life on the lower Don.[134] Scarcity, accentuated by periodic crises of the raiding economy, was increasingly undermining the exilic sovereignty of the Host.

A fracture appeared between northern and southern Cossack communities. There is evidence that the different factions debated the best ways to protect the autonomy of the space.[135] This strategic disagreement about the most effective combinations of voice and loyalty—most in the form of right of refuge and the exilic bargain with Russia—would later escalate into a division between loyalists and autonomists, a political division that would result in two intra-exilic wars after Bulavin's uprising of 1707–8. The main question before the krug in the 1660s and 1670s was whether the Cossacks should continue to emphasize strategic loyalty or attack the Russian state, abolish serfdom, and establish Cossack democracy in central Russia.

The Host was hurting. The problem of insufficient resources had to be addressed. This is when Stenka Razin appeared on the scene. First, he tried to revive the raiding economy, but ecological constraints and Russian interference foiled this strategy. Convinced that nothing short of war against Muscovy would protect the Host's autonomy, Razin decided to break the exilic bargain with the state. Stenka—"heretic and outlaw," the most colorful of all Russian rebels—was eventually captured by *domovitye* Cossacks (the wealthier, southern "householder" faction) and turned over to Moscow for execution.[136] The argument that loyalty, in the form of strategic dependency on Moscow, would better serve the interests of the exilic territory prevailed. Handing over Razin was portrayed as a voluntary sacrifice that enabled the Cossacks to keep the bargain intact. In one sense this seems correct. Tsar Alexei did not punish the Host, and he permitted his delegates to bargain with the Don representatives. The economic blockade instituted during the uprising was lifted. The exilic polity, it seemed, managed to get off "without even a slap on the wrist."[137] The bargain was not altered, and the original agreement guaranteeing autonomy and subsidy was restored.

In time-honored tradition, both the law and the renewed agreement were ignored by the Host. In 1671, one year after they turned over Razin and promised to serve "wherever the tsar would order," the Cossacks refused to send anyone to fight rebels in Astrakhan. Ataman Smarenin was almost thrown out of the krug when he tried to convince his comrades to accept a Russian plan to build a fort there. The response of the krug was clear: "Even if the Great Sovereign's subsidy of a hundred rubles were sent to [each of] us, we wouldn't construct and sit in those forts. We don't desire to sit in forts, and we are already willing to die for the sake of the Great Sovereign without forts."[138] In 1675 the Cossacks refused to deliver a bandit by the name of Buianka, reaffirming the right to refuge.

Why, then, did the state keep its end of the bargain? Boeck claims it was because the Don was a crucial piece of "a larger strategic puzzle that involved the Ottoman Empire."[139] The Cossacks provided necessary support to the state in its campaigns against Crimea and Ottoman coastal towns. Their role in the Crimean campaigns of the 1670s was of decisive importance.

Yet the Cossack advantage could not hold. Before long, the exilic fracture reemerged, this time as a full-fledged split between loyalists and autonomists. The loyalists advocated strategic dependency on Moscow and emphasized the independent role of the ataman, the politics of patronage, and an economy based primarily on the government subsidy. Some historians call them "pro-Government Cossacks" who exercised a "stabilizing influence" among the unpredictable grassroots.[140] Yet this characterization misses nuances of the exilic reality of the Don. There is no evidence to suggest that prominent loyalist politicians put the interests of the state before those of the Host. That would happen later, in the eighteenth century. The autonomists, however, believed that the exilic space was better served by strengthening the three pillars of autonomist politics: the raiding economy, the right to refuge, and direct democracy of the krug.

Both camps navigated a strategic middle ground between loyalty and voice, or between calculated allegiance and selective defiance. Loyalist politics was personified by the legendary ataman Frol Minaev, the first professional politician in the exilic territory, who used a refined balance of voice and loyalty. He united the Don territory and enjoyed the respect of both fellow Cossacks and their state neighbors in the north. In his communication with Russian officials, Minaev artfully argued that "unruly" defiance among the free people (*vol'nykh liudi*) of the Don was a result of an influx of Russian migrants. By interpreting state orders selectively, he defended their autonomy.[141] In 1683, he successfully sought an increase in the annual subsidy. His refusal to give up the right to refuge, a central component of the exilic constitution, managed to convey to the state that Razin's sacrifice was voluntary, the price for saving the status quo but not a precedent that could be repeatedly invoked by the government. More controversially, Minaev cultivated relationships with prominent Russian officials, including the influential diplomat Vasilii Vasilievich Golitsyn.[142]

Minaev's leadership benefited the exilic space in the short run. His emphasis on loyalty created new opportunities for raiding and the sovereignty of the Host remained intact. In the longer run, however, Minaev created a crack through which the forces of exilic disintegration could crawl: he was the first ataman to inform the Russian government of Cossack politics. While this selective divulging of information was strategic, his overreliance on the politics of personal patronage pushed a new generation of loyalist Cossacks into the smothering embrace of the government in the years following his death.

The exilic debates gained new momentum during the *raskol* (schism) in Russian Orthodoxy between 1677 and 1682. Old Believers who arrived in the northern Don after 1677 were recruited by autonomists to support a more "vocal" relationship with the state. The Old Believers' egalitarian tone and spirited criticism of the tsar, the patriarch, and "impious" Moscow melded with the egalitarian impatience of the autonomists, who were concerned about Minaev's strategic gambit of sharing information with Moscow. The Old Believers were welcomed to the Don, including the most influential of the new preachers, Kuz'ma Ko'soi, and sanctuaries were soon built for them around the Medveditsa River in the north.

Frol Minaev negotiated several clever moves within the krug. In late 1686, however, he joined the winter delegation to Moscow and was replaced in his absence by the autonomist Lavren'tev, who quickly embraced the Old Believers. Lavren'tev allowed an Old Believer priest to address the krug. His speech made a great impression on the assembled Cossacks. Then Kuz'ma

Ko'soi arrived at the Cossack capital Cherkassk, where his millenarian rhetoric about cleaning the world was well received.

Despite Minaev's success in outmaneuvering the autonomists, the state wanted more than just Ko'soi. A blacklist of sorts arrived at the Don; among others, Moscow officials demanded the extradition of Lavrent'ev, a respected autonomist Cossack. The ensuing feverish exchange of letters provides a unique glimpse into the nature of the exilic debates. Cossacks from the north reminded their comrades that "never before have they handed over their brothers." They were not afraid of the economic blockade, still fresh in the collective memory, since "they know how to feed themselves without it."[143] After many passionate debates and Minaev's temporary resignation, the issue was left unresolved until the winter, when prominent autonomists left with the delegation for Moscow. During the last krug to discuss the Old Believer question, in April 1688, an order from the tsar was read announcing that the lives of the Cossack delegation would be spared but demanding that Lavrent'ev be turned over. One autonomist exclaimed, "If you hand over Samoshka Lavrent'ev and his comrades to Moscow, then all of you who hand him over will get such a reward from your brothers . . . that none of your names will be remembered." The unfortunate man was murdered on the spot and his body removed from the krug, which decided that the most fervent autonomists, including Lavrent'ev, would be sent to Moscow after all. With "Liubo! Liubo!" shouts of approval, the krug was concluded.[144]

Exilic passions were running high, and the sovereignty of the Host was in jeopardy as civil war unfolded. Thousands of autonomists fled to the north and built a fortress on Medveditsa River. This turned out to be a mistake: their threats of civil war pushed many former autonomists into the loyalist camp. Frol Minaev consolidated the southern communities and stormed the "second Jerusalem" in the north. The surviving "free Cossacks," no more than a thousand men, escaped to the Caucasus, where they joined Tatars and Kalmyks. Their new sovereign, the Muslim ruler Shamkal, invited other Cossacks to join the ranks of the rebels:

> Come, Cossacks, to me the Shevkal and live together with your brothers who already live with me. There's nothing for you on the Don. From the tsars you [each] receive a subsidy of only twenty altyns. In my lands you will be able to dress in gold. The [Persian] Shah's ships, and also those of your Great Sovereign's merchants and traders, ply the sea with goods. You can raid them and there will be no prohibition from me, the Shevkal.[145]

This was not a sufficient incentive for other Cossacks to join. In fall 1692, this autonomist Cossack community was destroyed, save for a fragment that moved to Kuban and formed a new group of Kuban Cossacks under the protection of the Crimean khan.

This episode illuminates the complementary nature of exilic protective strategies. In order to protect their cooperative practices, the Kuban exiles used both voice (against the state *and* their fellow Cossacks, in the form of a millenarian revolt, not unlike Scott's Zomians) and alternative forms of loyalty (offered to the Crimean khan). This should not be surprising. There was nothing unusual or contradictory in the decision of "free Cossacks" to offer their loyalty to another sovereign—loyalty, as a protective strategy, was not limited to Moscow but offered to the extra-space actor offering the best bargain.

The civil war ended but the Host was exhausted and vulnerable to Russian intervention. The end of the generation of loyalists personified by Frol Minaev coincided with the accession of Peter as tsar. Peter wanted to control the exilic space of the Don for several reasons, most importantly its proximity to the Sea of Azov. The Cossacks were a significant military ally and provided a staging ground for military action against the Ottomans. Russian shipbuilding, Peter's favorite project, benefited from Moscow's relationship with the Host. The annual shipment of supplies to the Host was sent from nearby Voronezeh, and Peter decided to start his ambitious campaigns in Azov and also to build a navy. For this, he engaged the help of the Cossacks, who excelled in the sea campaign of 1692.

After the campaign, Peter continued to depend on the Cossacks to defend the newly established Azov colony from the Tatars and Ottomans. The state was not yet sufficiently strong to remove the "potentially lethal" edge of the Cossack blade; therefore, Peter left Cossack legal autonomy in place even as he endeavored to eliminate their steppe-raiding economy. Peter subordinated the Cossacks to imperial decrees and perpetuated aspects of local Cossack autonomy that did not interfere with imperial decrees and wishes.[146] The exilic territory was exempted from aspects of Peter's reform, and in return the Host helped him quell the Astrakhan rebellion of 1705.

The Cossack right to refuge was finally revoked by the krug in 1704, not as a result of state interventionism, but from a strategic assessment that the old exilic mechanism had outlived its purpose. Dominated by loyalists, the Host decided that the only way to confront the threat to sovereignty and material security posed by waves of fugitives from Russia and by the fracture between the autonomist north and the loyalist south was to renounce the right to refuge. The autonomists voiced their disagreement by refusing to be surveyed and by fomenting dissatisfaction on the river.[147]

The autonomist swan song came with Kondratii Bulavin's uprising in 1707–8, a relatively short rebellion that marks the transformation of the exilic space. The rebel army was destroyed, together with much of the Cossack territory. Afterward, the autonomist war against the state was restricted to a low-intensity form by the militia of Ignat Nekrassov. The period immediately after the rebellion was in many ways reminiscent of the aftermath of Razin's rebellion. The exilic territory was spared, and a new generation of loyalists emerged; this time, however, the new generation of loyalist Cossacks did not have the interests of exilic autonomy at heart. There was no ataman of Frol Minaev's political talents, and the patronage of imperial officials was sought by corrupt atamans. Their emphasis on loyalty to Moscow with increased power in the office of the ataman paved the way for the transformation of the exilic space from exit-with-autonomy to exit-without-autonomy. Interdependence with Russia was replaced by dependence on Russia, and cooperative exilic practices were gradually replaced by hierarchical, class-riven ones.

The Host was exhausted by years of intra-exilic warfare and debates. In contrast, the state (in no small part due to the military assistance of the Don Cossacks) was stronger than ever and ready to negotiate a new exilic bargain reflecting the new balance of forces. Under the new terms, voluntary service was replaced by universal military service. During the Russo-Turkish war, the Don was the first region in Europe to experience universal mobilization. Officially classified as an irregular army under the administration of the Military College, the Cossacks had no maneuvering space for noncompliance; the ataman, upon receiving imperial orders, had to assemble and dispatch the required cavalry regiments.[148] Between wars against Sweden and Suvorov's Alpine operations, "Don Cossack regiments served in campaigns that took them from the arid steppes of the Caspian basin to the frozen forests of Finland, from the populous northern European plain to the semitropical regions of Georgia and Transcaucasia."[149]

Cossack liberties were translated into rights, at the pleasure of the state. Now classified as privileged people of the Russian Empire, the Cossacks' new rights and privileges included some of the old liberties they had enjoyed since the sixteenth century: the affirmation of their status as free men; the right to common ownership of all territory within the Don Host's land; the right to sole use of Don water and land resources; the privilege of tax-free trade within the Russian Empire; and the privilege to sell and distill tax-free spirits.[150] Yet the so-called rights were nothing but a "cheap and convenient device to help insure that the Cossacks would always have sufficient resources to render their mandatory military service."[151] In terms of Russian foreign politics, the focus of the Russian and Ottoman relationship would shift from the Azov to the Caucasus.

ENTER THE CHANGING WORLD-ECONOMY

The history we have set out thus far suggests a historical pattern of changing exilic responses with respect to the Don Cossacks, and one that invites comparison with other exilic histories. The pattern moves in three phases:

1. *Exit-with-autonomy* (cooperative exilic practices of politics, economy, and membership).
2. *Exit-without-autonomy* (hierarchical exilic practices of politics, economy, and membership).
3. *Autonomy-without-exit* (ethnic and cultural exilic practices within an empire or nation-state).

The Don Cossacks traversed the three periods: between the sixteenth and late seventeenth centuries, they adhered to cooperative exilic practices that could be characterized as *exit-with-autonomy*. Between the early eighteenth and nineteenth centuries, they tended toward hierarchical exilic practices, or *exit-without-autonomy*. Finally, beginning in the nineteenth century, they were completely transformed into a privileged but culturally defined people within the empire: *autonomy-without-exit*. That phase has endured to the present.

The Don exiles' strategic dependence on the Russian state was initially beneficial to them. They were able to minimize external control and increase local community control. Loyalty to the emerging Russian state facilitated the process of exilic sovereignty-building. They were able to develop cooperative practices and structures characteristic of exit-with-autonomy. Loyalty, however, came with a price. The assistance received from Muscovy was not enough to completely avoid the exit-without-resource trap; Cossack communities were faced with economic hardship and material scarcity. More significantly, dependency on Russian resources eventually damaged exilic autonomy as the state became stronger and was able to squeeze the Cossacks by taking advantage of internal divisions. Yet the Russian state could not do this alone. Its most critical strength came from its changing position within the world-economy and, particularly, its holdings of critical resources and potential grain-bearing lands that were prized by European core economies. To understand how this affected exilic society on the Don, we must turn our attention once again to the changing capitalist world-system.

The transformation of the Don Host began in earnest under Peter the Great, with the most profound changes occurring during the reign of Catherine II (1762–96). The traditional life of the old steppe was extinct by 1800, and the transformation of the Don Host resulted in the Cossacks' socialization as Russians by 1835. As we have observed, the Russian economy consisted of agricultural production based on serf labor and the export of some basic manufactured goods. From 1450 onward, bulk goods from agriculture and forestry (skins, flax, hemp, pitch, tar, and potash) were exported in significant amounts from Novgorod. In the sixteenth century, exports shifted toward inexpensive and comparatively heavy bulk products like tallow and whale oil. Flax and hemp assumed new importance, and Russia began exporting cheap goods and importing expensive "luxury" items.[152]

The commercial exchange between Russia and the West in this period was important but not critical for the functioning of the world-economic system. In other words, Russia's economic dependence on Europe was not yet subordinated to the requirements of accumulation at the core of the capitalist world-system. Agriculture was concentrated in the production of grain, grown mostly in central parts of the country and sold in the northern lands as well as Siberia. Pressures to extend grain production provided a significant impetus for colonization and impelled the intensification of serfdom, on which agricultural production rested.[153] In the sixteenth century, Russia became a supplier of raw materials for the developing Europe-centered world-economy, but that relationship was not yet critical for the development of world-capitalism. It was significant enough, however, to influence the Russian expansionist politics that took the Stroganovs (Russia's richest business family) to Siberia in 1581. As a result of this form of development, the indigenous commercial bourgeoisie survived and cooperated with the expanding state. Cities, too, survived both the "long" sixteenth century and the crisis of the seventeenth century.

England was Russia's main commercial partner by the long sixteenth century. Ties became so extensive that Fyodor I, the last Danilovich ruler, was known as the "English tsar." English imports from Russia included raw materials like wax, hemp, hides, meat, flax, whale oil, tar, ropes, and masts for ships. In return, English ships arrived at Russian ports carrying luxury items such as lead, gunpowder, saltpeter, sulfur, and (probably) firearms.[154]

This trade benefited both sides. Ivan the Terrible (1530–84) used the Muscovy Company for his own strategic goals, particularly to bring Persia into his alliance against the Turks. Moscow was in dire need of direct access to European markets, while the English were trying to bypass the German and Swedish commercial dominance of the eastern Baltic. Trade through the Caspian was very lucrative and supported the flourishing of Astrakhan—a "veritable gold mine for the [Muscovy] Company."[155] Supplies from the Muscovy Company—the official supplier to the royal English fleet—were a significant factor in the rise of the English navy.

Attman portrays the period as the one of "fierce antagonism" between Livonian-Prussian cities and merchants from Atlantic states over access to lucrative eastern European trade.[156] Russian goods were originally traded from the Livonian cities Reval and Riga, but Ivan IV opened a new trade route in 1559 that allowed merchants to trade directly with Russia via Narva, avoiding the Hanseatic middleman. The situation changed again after Narva was lost to Sweden in 1581. From the occupation of Reval in 1561 to the conquest of Riga in 1621, Sweden came to dominate trade with Russia via the Baltic.

The rise of Dutch hegemony in the seventeenth century affected both Russian and eastern European commerce. Amsterdam had become the world center of the grain trade, and the Amsterdam market set the price of grain. Seventeenth-century grain-based trade with the United Provinces replaced the sixteenth-century raw-material trade with England. "Russian grain began moving westward in increasing quantities," writes Kagarlitsky,[157] as the price of grain rose in line with demand. In Nolte's view, the relationship between Moscow and Amsterdam was one of "oligopoly" because Russia could drive down the price by dumping large quantities of rye on the world market.[158] This made Russia a serious commercial partner in the eyes of the Dutch. As many as twenty Dutch ships a year set off for Russia, while only seven went to India. For its part, Russia was anxious to rid itself of the burden of duty-free trading with the English. The new commercial relationship with the Dutch, as well as the normalization of relations with Sweden, influenced the development of Russian commercial capital. Merchants from the United Provinces established a direct relationship with Russian merchants and with the Kremlin bureaucracy, forming a "united front of Dutch and Russian commercial capital."[159]

In the seventeenth century, global changes had increasing effects on the Russian economy. Russia was a country where everyone traded: tsars, boyars, and monasteries. A marked change took place at the time of the War of the Spanish Succession (1701–14), from which England emerged as the leading trading nation. By the eighteenth century, England had attained ascendance, even hegemony, in the capitalist world-economy. Russian trade with Europe expanded rapidly and its export composition changed dramatically, with primary products rising to 95 percent of trade value.[160] Major exports included vital raw materials for British manufacturing, grain, and shipbuilding materials, where Russia was often a more affordable alternative to North America. During the eighteenth century, England accounted for half of Russia's external trade. Almost all of England's flax and hemp imports (97 to 98 percent) came from Russia; most of its iron imports came from Russia and Sweden; tar came from Russia, Sweden, and the colonies; and timber from Norway, Baltic ports, and America. Attman notes that, "England's naval and mercantile fleets were manifestly almost totally dependent on the Russian market for the most essential raw materials."[161]

The relationship between the two countries was rife with tension and highly unequal: the English viewed Russians as military and political partners but not commercial equals. According to Kagarlitsky, "The British could now use Russian territory as an additional staging ground for increasing their commercial, political, and even military influence in Persia, Central Asia, and India."[162] Russia depended on foreign credits, and its eighteenth-century debt was high. Its wars against Turkey were expensive and financed by Amsterdam banks, from which Catherine the Great took as much as 7.5 million guilders.

The world market heavily influenced the local serf-holding economy, which supplied it with agricultural produce, raw materials, and semiprocessed goods. Organizing the rapidly increasing product for world demand meant the intensification of serfdom and the consolidation of the nobility and Russia's administrative apparatus. Kolchin describes the enserfment process:

> The debasement of the serfs was essentially a linear process; virtually every Russian monarch was responsible for some piece of legislation that further reduced the serfs' rights, with some of the most important acts being passed during the reigns of the reforming monarchs Peter I (1682–1725) and Catherine II (1762–96). By the middle of the eighteenth century the formal

power of the pomeshchik over his serfs was as great as that of the American slave owner over his chattel—almost total, short of deliberate murder.[163]

Peter the Great's serf legislation had obliterated the distinction between slaves and serfs. In 1722, he imposed the "soul tax" on *kholopy* (slaves). By the middle of the century, peasants were either serfs or state peasants. The nobility (*dvorianstvo*) was a landowning class, a service class, and a class with a defined hierarchy of ranks and duties. With shaved beards and Western manners, this class "held most of Russia's land, owned almost all the serfs, and dominated its government."[164] Peter I created the Ruling Senate (1711–22), transformed the army, and took important steps in the centralization of the state. He curbed decentralizing tendencies by absorbing the nobility's time and using them to force each other into ensuring better internal flows of surplus.[165]

Catherine II's accession in 1762 brought further incorporation into the world-economy and further intensification of serfdom.[166] Her provincial reform created a new administrative framework that distinguished between provinces, districts, and the *mir*, or village commune.[167] Administrative bodies combined locally elected and centrally appointed officials. Replaced by a civilian apparatus and a more organized bureaucracy, members of the nobility were now given time to focus on cash-cropping. Catherine's 1765 land survey facilitated the process of land concentration. Shifts in patterns of serfdom reflected this new orientation, as ownership and decision making over production became concentrated.[168]

This fundamental transformation of the system of government was accompanied by important economic decisions. The legal categorization of serfdom was fully developed during Catherine's reign, reaching a climax in the exclusion of most peasants from so-called personal legal status and creating a system capable of truly unprecedented exploitation of serf labor.[169] In a series of decrees between 1765 and 1767, landowners were allowed to send serfs to labor camps. It is no surprise that this all added a new impetus to escape, including migration to the Don.

The first quarter of the eighteenth century saw the construction of Russia's first large-scale factories, particularly the metallurgical industry in the Urals. Mostly established by 1720 and well integrated into global trade, its use of serf labor made Russian iron competitive on the world market. Ural factories brought together a disparate group of workers: industrial wage earners and skilled foreign workers; local artisans and metallurgists from other parts of Russia; and unskilled workers, auxiliary or "ascribed" peasants, and fugitives.

Part of this group became professional serfs after 1721, when factory owners were given permission to buy whole villages.[170]

The most important trend for the Cossacks of the Don was the steady rise of commercial agriculture. According to Lieberman, "From the 1780s cereal producers on the southern frontier became major suppliers to Mediterranean and northern European cities."[171] The rapid growth of grain exports was spurred by agricultural crisis in Europe and eventually led to Russia supplanting Poland as the breadbasket of Europe, as agriculture became "export driven to the same degree in which it was becoming commercial and market driven."[172]

Russia's cultivated acreage expanded by some 250 percent, chiefly on the steppe frontier. The effects were felt heavily in the Don. The exilic space of the Cossacks could hardly remain outside of world-capitalist accumulation; Catherine the Great (1762–96) had already incorporated the south Russian steppes into the Russian empire and opened the Black Sea ports to all nations in 1784. These ports assumed a growing importance for Russia's foreign trade. As Wallerstein documents, the intensification of coerced labor was not an accident but a result of policy decisions; "the increase in cereals production was facilitated by the abolition of internal customs in 1754 and the authorization of grain exports in 1766. The acquisition of the southern steppes and the Black Sea ports also furthered grain exports and hence integration into the world-economy."[173]

The changing pattern of revolt reflects these changes. The rebellion of Pugachev (1773–74) was arguably the most extensive rebellion in Russian history before 1905. A Cossack from the Don, Pugachev could not count on the help of the loyalist Host. His ideals were typically Don Cossack, including rebellion against modern ways of life, serfdom, and legibility. He was joined by Cossacks and Russians alike. However, as Kolchin observes, the silence of the exilic territory made a crucial difference and greatly influenced the outcome of the resistance movement: "The absence of such rebellions after 1774 indicates the degree to which the peasant wars were dependent on Cossacks operating in a sparsely settled frontier region and a government unable to respond quickly to trouble."[174]

Instead of making all men equal, as Pugachev had hoped, his revolt was followed by even more inequality, overarching administrative reforms, the full incorporation of the southeastern steppe within that new provincial system, and the strengthening of Russian military forces in the region.

Russia was fully incorporated into the capitalist world-economy by the mid-eighteenth century. It was not allowed to become too strong (in relation to western Europe) and, consequently, Russia's foreign policy was oriented toward eastern Europe, the Black Sea, and the Caucasus. Russia's integration into European economic networks had important consequences for the Don Cossacks. The Russian state had to guarantee the smooth operation of an integrated and expanding division of labor, to remove all obstacles to accumulation beginning with rival power centers. Thus, a condition of membership in the interstate system was the elimination and pacification of the exilic space on the Don.

As the steppes were no longer valueless from a world-systemic point of view, exilic practices were no longer tolerated. The advance of commercial agriculture and the demand for grain, dictated by the new developments on the world market, pressured Moscow to integrate the Cossacks into the Russian state-space. The incorporation of Russia was a process not only of integrating new territories into a systemwide division of labor but also of integrating self-organized, extra-state spaces such as the Don.

In a fascinating paradox, the Don Cossacks helped Russia become a strong state with semiperipheral rather than peripheral status. The Cossacks were victims of their own success and agents of their own demise, as they facilitated more favorable terms for Russia's incorporation into the capitalist world-economy, which then demanded their further political and economic subjugation. Before the eighteenth century, the Don exiles assisted not only the rise of the Russian state but also its ascent from peripheral status in the world-economy by policing Russia's frontiers against contending states and peoples, thereby creating a "buffer zone" that cheapened the cost of defending Russia's borders and maintaining regional hegemony. The divisions between loyalists and autonomists weakened the Don Host. It was unable to resist incorporation into Russian state structures and world-systemic structures of accumulation, and powerful sections of its established authority had a distinct interest in extending Russia's class society into the Don. The processes of exilic disintegration increased as the region was integrated more closely into the Russian state-zone and into world-systemic institutions and processes.

EXILIC DEMISE

As the Cossacks' exilic bargain with the Russian state eventually forced the end of exit-with-autonomy, so, too, did it complete the job of finishing exit altogether. Finally, in the last decades of the eighteenth century, exilic society on the Don was reduced to its ethnic and cultural aspects, to (cultural) *autonomy-without-exit*. The government subsidy was not nearly enough to avoid economic hardship and material scarcity. Full incorporation into the Russian state and economy, and thereby into the divisions of labor of the capitalist world-system, enabled some Cossacks to amass vast fortunes by accumulating land and growing grain, practices that had heretofore been anathema. Today, when one enters the Don by car from Volgograd, the flat vista of the steppe is no longer "furrowed with the hooves of horses" or "sown with the heads of Cossacks" but is, in summer, wheat as far as the eye can see and, in winter, rye. The people of the Don are mostly still poor, and still proud. But they are Russian, and large portraits of Vladimir Putin watch over the children in their classrooms and the atamans in their stanitsa centers.

The Cossacks helped in their own undoing. The transformation of the exilic space was not simply reducible to the rise of "friction-destroying technologies," nor were all of the negative changes in the exilic space simply results of imperial policy and the world-economy. Instead, change emerged from a *two*-sided bargain in which new Cossack upper classes, tied to the rising grain economy, built a stake in the new system of loyalty, not autonomy.

In the course of the eighteenth century, the exilic space based on voluntary association was transformed into an ethnic community based on ascriptive identity. This was a process that formally began with renunciation of the right to refuge in 1704, a strategic decision by Cossacks and not simply a result of government intervention or nativist elitism. As Boeck perceptively suggests,

> In order to preserve their separate deal with the Romanov dynasty, which guaranteed their personal freedom, immunity from direct taxation, and local autonomy, the Don Cossack community chose to disassociate itself from the larger, unfree, Russian population to its north. The starting point for this new analysis of Cossack identity is the fact that when the Don Cossacks concluded a deal with the new Romanov dynasty in the early seventeenth century they were an open multi-ethnic fraternity which replenished its ranks through in-migration. A little over a century later, they constituted a community in which membership was primarily acquired through birth and marriage. To facilitate this shift the Don Cossacks constructed an ethnic identity.[175]

In order to regain a form of autonomy in the eighteenth century, the Cossacks began to close ranks and create a pseudo-ethnic community. This was a decision of the Cossack Host in Cherkassk, albeit one that was taken in harsh circumstances.

Late eighteenth-century membership was not just restricted; the Don Cossacks were transformed into a closed society with birth-based identity. *Burlak* became an ethnic category. Don Cossacks were classified as *narod* (people), a privileged ethnic group within the empire.

According to Boeck, the eighteenth century brought a new relationship between documentation, economic exploitation, and territorial culture. Individual identity was verified and codified, and juridical differences expressed in ethnic terms. North and south came back together, but in a way that led to the disintegration (rather than reaffirmation) of exilic sovereignty: "The north was brought under the heel of the ataman." The first census was instituted in 1720 after a new deal with the state included an obligation to record the population of the Don. In 1734, the notoriously violent ataman Lopatin sent special officials to inspect the territory and look for non-Cossack fugitives. By the end of the eighteenth century, "the krug, once a symbol of Cossack democracy and liberty, had become an arena for punishing offenders of the boundary regime."[176]

Peter I had already brought changes to the exilic territory. The free movement of people around Azov was regulated by travel documents, checkpoints, and patrols.[177] In order to be able to conduct long-distance trade, Cossacks were required to possess a *voiskovoe pi'smo,* or letter of introduction from the Host. They needed passports not only to trade but also to hunt or fish. Cossack land was surveyed, and the names of Cossack warriors were recorded in books. Abstract knowledge of facts and figures replaced anti-state, place-based knowledge, allowing the state "to introduce its presence, control, and surveillance in the most isolated corners (which thus cease to be 'corners')."[178]

In 1733, the Don Host wrote to the empress: "By virtue of your Imperial Majesty's decrees ... our Cossacks do not cross the border for any reason without passports bearing the seal awarded to us by your ancestors.... Though a few dare to enter the Turkish border by managing to steal around checkpoints, we catch them and punish them without mercy in our public (*vsenarodnykh*) krugs."[179]

The eventual incorporation of the exilic Don space into Russian territory marked the beginning of the "intellectual privatization" of the Cossacks.[180] Under the new identity system, the Cossacks were more Russian than Russians themselves: valiant Orthodox crusaders, writing some of the most courageous but often reactionary pages of the Russian national history, now known as much for their participation in pogroms against Jews as for their valiant exilic exploits. Their history was appropriated by the state.

The exilic elements of the Don Cossack constitution were eliminated. No more cooperative practices that prevented class hierarchies from forming. No more the circular pattern of assembly discussion, delegation, and justice; nonspecialization of governing; insurgent identity; decentralization with coordination. Corruption became more rampant and, for the first time, lucrative.

The history of the exilic space between 1670 and 1835 is a history of struggle between the autonomists and the loyalists, both of whom were at first interested in protecting state-refusing exilic practices. The most dramatic transformation in Cossack society, the gradual disintegration of Don Cossack autonomy and exilic sovereignty in the eighteenth century, resulted from the appearance of the new generation of loyalists. A vacuum of leadership in the loyalist camp emerged following the death of Frol Minaev, and autonomist hopes rested on the success of Bulavin's uprising.[181] During the confusion that followed its brutal demise, a new politics emerged that favored the Russian policy of "subordination and centralization at the expense of the Cossack autonomy."[182] The confluence of two trends, state interventionism and internal socioeconomic conflict, resulted in the erosion of democratic practices. After Bulavin, says Menning, the "Tsarist State was not using force as much as a combination of administrative measures and the astute utilization of social change."[183] The new face of power on the river was concentrated executive power, influence on elections, control over distribution of the imperial subsidy, corruption, and nepotism.[184] The direct democratic elements of Cossack exilic practice were replaced by imitations of state institutions and imperial models. Peter I (1672–1725), and especially Catherine II (1729–96), demonstrated considerable skill in turning this process of social differentiation against exilic autonomy.[185]

The process of restructuring the ataman's role began with Peter Emilianov. A decree issued by Peter I in 1710 confirmed Emilianov as ataman in perpetuity, without any prior communication with other office holders.[186] This transformed the office of the ataman from elective to appointive; the ataman was now, for all intents and purposes, an imperial client. As Emilianov himself pointed out (not without some pride), "In order to be ataman one has to have a decree from the Great Sovereign and not simply be self-proclaimed."[187] Emilianov not only transformed the office of ataman, but also successfully "defied the krug with impunity, and used control of the Host's chancery to augment his authority. He and his allies employed imperial patronage ties to silence and undermine their opponents."[188]

As a result of the Emilianov era, the relationship between people and power in the Don region was forever altered. Around 1730, the Military College created the rank of elder (*starshina*) for those who distinguished themselves in government service. This had far-reaching consequences for the exilic territory. As Boeck explains, "For ordinary Cossacks opportunities for upward mobility all but disappeared as a result of the government decision to grant seals of approval to a group of leaders it christened as the starshina."[189] By 1734 there were already twenty-seven Cossack starshina, by then a separate category of the Cossack population. Through influence, judicious appointments, and administrative fiat, tsars including Catherine II and Paul I "turned the process of social differentiation that had spawned the elders to the advantage of the State ... St. Petersburg fostered the emergence of the elders, assumed control of their selection, and, by bowing to their limited interests and aspirations, transformed them into docile collaborators of Imperial rule in the land of the Don Host."[190] This was a stunning blow to autonomist forces in the Don. Power was reshaped according to the Russian imperial model. The practice of submitting the ataman's actions and decisions to the krug was ended.[191]

Ataman after ataman surpassed his predecessors in abuses of power. During 1738–1772 only two men were appointed atamans. Their rule became synonymous with corruption, and they subjected their fellow Cossacks to intolerable violence. In a document submitted to the court in Moscow, a certain Serebriakov complains about the

> intolerable violence of Ataman Danila Efremov. Elders and other people dispatched by him upstream and along the Don, Donets, Medveditsa, Khoper, and Buzuluk to all the stanitsas have taken extremely oppressive measures. They unmercifully beat the stanitsa atamans and the Cossacks and take large sums of money, which they divide with the Ataman [Efremov], with the result that stanitsas have fallen into great debt ... everyone cries bitterly, not having any kind of defense.[192]

The Efremovs, who traveled around the Don with bodyguards, aspired to the rank of Russian nobility and attempted to make the institution of ataman hereditary. In 1775, on the recommendation of Prince Potemkin, Cossacks could become members of the nobility by virtue of their military service. By the 1770s, 89 elders had been admitted to the nobility, rising to 206 in 1796. This was a "closed society within a closed society," a Cossack oligarchy where equality once prevailed.

If the disintegration of exilic politics during the eighteenth century meant independent power for the ataman, it also meant declining power for the krug. The krug continued to exist, but with an ever diminishing sphere of competence. After 1732, it was no longer able to elect campaign atamans; in 1755, it lost the right to choose Host elders; in 1775, it stopped meeting regularly; and in 1776, it lost the right to elevate Cossacks to the rank of officer. Its only prerogative by that point was the election of the Host esaul (head clerk). During Catherine's reign, the ancient Cossack Assembly became largely a ceremonial body.

The krug was gradually replaced by the Chancery of Elders. This was a victory for "centralization, against the old forces of autonomy as embodied in the Krug."[193] Catherine's administrative reform of 1775 reorganized the Cossack nobility. According to Menning, her changes were "an impressive gain in the struggle to bring the Cossacks under closer legal and administrative control."[194]

Voices for Cossack autonomy were effectively stifled. The Host had survived Pugachev's uprising and valiantly served the empress in the Russo-Turkish wars, but it barely survived further reforms administered by Potemkin. Direct democracy, that exercise of effective power, was removed from the exilic life of the Cossacks. Directly democratic aspects of "noncoercive power" were replaced by representative governance. The final chapter in the dissolution of the exilic autonomy of the Don Host was the statute of 1835, which defined the Cossacks as a separate ethnicity that managed to survive only as an "anachronism, a military class whose service was based on the collective ownership of land."[195]

On the economic side, the raiding economy was replaced by settled ranching, agriculture, and commercial fishing. The introduction of serfdom, land alienation, creeping poverty, and bitter disputes over the increasing land shortage brought the exilic territory to a state of "impending breakdown."[196]

Economic crisis had already weakened exilic autonomy. In a letter from 1694, the Don Host notified the tsar that they would no longer be able to build ships "because we have no source of ship hulls (*lotoshnye truby*) and from Rus' delivery of such hulls has ceased."[197] This was due to depletion of old-growth forest in the Don by a century of building ships for the raiding economy. The ecological crisis, combined with a more aggressive imperial politics, left Cossack sea adventures at the mercy of the emperor. The sea was no longer free—the mouth of the Don was under the control of the state, with the steppe being the only remaining arena for raiding. Two decrees at the beginning of the eighteenth century, one from the Host and the other from Moscow, reveal that raiding was now considered *vorovstvo* (felonious) behavior.[198]

Although commerce with the Azov colony was significant, the onset of agriculture on the Don was indicative of the new age. Spaces where before "no lands whatsoever were plowed and no grain was sown" were now under the plow.[199] At first, the Host categorically forbade plowing and sowing in Cossack territory: "No one in any place is to plow or sow grain. If they start to plow, the guilty party is to be beaten to death and deprived of property . . . Whoever desires to plow, should return to their previous place of residence, wherever they have [previously] lived."[200] Two decades later, Don Cossacks were fighting with Azov colonists over the fisheries in the lower Don.[201]

While the struggle to prevent the Russians from taking over lucrative fishing spots was successful at this time, the Cossacks were not able to defend the forest preserves that Peter desired for shipbuilding.[202] State-sponsored enclosures of exilic spaces during Emilianov's tenure as ataman marked the beginning of the privatization of fisheries and forests.[203] Emilianov had a lucrative construction business, building ranches and farms in the north. Fisheries and trading stalls were rented to other Cossacks, and massive alienation of land was afoot.[204]

Emilianov traded on two loopholes in existing custom: free homesteading (*zaimka*) and the lease system known as *otkup*.[205] The "inalienable right to the sole use of the land" was a cornerstone of the Cossacks' new deal with Peter; yet, even after 1711 there was no private ownership of land in the Don. However, the custom of *zaimka* inadvertently introduced land inequality through the back door. According to the custom, each Cossack was entitled to as much land from the *stanitsa iurt* as he or his hired peasant laborers could work. For a time, attempts to manipulate land ownership were remedied by its periodic redivision. However, the redivision of *iurt* land was extremely rare in the eighteenth century, and the elders (and later nobles) accrued a disproportionate amount of land.[206] The *voiskovaia* (unoccupied) land, a large expanse of more than 6.5 million acres, was subject to a similar process of slow accumulation in the hands of the wealthy elite. Some of these estates were enormous, exceeding one hundred thousand acres. Available statistics from 1821–22 reveal that 4 percent of the Cossack population controlled over 27 percent of usable land in the Don.[207] The autonomists and rank-and-file Cossacks were not just idly watching this appropriation of sta- nichnaia land; documents from local assemblies reveal a fierce struggle against both legal and illegal attempts to appropriate land.[208]

Similarly, the lease system (*otkup*) benefited the emerging group of soon- to-be-wealthy Cossacks. *Otkup* was practiced in fisheries as well as in the milling of grain and distilling of wine.[209] The only exempt resource was salt from the lake region of the trans-Don steppe. Fish and fish processing became a central economic activity after the demise of the raiding economy, and their control was highly sought after. In the nineteenth century, under Ataman Platov, a new class of professional merchants appeared, so-called "trading Cossacks," who were exempt from military service.[210]

The first evidence of the institution of serfdom in Cossack territory is from 1734, when Ataman Danila Efremov imported thirty serfs from Russia even though serfdom was still illegal. The total number of serfs in the terri- tory remained below one thousand souls in the nineteenth century, although this did not include non-Cossacks, who instead of payment in cash started to receive crude labor contracts. Being a *burlak*, or a non-Cossack, was not identical with serfdom, yet the threat of deportation made *burlaki* working conditions virtually indistinguishable from bonded labor.[211]

The final chapter in the transformation of the exilic economy occurred between 1775 (Catherine's administrative reforms) and 1835 (Tsar Nicholas I's statute codifying Russian law), after the imperial strategy of undermining Cossack autonomy backfired. The resulting excess of nobility-induced land shortages undermined the collective ownership of the land and, conse- quently, the ability of the Cossacks to perform their military service. In reac- tion, Catherine the Great decreed that all peasants had to be registered with the officer on whose land they worked. The chief aim of this decree was to enable the collection of a head tax.[212] The next step was a 1796 regulation in which Tsar Paul ruled that peasants living in the Don were "considered by law [to be] the serfs of the officer or stanitsa in whose name they were regis- tered."[213] A report by Prince Gorchakov, personal representative of Tsar Alexander I, after his inspection of the Don Cossack Host in 1801, claims that Don society was "on the verge of a breakdown."[214] The report empha- sized that the cardinal problem was the system of landholding, "the very cornerstone of the whole system by which the Cossacks rendered their valu- able military service to the Tsarist State."[215] There was unrest among serfs in the Don and even a serf uprising in 1821. These moments led to Ataman

FIGURE 2. Autonomy without exit. Uniformed Don Cossacks today as an ethnic/cultural group within Russian society. Viacheslav Yaschenko.

Denisov's decision to codify Don Cossack law. All that remained of Don Cossack exilic society were its cultural traditions, which, although colorful even today, slowly became anachronistic.

By the time we visited the Don, in 2012, it was clear that a proud history was reenacted in a shell of interesting cultural displays such as dancing and horsemanship, which were handed down to new generations in public schools—under the watchful eye of Vladimir Putin's portrait. The ataman, although commanding some respect in the community, had limited power and was largely a figurehead who presided over public exhibitions and organized rare VIP visits (we were welcomed quite warmly in the ancient stanitsa Ust'-Medveditskaya, where we were told that "a visit by such distinguished professors is as rare a sight on the Don as the yeti"). The ataman presides over the initiation of visitors into the Cossack Host, laughingly pretending to beat them with a Cossack whip after they drink moonshine off of a Cossack sword blade . . . the whole ritual taking place in the stanitsa museum.

A major bone of contention and item of debate among Cossacks is the new uniform forced on them by the Russian state, which reflects post-Soviet military style rather than the much-preferred Cossack fur hats and tunics. Only the red stripe down the pant leg remains to show that these are Cossacks. The exilic economic practices of old are few, mainly some fishing for household consumption, some beekeeping, and some moonshine distillation. The main public face of the loyalty bargain with the Russian state is the neofascist gangs of Cossacks who terrorize the Moscow metro and who policed the 2014 Olympics in Sochi, enforcing "order."

In interactions with the residents of Ust'-Medvetitskaia and its environs, once the proudest district of the Don Host, made famous in fiction by works such as Sholokhov's *Tikhii Don* (*And Quiet Flows the Don*), the sense of pride mixed with loss is profound. The long historical erosion of the exilic space was colorfully encapsulated in a conversation we had with a resident of the stanitsa, a few meters from the Don.

"My grandfather was a Cossack," he told us, "my father was the son of a Cossack, and I am nothing but a dog's rear end."

CONCLUSIONS

Our main task in this chapter was to describe the fascinating historical process in which exilic space was affected and transformed by its relationship to the state and the changes in the world-economy, influencing, at the same time, the territorialization of Russian state and its incorporation into the capitalist world-system.

In the first chapter of their exilic history, the communities on the Don were external to the capitalist world-system yet still dependent on the state in Moscow. Cossack autonomy was dominated by the raiding economy, which was located outside of "formal economy" to the extent that things were provided according to usefulness, availability, and need rather than market value. Resource-uses and distributional questions were decided by agreement and direct democracy rather than market price and ability to pay. Equality was placed at a premium. However, the economy of the steppe was always, to a large extent, parasitic in its reliance on raiding and government subsidy.

After Russia's incorporation into the European-centered world-system, the Cossacks' substantive economy came under persistent and violent attack by the formal economy and was transformed by capitalist accumulation and the extension of the law of value. A result of Russia's semiperipheral incorporation was the disintegration of exilic space. The hegemonic shift from

Holland to Britain and the accompanying industrial revolution created strong pressures for peripheral and previously external regions such as Russia to produce inputs for the industrial economy. As Russia became a "breadbasket" for the West, the resulting pressure to introduce farming and produce for the world market impacted the Cossack exilic regime. These pressures induced the transition of Cossack production from herding to farming, which in turn imposed pressures for the creation of a landed upper class and serf or serf-like classes.

The history of the Don Cossacks complicates Scott's proposal for the study of nonstate spaces. The republic on the Don was exilic. Once we place the Don in the context of world-capitalism, however, the term "nonstate space" no longer seems to capture its historical complexity. Before the eighteenth century and during the initial stage of incorporation, the Cossack territory was a "black hole": a self-organized space instituted before Russia was included in the hierarchical organization of the capitalist world-economy. Structured outside the realm of the interstate system and capitalist accumulation, Cossack exilic space was produced as an instance of infrapolitics of the capitalist world-economy, a form of place-based politics that was later disfigured and deformed in the process of world-system incorporation.

Putting things this way situates the Don Cossacks within "world time": that is, within the world economy's rhythms and patterns of organization and change; cycles of accumulation and their associated divisions of labor and technologies of production and control; changes among hegemonic regimes and their geographic priorities, leading sectors, and global reach; and general world development and its impact on the abilities and desires of the Russian state to impose control over populations and labor within its territories and desired territories.

The story of the Don Cossack Host diverges strongly from Scott's account of Zomia. As core powers incorporated the Russian external arena into the capitalist world-economy, the exilic territory—a former "black hole" constituted outside of the "world time"—was fundamentally transformed. World-systemic incorporation captured these spaces by bringing them into global divisions of labor and associated trading regimes; it imposed new economic units of production and trade, new ways of acquiring and controlling labor, new institutions of state control, and new infrastructures. All of this made it impossible for the exiles of the Don to use the strategic combinations of voice and loyalty that had served them previously. Although state pressures transformed loyalty into obeisance, the Cossacks themselves contributed to the final outcome.

It is best to be skeptical of economic determinist explanations that elide local dynamics, as the case of the Don Host reflects. Exilic specificities were particularly important in the way that the Russian state and the Cossack community bargained and interacted, as well as in the outcomes of those interactions at any given time. Local specificities were foremost in determining the availability of different strategies of exit and voice, Cossack chances of successfully maintaining their autonomy, and the nature of exilic production possibilities and of loyalty bargains between the Cossack communities and Russian authorities. These were not just local bargains between the Host and the state; they arose in the context of the world-economy. Viewed from the perspective of the world-economy, the Cossacks helped Russia become a strong semiperipheral state and facilitated the process of Russia's semiperipheral incorporation into the capitalist world-economy.

Before the eighteenth century, the Don Cossacks policed Russia's frontiers against contending states, becoming a "buffer zone" that cheapened the cost of defending Russia's borders and maintaining regional hegemony. The loyalty of the Host allowed relative territorial safety for the state-space in relationship to Tatars; a complex, and ultimately successful military and diplomatic struggle against Turkey; and the development of modern territorial sovereignty that began with the establishment of the Belgorod line and climaxed with Catherine's territorial organization. The exiles from the Don were an important part of Russia's diplomatic and political struggle with the Ottomans during the Azov and Crimean campaigns. They assisted Peter in building the navy and also in quelling the Astrakhan rebellion. Later, when the center of gravity in Russo-Turkish relations shifted to the Caucasus, the Don Cossacks constituted a valuable military and human resource. They stayed loyal to the state during delicate moments of Pugachev's rebellion. During all this, the Russian state allowed autonomy to continue in its bargain with the exilic space. But the Cossacks paid an increasingly high price of loyalty.

Analytic categories of exit, voice, and loyalty suggest a relationship between the state and exilic spaces that recognizes Cossack agency. The exilic bargain with the early Russian state allowed exilic formation. Similarly, the exilic sovereignty of the Host was developed in tandem with the territorialization of Moscow's rule—the territorialization of exit was both a consequence and a victim of the erection of the Belgorod imperial boundary.

The great Cossack contradiction, between freedom and right to refuge, on one hand, and limited resources on the other, made it impossible for the exiles to resist the advent of agriculture and the state they themselves had helped to make so powerful. In the eighteenth century under Peter and Catherine, Russia underwent a profound transformation as it was incorporated into the world-capitalist economy. The result and the main consequence was a considerable narrowing of the choices available to the Don Host. The new organization of the economy allowed very limited maneuvering space. The Cossacks' reliance on loyalty, despite its strategic benefits between 1680 and 1700, made the eighteenth-century Host vulnerable to the state's attempts to promote internal sociopolitical differentiation. The socialization of the Cossacks would have been impossible without their own complicity. The ataman of the Host had already become an imperial client during Peter's reign, and Catherine's politics of "grooming of the local nobility" set the nail in autonomy's coffin.

Further, the presence of exit made the use of voice much more likely. The Bolotnikov and Razin rebellions of the seventeenth century, which erupted before the encroachment of capitalism, are different in character from the eighteenth-century uprisings of Bulavin and Pugachev. The former were about spreading exilic autonomy as a way of strengthening exilic society and ameliorating resource constraints. The fact that the pretender phenomenon, the rebellious cosmology of the "returning tsar," reached its peak under Catherine is hardly surprising. The revolutionary nature of revolts was most directly expressed with Pugachev, who led a class-conscious uprising that enveloped Russia during the most violent phase of capitalist incorporation. By that time, the Don was in retreat.

Russia's semiperipheral incorporation accompanied the disintegration of the exilic space. The industrial revolution created strong pressures for previously external regions such as Russia to produce inputs for the industrial economy. As Russia became a "breadbasket" for the West, the resulting pressure to produce grain for the world market infected the Cossack exilic regime. Cossack production went from herding to farming, which in turn applied incorporative pressures that encroached on Cossack political autonomy. As the Russian state became stronger and was itself incorporated into world-economic structures, the terms of its exilic bargains with the Don turned progressively in its favor and eroded the exilic nature of the Cossack space.

The Cossacks from the Don managed to survive as an ethnic community, and the argument has been made that the Host benefited in important ways.

Unlike their Tatar neighbors, the Don Cossacks survived. Menning points out that the Cossacks were "far better off in a material sense than the average Russian or Ukrainian peasant."[216] Similarly, Boeck writes that the Don Cossacks not only entered the Russian Empire in the early eighteenth century on a superior footing to the enserfed Russian masses, but also maintained privileges as a military caste and ethnic community, with a special place in the Romanov dynasty.[217]

The development and consolidation of the interstate system brought about a modern state in Russia, an increasingly powerful and effective (semi-peripheral) unit that required a monopoly over the legitimate use of force in spaces it hoped to control. The moment the state was strong enough to remove the threat the Cossack exilic space represented to the Russian monopoly of power, it did so. The alternative exilic practices of the Host—its democratic/substantive institutions such as the krug and the raiding economy—were eliminated and replaced by new structures and relationships.

Yet Menning asserts that "nearly 200 years of Imperial rule failed to erase the krug from Cossack consciousness."[218] On the eve of the Russian Revolution, in 1917, the first action of the Don Cossacks was to rehabilitate the krug and direct democratic politics. Delegates were once again appointed collectively. Cossack leaders like Philip Mironov, today a rehabilitated hero of Ust'-Medveditskaya, re-created their people's historic adherence to direct democracy under the banner of "All Power to the Soviets" . . . until that slogan itself became a threat to Soviet state centralism and leaders like Mironov were obliterated.

Today, it might appear that the possibilities of exilic creation have been completely undermined. One might conclude, as does Scott with respect to the incorporation of the peoples of Zomia, that modernity destroys "friction of distance," making the "art of not being governed" a thing of the past and not a living reality. This is not our intention, nor our conclusion. Rather, the history of the Don reminds us just how difficult it is to build and reproduce exilic society in the conditions of contemporary capitalism. The Cossack experience of exilic disintegration is an antidote to naïve utopianism and points to dangers of exilic society, including the difficult politics of the loyalty bargain. Yet, even here there are glimmers of hope. The enthusiastic emergence of decentralized soviets on the Don gives testament to Kropotkin's thesis about the degree to which human desires to practice mutual aid are lurking beneath the surface of modern or postmodern possessive individualistic institutions, looking for opportunities to break out. Further support for this thesis lies in the degree to which contemporary exilic societies and practices exist, within the fractures or "cracks" of world-capitalism. To examine these questions, we turn to two contemporary instances of exilic space: the voluntary exile of the Zapatistas in southeastern Mexico and the forced exile of isolated prisoners living in the most restrictive bare-life conditions.

FOUR

Zapatistas

Before us looms a horizon of mountains and forest. It may not be the heart of darkness, but the Lacandón Jungle has its specters, and is known colloquially as the Desert of Solitude. Once, this vast, lush rainforest, covering 6,000 square kilometers was mostly uninhabited, but waves of twentieth-century migration by displaced and landless migrants from Oaxaca and Guerrero ensured the slow but steady colonization of this virgin territory. By the 1980s, the rainforest was reduced to about one-third of its original size as, alongside the massive colonization, the government intensified exploitation of the forest with logging and mineral extraction, and large-scale cattle ranching cut vast swathes of pasture from forestland. In this fertile wilderness, campesinos cut out a basic living. The population increased from a few thousand to roughly 400,000. Industry and subsistence farming came in conflict over limited resources. The migrants were caught between their own farming and seasonal work as peons on the farm estates or coffee plantations of wealthy landowners. Poverty and misery, pervaded by a sense of hopelessness, was their lot. Despite the promise offered by the forests, canyons, and glens of the Lacandón region, from the back lands of Chiapas came not development or progress but its antithesis: rebellion. Some people's solitude or fear is other people's refuge. It was here amongst the population—the poorest of the poor—that the Zapatista resistance took root. As Subcomandante Marcos has remarked, "That's why the Lacandón is what it is—a kind of breathing space at the end of the country." For ten years the Zapatista rebellion grew in the shadows of the Lacandón Jungle and emerged on January 12th, 1994, as a state-wide insurgency. And so, from a semantic perspective, from the Desert of Solitude was born the War against Oblivion.

RYAN, *Zapatista Spring*

THERE ARE STILL TERRITORIES of exit. In January 1994, on the day the North American Free Trade Agreement (NAFTA) between Mexico, Canada, and the United States took effect, a group of indigenous Mayan people declared war on the Mexican government and seized several municipalities in the southern state of Chiapas (see map 3). They were mostly from the jungle but also from the cool mountain highlands of Chiapas, known to anthropologists through ethnographies such as *Juan the Chamula*.[1] In the First Declaration of the Lacandon jungle, released on the day of the uprising, the Zapatista Army of National Liberation (EZLN) expressed their demands: work, land, housing, food, health care, education, independence, liberty, democracy, justice, and peace. They cited article 39 of the Mexican Constitution: "The people, at any time, have the right to change or modify the form of their government." As the Mexican military moved to suppress the uprising, millions of people around the world demanded that the army end its attack on the Zapatistas. The EZLN withdrew from municipal headquarters, but the land they occupied became "territory in rebellion." They eschewed violence yet remained a guerrilla force committed to "autonomy": territorial self-organization and self-administration of politics, justice, education, health care, and the economy.

Zapatista territory shares exilic characteristics with the early Don Cossacks: friction of space, agriculture of escape, decentralization, egalitarian and flexible social structure, escape-based cultural identities, and an ecology of escape, as well as a rebellious cosmology. Both groups employ three complementary escape strategies: exit (state- and capital-refusing practices), voice (they are a guerrilla movement and an example to non-exiles), and loyalty (strategic dependency on extra-space actors). Their "exit-with-autonomy" is characterized by *cooperative practices* such as decentralized organization of territory; directly democratic assemblies; "leading by obeying"; and egalitarian structures of production, distribution, and provisioning. Unlike the Cossacks, they practice strategic loyalty toward national and international *civil society*, which reduces their dependency on the state. The threat of voice has kept the state from using the "high-intensity" military option . . . so far.

Zapatista escape happened within the context of world-economic restructuring: a newly emerging hegemonic power hierarchy, new leading economic sectors, new global divisions of labor, and neoliberalism under the "Washington consensus." The Zapatistas are not outside of this system, but inhabit a paradoxical extra-state location within it. Autonomy is contested

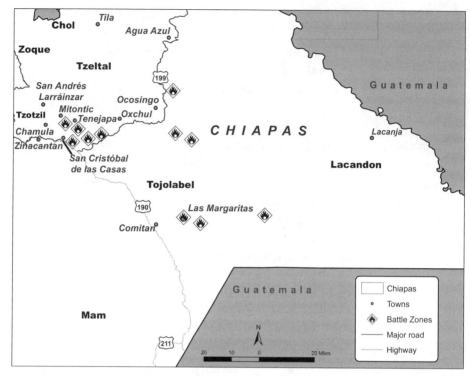

MAP 3. Principal Mayan linguistic groups and points of battle between the EZLN and the Mexican army, 1994–95. Kevin Heard, Binghamton University GIS Core Facility.

and partial, contradictory and incomplete. But it generates new social relations and resists incorporative pressures.

Land is at the heart of Zapatismo.[2] After the Mexican Revolution, peasants received not "land and freedom" but land and *the state*. Land reform, through the establishment of the communally owned *ejido*, was an important link between state and people in Chiapas. Its promise and shortcomings gave rise to things that were favorable to exilic formation: perception of the state as an unreliable provider of public goods, resentment and caution toward state institutions, and a growing conception of the state as "bad government." Land reform in Chiapas was substantial, but did not instigate profound sociopolitical transformation or even end the *finca* (large estate) as a productive unit. Furthermore, the relationship between *ejidatarios* (farmers working on communal land) and state bureaucratic agencies had a formative influence on self-governance and the possibility of "delinking" from state structures in many localities.

Mexico experienced an armed revolution during 1910–1920, followed by a period of regime consolidation and state-building from 1920 to 1940.[3] The revolution was not a single event but a set of processes and overlapping struggles.

Emiliano Zapata came to represent the landless rural people of southern Mexico after he helped organize a small guerrilla movement in 1911 in response to Francisco Madero's 1910 call to arms to remove the dictator Porfirio Díaz from power.[4] In 1911, Zapata issued Plan Ayala, which articulated the Zapatistas' key demands. The plan asserted that the land belongs to those who work it and called for the nationalization of land and juridical review of all cases involving rural real estate.[5] It also insisted on the people's right to choose their own representatives.[6] As Gilly asserts,

> Emiliano Zapata did not set out to destroy the capitalist system: his ideas sprang from the peasantry, not from a socialist program. However, implementation of the Ayala Plan would have effectively smashed the living roots of capitalism. For it would have involved nationalization of all the property of the ruling classes. More important still—because actually applied by the peasantry—was the principle that the people themselves should decide, "arms in hand"; that, instead of waiting for the revolution to triumph and enact the necessary legislation, they would begin cultivating and defending the land.[7]

When Zapata and his chiefs signed the Ayala Plan, they declared themselves in rebellion against Madero's federal government. At Aguascalientes in October 1914, a "minimal program" of the revolution was adopted by Pancho Villa and Zapata, calling for the withdrawal of US forces from Mexican territory, the return of communal lands to villages, the destruction of large landholdings and the return of land to the people who worked it, the nationalization of property belonging to enemies of the revolution, and freedom of association and the right of workers to strike.[8] The Ayala spirit was reflected in the Zapatistas' Agrarian Law of October 26, 1915, which "codified the right of all Mexicans to possess enough land to cover their needs and those of their family, the rights of sharecroppers to own the land they work, and decreed inalienable the land ceded by the government to communities and individuals.[9] The Zapatistas seized major centers of sugar production, commerce, communication, and government administration, and ran them as self-governed communities.[10]

After a brief occupation of Mexico City, the peasant armies withdrew, possibly because the exercise of state power was incongruent with a revolution from below that still had not triumphed.[11] The failure to institute a revolutionary regime halted the grassroots trajectory of the revolution. In 1917, Carranza, the "first chief of the Constitutionalist Army," became president of Mexico. Zapata was assassinated on April 10, 1919.

The legal mechanism binding the rural population to the postrevolutionary regime was the Constitution of 1917, which called for agrarian reform much less extensive than that advocated by the Zapatistas. The model of a strong central government written into the constitution severely limited the autonomy of local communities and conditioned what rights they had on support for the government, which bestowed *ejido* (communal property) rights on behalf of the nation.[12]

In the 1917 Constitution and the institution of *ejido*, the promise of land redistribution was given on the condition of popular acceptance of the state. Articles 27 and 42 made land distribution a mechanism for peasant demobilization and for undercutting more radical agrarian reforms.[13]

The Mexican Revolution, then, was not an emancipation but "a new order of capitalist control."[14] *Ejido* was simultaneously a fragile compromise and a meaningful accomplishment. Campesinos gained land, articulated a particular political consciousness, and took up the revolution as their own. Yet the *ejido* became a fundamental cornerstone of state power, a state grant in perpetuity, carved out as a new spatial form from a myriad of properties rather than a "return" of land to communities.[15]

Some *ejidatarios* held and worked the land collectively, as intended, while others rented out or mortgaged the land in ways technically illegal. Put differently, the *ejido* in the 1920s was constructed and reconstructed in politically volatile and regionally specific circumstances.

The most immediate task of the postrevolutionary state was the centralization of rule.[16] Land redistribution was especially important for extending control over the rural population. In 1921 and 1922, legislation was passed according to which only the president could grant land titles. As a result, there was "much correspondence between local *ejido* authorities and Mexican presidents in the struggle to secure land."[17] The number of hectares expropriated by presidential decree fell from 956,852 in 1925 to 502,700 in 1926 and only 289,933 in 1927.[18]

Education of indigenous peoples was also an important instrument in the centralization of power. The focus of rural education in the 1920s was to integrate individuals into the market economy, and communities into the nation.[19] The new politics of the Mexican state was founded on the assimilation of the indigenous through public education, state policies, and economic development.[20] This was a very simple solution to the "Indian problem."[21]

The attempt to centralize governmental power took on new momentum during 1934–40 under President Lázaro Cárdenas, the chief architect of the corporatist postrevolutionary Mexican state. Cárdenas's main accomplishment, premised on a realization that institutionalizing the revolution was the only way to consolidate power, was to articulate a new and more intimate relationship with the people.[22] This was established through, among other things, the creation of national worker and peasant confederations, carefully managed from above but in the name of the revolution.[23]

The Cárdenas administration organized ejidatarios into the Confederación Nacional Campesina (National Peasants' Confederation, or CNC), and set about promoting a national popular culture around a particular interpretation of the Mexican Revolution. This was accomplished through the growth of rural education; "thousands of rural schoolteachers, engineers, and other government personnel fanned over the Mexican countryside and attempted to connect its farthest corners with the central government." The state appropriated and "sanitized" Emiliano Zapata:

> The writing of songs about the Revolution, the promotion of civic rituals on the day of Zapata's death to reinforce his memory, the use of the Mexican Revolution, Plan de Ayala, and Zapata's image to sell, celebrate, and codify agrarian reform and agricultural programs, the SEP-sponsored radio shows emphasizing the revolution—all of these events, texts, and interactions created a common set of national symbols received in widely varying segments of Mexican society.[24]

Khasnabish contends that the power of the PRI, which succeeded the PNR, "radiated not only from its material, institutional and coercive capacities but from its appropriation and deployment of a revolutionary heritage which it at least needed to appear to nurture and defend."[25]

But the effort to centralize state power was far from complete. Regional power blocs resisted the Cárdenas regime, in spite of his vast popularity. The ideological deployment of revolutionary heritage in local contexts exhibited tremendous variation.[26] The incorporation of Zapata into local and regional culture came much later in eastern Chiapas, in the 1970s and 1980s, and from below, through the creation of regional peasant organizations in conjunction with organizers from the urban Mexican left.[27]

By 1940, corporate institutions were in place that would allow the postrevolutionary state to successfully manage economic growth and political dissent until 1970. The first moment in the delegitimization of the PRI was the 1968 student movement. The Tlatelolco massacre in October of that year was one of the first indicators that the postrevolutionary social pact had been broken.[28] Students and militants, including founders of what was to become the EZLN, were convinced that institutionalized politics could not bring fundamental change and turned to guerrilla activities. The long "dirty war" by the state against these organizations further eroded the postrevolutionary social pact and "organizing among indigenous peasants of Chiapas took on an increasingly militant and independent character."[29]

Beginning in the 1970s, Mexican governments, in the context of global restructuring, attempted to shift the emphasis of rural policy away from land redistribution toward the modernization of production and marketing.[30] Neoliberalization of Mexican economic and social policy, along with corrupt actions such as the 1998 electoral fraud, which kept the moderate left Party of the Democratic Revolution (PRD) from taking office, further eroded the popular social base of the PRI.

Finally, support for government was broken in places like Chiapas with the announcement of the North American Free Trade Agreement (NAFTA) and the revision of article 27 of the constitution to allow privatization of collectively held land. This alienated many peasants in Chiapas and lent support to the armed option offered by the EZLN, which had been organizing in remote areas of the state for nearly a decade.[31]

The Zapatista rebellion in Chiapas began on January 1, 1994, the day NAFTA went into effect. At the national level, the PRI subsequently lost the presidential elections of July 2000 to the National Action Party (PAN), ending more than seventy years of one-party rule.

LAND REFORM AND THE ORIGINS
OF EXILE IN CHIAPAS

Land reform in Chiapas was uneven. In some areas, notably the central highlands, the postrevolutionary state had a much greater presence than, for example, in the Lacandon forest. From the 1960s, migrants in the forest "constructed a new social order largely at the margins of the state."[32] This is an example of how many of the social, political, and economic relationships that contributed to the emergence of Zapatismo in 1994 can be traced to regionally specific processes of state-building and agrarian reform between 1920 and 1994.

In the 1920s, the Mexican Revolution was characterized by inter-elite struggles between Ladino (non-indigenous) factions.[33] The indigenous, who referred to this period as the "time of hunger," were excluded from these events. According to Hasketh, the revolution in Chiapas "was really a struggle between elite classes to control land and Indian labour—the state's most precious commodity."[34]

The real revolution, or the "Time of the Indians," arrived with activists and teachers sent by President Lázaro Cárdenas (1934–40). They brought a revolutionary process that reached Mayan peasants in the form of agrarian reform, labor unions, and an end to debt peonage. Land reform connected the state to the peasantry, especially in the central highlands. This "ambivalent revolution" brought Indians new rights but also "led to a more intimate form of domination" as the state "reached inside" the communities, "changing leaders [and] rearranging the governments."[35] In many Indian communities, a "bossism" penetrated communities that had previously resisted outside intervention. Indigenous traditions were harnessed to the state and used to legitimize the rule of the PRI.

Local elites also co-opted the more radical initiatives of the central government. The Union of Indigenous Workers (Sindicato de Trabajadores Indígenas), originally intended by Cárdenas to ensure the payment of a minimum wage, fulfillment of labor regulations, and the substitution of collective for individual contracts, became an agency serving the interests of employers and local landowners.[36] As a result, the economic power of landowning cattle ranchers was firmly established.[37]

The tension between federal and local/regional projects was further aggravated by the founding of the federal National Indigenous Institute (INI), which opened its first regional center in Chiapas in San Cristóbal de Las Casas in 1951. INI employees, committed to ending the supposed isolation of indigenous cultures, discovered not only that the indigenous people were well integrated into the regional economy but also that numerous abuses and illegal practices were used against them.[38] They clashed with coffee planters and labor contractors over the continued enforcement of debt peonage; with the state treasurer and leading distillers over the state liquor monopoly; and with the state governor and local political bosses over indigenous legal rights, liquor monopoly, and land claims.[39]

Systematic agrarian reform began in Chiapas after 1940, when it was slowing in Mexico as a whole. In 1934 agrarian legislation became federal, and debt peons were finally allowed to petition for ejidal grants. Land reform increased considerably between 1930 and 1939, when 290,354 hectares were granted to more than twenty thousand petitioners across the state.[40] Land reform was concentrated in a few municipalities. During 1950–59, 46 percent of the redistributed land was located in just twelve municipalities, mainly in unexploited regions of the Lacandon forest and the frontier. Similarly, 28 percent of all land granted to ejidatarios during 1970–79 and 12 percent in 1980–84 was located in that same region.[41] This was the seed of exilic formation.

By 1993, approximately 3.8 out of 7.4 million hectares—over 50 percent of the total territory of Chiapas—were held by *ejidos* and peasant communities. Only 3 percent of land owned by Ladinos was private property.[42] *Fincas*, or *ranchos*, continued to exist in the northern and eastern parts of Chiapas, but elsewhere land redistribution programs transferred considerable amounts of land to the peasants in the years before the Zapatista uprising.[43]

Still, important limitations to land reform would later cause conflict. Properties under three hundred hectares that were engaged in export agriculture were immune from redistribution. Certificates of exemption (*inefectibilidad*) protected ranches from expropriation, and after 1984 also protected most of the remaining private property in Chiapas.[44] Individual colonization prior to 1962 also increased private property holdings. *Ejidos* next to commercial *fincas* provided a source of labor, and land granted to peasants in those areas was often unofficially occupied by cattle ranchers and logging companies. Many presidential decrees granting land to petitioners were either not executed or significantly delayed.

These practices created regional differences in peasant perceptions of the state. Land reform in eastern Chiapas brought an unprecedented insertion of the state into the rural countryside. Yet the capacity of the state to govern was incomplete, and many indigenous people came to consider it "bad government" (*mal gobierno*).[45] Instead of being an institution with the moral obligation to defend the poor against wealthy landowners, the state was either ineffective or predatory.

This explains Van der Haar's claim that the "the historical experience of engaging with the State . . . allowed the Zapatistas both to imagine and to organize governance 'beyond the State.'"[46] Land reform established the *ejido* at the center of the rural landscape. Then, it was appropriated and resignified by local indigenous populations. The reform bureaucracy was a main conduit for obtaining ejidal land, but it had limited regulatory presence in the autonomous life of the *ejido* community.[47]

The indigenous peasants' relationship with the state soured in the Cañadas region after it created a biosphere reserve next to the common property of the Lacandon Indians.[48] This was part of a much wider scheme organized by the state forestry company to exploit rare woods in the forest.[49] When numerous *ejidos* were suddenly classified as "invaders" and listed for relocation, confrontations broke out between independent peasant organizations and the government. Widespread repression of unions and evictions were combined with the selective distribution of land.[50]

Opposition to "bad government" was already organized, therefore, in the 1990s when peasants in Chiapas heard of President Carlos Salinas's measures to privatize the *ejido* and abolish the constitutional obligation of the Mexican state to provide landless peasants with land. Those still waiting to receive land could not believe that they now would not obtain any. Moreover, when article 27 was changed, Chiapas had the greatest number of unresolved land conflicts of any state in Mexico. Politically powerful ranchers' associations, representing more than twelve thousand *ganaderos* (ranchers) organized in sixty local associations, supported the reforms to article 27.[51] Fear of farm foreclosures and loss of land rights was widespread.

To facilitate the privatization of Mexico's 27,410 *ejidos*, the Procuraduría Agraria agency was created in 1992. Bureaucrats brought a new message to rural Mexican citizens: protect your individual rights to land. They "brought the philosophy of NAFTA to the countryside."[52]

EXILIC FORMATION

> Zapatismo is not a new political ideology or a rehash of old ideologies. Zapatismo is nothing. It doesn't exist. It only serves as a bridge, to cross from one side to the other. So everyone fits within Zapatismo, everyone who wants to cross from one side to the other. Everyone has his or her own side and other side. There are no universal recipes, lines, strategies, tactics, laws, rules, or slogans. There is only a desire: to build a better world, that is, a new world.
>
> Quoted in Ryan, *Zapatista Spring*

The exilic colonization of the Selva Lacandona and the Cañadas region became the cradle of Zapatismo. When the first members of the future EZLN arrived there they encountered "forgotten" but militant peasants with decades of experience in organizing via independent peasant organizations, and with experience in life outside of the state-regulated structures of government.

The ELZN's largest base of support came from indigenous communities in the Lacandon rainforest, a region reclaimed by tropical forest after pre-Columbian Maya groups abandoned it centuries before. The first wave of exilic colonization there began in the 1940s, when the first *ejidos* were granted.[53] This multi-ethnic process was led by poor youths determined to gain access to land. The inhospitable and remote terrains of Las Cañadas and the Selva Lacandona became home to a new generation of indigenous peasants.[54]

Perhaps, colonization of the Lacandon was a safety valve for the government. According to Harvey, it "was encouraged as a means to avoid affecting the interests of private owners in the parts of Chiapas."[55] For young indigenous immigrants, however, colonization opened the possibility of forming "communities of experiment." Left to themselves, they would become "the base and backbone of the Zapatista movement and their assembly-based form of direct democracy would become one of the hallmarks of Zapatismo."[56] These campesinos, former peons and landless laborers who had worked on the *fincas* and coffee plantations in other regions of Chiapas, left the world of the state for the jungle as soon as they received *ejido* titles. They were principally Tzeltal-, Ch'ol-, and Tojolobal-speaking Mayans from the northern and eastern highlands who had lost their land as a result of the encroachment of local elites.

The flow of migrants to the Lacandon grew rapidly after 1950, increasing the population from around 1,000 in 1950, to 10,000 in 1960, 40,000 in 1970, 100,000 in 1980, and 150,000 in 1990.[57] The population of Ocosingo, the region's largest municipality, more than doubled between 1950 and 1970, doubled again in 1970–80, and grew by another 56 percent in 1980–90.[58]

By 1970, 738,000 hectares of land in the Lacandon were *ejidos*, and only 300,000 hectares were held as private property. Yet the *ejido* sector was increasingly vulnerable to the fluctuation of coffee prices, economic reforms, trade liberalization, and cheaper imports.[59]

The colonists referred to themselves as the forgotten ones (*los olvidados*), since they did not receive any support from the state.[60] They established independent peasant cooperatives and new self-governing communities with horizontal social structures and new cultural-political identities.[61] Rather than breaking completely with their earlier culture, they transformed it, introducing communal democracy without political bosses.[62] Indians from different language groups had to learn each other's languages and modify their customs to get along. They worked plots of unusually poor quality, yielding just enough maize for basic subsistence. State agents were rare, so the colonists were left alone to develop their own exilic governing structures and organizing practices. These areas would later become the key areas of support for the Zapatista movement.[63]

In conditions of economic hardship, autonomous forms of organization replaced the state. ARIC (Asociación Rural de Interés Colectivo), the independent federation of *ejido* unions, became the de facto subterranean government of the region, organized "by way of communal assemblies who elected their own officials and staffed their own police as well as committees for health and education."[64]

The *ejidal* unions were first established as a response to the modest agrarian reforms of President Echevarría in 1971. The unions had two immediate goals: to pressure the government to issue new land titles and to administer promised government credit. Both the ejidal union and the *ejidos* served as organizational paradigms for Zapatista communities, especially in the recovered territories (*tierra recuperada*) taken over after the 1994 uprising. Even though these institutions were imposed as part of the land reform process, they were appropriated by indigenous peasants as autonomous structures and had "considerable scope for rendering themselves opaque and for keeping their internal affairs largely out of the reach of the State administration."[65]

Hidden from the state's view, the main structural components of Mexican ejidal communities were the *comisariado ejidal* (ejidal commission), the *consejo de vigilancia* (council for land control), and the *agencia* (police). Their head officers constituted a council of authorities (*consejo de autoridades*) who, together with the *ejido* assembly (*asamblea*), constituted de facto local governments that operated relatively autonomously from the state on matters of everyday communal administration, justice and internal affairs, and land-related questions, including frequent conflicts and forest use. Local experts led committees on education, health, and other matters.[66]

In 1972, the government decided to give 614,000 hectares of jungle land to indigenous people in the Lacandon and forcibly resettled seven thousand Tzeltal and Ch'ol colonists. The struggle against this forced expulsion

FIGURE 3. Cooking a festival meal in the Caracol of Morelia. The slogan on the wall reads "with insurgent fire." Charlotte Saenz.

influenced the funding of the Union of Unions (Unión de Uniones Ejidales y Grupos Campesinos Solidarios de Chiapas, or UU), the first and largest independent campesino organization in Chiapas, representing twelve thousand mainly indigenous families from 180 communities in eleven municipalities. According to Barmeyer, the UU organized the Cañadas into a de facto autonomous region with regional authorities able to control the provision of services to the population.[67]

The Indigenous Congress of 1974 further heightened the communal identity of the inhabitants of the Lacandon. Governor Manuel Velaso Suárez invited Bishop Samuel Ruiz of Chiapas to help organize the conference "as a means to co-opt new indigenous leaders into the expanding state apparatus."[68] This action backfired. Instead, Liberation Theology, insurgent ethnic identity, and new forms of agrarian activism met in one setting.

The event "stunned conservative San Cristobal."[69] Delegates included 587 Tzeltals, 330 Tzotziles, 152 Tojolobales, and 161 Ch'oles, together representing 327 communities.[70] In Benjamin's words, "Never had Tzotziles, Tzeltals, Tojolabales, and Choles spoken with one another like this, listened to others with similar problems, or viewed themselves as one people . . . It was a revelation. Giving voice to one's problems is a requisite to solving them."[71]

Delegates demanded the titling of *ejido* land and denounced encroachment by ranchers. Back in their communities, they became "missionaries of inter-community and inter-ethnic activism and organization."[72] They founded new producer, transport, and consumer cooperatives; brought in health specialists and founded bilingual schools; and encouraged translations of scientific, historical, and political texts into local Mayan languages. The Indigenous Congress proved to be a catalyst for grassroots organizing, and many delegates eventually joined the EZLN.[73]

In response, the state-sponsored Confederación Nacional Campesina (CNC) organized its own congress in 1975, but this could not prevent the radicalization of the Lacandon colonist communities by veterans of the Indigenous Congress. Several independent organizations arose in the years after the congress: the Emiliano Zapata Peasant Organization (OCEZ) worked primarily on agrarian reform issues to help peasants to stay on their land and gain title to contested lands, and the Independent Confederation of Agricultural Workers and Indians (CIOAC) employed Mexico's labor laws to protect peasant workers.[74]

After the congress, the bishop met Maoist activists from the nationwide movement La Linea Proletaria, which focused on building popular power rather than seizing state power.[75] The leftist students and communist militants began a "systematic and intense" incursion into the new frontier.[76] The first members of the mass organization arrived in the Lacandon in 1977 as part of the wave of militancy unleashed by the 1968 repression of the student movement.[77]

These activists, still remembered in the exilic territory as "the advisors" (*asesores*), joined forces with *catequistas* and liberation theologians preaching about the exodus. They contributed to the organizational culture of the colonists by instituting small assemblies (*asambleas chicas*) in order to break the centralized political culture of the communities, including their emphasis on collective production and the establishment of commissions. They were aware of the political significance of the absence of the state. Van der Haar quotes one of these "early arrivals": "First the Church arrived, then we did . . . and finally the State."[78] Forbis writes that "at the time of the EZLN uprising in the Cañadas, the state form was a 'lack,' a permanently incomplete promise of liberation to most campesinos. The state was felt as suffering, as need, and as violence in its absence."[79] And in its absence, other actors responded to needs for transport, water, health care, education, and conflict resolution.

In response, the state police, federal army, and paramilitary groups, funded by the ranchers, carried out countless evictions and killings. As repression increased, so did the political awareness of the population. As a result, "when the first EZLN members initiated contact with the indigenous communities in the early 1980s, they found a cadre of well-prepared, well-respected indigenous leaders in the communities and a population familiar with discourse on the rights and value of the poor."[80]

THE ZAPATISTA ARMY OF NATIONAL LIBERATION (EZLN)

When a new generation of Maoist activists returned to Chiapas in 1983 they encountered a different situation than their comrades had a decade before: a lively autonomous political culture. These activists, including the man who would become famous as Subcomandante Marcos, soon realized that their survival depended on their ability to adapt and learn from these indigenous ways.[81]

The Zapatista movement combined elements of urban mestizo political culture (predominantly Maoism) and indigenous-campesino traditions. The indigenous population "inverted the traditional leader-mass relationship" and replaced it with popular and democratic organization.[82] Learning indigenous languages and understanding their interpretations of history and culture taught the formerly urban guerrillas the importance of patience. After a decade, instead of emerging from the university, like previous movements, the EZLN emerged from the mountains and jungles, from the world of the indigeneous campesino, like Zapata himself. Armed students and indigenous colonists in exile created a hybrid of local and national ideas and practices. As a result, "the Zapatismo that emerged in 1994 was something still in process."[83]

Setting up "the organization" took time. The ELZN's health and literacy campaigns, including simple projects such as digging latrines, giving vaccinations, and teaching women to read, were critical in winning over the communities. In the early 1990s (probably around 1991), the EZLN built its first safe house on *ejido* lands.[84]

In interviews given to sociologist Le Bot, Subcomandante Marcos says that an important motivation to organize the EZLN was the colonist communities' need to protect themselves from the police and landowners. Zapatismo in the Lacandon was hardly a coherent political ideology. As Marcos puts it:

> When we made our appearance on the first of January of 1994, we had only vaguely defined what Zapatismo is. It was a very vague initial synthesis, a mixture of patriotic values, of the historical inheritance of what was the clandestine left in Mexico in the decade of the 1960s, of elements of indigenous culture, of military elements of Mexican history, of what were the guerrilla movements of Central and South America, of national liberation movements.[85]

The EZLN grew almost invisibly through social networks in the indigenous communities.[86] Land reform and its consequences, including the colonization of the Lacandon, the organization of new communities, and the formation of ejidal unions, shaped the political imagination and organizing practices of indigenous campesinos. In the absence of and growing antipathy toward state structures and institutions, autonomous organization had already emerged. The EZLN first appeared in public under other guises, such as the Alianza Campesina Independiente Emiliano Zapata (ACIEZ), which formed in Chiapas in 1989. In early 1992, it changed its name to ANCIEZ by adding "Nacional" to its title, claiming member organizations in six central and northern states. A letter from ANCIEZ to the president of the republic in 1992, concerning the revision of article 27 of the constitution to make way for NAFTA, stated directly that "a few months ago our most precious historical conquest was extinguished: the right to land."[87]

In 1992, as one of seventeen organizations to join the Common Front of Social Organizations 500 Years of Struggle and Resistance of the Chiapas People, ANCIEZ organized a "counterquincentennial" against the invasion of the Americas in the town of San Cristóbal. The protestors denounced colonization and its modern continuation through Salinas's neoliberal policies as "500 Years of Robbery, Murder, and the Destruction of Indigenous People." Speeches in Tzotzil, Tzeltal, and Tojolabal declared that "Indian unity is the only way to end five centuries of injustice."[88] The event ended with the protestors pulling down of the statue of the conquistador Mazariegos.

Although the march seemed spontaneous to onlookers, many ANCIEZ militants were already part of the clandestine Zapatista Army of National Liberation (EZLN),[89] which had been in the communities of the Selva Lacandona for nearly a decade, discussing the merits and drawbacks of rebellion. In January 1993 the communities voted for war, and the Clandestine Indigenous Revolutionary Committee of the Zapatista Army began preparations for a military uprising. A year later, NAFTA and its associated policies provided the impetus for a clandestine, practically invisible movement that would emerge as a public rebellion.

EXILIC CONSTITUTION

> Zapatista territory, it is worth noting, is one of few places in the entire nation that is not riddled with or dominated by drug trafficking, not simply because of their internal laws against use and cultivation, but because they control their territory in a way that few communities or cities have been able to do. The entire system of autonomy—the difficulty in corrupting the governing councils because of their rotating function, the involvement of the entire community in the governing structure, the investment of communities in maintaining their own economic and physical health—make the formation of the networks necessary for drug activity, which usually include politicians and police officers that have been bought off, locally compliant or coerced business owners, and a population of disenfranchised young people available for the riskiest of activities, unavailable and almost impossible to form.
>
> KAUFMAN, "We Are from Before"

This remarkable passage captures the Zapatistas as an example of exit-with-autonomy, reminiscent of Cossack territory before the eighteenth century. As with the Don Cossacks, theirs is an exilic space that rests on the selection of state- and capital-subverting practices and autonomous mechanisms of cooperation. Its exilic constitution, referred to by the Zapatistas as autonomy, prevents the recapture of exiles and partly thwarts world-systemic forces that pull the exiles back into the interstate system.

Zapatismo policy and practice is constantly refined and reinvented. Is such flexibility inscribed in the general organizing logic of exilic spaces, in the need to create structures of escape that thwart the structures of capital and state? It would seem so. But Zapatismo also comes out of a political and activist philosophy that is less prescriptive of future structural forms and practices than most orthodox Marxist movements, following the motto of the alternative education movement, "We make the road by walking."[90] Slowly, Zapatismo became a conscious political project: exiles arrived at the realization that a community practicing mutual aid, rather than competitive rivalry, is more likely to survive in a hostile environment, in this case the Mexican state and its attempts to reincorporate them into capitalist economic processes.

Autonomy. Among Zapatista scholars, the concept of autonomy has been much debated. Is autonomy derived from preconquest communal traditions of indigenous Latin America?[91] From discussions originating with the Indigenous Congress of 1974?[92] Or a new concept that emerged and matured in practice after 1994?[93] All three interpretations may be correct. Autonomy has roots in Mayan customs and practices but is constantly reinvented in practice.

Zapatistas are not the only example of autonomy in Chiapas. A privileged marginal status, akin to *autonomy-without-exit* in the late eighteenth-century Don region, exists in the seven pluri-ethnic regions that were established on January 21, 1995. Pluri-ethnic regions (PARs) are based on a program of regional cultural autonomy; they receive government aid and seek participation in the electoral process.[94]

The Zapatistas have a very different take on autonomy. As a consequence of being "abandoned by the state" and in need of basic services, the indigenous communities of Chiapas have opted to resolve their problems through self-organization. In other words, they implemented autonomy themselves.[95]

Zapatista practice suggests that the meaning of autonomy is fluid.[96] Barmeyer cites one villager who told him, "We've got *educación autónoma*. Our community teacher is not paid by the government. He teaches our children what we want them to learn."[97] A *promotore* (teacher) in the Zapatista community of Oventic told one of the authors of this volume, "Everything you see around you, we built; we take nothing from the state. We built our own infrastructures, our roads and houses, schools and health systems." When asked, "What about the electricity?" he replied, "Well, we liberate that!"[98] At the time, however, the Zapatistas were, with the aid of electrical workers from Mexico City, building their own generating stations. They were also installing independent pipeline systems to provide fresh drinkable water and communications towers to link the communities to the internet. A boot factory in Oventic provided belts and boots for EZLN guerrillas at a subsidized price far below that paid by others.

Autonomy is something material, something tangible. For many people, the core meaning of autonomy is the ability to subsist independently. In practice, finding the resources to do so may be the biggest threat to exilic life.

There have been three distinct periods in the development of Zapatista autonomy. The first was the struggle to get land, learn how to use it, and govern those who are on it. This was self-government, but not yet independent of state subsidies and resources.

Second, between 1997 and 2005, during the *resistencia*, the Zapatistas began refusing government subsidies. This was an "era of silence" when a unilateral autonomy "in practice" began to take form. "Because autonomy means to govern ourselves. We no longer have to depend on the federal government who made the decisions. It didn't ask, it just informed. However, our autonomous government invites and promotes rather than orders."[99]

The third stage (2005 to the present) relates local practices to the Other Campaign (*La Otra*). With land and resources, the Zapatistas became productive but they still needed markets for their surplus products. The Other Campaign, among other things, was an attempt to open autonomy elsewhere in Mexico to achieve this objective. This raises the question, as with the Don Cossacks, of exit and *loyalty*. Let us look at each of these periods and constitutional aspects of the exilic space in turn.

Exilic territory. There are multiple aspects to the concept of exilic territory. It is a mode of geographical escape; it is a safe haven to communities and municipalities in rebellion; and it is the land that was "recovered" from the latifundistas. The territory is home to a comprehensive set of self-governing systems and projects in food security, the administration of justice, health care, education, production, and communication. For Harvey, "The community has been converted into a strategic resource for the reconstruction of the bonds of solidarity and the defence of natural resources."[100] Zapatista territories are people, not settlements.[101]

The rebel territory was enacted through the creation of thirty-eight autonomous municipalities (MAREZ) in December 1995.[102] Two years later, the terms "indigenous" and "autonomous" were linked to "rebellion" in Zapatista descriptions of these municipalities. During the first months of the rebellion, the Zapatistas "recuperated" five to seven hundred thousand hectares of land (around 1.2–1.7 million acres, or 1,900–2,700 square miles) from latifundistas,[103] providing a material base for the construction of the exilic territory. As EZLN lieutenant colonel Moisés explained, "The land where the [Zapatista] compañeros and compañeras are now is their own property, land we recuperated. We discovered . . . that what [capitalism] does is make us prisoners of where we work. That's how capitalism functions: you work on ranches, or work in factories, and the profit is not for the people who work. Without this, we wouldn't be where we are today. It is clear to us as Zapatistas that since we became owners of these lands, as they are our means of production, this is the base from which to attack capitalism."[104]

Municipalities were clusters of communities, in all, more than one thousand communities and around three hundred thousand individuals.[105] They were governed with three sets of laws: the 1917 political constitution of the United States of Mexico, the Zapatista revolutionary laws of 1993 (implemented with the uprising), and the local laws of the autonomous municipal committees. This was an act of direct autonomy. According to Comandanta Esther, "The political parties conspired to deny us our rights . . . Now we will exercise our rights ourselves. And we don't need anyone's permission to do so, especially that of politicians . . . In practice, what we are doing is forming our own autonomous municipalities, and we haven't asked anyone's permission."[106]

The municipalities were in turn organized into five autonomous zones, or *aguascalientes* (zones of encounter, later renamed *caracoles*), which opened relationships with (inter)national civil society and were primarily under the control of EZLN army commanders (see map 4).

Since at least 1996, the Zapatistas have faced three major problems in establishing exilic sovereignty on their territory. First, Zapatista municipalities are "alliances of villages with a variety of historical backgrounds."[107] Many Zapatista-dominated communities border villages loyal to the PRI. In some villages and towns, separate administrative structures exist for Zapatistas and national parties. In the mountain town of San Andrés, for example, the

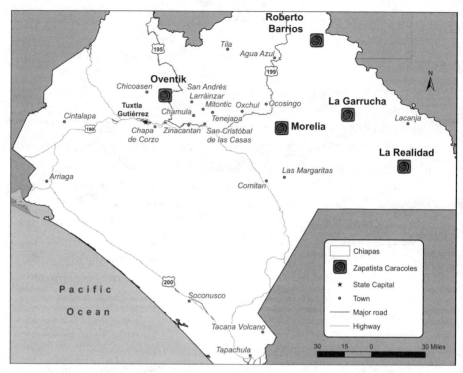

MAP 4. Zapatista *caracoles* in Chiapas, Mexico. Kevin Heard, Binghamton University GIS Core Facility.

Zapatista *municipio* runs the public toilets and the central market while the state *municipio* maintains other parts of the town with state funds.

The problem of divided and fluctuated loyalties was especially painful from 1997 to 2004. The exception was the *nuevos centros de población*, new communities on recovered land where support for Zapatismo was almost unanimous. New communities are obliged to give support to the EZLN. To leave the movement, they would also have to leave the homestead. This exilic mechanism ensures participation in and local support for the guerrilla movement and the exilic project.[108]

The second challenge is the presence of Mexican military forces. The announcement of the MAREZ was greeted by a federal army attack in February 1995. Autonomous authorities were arrested and administrative buildings destroyed. This strategy was ultimately unsuccessful and the Mexican state had to tolerate judicial and governmental pluralism in Zapatista regions.

The third challenge to Zapatista exilic sovereignty was the interference of the EZLN itself in community self-government and organization. As the EZLN later admitted, the democratic structure was "contaminated" by a nondemocratic institution: a hierarchical military structure that exercised a nondemocratic decision-making force over the communities.[109]

Sovereignty in the exilic territory was consolidated in three phases: 1994–97, 1997–2003, and 2003–present. During the second period, and especially after the government betrayal of the San Andrés Accords in 2001, a comprehensive political restructuring occurred. Those years of "public silence" were dedicated to creating conditions for the even development of municipalities with the removal of the EZLN from civil affairs and the return of decision making to the communities themselves. In August 2003, the Zapatistas announced the creation of *juntas de buen gobierno* (good government councils) to govern the five autonomous spaces, now called *caracoles*, and especially to coordinate activities regarding health, education, and agriculture.

Exilic membership. As with the Don Cossacks, exilic membership was extended widely, both to exiles who self-identified with the project of autonomy (Zapatismo) and to the community of exiles. The Zapatistas replaced the state with the exilic administration of justice, education, democratic organization, production, and health care. "Being Zapatista" has given self-confidence and a sense of belonging to an insurgent community that transcends ethnic difference and that was constructed in opposition to *mal gobierno*. This escape structure includes a change in gender relations *and* a new definition of exilic citizenship: a multivalent insurgent identity that challenges neoliberal multiculturalism.[110]

Asking, "Who are the members of the Zapatista exilic space?" Levya Solano and Olesen refer to exilic membership as an "imagined community" of those who share the feeling of belonging to Zapatismo.[111] At times, this may include national and international solidarity activists and civil society supporters. In the Zapatista territories themselves, the question of membership is clear. We asked a Zapatista in Oventic, "Who is a member of the community, with rights to participate in public assemblies?" He answered, "Anyone living here who has *buen pensamiento*" (good thinking). We asked, "How do you know they have *buen pensamiento*?" He replied, "Because they are here."

Depending on age, gender, or strength of political affiliations, members can enter the EZLN as *insurgentes* (insurgents), *milicianos* (militia members), or members of the *base de apoyo* (support base). Members of the base do not take part in military training or actions but provide logistical and material support. *Milicianos* are irregulars: they receive military training but are mobilized only in case of emergency. Members of the *base de apoyo* participate in communal affairs, from weekly general assemblies to economic activities. Insurgents are active guerrilla fighters and do not share in communal responsibilities. Their upkeep is a toll on the base of support but is "regarded as an investment that the Zapatista base makes into its future."[112]

The EZLN has always regarded gender as a constitutive part of the movement, and they claim to work actively to establish gender equity in autonomous governance. A third of Zapatista insurgents are said to be female, an unusually high number, especially in such a patriarchal context as Mexico. The commitment to building new social relations is evidenced by the EZLN's Women's Revolutionary Law, "imposed" by Zapatista women on March 8, 1993, and frequently described as the "revolution before the revolution." One Zapatista woman explained, "Some things must be asked for, and others must be imposed ... [O]ur freedom and dignity are things which we shall impose, whether or not they are recognized by the government or by our partners."[113] Women were the driving force behind the ban on alcohol in Zapatista communities, which occurred around the time of the Women's Revolutionary Law. A young Zapatista cited by Forbis explained, "We women were tired of having to deal with these men and their problems."[114] Laws regarding indigenous women's rights were immediately enforced in the Chiapas towns taken by the insurgents during the 1994 uprising.[115]

The involvement of women is of extraordinary importance for the cohesion of the exilic space.[116] As Forbis notes, "The presence and leadership of women from the beginning of the movement has been a key part of undermining [the] particular kind of organization that fosters centralism and homogenization."[117] In one village, at least, most insurgents were women: "With the ban on alcohol and guaranteed equal rights enshrined in the revolutionary laws," speculates Barmeyer, "EZLN membership may just have a special appeal for women."[118]

Zapatista exilic citizenship, or "insurgent identity," disrupts the state's dominant definitions of "multicultural" identity. In response, first the Salinas administration (1988–94) and then that of Vincente Fox (2000–6) promoted a conception of indigenousness that was more economistic (Indians need "development") and narrowly ethnocentric.[119]

FIGURE 4. Daily life: Eating beef stew in the Lacandon jungle. Festivals and celebrations are an important part of Zapatista life. Charlotte Saenz.

The Zapatistas' exilic membership, sometimes referred to as the "Indianization of autonomy," is built in active opposition to the state-endorsed *mestizaje* ideology. Exilic identity formation in some ways reflects the fluidity that Scott finds in the movement of people of Zomia from valley to valley and across language barriers. Zapatista membership crosses four main linguistically distinct peoples of eastern Chiapas: Tzeltal, Tzotzil, Tojolabal, and Ch'ol. It also crosses religious divides. But a difference from Scott's Zomia appears to be a shared ideology/identity that brings together those diverse Mayan groups. This is a common identity of practice.[120] Exilic citizenship is best tested on the ground, in practices that include bilingual and bicultural (critical) education and the many other educational initiatives that counter the notion of culture as bounded and historical. It is also about the recovery of collective joy. Forbis finds that "fiestas punctuate the calendar just as planting and harvesting do. Parties are thrown for religious celebrations, Zapatista holidays, and other special events. Some are held just for the community, others are regional with visitors arriving from the neighboring communities or the zone. Although there may be sports tournaments and speeches, there is always food and a dance. Dances were a key event for seeing how intimate and spatial gender relations are enacted."[121]

Exilic membership is a process involving the reappropriation and recovery of traditional customs and culture, as well as a critique of inherited authoritarian and patriarchal elements. Indigenous women have a key role. As Mora argues, Zapatistas offer a third way, "between-and-against" assimilationist and multiculturalist ideologies and governing techniques.[122] Their exilic membership pivots on linking insurgent political identity to self-governing institutions and substantive economic practices.

Exilic politics. The *asamblea*, a gathering of all community members that is presided over by three community representatives and usually a fourth appointed by the EZLN, governs each community. The *asamblea* directly elects committees for specific tasks. Municipal committees consist of rotating members from constituent communities; representatives for an autonomous municipal council are elected biannually by member communities and are instantly recallable. They do not receive financial compensation, but receive help with work on their *milpa* (food plot) while in office. Councils deal with applications for justice based on customary practice. Regional government consists of five *juntas de buen gobierno*, with rotating members. Since August 2003, five regions and five regional governments have administered twenty-nine autonomous municipalities.[123]

The system of regional juntas provides coordination without centralization. Their official responsibilities include balancing unequal development across the autonomous municipalities; mediating conflicts between autonomous municipalities and between autonomous municipalities and state municipalities; investigating and correcting human rights violations; overseeing municipal projects; overseeing the implementation of laws; attending to national and international guests who wish to visit the communities, propose projects, install peace camps, or do research; and promoting the participation of community members in other movement activities.

In La Garrucha, the *junta* is staffed by an eight-member team with two members from each of the four municipalities, who in turn represent around 211 communities. La Realidad has a seven-member team, also representing four municipalities and around 150 communities. Their term of office is limited to fifteen days! Term lengths and rotation are decided locally by each zone, ranging from turns of one week to three months.[124]

These rotations are among the most interesting state- and capital-avoiding features of Zapatista governance. The corruption of political delegates is

FIGURE 5. Zapatista self-government: *Junta de buen gobierno* in Oventic receiving international solidarity delegation. Charlotte Saenz.

prevented by the structure of the institution itself. There is no professionalization of politics and no politicians; everyone can govern. Politics is not a separate sphere of life, but an integrated one. However, local people such as teachers reported problems inherent in this form of governance. If a project is approved by a staff member of the *junta* at one point, it may have to go back to new staff, to be approved again, over and over.

A parallel hierarchy of military functionaries is appointed by the EZLN command rather than being freely chosen by the *asambleas*. The EZLN sought to ameliorate the impact of this on community democracy in 2003 by reducing its presence in communal affairs. An EZLN civilian steering committee is made up of delegates elected by community *asambleas* and sent to the General Command (*Comandancia General*). The role of these delegates is to steer the guerrilla movements in times of crisis, keeping the vertical military hierarchy in check.[125]

Another important institution in *ejidal* communities is the *consejo de vigilancia*. Only holders of an *ejido* title are entitled to staff this institution. The collective meetings of *ejidatarios* mediate conflicts. In some older villages, where access to the *consejo de vigilancia* was restricted to titleholders, it became an obstacle to democratic processes. This was mitigated when recuperated lands were shared among formerly landless Zapatistas, thus qualifying them to participate in the *consejo*.

Two principles are widely associated with Zapatista direct democracy: consensus decision making, and *mandar obedeciendo* (leading by obeying). The consensus process, which has been widely analyzed,[126] appears to stem from the encounter between indigenous tradition and Maoist activists. A popular priest in the Zapatista region once complained to us that indigenous church meetings can take days instead of hours, because according to indigenous tradition all attendees must have their say and the meetings must end in consensus. *Asambleas chicas*, smaller assemblies created to confront centralism, reinvent this indigenous tradition in the spirit of Maoist cells. Another important Maoist contribution is *autocrítica*, or self-criticism, which is widely practiced within the EZLN and base communities, constituting "the essential element of evaluating collective actions in the communities."[127] This device serves as an anti-hierarchical mechanism that allows lower ranked insurgents to criticize their superiors.

The general assembly meets every week and then splits into ten smaller assemblies. Attendance is mandatory, and the promise of public shaming motivates regular attendance. Consensus was important in meetings that were summoned in important moments in Zapatista history, such as the decision to start the uprising in 1994 (we were told that Marcos and much of the leadership opposed the uprising at that time but acceded to the decision of the communities). This system of consultation is a directly democratic form of gauging the "exilic public opinion" at any given moment but of course it is also used to build support for leadership positions and programs.

The idea of leading-by-obeying was introduced in the second declaration from the Lacandon jungle and has been one of the guiding principles of Zapatista politics ever since.[128] This local concept is rooted in the Mayan traditional of considering public office as a *cargo* (charge) that is to be fulfilled on behalf of the community. Only those things that are asked of a leader by the community are to be undertaken. *Mandar obedeciendo* is a complex notion built on seven principles: "To obey, not to command; To represent, not supplant; To step down, not climb up; To serve, not to help oneself; To convince, not to defeat; To construct, not destroy; To propose, not impose."[129] The basic premise is that every individual administrative position needs to benefit the collective; at the same time, however, every individual administrative position needs to be supported by the collective. Elected delegates are obliged to check that all agreements made on the community level are being observed on the municipal level. The escape structure is governed by the reciprocal relationship between the respective *encargado* and the village population. Cargo holders are always recallable and at the first hint of impropriety they are to be removed from their positions and replaced. Again, cargo holders do not receive financial compensation, but are helped with their fields by the community. The nonremunerative character of positions, nonspecialization of governing, and nonlucrative nature of corruption are designed "to ensure that in Zapatista rebel territory, whoever rules, rules by obeying."[130]

The same ethics govern the justice system. Five aspects in particular stand out. (1) Legislative, juridical, and investigative institutions are *integrated*. (2) Judicial councils, which are regionally organized and whose jurisdiction includes everything from petty crimes to more serious violations, are *decentralized*. Every regional unit has the freedom to decide on the specifics of the punishment according to local context. Regional jurisdiction includes the increasingly contentious issue of recovered lands, targeted as they are by state counterinsurgency measures and paramilitary violence.[131] (3) *Indigenous languages* are used (in contrast to Mexican state territory, where courts rarely provide adequate translation from Spanish). (4) Conflict resolution is achieved by way of *transformative justice*, and rarely involves incarceration: the most immediate concern is the cohesion of the community. Prisons do exist, as do community police, but cargo holders who decide on the nature of the punishment often demand a *multa* (a monetary fine) instead of imposing incarceration. The emphasis is on transformative rather than punitive justice. The parties involved can negotiate compensation, and when the perpetrator has to take a loan from relatives to pay the fine, the participation of the family helps prevent further transgressions.[132] (5) The everyday life of the community is characterized by *transparency and integration*. Autonomous councils have open-court days, which are attended by those who mistrust the official justice system. Punishment often involves an "introduction to the principles of autonomy" and community work. For example, the punishment for drug use in one zone is ten days collective labor and six months suspension from the organization. If the lecture and community work are not enough, upon a second offense the perpetrator may be sent to the penal system of the "bad government."

Educación autónoma. Autonomous education is perhaps the most advanced aspect of Zapatismo.[133] Education does not separate intellectual from moral or manual activity. It is built on a principle of horizontal communication of knowledge where "no one educates anyone else, no one educates oneself."[134] As with the justice system, there is significant local variation in the curriculum, but the goal is to integrate it into the life of the community. *Promotores* (not teachers) come from the communities where they work, and their work is understood to be a cargo that is performed in exchange for community help on their *milpa*. The first autonomous high school, the Autonomous Zapatista Education System in Rebellion and for National Liberation, is essentially a promoter-training academy, based in Oventic but with alumni from across the Zapatista territories. Since the alumni (not students) in this school come from far and wide and live in dormitories, the community is responsible for their upkeep.

The pedagogical premise is that, in the context of good government, education "springs from the people."[135] All children in Zapatista territory receive a primary education and 37 percent receive higher levels of education. In comparison, only 20 percent of children in the divided or pro-government communities received higher education.[136] The results of Zapatista education, however, are limited due to the fractured sovereignty of the exilic territory and the presence of state schools.

Nonetheless, we observed remarkable things in the *secondaria*, where learning takes place primarily outside of the classroom but also involves formal reading and learning. A group of young people about fifteen years of age, few of whom spoke any Spanish before attending the school, discussed the international financial system with an understanding that would make most undergraduate professors in US universities jealous. None of them had ever been outside of Chiapas, nor had they even been in an airplane; they built their understanding of international finance by beginning with their own experiences of poverty and then tying them upward into regional, state, and international neoliberal institutions.

"Paulo Freire already laid out this kind of education in great detail," we remarked. "Aren't you just reinventing the wheel?"

"Maybe so," came the reply from a Zapatista *promotore*, "but it is *our* wheel."

The Zapatista autonomous health system is based on the same principles: holism and de-professionalization. In autonomous clinics, Western medical technology coexists with traditional remedies and herbal pharmacies.[137] Special emphasis is given to women's reproductive health, with well-trained midwives holding knowledge of both traditional and modern technologies.

FIGURE 6. Zapatista health clinic, Caracol of Oventic. Most of the equipment and medical supplies are donated by international supporters. Charlotte Saenz.

Health is understood as a collective phenomenon; prevention, or "knowing how to care for and heal oneself," is part of all health campaigns.

When Zapatismo first emerged, Chiapas had the lowest ratio of doctors to population in Mexico and abysmal maternal and infant mortality rates. Students from the Metropolitan Autonomous University of Mexico City, together with other national and international volunteers, constructed an expansive system of health-care institutions where patients could speak in their own languages. But the construction of the autonomous health-care system really started in 1995 with the election of health promoters in all participating villages. A second phase began in 2004 with the establishment of the juntas, when the Zapatistas started vaccination programs directed against tetanus and typhoid. By 2007, there were two hundred community health clinics together with twenty-five regional clinics and several hospitals (to put this in context, the first serious state hospital in Chiapas was built in 2006). Even smaller clinics take as many as thirty patients a day.[138]

Regional variances exist in health care, with regional systems of knowledge, specific local problems, and different natural remedies in each zone.

Each region contains seventy to three hundred health promoters, many of them women. One zone boasts an ophthalmology center, while another one has a dental center, a laboratory, and a gynecological center. At least two zones now have ambulances. Exaggerations of activists and scholars notwithstanding, the autonomous health-care system is a remarkable achievement. In one zone, three hundred female doctors, midwives, and bone-setters have been trained.[139]

Exilic economy. The Zapatista economy developed in two distinct periods: 1994–98 and then during *la resistencia*, starting in 1998. The primary goal is self-sufficiency—*active* independence from the state and its social programs. The primary method was growing and selling agricultural produce. This was arrested, however, by communal conflicts and large numbers of villages leaving the organization. Starting in 1998, there was a considerable effort to boost (autonomous) production. In 2001, a program for production and commercialization was initiated to improve living conditions by promoting cooperation, democracy, and communal organization. This included many microprojects and a schooling farm in Zona Selva Tojolabal focused on sustainable management, cattle vaccination, and basic agrarian training. Agricultural projects include the development and use of composting and organic technologies, preservation of soil and conservation of native seeds, and the rejection of genetically modified seed and chemical treatments.[140] Products are sold to local, national, and international customers, while financial management remains in the hands of community members. One example of this is the women's collective from Oventic, Mujeres por la Dignidad (Women for Dignity). The cooperative was formed in 1997 and now has more than seven hundred members from four municipalities. Products from Zapatista communities, including clothing, artwork, and coffee, are sold at a solidarity cafe in San Cristóbal. This strategy ensures that primary producers, not middlemen, receive the full benefit of their labor. But is the solidarity economy just providing breathing room for the exilic economy, or is it indispensable for its survival?

In many villages, communalism coexists (uneasily) with individual entrepreneurship. Communal projects often compete against the desire for individual profit, and private enterprise can stand in the way of a communal economy. In one village, people work their *milpas* and cultivate maize during the week. On Saturday, the whole village assembles to accomplish a collective task that will benefit the community as a whole. Participation is obligatory and regulated by a rotation system. Most Zapatistas see no contradiction between participating in the collective project *and* increasing the profitability of their land.[141]

Yet production is not limited to subsistence; commercialization and trade yield a collective surplus. Small-scale production and commerce include cooperatives, coffee shops, artisan shops, bakeries, and various cooperative ventures. In La Realidad there is a bank that provides loans at 2 percent interest.[142]

Statistics are hard to come by, but collectivized surplus is used in two principal ways: to acquire products that autonomous communities cannot produce themselves and to reinvest in other community projects.[143] According to Kaufman,[144] a third form of surplus-distribution goes into national and international solidarity projects: in 2005, corn was sent to Cuba, and in 2006 to Oaxaca and San Salvador Atenco.

When we visited a women's handicrafts cooperative store in Oventic, though, we were told that this was the one economic venture in the village where the participants kept a share of their profits (the boot factory nearby is entirely nonwaged labor). We were told that putting cash in the hands of women was a way to positively transform the gender inequality that is endemic in the community (as everywhere) while *re*valuing the indigenous dress that the women wear and sell (Zapatista men commonly wear cowboy boots and jeans while women wear the traditional handmade *huipil* blouse and skirt).

As with the Don Cossacks, there is an acute problem of the "ecology of escape": slash-and-burn agriculture jeopardizes the environment of the Lacandon jungle and highlands alike.[145] There are efforts to use locally adaptive and nutritionally rich inherited methods. For example, the cultivation of organic hibiscus combined ecological standards with indigenous agricultural techniques.[146] However, these efforts are endangered by massive agro-industrial campaigns to produce and distribute genetically modified seed. Frequent seasonal failures are another obstacle.[147]

One of the most pressing problems of exilic economy is intercommunal conflict. In several villages, communal organization was suspended and then resumed after several years of intercommunal conflict. Barmeyer reports on considerable difference and regional variance. For instance, many residents in villages that were unanimously Zapatista migrate regularly as seasonal workers to the oil fields of Tabasco. In divided villages, the practice of seasonal work in Tabasco was prohibited to prevent economic inequalities and internal conflict.[148]

FIGURE 7. Zapatista women's handicraft cooperative in Oventic. The women who run this cooperative receive a portion of the proceeds from their labor. Charlotte Saenz.

As with Cossacks, however, one of the main threats to autonomy comes from the difficult loyalty pact, although in this case not with the state but with national and international supporters who provide material aid. One element of the founding of the *juntas de buen gobierno* was a drive to increase local control over what did and did not come into the communities by way of aid. In April 1994 Subcomandante Marcos wrote of the problem,

> To those from civil society who came to the communities . . . we know that you are risking much to come and see us and to bring aid to the civilians on this side. It is not our needs which bring us pain, it's seeing in others what others don't see, the same abandonment of liberty and democracy, the same lack of justice . . . I saved an example of "humanitarian aid" for the chiapaneco indigenous, which arrived a few weeks ago: a pink stiletto heel, imported, size 6½ . . . without its mate. I always carry it in my backpack in order to remind myself . . . what we are to the country after the first of January: a Cinderella . . . These good people who, sincerely, send us a pink stiletto heel, size 6 and ½, imported, without its mate . . . thinking that, poor as we are, we'll accept anything, charity and alms. How can we tell all those good peo-

ple that no, we no longer want to continue living Mexico's shame. In that part that has to be prettied up so it doesn't make the rest look ugly. No, we don't want to go on living like that.

In July 2003 he wrote:

> The other pink heel never arrived, and the pair remained incomplete, and piling up in the "Aguascalientes" were useless computers, expired medicines, extravagant (for us) clothes, which couldn't even be used for plays ("señas," they call them here) and, yes, shoes without their mate. And things like that continue to arrive, as if those people were saying "poor little things, they're very needy. I'm sure anything would do for them, and this is in my way."
> And that's not all. There is a more sophisticated charity. It's the one that a few NGOs and international agencies practice. It consists, broadly speaking, in their deciding what the communities need, and, without even consulting them, imposing not just specific projects, but also the times and means of their implementation. Imagine the desperation of a community that needs drinkable water and they're saddled with a library. The one that requires a school for the children, and they give them a course on herbs.[149]

Aside from the issue of local control, the quality and amount of aid from civil society diminished over the years, challenging the Zapatistas' ability to maintain material sustainability along with autonomy. One observer asked, "How does entering into market relations, even in areas such as fair trade coffee and artisan production, affect the autonomy project?"[150] Finding enough land for subsistence farming was one thing, but the cost of maintaining communities in the face of continuing low-intensity warfare against them by the Mexican state and entry into market relations was more difficult.

Zapatistas display considerable ingenuity in meeting these obstacles. They created a system of collective warehouses in the jungle zone to avoid market fluctuations, dependency on coyotes (or intermediaries), and prohibitive transportation costs.[151] Flexibility was important: when one association of Zapatista producers failed to raise enough money to build a community warehouse, they bought a communal truck instead, to take their produce to the local market and bring back essential goods like soap, sugar, and tools bought at wholesale prices. Some large collective purchases are made to alleviate intensive, usually gendered labor (e.g., corn-grinding machines) or to get a better price (livestock). Ad hoc committees operate in situations of communal emergency, for example, to obtain food or to raise cash by harvesting rare timber.[152] Finally, new population centers have an important economic role as recovered land is often ideal for cattle pasture or coffee plantations. New communities provide a crucial resource for the survival and economic autonomy of the whole Zapatista territory.

How, then, should one think of Zapatista production? Zapatista economic activities are not outside of capitalism, but they are not completely capitalist, either. Some autonomous production, like the production of organic food, is done on a smaller scale and the surplus is (for the most part) retained locally. Some Zapatista products, however, are exported to capitalist markets, although primarily niche solidarity markets. Coffee earnings are linked to the world market, and the territory is also increasingly dependent on seasonal work, migration, and remittances.[153]

There is an apparent paradox: can one engage in capitalist markets without replenishing the reproduction of state and capital? Zapatista exilic economic activities undoubtedly increase their independence and encourage new social relationships in the territory. However, if the ambition is to organize an autonomous productive base outside of the relationships of accumulation of the capitalist world-system, then there is no evidence that this kind of complete exit exists. The Zapatista economy is paradoxical, simultaneously inside and outside of the system: extra-state but intrasystemic.

We describe the economic activities of the Zapatistas as *contradictory substantive practices*. They are not in direct antagonism to the capitalist law of value, but they are undoubtedly transformative. They are capital and state resistant, as they prevent complete incorporation into world-capitalist institutions and processes. They are anti-capital in certain respects or at certain times, but sometimes supportive of capitalism, even simultaneously.

Zapatistas communities live beyond minimum subsistence, and hunger has been almost eradicated. Yet there is no autonomous productive base independent of the commodity chains and hierarchical processes of the capitalist world-economy. Even the *milpa* requires tools and other inputs from external markets. Contradictory substantive practices, by collectivizing surplus, strengthen cooperative activities, and at the same time allow some private property. They also depend on international solidarity—money brought to the communities from outside—and this "loyalty bargain" brings with it many distinct problems. The result of this exilic construction is *exit-with-autonomy*, organized around a set of cooperative practices that aspire to be more capital and state resistant.

Many scholars emphasize the unusual strategic flexibility of the Zapatistas. Kaufman notes that "the EZLN seemed to employ indigenous claims to emphasize the particular and contextual nature of their struggle, nationalist language to displace indigenist sectarianism or secessionist claims, internationalist language to displace nationalist dogmas and identities, and then return to an emphasis on indigenous thought as an attempt to reach from the particular toward the universal, a being beyond nation-state-defined subjects and citizens."[154] This was no accident, nor is Zapatista eclecticism unique. To the contrary, it seems to be a standard exilic response to states and capital, much akin to the Cossacks' use of strategic language when addressing Muscovy and other outsiders.

Flexibility is necessary for the simultaneous enactment of exit, voice, and loyalty. After the breakdown of negotiations with the Mexican government in the late 1990s, the Zapatistas reemphasized exit and loyalty (to civil society rather than the state, unlike Cossacks), but they were actively pursuing all three strategic options from the very beginning. In the San Andrés Accords, the Zapatistas engaged the state to seek recognition of their rights, but they also gained the attention of Mexican society. They "anchored that demand in the belief and practice that such rights and their protection will only arise as a result of struggle."[155] This understanding provides the real meaning of an otherwise confusing statement by Muñoz Ramírez that "the dialogues with the federal government, the EZLN has stated, were in the end only secondarily about speaking with the government; they were principally a place of encounter, acquaintance, and alliance with other sectors of Mexican society."[156] Negotiations and cooperation with the government (loyalty to the state) were a strategic maneuver, used not only to define extra-state loyalty bargains with civil society but also to seize an opportunity for the development of structures of exit ("autonomy"). Some observers agree. With respect to the 2001 appeal to the Mexican Congress to enact the San Andrés Accords, Barmeyer observes that "local Zapatistas were fully aware of the somber prospects of a law that endorsed real autonomy. I think they half expected that their twenty-four comandantes would not come up with the goods but realized that the political theater of the march on Mexico City was also about mustering national and international support in the interest of their own long term agenda."[157] Strategic engagement with the state not only provided an opening for voice but also assured that this use of voice would reach ears

(Mexican and international civil society) that would enable the movement to withdraw altogether from its engagements with the state.

At the beginning, say the Zapatistas, there was fire. The open rebellion started symbolically on New Year's Day 1994, when several thousand Zapatista fighters took over several towns in Chiapas. The government responded with force, and more than four hundred poorly armed rebels were killed in the "battle of Ocosingo." Images of wounded indigenous rebels, inadequately armed, prompted civil society into action; Salinas declared a cease-fire after only twelve days.[158]

On February 1, the EZLN command faxed a call for help to NGOs throughout Mexico, asking them to provide a "belt of peace" and safety for negotiations between the EZLN and government representatives in San Cristóbal. The EZLN did not ask NGOs to take sides, but emphasized their potential to construct a broad alliance across civil society to promote a new national project by bringing about democratic change.[159]

Mexican and international civil society responded by recognizing the legitimacy of the Zapatista rebellion, condemning violence, and demanding a political process.[160] The EZLN and the government negotiated one of the quickest transitions from guerrilla uprising to peace process in world history. Negotiations were held in San Cristóbal Cathedral in February 1994, mediated by Bishop Samuel Ruiz. The EZLN organized a consultation among its base communities to decide their next moves. They also received a number of distinguished visitors.

The impact of the uprising undid the government's work to restore public confidence after the fraudulent elections of 1988 The government sought to isolate the Zapatistas by organizing campesino and indigenous groups into the *Consejo Estatal de Organizaciones Indígenas y Campesinas* (CEOIC), a state-sponsored indigenous organization that included nearly three hundred different groups who "rejected the violent option" promoted by the EZLN. Concurrently, the government initiated an ambitious land-redistribution program. The EZLN's response was the convocation of the National Democratic Convention (CND), which mobilized a broad spectrum of civil-society actors. Then, they announced the formation of autonomous municipalities, their official declaration of "exit" from the Mexican state.

The state responded with a raid by the Mexican army, which failed to capture the EZLN leadership and instead led to the militarization of exilic territory. Zapatista base communities collectively decided to promote a civic, nonpartisan front and an alliance with Mexican civil society. The NGO network

CONPAZ and the San Cristóbal Catholic diocese responded by instituting peace camps that enabled most refugees to return to their villages.

A second round of negotiations started in 1995 under the auspices of the diocese. Negotiations were soon moved to the highland town of San Andrés. The EZLN used the talks to publicize its issues: "From its situation of military siege, the EZLN was able to capitalize on the negotiations by inviting indigenous leaders and experts and by issuing frequent communiqués that kept the guerrilla movement in the public discourse."[161] Not surprisingly, the negotiations failed. Only one topic—indigenous rights and culture—was agreed upon, while others, including democracy and justice, living standards and development, women's rights, and peace with justice and dignity, were left unattended. The negotiations were suspended in 1996.[162]

In one of the formative and most decisive moments in conjuring a new form of loyalty and strategic extra-space dependency, the Zapatistas immediately responded to the breakdown of negotiations with a flurry of activity directed toward civil society. The Fourth Declaration of the Lacandon jungle in January 1996 invited civil society to create a Zapatista Front for National Liberation (FZLN) to promote the ideas of Zapatismo. The Zapatistas also convened the National Indigenous Forum (CNI), with representatives from thirty-five indigenous groups from across Mexico. The forum produced a document that provided the basis for the San Andrés Accords on Indigenous Rights and Culture, signed by the government and the EZLN in February 1996.[163]

In the summer of 1996, pro-Zapatista solidarity groups from Europe organized Against Neoliberalism and for Humanity, a conference in Berlin, followed by the Intergalactic Meeting against Neoliberalism and for Humanity, held in Chiapas in exilic territory.[164] After President Zedillo decided not to present the San Andrés Accords for ratification in the Mexican Congress, the Zapatistas entered a period of "strategic silence" and heightened alert in the exilic communities.

The EZLN then initiated a series of initiatives to relaunch the political process, including a journey by 1,111 Zapatistas to Mexico City to participate as observers in the September 13–15 founding of the Frente Zapatista de Liberación Nacional (FZLN). Counterinsurgency measures by the state were numerous. The number of paramilitary groups increased, supported by farmers who had lost land to Zapatista "recoveries." Poor young men were recruited. At the height of paramilitary activity, in 1997–98, several thousand Zapatista villagers were displaced. A more insidious form of counterinsurgency was the issuance of "development money" to government loyalists and a large-scale development program for eastern Chiapas.

Two programs in particular defined the new relationship between the Zapatistas and the state. The Program of Rural Provisions (DICONSA) aimed at providing marginalized populations with staple foodstuffs like maize, sugar, beans, and other nonperishable products. These were delivered to stores in indigenous areas and sold at competitive prices. The majority of inhabitants of the Zapatista territory in the canyons and the jungle were eligible to obtain these basic goods in designated stores. PROGRESA, the Program for Education, Health, and Nutrition, was initiated in 1997.[165] It gave as many as 2.4 million stipends for Mexican children to attend government schools. With a special focus on rural women's integration into medical and income-generating projects, PROGRESA was a direct challenge to Zapatista autonomy.[166]

At the same time, the military blockade was intensified by the multiplication of bases, patrols, and roadblocks. Tens of thousands of soldiers transformed local communities into barracks, while paramilitary groups and state security forces constantly intimidated and harassed them. The Zapatistas responded by founding new population centers (*nuevos centros de población*) on occupied land and installing NGOs as protective buffers around exilic villages. These responses met with repression, paramilitary violence, and blackmail.

When forty-five pacifists who were sympathetic to the Zapatista movement were slaughtered by paramilitary forces in the village of Acteal in December 1997, however, (inter)national civil society and human rights advocates were outraged. Against this complex background, the Zapatistas declared themselves "in resistance" to all government programs, including money, food, and educational and medical aid. Communities in exit were urged to refuse the "alms of the state."[167] In 1999, the Zapatistas announced a *consulta* on indigenous autonomy.[168]

Then, a dramatic change altered the Mexican electoral landscape: in December 2000 the PAN (National Action Party) replaced the PRI after seventy-one years. The historic defeat of the PRI was widely regarded as a consequence of the Zapatista movement. As an "external challenge" to the PRI, and to the national political system as a whole, the Zapatistas accelerated Mexico's democratization.

The new president, Vincente Fox, declared his intention to "solve the Chiapas problem in 15 minutes." Fox never defined what he meant, exactly, but it soon became obvious that he did not intend to fix the structural poverty of the indigenous population. Rather, he proposed to fix a perceived lack of investment opportunities through a neoliberal project called the Plan Puebla Panamá. This "mega-project" included the construction of *maquiladoras* (assembly factories) in low-wage areas, along with airports, roads, and other infrastructure. The so-called biological reserve corridors were targeted for pharmaceutical and seed companies. Fox made some symbolic conciliatory gestures: he removed seven military bases (out of three hundred or more) and released one hundred political prisoners.[169]

The Zapatistas, after extending and consolidating their exilic territory during the period of silence, decided to revive the San Andrés Accords. They undertook a march to Mexico City in 2001. On the way, they participated in the third National Indigenous Congress, underscoring their role as champions of the indigenous. On the road, their reception by hundreds of thousands of Mexicans was spectacular: "Greeted as beloved heroes in towns and cities along their journey, they arrived to the center of Mexico City where over 300,000 people were gathered to receive them."[170] They addressed the Mexican Congress, which, as predicted by many members of the Mexican civil society, rejected their right to self-determination and economic autonomy. Then, after a remarkable journey carefully used to promote the message of exile, they retreated back into the jungle and several years of strategic silence.[171]

The silence ended again in 2002 with a string of communiqués issued by Marcos. He presented the results of exit, of building an autonomous society in exile, and announced the restructuring of their exilic space through new governing bodies called *juntas de buen gobierno*. Since then, the exilic government has consistently rejected state programs and institutions and executed its own autonomous policies of social development. This was the second phase of Zapatista autonomy, in which the Zapatistas decided to reject "government alms" and reduce their dependency on the state. The challenge to the state had become "direct and everyday." The base communities faced a big ask: support the EZLN without any outside help. A "bundle of hardships" included the suspension of schooling for children, the end of monthly infusions of cash for those who claimed PROCAMPO grants, and higher costs for basic goods. The state showered non-Zapatista communities with infrastructure and development aid. Roads went into forgotten parts of the jungle. Power lines were extended and "real" schools expanded. As a result, families who were insufficiently integrated into exilic society opted for inclusion into

FIGURE 8. Loyalty bargain. Ambulance donated by Italian supporters from the Ya Basta! network. The names of two Italian activists killed by the Italian police and fascists in the early 2000s appear on the side of the ambulance. Charlotte Saenz.

the "institutional world." By the end of the 1990s there was hardly a settlement without factional splits.[172]

This could be considered an example of *refused loyalty*, a situation where the political costs of loyalty are perceived to be greater than its economic advantages. Yet there are high risks involved in state refusal, just as there are with the loyalty bargain, because the state has power and resources to punish the disloyal. In this case, state social programs were mechanisms to divide and co-opt. One particularly effective counterinsurgency measure was the already mentioned PROGRESA, in which rural women were integrated into income-generating medical projects, in direct competition with Zapatista health and education projects. Under the Fox administration, PROGRESA was replaced by Oportunidades, which came to be known as the model poverty-eradication program of the continent. Giving cash transfers of between 150 and 1,050 pesos to poverty-stricken women with school-age children, Oportunidades had the largest budget of any federal program: 25 billion pesos in 2004, 33 billion in 2005, and 36 billion in 2007.[173] The program was said to benefit five million people directly and twenty-one million indirectly—a fifth of the Mexican population. According to documents from the Secretaría de Desarrollo (Ministry of Development), five hundred thousand families in Chiapas were beneficiaries in 2004, a tenth of the beneficiaries in the nation, and it was projected that 70 percent of the state's population would receive benefits by 2007.

Plan Puebla Panamá (PPP) was launched in 2001 in active collaboration with the Inter-American Development Bank, with the ambition to "fully incorporate southern Mexico and central America into the global economy through the urbanization of the countryside."[174] In 2008 this program was replaced by Proyecto Mesoamerica, but Plan Puebla Panamá continued in all but name.Rural cities are the centerpiece of the PPP, but in addition to the rural cities program, the spatial marginalization of Chiapas includes infrastructural networks and economic corridors designed to spatially and legally marginalize communal land. The Zapatista territories are increasingly infiltrated by the roads, plantations, and rural cities in an attempt to reduce them to "mere zones of confinement within an expanding urban fabric."[175]

The control over space—Hasketh's "clash of spatializations"[176]—plays an important part in the aim to recapture exilic territory and draw exiles back into regional and world markets. The Zapatistas and other indigenous people have met these "normalizing spatial practices" of state and capital, facilitated by paramilitary violence, with continuous resistance, including opposition to the forced displacement of communities, blocking the construction of the San Cristóbal–Palenque Highway, and the resistance of the Zapatista community of Bolon Ajaw, which occupies part of the proposed site of the Palenque–Agua Azul integrally planned center.[177]

Another state approach is to pit ethnic groups against each other in order to "make way for capitalist development." Although the Montes Azules Biosphere Reserve had been overlapping the controversially established Lacandon community territory since 1978, the state began evictions of Zapatista communities there in 2000.[178]

The other edge of the Mexican government's strategy was low-intensity warfare. In February 1995, after President Zedillo issued judicial orders for the arrest of the EZLN leadership, the army moved into Zapatista territory and ransacked villages, causing thousands to flee into the mountains. By 2000, state forces (military, police, and immigration authorities) held 502 fixed positions (camps, offices, bases), sixty permanent checkpoints, and ninety-three "intermittent" checkpoints. In the Ocosingo municipality alone, there were eighty-one fixed positions and checkpoints and thirty-two intermittent checkpoints. Between sixty and seventy thousand soldiers were stationed in Chiapas—30 percent of the Mexican total for only 4 percent of its population. Paramilitary forces were also considerable. Supporters of the PRI from divided communities were recruited into armed groups, trained and supported by the police and army. According to the human rights organization Frayba, as many as twelve different paramilitary groups operated in Chiapas by the end of the 1990s.[179]

Military action introduced a new reality into the exilic space. According to Stephen, utopian segments of Zapatismo, including collective agriculture, women's rights, children's rights, cultural and individual respect, all have to compete with "the reality of daily survival in what has become a long-term war."[180] For many communities, this means constant surveillance, harassment, and restricted mobility.

The worst massacre of the state war occurred in the village of Acteal in December 1997, when forty-six Tzotzils were gunned down by paramilitaries in a five-hour killing spree that began with the storming of the village church. This was followed by a series of repressive acts in the highlands and jungle regions. During the first two weeks of January 1998, fifty military raids were registered in Zapatista communities, resulting in the death of at least eight Zapatistas, the detention of hundreds, the destruction of houses, and the expulsion of 120 human rights observers. In the spring and early summer of 1998, security forces carried out raids in four Zapatista communities, leaving one Zapatista and one federal soldier dead.[181]

Mora sees this process as a transition toward a police state. Yet the election in 2000 of Governor Pablo Salazar, who adopted a reconciliatory posture and professed adherence to the San Andrés Accords, along with the election of President Vicente Fox, finally allowed for the relatively unhindered functioning of exilic municipalities.

The state's reaction to *refused loyalty* put great pressures on the exilic community. To withstand them, the exilic project employed several counterstrategies. One was to seek a new loyalty bargain with other extra-space partners who could replace some of the resources lost when relations with the state were broken. Another was to find ways to intensify cooperative exilic practices of solidarity and mutual aid within the community.

The Mexican Revolution and national identity. The loyalty given to the state by Zapatista engagement in the San Andrés negotiations was merely strategic, but it led to new and more sincere forms of loyalty to civil society. In the process, the Zapatistas appropriated nationalism and especially the legacy of Emiliano Zapata. According to Stephen, the Zapatistas offered an alternative model of nationalism from below, based on identification with the national hero and the struggle for land, political participation, and self-determination.[182] Like the Morelos revolt in the 1910s, the Chiapas rebellion was an indigenous revolt *and* it was justified by the "right to rebel" against illegitimate government, enshrined in article 139 of the 1917 constitution. The rebels thus disputed the Mexican government's legitimacy by recovering "betrayed" national symbols and heroes.[183]

The legacy of the Mexican Revolution became an important terrain of contestation between state and exiles. The governments of Salinas de Gortari (1988–94) and Zedillo (1994–2000) consistently put forward their own vision of Mexican nationalism, with Zapata defending free-trade agreements and foreign investment, as well as freedom to choose one's *individual* land. The PROCEDE marketing campaign celebrated Zapata as a neoliberal defender of individual property rights. On the seventy-fifth anniversary of Zapata's assassination in 1994, President Salinas de Gortari seemed to be in "a virtual war of words with Subcomandante Marcos of the Zapatistas over who could gain the most press coverage linking him to the legacy of Zapata."[184] Bureaucrats from the government Procuraduría Agraria agency launched a widespread campaign to commemorate the anniversary. National television and newspapers sponsored tearful homages to Zapata, while national newspapers printed pictures celebrating him. President Salinas de Gortari declared publicly that "Zapata's struggle continues."[185]

In contrast, EZLN Comandanta Ramona offered a present to one of the surviving compañeros of the Mexican revolutionary hero Rubén Jaramillo: a Mexican flag brought from the Chiapas jungle. Ramona said, "This [flag] is so that they never forget that Mexico is our patria [native land] and so that everyone recognizes that there will never be a Mexico without us."[186] The exiles disputed both the legitimacy of the Mexican government and the symbols of its rule: they offered an alternative model of collective identity, undermining the state's claims on Mexico's revolution.

Indigenous affairs. While movements for indigenous autonomy, in the form of regional indigenous rights networks, have a long history in Mexico, the

Zapatistas inspired the first genuine national network of indigenous groups. The key institution is the National Indigenous Congress.[187]

The EZLN is not simply "the vanguard of Mexico's indigenous peoples"[188]; it also aims to reinvent indigenous identities. This has been achieved by associating indigenous unity with autonomy, a model that transcends local and regional differences and builds on the multilayered identities of most indigenous Mexicans.[189] The San Andrés Accords, signed by the EZLN and the federal government in February 1996, have become the paradigmatic reference for the debate of indigenous peoples and the state in Mexico.

This politics was, however, contested by the state-sponsored multiculturalism of the Fox administration after 2000. Fox implemented a combination of neo-indigenous politics with "neoliberal multiculturalism"[190] through the Commission for the Development of Indigenous People (CDI). This unusual institution encompasses several components: the co-optation of indigenous professionals into bureaucratic structures, sponsorship of community development–cum–counterinsurgency, the creation of new municipalities, the initiation of intercultural universities, and the celebration of inclusion and diversity.[191] Anna Tsing points to the process of strategic "conflation" of indigenous and peasant rights and demands, a process in which "peasant activists became indigenous activists to utilize the international cachet of indigenous politics."[192]

Human rights. The discourse surrounding human rights is a major area of contestation/competition between the exilic space and the state. As Speed and Collier maintain, "Given the crucial role that the human rights discourse is playing in limiting state power in Chiapas, it is not surprising that both the federal and state governments are increasingly trying to adopt or co-opt the discourse."[193] Beginning in 1996 in particular, the human rights became an indispensable part of the language employed by the state and its Chiapas-based institutions, the National Human Rights Commission (CNDH) and the State Human Rights Commission (CEDH).

The Zapatistas use human rights to their own advantage by employing language from the United Nations International Covenant on Economic, Social, and Cultural Rights (1966). They seek to recast human rights as the economic and social rights of Mexico's excluded citizens, removing the exclusive emphasis on the rights of individuals. The Zapatistas also seek support for indigenous rights. Countries such as Canada, the United States, Denmark, Italy, Spain, and Germany urged the Mexican government to comply with the 1996 San Andrés Accords on Indigenous Rights and Culture.[194] This aspect of the Zapatista interpretation of human rights discourse is part of the global trend of indigenous activism reignited by the 1992 quincentennial of the conquest of the Americas.

Threat Of Dispersal One of the most intriguing and least mentioned strategic innovations by the Zapatistas is their own version of the Don Cossacks' "threat of dispersal." In an interview with Spanish television, Marcos said that the Zapatistas are aiming for a relative autonomy similar to that of Catalonia or the Basque Country.[195] It is, of course, possible to see this gesture as a strategic device with more than one purpose, as a way to establish strategic relationships with partners outside of Mexico and to establish an exilic bargain with international civil society.

CIVIL SOCIETY: AN ALTERNATIVE FORM OF LOYALTY BARGAIN

In 2004, the EZLN published a communiqué describing the contemporary history of Zapatista indigenous communities. Subcomandante Marcos, referring to the Zapatistas' "third shoulder," conveys the importance of national and international civil society for the survival of the exilic space:

> To the two shoulders that the usual human beings have, the Zapatistas have added a third: that of the national and international "civil societies." ... We believe that we have been fortunate. From its beginnings, our movement has had the support and kindness of hundreds of thousands of persons on the five continents. This kindness and this support has not been withdrawn, even in the face of personal limitations, of distances, of differences of culture and language, borders and passports, of differences in political concepts, of the obstacles put up by the federal and state governments, the military checkpoints, harassment and attacks, of the threats and attacks by paramilitary groups, of our mistrust, our lack of understanding of the other, of our clumsiness.
>
> No, in spite of all of that (and of many other things which everyone knows) the "civil societies" of Mexico and the world have worked because of, for and with us.[196]

To reduce dependency on the state, the Zapatistas created extensive relationships with the "outside world." International organizations, not the base communities, obtained most of the necessary funds to build autonomous community infrastructures.[197] The "expert" role of international volunteers became indispensable for training and building infrastructure projects. Thus, exit-with-autonomy was achieved at the cost of new dependencies, which were in turn made necessary by the common exilic problem of *exit-without-resources* that we showed to be a chronic problem for Cossack autonomy. Barmeyer contends, "In return for assistance in the autonomy project, the guerrilla organization has also made itself available as a campaign engine for national and international social movements."[198] This exilic bargain required the Zapatistas to serve not only their base but also their supporters.

Was this new bargain, this loyalty to the civil society, a better alternative than dependency on the state? We believe that the answer must be yes. Even if the alliance with civil society created a dependency on outsiders, it enabled local community control.[199] Funding and training were initiated by outside agencies, but most projects were initiated and controlled by exilic municipalities.

The relationship between the Zapatistas and civil society was established gradually. The first organization of NGOs in Chiapas was CONPAZ (the Coordination of Nongovernmental Organizations for Peace), which monitored human rights abuses and coordinated the work of NGOs in Chiapas. The key institution used to minimize Zapatista dependence on the Mexican state was the Fray Bartolomé de las Casas Human Rights Center (also known as "Frayba"). In 1995, after the raid of the Mexican army, Frayba helped the Zapatistas organize peace camps populated by national and international observers in fifty indigenous villages.[200] The presence of outsiders, including non-indigenous Mexicans, was essential in deterring government military plans. Yet the Zapatistas were forced to introduce a maximum stay of six weeks due to the tensions caused by the international presence in base villages; among other concerns, activists were perceived to disturb the communal balance by establishing relationships with individual community members rather than with the community as a whole.[201]

The democratization of exit influenced the dynamics between independent outside actors and Zapatistas. During the process of democratizing the communities and reducing perceived EZLN authoritarian tendencies, solidarity work came under more scrutiny with respect to indigenous project management. Projects now needed approval from councils of elected delegates. The tension between councils and the EZLN command was palpable, however, as the EZLN still had the final say in approving projects.[202]

During 1997–2001, in answer to NGO-related tensions, the EZLN established a new project-coordinating body, *Enlace Civil*, which maintained a direct link with the EZLN *comandancia* and coordinated incoming requests from the base communities. Solidarity groups—first from Mexico, then from western Europe, the United States, Argentina, and Chile—joined this reciprocal partnership, many if not most of them founded in the aftermath of the two "intergalactic meetings" for humanity and against neoliberalism in 1996 and 1998.[203] They were members of the Zapatista-inspired antiglobalization network called Peoples' Global Action.[204]

After the 2001 Zapatista march on Mexico City, changes associated with the founding of *juntas de buen gobierno* forced further regulations on external civil society. A major motivation for the changes was the problem of uneven exilic development, whereby roadless villages on the periphery of the jungle received far fewer resources than municipal centers. Such imbalances of the loyalty bargain led the EZLN in August 2003 to publish a series of communiqués signed by Subcomandante Marcos under the title *Treceava Estela* (Thirteenth Stele). In addition to announcing the closing of the *aguascalientes* and the creation of *caracoles* and *juntas de buen gobierno,* Marcos delivered a humorous critique against disrespectful and damaging "handouts and sympathy" from outside supporters. He criticized the paternalism of NGOs and solidarity activists. While grateful for their help, he invited them to leave the attitudes of social workers behind and to engage in the process of sharing, mutual learning, and multidirectional solidarity.[205] This was a clear attempt to preserve autonomy-with-exit.

International solidarity groups responded favorably to the changes. In 2004 alone, according to Barmeyer, aid rose to Mex $12 million (US$ 1.2 million).[206] In the same year, forty-five hundred people from over thirty countries visited the Caracol of Oventic, many of them solidarity activists who worked on projects like water and communications systems. Both Enlace Civil and Frayba established a rigorous set of procedures and regulations regarding the visits of solidarity activists. As Barmeyer notes, "Whereas experience, skill, and particularly contacts to the comandancia (central command of the EZLN) were a prerequisite for running an NGO in rebel territory, the smooth operation of the projects required volunteers who felt honored to take part in a clandestine enterprise, did not ask too many questions, and got on with their job." This is why "project volunteers represented a further step on the scale of logistical aides for the Zapatistas' efforts to consolidate their independence from the Mexican state."[207] Much help came from Mexican universities, where student groups had organized since 1994. North American NGOs and European solidarity groups provided cash for infrastructural, educational, commercial, and health-related projects.[208]

With the post-2003 changes in exilic governance, a clear division of labor emerged between international NGOs, external support groups, and community-based NGOs and projects in Chiapas. The large international NGOs simply provided money for local projects. The money "radicalized" as it flowed down the line: "Donor organizations that channeled funds to Chiapas had a broad base among urban liberals or Christian congregations in the United States who adhered to a moderate humanist approach towards development, while the people running local projects in Zapatista base communities sought to support and further revolutionary social change."[209] In a parallel effort, solidarity groups (who could raise less money but were able to be more honest with their constituencies) sent trained activists directly to the communities to work on projects. NGOs funding groups like TENAZAS and SHOXEL "shroud[ed] their revolutionary clients with the inconspicuous veil of 'indigenous communities in need.'"[210] Another organization, Schools for Chiapas, recruits people for caravans to Oventic, where they assist the local Zapatista secondary (teacher training) school. They provide funding for the Zapatista base communities by employing "package zapatourism." They have also assisted in the creation of the Institute for Mayan Languages, where international students engage with Spanish and indigenous languages and the history of the Zapatista struggle.

The mechanism of fund-raising is fairly straightforward: international funding organizations raise money by promoting the projects of small local NGOs in the global South to the donors in the global North.[211] In the mid-1990s, better-known Zapatista strongholds like La Realidad were inundated with offers for projects designed by outsiders; but these projects did not always meet local needs or realities.

In 2006, the Zapatistas publicly launched the third phase of their exilic journey in typical Marcos fashion. On June 21, 2005, the EZLN sent all of its national and international supporters "a goodbye that is not a goodbye," stating,

If there is one thing that we as Zapatistas treasure it is keeping our word. All this time we have told you we would fight for the indigenous peoples of Mexico. And that is what we have done. We told you we would try the paths of dialogue and negotiation to achieve our demands. . . . And that is what we have done. We have also said, falta lo que falta [what is missing is yet to come], and well, it is time to start looking for that missing piece. Not looking, building. Building something else, something "other." . . . It has been an honor to work with you. If you decide to delink from us as we take this next step, you are free and welcome to do so. If you want to take this next step, to build this "other" thing with us, you are free and welcome to do so.[212]

The decision to start the "Other Campaign" (*La Otra*) was made after an exilic referendum that resulted in 98 percent approval for the new departure. It was announced in the June 2005 Sixth Declaration of the Lacandon jungle, which claimed that the Other Campaign was a "National Campaign for building another way of doing politics, for a program of national struggle of the left, and for a new Constitution."[213]

The timing was provocative: the middle of a Mexican presidential campaign in which popular leftist candidate Andrés Manuel López Obrador was leading the polls. For their part, the Zapatistas made it clear that theirs was an alternative to electoral politics, a blatantly anti-capitalist movement to change society from below. Much of the left, including longtime supporters of the Zapatistas, were horrified, as they felt Mexico was on the verge of a leftist electoral breakthrough. According to Kaufman, "The great majority of recognizable leftist actors and institutions in Mexico, as well as in other parts of the world, met the announcement with a mix of confusion and rage." Such a move was simply not appropriate in the "current conjuncture."[214]

The first "exodus" of Zapatista supporters in 1997 occurred as a result of politics of *resistencia*; this second exodus occurred in response to La Otra, which was a complete break not only with the institutional left in Mexico but also with a considerable segment of civil society. Some authors saw the Other Campaign as a way out of the exit-without-resources trap, an attempt to find new markets for Zapatista products in the face of economic stagnation. Others read it as an explicit anti-capitalist turn from the (largely external/ European) interpretation of the Zapatistas as a cultural identity movement.[215] This is true only to a degree; the Zapatistas were always concerned primarily with material issues such as the health and livelihood of indigenous people, especially women. Zibechi calls La Otra an attempt to launch an approach to politics that is both beyond and against the state, and thus extra-electoral, that unifies popular movements "from below." From this perspective, the shock and outrage expressed by celebrities and parts of civil society did not concern them, for their target audience was distinctly different as they were redefining the exilic bargain.

"We see how the Zapatistas approach politics," wrote Zibechi, "by building within spaces that are invisible to the powerful, political parties, academics, and intellectuals linked to power. Starting out from the creation of spaces for listening, they hope to create new spaces for a new vocabulary for those from below who are in struggle."[216]

The Zapatista statements about the Other Campaign did not just target Mexico's poor, but also a "rainbow" of "others," such as LGBT (as it then was). In the words of Marcos:

> Before leaving, [Comandanta] Ramona gave me this embroidery which she made while she was recovering in Mexico City. She gave it to someone from civil society, who returned it to us in one of these preparatory meetings. She told me: "This is what we want from the Other Campaign." These colors, no more, but no less. Perhaps what we need to do is understand unity like Ramona's embroidery, where each color and form has its place; there's no uniformity, nor hegemony. Finally, to understand unity as the agreement along the path.[217]

Undoubtedly, La Otra signaled a new phase in the relationship between Zapatistas and Mexican civil society, a new "loyalty bargain." Their communiqués state that one of their objectives is to articulate their practices of autonomy in Chiapas with other social struggles throughout Mexico in an effort to create a new political space beyond the exilic territory. Many scholars have noted the specific use of the term "capitalism," which had been mostly absent in Zapatista statements since 1994.[218] According to the EZLN,

> This is what the Other Campaign means to do: name the enemy, capital, and the ally of this enemy, the political class . . . we intend the defeat of this government and the destruction of capital. And then, like someone said once, we will have only just won the right to start over, but we will have to start where one always has to start, from below.[219]

According to Harvey, until the Other Campaign, the Zapatistas focused mostly on internal aspects of the movement, including the consolidation of autonomy.[220] Their relationships with other groups were "organized with this task in mind," in other words, in the context of what we have called the loyalty bargain that was made to protect indigenous autonomy. Yet the Sixth Declaration of the Lacandona calls for groups on the left "to work with the Zapatistas in developing a national program for the political and economic transformation of Mexico, the formulation of a new constitution and the promotion of the new forms of political engagement."[221]

Through La Otra, the Zapatistas strove to prevent recapture by employing a new form of exilic communication: calling on potentially rebellious groups throughout Mexico to exercise new forms of politics outside of electoralism and from below. In so doing, they hoped to turn the loyalty bargain on its head by taking full political control of their alliances with external civil society. These strategic choices are constitutionally related. The Zapatistas were able to reduce their dependence on the state (something that the Don Cossacks could not have done) by substituting a loyalty bargain with civil society for one with the state and thereby increasing their control on the local, community level. Their cooperative exilic practices, characteristic of exit-with-autonomy, were enabled by these dynamics of voice and loyalty, which nonetheless required periodic fine-tuning, as with the refusal of certain offers of aid from international civil society that accompanied the reforms tied to the *juntas de buen gobierno*. But, as we saw in the case of the Cossacks, these dynamics are defined by, or at least heavily impacted by, the rhythms and patterns of change in the world-economy. How did these world-systemic changes affect Zapatista autonomy?

MEXICO'S CHANGING ROLE IN THE WORLD-ECONOMY

There are those who are devoted to imagining that the rudder exists and to fighting for its possession. There are those who are seeking the rudder, certain that it has been left somewhere. And there are those who make of an island, not a refuge for self-satisfaction, but a ship for finding another island and another and another.

Subcomandante Marcos, quoted in Zibechi,
Territories in Resistance

While the implications of the world-systems approach require a rethinking of the meaning of contemporary de-territorialization, the more traditional interpretations of world-systems analysis omit what we call the infrapolitics of the capitalist world-economy—the production of exilic spaces and practices in the capitalist world-economy as a manifestation of territorial and structural refusal of capitalist modernity. While one can observe structural exit from the processes of the world-economy by social groups who are excluded (or forgotten, as the Zapatistas like to say) from the core processes in the world-economy, escape from capitalist modernity can also be informed by the "recovery" and reinvention of social utopias and alternative paths to sociopolitical organization. Exilic self-organization is thus the "exclusion of the excluders by the excluded."[222] In this context, the Zapatistas represent a form of structural escape from the spaces of capitalist modernity. As exiles, they reject specific material and cultural implications of processes of the capitalist world-economy. The territory itself becomes part of an escape social structure that prevents the incorporative pressures of the capitalist world-economy, or at least helps the group deal with these incorporative pressures on its own terms. "Spaces-of-exit" are structural and territorial forms that are simultaneously outside and inside the capitalist world-system.

The explanations for Mexico's development trajectory, then, must be located within the world-economy and not just in Mexico. One can observe the global, neoliberal production of state and exilic spaces within the context of the periphery, specifically, the Latin American developmentalist model and its discontents. Eastern Chiapas is a produced space, a site that reflects the contradictions and limitations of capitalist incorporation. The complex and contradictory history of this exilic instance were determined by the (relational) specificities of regional development, the Mexican state, and the world-economy as whole.

Zapatista exit is a product of peripheral capitalism. The incomplete incorporation of Chiapas into the interstate system of the capitalist world-economy allowed for a concrete, geographic space where new social and political relationships were improvised largely independent from the state. In a sense, indigenous Chiapas was always prone to this. At times, indigenous labor was desired; for example, as bonded labor in the coffee fincas and mahogany forests of the region. Yet when the resource died out or global markets turned sour, that labor, no longer desirable, once again disappeared into the mountains and jungles from whence it had been taken. Such patterns are complicated by the mismatch between borders and peoples: Mayans, like Kurds and Basques and numerous other peoples, often treat such borders with disdain, especially when the ideologies that are created to solidify the "nation" (in Mexico, *mestizaje*) do not really apply to them.

The Zapatistas represent a type of exilic space or "black hole" that appears during crisis and restructuring of the world economy, with a new hegemonic power hierarchy, new leading economic sectors, and new global and regional divisions of labor. To the extent that the exiles are adept in escaping incorporative pressures, they constitute an obstacle for capital accumulation strategies in the region. The reincorporation of an area, which is a part (in this case) of neoliberal restructuring, imposes pressures on geographic exiles, who must make political bargains to extend their periods of escape, go further into the hinterlands beyond incorporation, or try to find new forms of structural escape as they are "captured" geographically.

In Mexico, the dynamics of infrapolitics are inscribed in space. The neoliberal phase of "inverted developmentalism" and reperipheralization sought to de-territorialize space before re-territorializing it in order to forge new global-spatial divisions of labor for the increasing (and increasingly limited) accumulation of capital. In what Hasketh terms a "clash of spatializations," the Zapatistas, as an exilic group produced by the new moment in the organization of the world-economy, seek to re-territorialize and reappropriate space.[223]

The production of exilic space in Chiapas should be viewed in relation to the hegemonic shifts and restructuring of the world-economy. The change in world time made it impossible for the Mexican state to use the military option and annihilate the Zapatistas, as was the case during the so-called dirty war in the 1970s and 1980s and, even more à propos, as in the US-sponsored genocide against Guatemalan Mayans in the early 1980s, one of its proxy wars against national liberation in the region. The rebels are protected not only by their own weakness but also by the weakness of the Mexican state within the changing structures of the world-economy. This weakening of the state has created a "stalemate" between state and exiles; the state has had to resort to the tactics of low-intensity warfare, and the exiles to the *threat* of voice combined with the support of an international community that is tied to the Zapatistas by a loyalty bargain.

Another consequence of the neoliberal peripheralization of the Mexican state is its inability to sign the San Andrés Accords. The state could not keep its word. The degree of autonomy incorporated in the San Andrés Accords was in direct conflict with national and transnational investment interests in the oil, water, mineral, and biological resources of the region. Permitting autonomous governance would paralyze Mexican state attempts to "make ready" the indigenous people for the displacement and destruction implied by such projects.

These emerging forms of power, communication, and technology created new strategic ways out of the "exit-in-isolation" and "exit-without-resources" trap. The Zapatistas' strategic loyalty relationship with nonstate extra-space actors has reduced their dependency on the state. This alternative form of extra-space dependency has encouraged community control and a contradictory independence from capital and the state, as well as making the developmentalist project of taking state power strategically unnecessary.

Finally, *infrapolitics*, the production of exilic spaces and practices in the capitalist world-economy, is a constant, if neglected, aspect of global politics. During the normal historical life of the capitalist system, infrapolitics is largely invisible, or, in James Scott's terms,[224] part of the "hidden transcript" of the capitalist world-economy. During times of hegemonic shift and deterritorialization, the production of exilic spaces and circulation of exilic practices become visible, part of the "public transcript" of the world-economy. By highlighting the contradictions of capitalist relations in the process of hegemonic transition and global restructuring, the Zapatistas produced an exilic model that resonated well beyond the local and national context.

Despite these factors, we can identify tensions in the exilic project.

EXILIC TENSIONS

> All of this now, everything we have and do now, good or bad, it is we as Zapatistas that decide and do it, not the bosses/masters. This is why our people hope that [our account of] our practice is useful to you, brothers and sisters from elsewhere, Mexico and other countries. Because when the people rule, no one can destroy them. And also, we have to realize that the people, our peoples, can fail, can make mistakes. But then, well, there's nobody to blame.
>
> LIEUTENANT COLONEL MOISÉS,
> quoted in Kaufman, "We Are from Before"

Tension in exilic territory and membership. From 1994 to 1997, exilic members were dual citizens, receiving PROCAMPO money from the state and organizing insurrection at the same time. The politics of *la resistencia* put an end to this. Barmeyer contends that the initial strategy of "pirating" state resources came under public scrutiny and therefore had to be scrapped as incompatible with the EZLN's image.[225] Yet, it seems more likely that the EZLN calculated that dependency on the state was far more costly than depending on (inter)national civil society. Simply put, the Zapatistas sought nonstate partners, and unexpected global enthusiasm for their rebellion guaranteed national and international support for exit-with-autonomy.

Like the Don Cossacks, the Zapatistas made a difficult strategic decision—and they paid a price. By the end of the 1990s, Zapatista territory was rife with factional and communal divisions. Economic hardship coupled with a sense of abandonment precipitated an exodus from the exilic territory. Former Zapatista villages became PRI strongholds. As a seventeen-year-old villager testified, "Instead of our leaking zacate roofs we now have rainproof corrugated iron over our heads. Things are looking up, we'll be able to buy cars and tractors."[226] Re-entry should not be dismissed as treason against the exilic cause. Those who left the Zapatistas did so on the pragmatic assessment that the sacrifice of exilic membership was too great. Legitimate, dire needs in the community made the government's counterinsurgency measures effective and influenced many exilic members to consider material support for the EZLN to be too great a sacrifice.[227]

Communal divisions were not always confrontational. Villagers supported the EZLN as insurgents, militia, or *bases de apoyo*, with different motivations and different levels of integration into exilic organization. In reality, different factions sometimes just let each other "go their separate way" (*yo cada quien con su camino*). This coexistence, however, worked only if the communal dispute did not involve land. The new population centers were resource rich: landless peasants received fertile land in return for political allegiance. Exilic membership in these centers was homogenous. The potential problem, however, was hidden precisely in the better quality of the land. A geographical split of exiles along economic lines was inherent in the difference between the new settlements, with land and better living standards, and the older, less affluent communities, which were riddled by political division.[228]

The 2003 reforms aimed to rectify this situation and provide uniform development in Zapatista territories. However, the new regulations led to defections in new settlements on former finca lands, where settlers wanted to benefit from productive coffee lands or cattle pasture, yet were prevented to the degree that their surplus was transferred to poorer exilic regions to reduce regional inequality.

Another source of tension is the integration of non-Zapatista communities with access to autonomous law courts, schools, and clinics. The Zapatistas followed an open-door policy to entice villagers into the exilic project.

However, shortages caused this generosity to backfire and exacerbate political divisions.[229]

There are many reasons for this relatively weak or inefficient sovereignty: low-intensity warfare; the lure of state-provided resources; and the economic hardships caused by the need to support guerrilla forces, teachers, administrators, as well as poorer regions through transfers of wealth. Barmeyer also cites authoritarianism as a possible reason for relatively weak exilic sovereignty before 2003.[230] It is natural that the guerrilla organization would exercise control over exilic society during the initial period of exit, not least for reasons of security during a time of government suppression. Over time, however, the exilic communities themselves began to express a desire for more autonomy . . . *from the guerrilla*. Moreover, international civil society demanded a "clean guerrilla" in return for its support. This led Marcos to intervene and charge the EZLN with "contaminating a tradition of democracy and self-governance."[231] Local aspirations, along with the kind of strategic loyalty that Zapatista exiles chose, demanded further political transformation and the democratization of community life.

Thus, the new *caracoles* and *juntas* were an alternative way of sustaining local hegemony, particularly in core communities. This administrative reorganization, a consolidation of exilic sovereignty, was an attempt to achieve community hegemony along the lines of Zapatista ideology *without* becoming a state. It appears that the increasingly democratic and cooperative practices within Zapatista communities resulted in the return of many members and many villages to the exilic space.

Sometimes, when you fix one problem another appears. Just as the Zapatistas closed one source of exit of disaffected members, a new source appeared: migratory flows to Mexican cities and the United States. The Zapatistas were able to contain the migration of Zapatista youth for many years, but this changed with the first wave of migration in 2002–3.[232] Migration is now one of the most consistent factors threatening the exilic sovereignty of the Zapatistas.

"We are losing our most precious resource, our youth, to migration. First, to the cities of Mexico but even more so to the United States," a Zapatista activist told one of us in 2004.

Especially worrying is the migration of members of Zapatista youth groups (*grupos juveniles zapatistas*), because youth migration is regarded as a form of "civil death" that threatens the reproduction of the indigenous community. Zapatista militants often consider such migration to be a form of defection.[233] The Zapatista revolution is a daily practice and a way of life, so it comes as no surprise that migration would be ill-received.

Calling migration defection could be considered extreme[234]; many exiles defend it as a legitimate way of obtaining economic resources. According to Aquino Moreschi, these two projects—one based on collective organization for the common good ("the autonomous Zapatista project") and the other based on personal or family needs and aspirations ("the migration project")—coexist in tension and permanent negotiation throughout the territory.[235] In the beginning, the communal reaction to transnational migration was one of confusion; previous migration had been short-term and subject to community or at least family approval. Currently, Zapatistas may migrate to the north if the assembly gives its collective stamp of approval. Different agreements regulate the length of absence, the amount of communal work that the absent member owes to the collective, and/or the amount of money paid in cash. A sort of a taxation system has been established whereby a migrant keeps his exilic citizenship if he pays a certain amount of money in exchange for the communal services lost to the migrant's family. These communal agreements are often reassessed and renegotiated. Recent research shows that many militants have adopted a more receptive, benevolent attitude toward migration since 2003. In some cases, it has been recognized as a strategy through which one can earn a living *and* support the exilic project from abroad,[236] a solution to the problem of *exit-without-resources* and a new kind of loyalty bargain.

Still, several aspects of migration cause tension. The loss of productive males threatens "exilic reproduction." Remittance money (*remesas*) enriches certain families and jeopardizes solidarity within the community.[237] And emigration has special consequences for women, as migrating husbands mean single parenting.

One important source of exilic tension is the pervasive exclusion of women. Indigenous peasant women who became integrated as combatants or in "support networks" (*bases de apoyo*) account for a third of EZLN membership.[238] The Revolutionary Women's Law, as well as egalitarian and cooperative exilic practices in the everyday life of the communities, have strengthened the position of women and challenged the traditional indigenous model of womanhood. The situation, however, is far from ideal.[239] Cooperative practices are hampered by patriarchal practices in Zapatista base communities. Progressive attitudes among the guerrilla forces are constrained by long-standing local traditions, including *linkerobo*, a particularly abusive custom whereby a woman is abducted by her future husband. Sexual violence also still exists and in some communities patriarchal culture excludes women from holding public office.

Mexican feminists made demands on the EZLN almost immediately after the uprising. During the National Democratic Convention in August 1994, the guerrillas were presented with demands including the revision of the vertical military structure and suspension of patriarchal sanctions against the bending of "traditional" gender norms. According to Olivera, the situation for indigenous women has been affected by two contradictory developments: "On the one hand, events have reproduced and reinforced . . . the situation of subordination in which women lived before. On the other hand, events have encouraged not just the political participation of women, but also their rebellion against the subordinate position they have been assigned in the gender, class and ethnic hierarchies."[240]

As with other aspects of exilic life, Zapatista gender politics is influenced by war. Low-intensity warfare is, among other things, a campaign of terror aimed at indigenous women that is intended to discourage their support for the EZLN. Indigenous women constitute a majority of the displaced population, and more than six thousand women still cannot return to their homes.[241] The problem of safety is grave. Practices such as gathering wood in the forest and working on coffee fincas or in cornfields have become unsafe. In addition, material scarcity and insecurity has been a factor in the increase of domestic violence in many exilic communities.

The ecology of escape is not progressive by definition. We have seen how environmental degradation and deforestation of the Don helped seal the fate of the Cossack exilic space. Something similar may be happening in Chiapas. Earle and Simonelli maintain that the alternative exilic development model permits campesinos to subsist in agriculture.[242] But in an ecosanctuary like the Selva Lacandona, the subsistence agriculture of escape constitutes an interference in the tropical rainforest, with negative effects on existing ecosystems.[243] *Milpa* cultivation requires clearing of rainforests, hardly a long-term solution. Lack of capital encourages slash-and-burn agriculture with tools like machetes, chemical fertilizers, and fire. One solution would be more widespread use of organic farming methods, including permaculture, nitrogen-producing vines, and compost. The central question is whether it is possible for the exiles to adapt to this fragile ecosystem. Can they achieve higher yields with little cash input, using organically grown maze derived from a genetically diverse strand, or will the current practices of "sacrificing the forest"[244] continue to dominate?

Tension in exilic politics. The most prescient question regarding the new political system is whether the exilic political model has successfully replaced the former system of clientilism, authoritarianism, and electoral fraud. In this regard, the first and perhaps most crucial source of tension is the parallelism between civilian and military administrative structures. In the aftermath of the uprising, militarization of democracy dominated all levels of communal governance. Before the 2003 reforms, administrative centralization and the appointment of officials by and from the EZLN hampered direct democracy.

Mandar obedeciendo has been applied with significant local variations. As with the Don Cossacks, regular village assemblies in themselves are not a sufficient safeguard against patriarchal, gerontocratic, or clientilistic practices, even in the context of a consensus decision-making system. Administrative practices before 2003 were marred by nepotism and clientilism, resulting in uneven municipal development. This should not come as a surprise, as the political culture of rural Chiapas has long been marked by *cacicazgos* (violence), fraud, and co-optation. As Rus has shown, the story of governance in indigenous Chiapas after the ascent of PRI is a tale of personal power and control of local resources.[245] There is a lot of history for the exiles to contend with.

Another possible source of exilic tension are differences between the heterogeneous and politically divided communities and the homogenous base of new population centers, where democratic practices are far more advanced. A very encouraging result of the 2003 reform has been a steady "municipalization" of exilic governance. Zapatista governance is in the process of being integrated into the community; there is not yet enough evidence to conclude whether these reforms have dominated all communities. From our observations, the difference between EZLN functionaries and "ordinary" exilic members is still noticeable.

Tensions in educación autónoma. A different kind of tension exists in the realm of autonomous education. The lack of communal support and competition with "real schools" have influenced some exilic members to change their political affiliation. Community teachers are often inexperienced, and the involvement of urban Mexican and international solidarity activists creates tensions in terms of both dependence on outside assistance and alienating the local population, who are often unable to identify with the education project.[246]

Tensions in the exilic economy. The temptation to see exilic spaces as a reverse image of world-capitalism is not entirely accurate. Zapatista exiles are indeed attempting to escape capitalist processes and to allocate their energies and resources more according to usefulness to the community than to the production of exchange value. But this does not automatically translate into desirable results. Exilic spaces encourage cooperative economic projects, but these have not become their defining characteristics, nor will they necessarily become so—the reality of the everyday struggle tends to be messier. In a much-quoted description, Earle and Simonelli offer an interpretation of exilic economy as a "restraint on the hegemonic appetites of international development."[247] Moreover, it is an example of "social capitalism" that has created an alternative to migration by retaining the milpa-based subsistence agriculture as a model of autonomous development.

Yet capitalism, as a unitary world-economy, does not allow a complete outside. Zapatista territory is a contradictory location: extra-state and intersystemic. The exiles are (relatively) independent of the state but dependent on (inter)national civil society and, increasingly, on remittances from the United States. Their territory includes private property and private enterprise. They depend on regional labor markets for income, and world trade networks for commodities to supplement their own produce and for markets for their own produce. Economic autonomy from the state implies a reliance on fair trade and economic solidarity networks. Possibly, exilic economic structures that are centered on provisioning actually *cheapen* the labor that moves to regional markets, as day or casual workers can work for less money.

Yet the Zapatistas have made tremendous efforts to develop structures and institutions for self-provisioning on the household and community levels. Zapatista territory is predominantly cooperative and communal, and much of its surplus is collectively distributed. Therefore, exilic economic activities are *contradictory substantive practices*: anti-capital in certain respects but supportive of capital in others; both self-provisioning and producing for external markets. The crucial question before the Zapatistas is whether and how they can develop those activities that might strengthen their position of autonomy from regional and world-capitalism.

Undoubtedly, NGO involvement in Zapatista affairs produces new contradictions. Some anthropologists even compare those NGO projects with rural development programs of the Mexican state, which the PRI used for decades to influence people in rural Chiapas. On a world scale, this is what the World Bank and other international financial organizations understand as development: such institutions use "development projects to integrate peripheral communities into the world market."[248]

Does the Zapatistas' relationship with NGOs imply the integration of exilic communities into the world market? Does NGO involvement "empower" a workforce to be integrated into the world market as producers and consumers? Or does cooperation with NGOs who are sympathetic to exilic struggle and vetted by the exilic organization help indigenous communities *avoid* mainstream "development" and deal with the outside world on their own terms? Exilic spaces like those in Chiapas require research that examines these exilic tensions, and the limits of self-organizing possibilities, in their full variation and regularity.

Even if contradictory substantive practices are more empowering than disempowering on balance, tensions remain. Barmeyer's research points to at least three areas of tension: the partisan involvement of NGOs (1994–97), the relationship between NGOs and local communities (1997–2003), and the introduction of capitalist models of production (2003–present).[249]

The partisanship of NGOs can go too far. Water systems built by NGOs like SHOXEL, in villages with fluctuating affiliations, may instigate serious communal divisions. If affiliations are fluctuating, then building a large water system that delivers water to Zapatistas but not to the PRIstas can worsen intercommunal conflict and prevent the potential return of former exiles. Sometimes promised NGO projects never materialize, which reflects poorly on the Zapatistas, caught in a competition with state social programs.

There are many poignant examples of tensions caused by relationships between exiles and NGOs. Where international solidarity activists tend to be sensitive to local *usos y costumbres* when integrating locals into a project and developing long-term relationships, this is not always true of NGOs.[250] In one case, a salaried NGO worker noticed that dry-compost latrines were highly sought after once they were introduced to the communities. Instead of facilitating their introduction through exilic channels, he started his own business to supply them.[251] The replacement of one kind of extra-space loyalty with another is not without complications, even when the state is replaced by supposedly sympathetic NGOs.

Exilic polities can also foster divisions and clientelism. Barmeyer observed that whenever a group of experts got privileged access to information, material, and money, there was a danger of breeding new elites or power brokers who could undermine exilic democracy.[252] Just giving cash to a villager to spend on subsistence commodities hardly seems like a new indigenous elite in formation, but it can have detrimental repercussions on the balance of power in the community.

Another source of exilic tension is the fact that many NGOs and solidarity activists "adopted" the most accessible and colorful Zapatista zones, such as mountainous Oventic, creating inequalities in the distribution of the solidarity aid between regions. Professional NGO managers have to be observant of funding realities; the competition is fierce and is often not based on need but exposure; thus, they choose cases to support that ensure their own survival.[253] Many roadless villages therefore find themselves "off the solidarity grid."

Internationals can also bring negative externalities. The real or imaginary world of a revolutionary holiday in a rural utopia, with unlimited cellular calls, uninterrupted electricity and internet, and so on, is attractive to many young visitors. In 2004, at the beginning of the period of *caracoles*, a Zapatista activist who coordinates the building of water systems complained to us about how the leadership of many *caracoles* was spending money on communications towers, ostensibly to satisfy the limitless appetite of visitors to "be connected" when the money could have been used to serve the basic needs of the communities. However, this is not always a one-way relationship. Barmeyer describes an experience of one community that resisted the creation of a lockable private space in a newly built bathroom, thus embracing a new technology without cultural impositions brought by solidarity water workers.[254]

Other visiting activists encounter negative local reactions to their attempts to support feminism. Their efforts to hold women-only workshops are often frustrated by male-dominated assemblies. Despite the insistence of the visitors, the workshops are often gender mixed because the assembly fears splits in the communities. The feminist group COLEM reportedly organized a gender-mixed workshop in a Zapatista village in the mid-1990s. Their talk about patriarchal exploitation left the audience in a great deal of distress. The organization was eventually expelled from Zapatista territory on the basis that it had incited "gender war."[255]

Market integration also reveals the contradictory nature of exilic substantive practices. Some NGOs assist women in setting up cooperative artisanal workshops with the aim of enhancing women's empowerment. The products are sold in Mexico City or in solidarity markets in the United States or Europe. Zapatista coffee is also distributed worldwide through a solidarity network. These activities can indeed be locally empowering, but they can have negative impacts, too. Members of coffee cooperatives have been known to hire landless seasonal workers from other regions, which threatens both community cohesion and collectivity. Some of the more successful Zapatista coffee-producing villages left the movement following success in exporting their organic coffee to Europe.[256] Nevertheless, products sold on the capitalist market may still have a positive impact if the production process is collective. Not only that, but indigenous women have a choice other than leaving to find work in multinational corporations. Work in local, community-based collectives provides them with skills they would not be able to acquire in the narrow patriarchal context of the village.

With regard to visitors and their projects, Zapatistas say proudly that "our first answer is 'yes,' then we talk about whether there are reasons to say 'no'" (personal information). After the 2003 reform, however, Zapatista communities began to say "no" more often. Increasingly, the refusal came from local communities themselves. This gives reason for cautious optimism. If it is desirable for Zapatista communities to become self-sufficient, or at least far less reliant on extra-space help, then they must find ways to wean themselves from their reliance on NGOs and solidarity groups. Barmeyer proposes that "alternative development projects that prove to be both successful and sustainable in the sense that locals can maintain them without further input could well become organizational models for a whole society." He suggests that this would be even easier if, for example, the communities of Chiapas gained control over the resources in their territories, including "oil, hydroelectricity, minerals, and pharmaceutical resources, and also over the yields of an environmentally and socially responsible tourism."[257] The Zapatista reforms of 2003 indicate that the Zapatistas are aware of the tensions involved in external dependencies, even those that do not involve the Mexican state.

The first steps to restructure the relationships between NGOs and the rebel municipalities date to 2002, after the subject was debated in Zapatista municipal councils. Kaufman and Barmeyer speak of two positions in the debates: one favored centralized administration and the other, which was adopted, favored local control over outside projects.[258] *Juntas de buen gobierno* now coordinate solidarity and NGO projects. Regional *juntas* and municipal autonomous councils review them to decide on the terms of their implementation. One interesting innovation is a community tax amounting to 10 percent of the total cost of the project, which is redistributed to other communities in the region, chosen by the *juntas*, "to balance out the economic development throughout Zapatista territory."[259] In addition, surpluses or bonuses for the sale of products from cooperatives are to be made available to *juntas* for distribution "to help those compañeros who do not receive any kind of aid."[260]

To conclude, cooperative practices predominate in exilic Chiapas. Production consists of autonomous, self-provisioning activities, and the institution of exilic authority protects collective rights over the surplus, safeguarding the community against private accumulation and the resurgence of inequalities. Yet undemocratic tendencies are still present, patriarchy is resistant to change, and there are still inequalities, some of which are tied to the persistence or reappearance of private property.

The Zapatista economy can hardly "de-link" from world-capitalism, even though Zapatista society has largely de-linked from the Mexican state. Zapatista economic activities are contradictory substantive practices, anti-capital in certain respects, supportive of capital in others. Observers who paint a rosy picture of "complete autonomy" in the Zapatista territory do no favors to the exilic project. The reality is often messy, contradictory, and confusing. Are *juntas de buen gobierno* going to eliminate all the inequalities and tensions that produce *el mal gobierno*? Probably not. Is the exilic reform from 2003 enough to curb tendencies of possible exilic disintegration? It is too soon to tell.

CONCLUSIONS

Despite extreme differences in historical time and external conditions of exile, Zapatistas and Cossacks display interesting similarities. These indicate, as Kropotkin argued, that people who are faced with bad government and institutions of social regulation will try to produce alternative institutions of mutual aid and autonomy. Yet there are also instructive differences in the two cases that are not just due to different historical times but also to different relations with the state and capital, and therefore different strategies for dealing with them.

For a time, the Cossacks had bargaining power. Not only were they in a unique position to protect the nascent Russian state from external threats, but they also inhabited a territory that itself posed a threat to that state, and therefore the state had real interests in making a loyalty bargain with them that was in both sides' mutual interest. Mayans, on the other hand, are forgotten rather than useful. Even worse, they are in the way of ranchers and resource hunters who see in the Lacandon rainforest a *terra nullius* that from their perspective should be opened to exploitation. It is no surprise, especially in the age of neoliberalism, that the Mexican state favors the fortune hunters over the exiles. Thus, the Zapatistas' ability to strike a favorable loyalty bargain with the state is limited. They achieved some power through voice and the state, failing to suppress that voice by military force alone, was willing to probe the possibilities of a bargain in the form of a peace accord. But the Mexican government apparently never intended to follow through on the bargain, leaving the Zapatistas no choice but to look elsewhere for partners. They found them in national and international civil society.

Exit-without-loyalty created resource problems for the Zapatistas, but it also enabled them to avoid the recapturing strategies employed by Muscovy against the Cossacks, strategies that eventually led to the end of Cossack autonomy. Instead, the Zapatistas faced scarcity after implementing internal changes that improved direct democracy *and* self-provisioning of the community, especially in education and health but also in key material infrastructures like water. They explicitly spurned the state by turning to other providers. In contrast to Cossack society, which faced the problem where the state uses subsidies as leverage and sponsors loyal factions against the autonomists, Zapatista society has been based on autonomy. Without it, exile would not mean anything. Instead of the state, the Zapatistas had to find new ways to secure resources, through a loyalty bargain that would not threaten autonomy. Whenever their bargain with civil society threatened the solidarity of the community, the exiles rather masterfully changed the bargain, sometimes taking advantage of a narrative that insists that activists and donors are serving the needs of their target communities (the Zapatista communities) rather than the other way around.

Exilic economic activities, while substantive and tending toward mutual aid, are always both inside and outside of regional and global economic processes, never totally independent. We have seen this with respect to the importance of getting exports into markets, such as solidarity or fair-trade markets, for coffee, handicrafts, and other products. But communities have also found it necessary to purchase market inputs for exilic economic activities. The communities have tried to overcome this market dependence for many infrastructural goods and services but also for some consumer goods such as boots and other leather goods.

Yet problems with de-linking from world-economic processes have been exacerbated by changing world-systems trends such as the sudden rise in emigration, especially among youth. Even here the balance is unclear: remittances can be good, but the loss of youth could be fatal to communities. Some have suggested that the Other Campaign is partly an attempt to avoid the exit-without-resources trap. Like Stenka Razin, the Zapatistas apparently decided that their exilic community can only move forward if it brings other Mexican communities in with it. If there can be no "socialism in one country," can there be "exile in one territory"? Unfortunately the results of the Other Campaign have not been too favorable thus far, even though there is considerable sympathy with the Zapatistas throughout Mexico and a growing number of autonomy movements in other states, such as Oaxaca and Guerrero. La Otra is a high-risk strategy; if it eventually succeeds, the question arises whether the Zapatistas can outlive the growing pains experienced by other exilic communities.

Perhaps the most important result of our study of the Zapatistas is that they give some hope that exit-with-autonomy is still possible, even in a world-system that has become more and more hostile to such experiments.

Both the Cossacks and Zapatistas are examples of voluntary exile, one losing its autonomy over time and the other (so far) maintaining and even strengthening it in important ways. But what of involuntary exile? We now turn to an example where exile is forced and exiles are under heavy state control and discipline, even going so far as to try and keep the exiles in strict isolation from one another. Can a society built on principles of mutual aid and solidarity be built in such extreme circumstances as long-term prison isolation, and among petty criminals, drug dealers, and murderers?

FIVE

Forced Exile

PRISON SOLIDARITY

SO FAR WE HAVE EXAMINED a historical case where the conditions of the world-economy and the emerging states within it provided both the reason and the opportunity for escape. The open geographical spaces of the eastern European steppe and frictions of territory made successful escape possible, while exilic Cossacks developed an economy of escape based on cattle herding and raiding. The long historical experience of Cossack exilic life made it possible for us to follow a change in what we have termed a "loyalty bargain" with the Russian state. Renegotiating this bargain in the context of a changing world-economy worked to the advantage of the core power and produced a pattern of change: from exit-with-autonomy and exit-with-resources, to exit-without-autonomy, to autonomy-without-exit. This long historical pattern suggested that exilic communities may face special and possibly increasing difficulties when they enter such loyalty bargains with dominant states, whose built-in advantages wear away exilic autonomy as bargains are remade again and again in the context of the changing conditions of the world-system. These problems appear to be tied to state power and to the rhythms of development of the world-capitalist system, leaving open the question of whether the long-term survival of exilic communities and practices depends on the undoing of capitalism. They also suggest that tensions such as class formation related to changing economic opportunities may threaten the solidarity of exilic communities.

Our second example was a contemporary one: the Zapatistas of southeastern Mexico. Again, we see two remarkable features. One of these is the tenacity with which an exilic community clings to practices and institutions of mutual aid in the face of an environment of possessive individualism: in this case, an increasingly neoliberal Mexican state and local land regime that aimed to destroy the institutions of communalism, the *ejidos* that were won in the Mexican Revolution. While the *ejido* existed more in promise than in fact, the attempts of the Mexican state to undermine it, in the context of an emergent North American free-trade regime, mobilized indigenous groups not only to save it but also to make it meaningful by building a society based on mutual aid, communal landholding, and direct democracy. But another feature of Zapatismo has been the difficulties associated with its strategic dependence on extra-space actors. External supporters make demands on the movement—a problem that the Zapatistas sought to ease by reforms associated with the creation of the *juntas de buen gobierno* in 2004. Further, a paucity of resources forces many Zapatista children to migrate regionally and even to North America in search of work. We can admire the creativity and perseverance of the Zapatista community, but we must also recognize the dangers and restrictions that they face.

Our third case is quite different from the others. It may seem counterintuitive, but some of the most common and utopian experiences in exilic community formation in recent times have been developed by prisoners (especially, but not exclusively, political prisoners). These are cases of forced exile and incomplete escape. In this chapter we examine such prisoner experiments generally, but then focus in detail on the experiences of Irish political prisoners in the "blanket protest" in Long Kesh Prison outside of Belfast during the late 1970s (a prototypical case of a developed exilic community), Turkish/Kurdish prisoners in "F-type prisons" since 2000 (a largely quashed exilic experience), and US supermax prisoners since the 1980s (sporadic and partial but hopeful experiences).

PRISONS AND EXILE

Before embarking on our analysis of isolated prisoners as exilic communities, let us briefly return to concepts that we mentioned in chapters 1 and 2. The first is Goffman's concept of *stripping*.[1] For reasons we have already outlined, we find this more fruitful than Agamben's concept of *bare life*.[2] It is in prison that the starkest form of stripping occurs: clothes and other items are literally taken away, to be replaced by institutional uniforms; the day is filled with prescribed work and uses of time and space. The prison is meant, at least in theory, to transform identity and produce a new subjectivity. Yet prisoners not only resist this subjugation but often build upon the advantages of stripping to create their own subjectivities. They tattoo, they paint, they write, they *congregate*. As one reviewer of this volume put it to us, this is a contest over what kind of human beings are to be produced: those who are committed to possessive individualism or those committed to mutual aid.

Perhaps nowhere is this battle fought more directly than in prisons. It is the same essential conflict that we have observed among Cossacks and Zapatistas, yet carried out in more direct, almost laboratory conditions. Among prisons, perhaps nowhere is the battle fought as directly as in institutions of solitary confinement such as contemporary security housing units (SHUs) in the US, where the state deposits captives who refuse to take on institutional identities of individualism, conformity, and snitching. Since at least the 1960s, the US prison system has promoted an intense campaign of behavior modification that was explicitly modeled on Chinese brainwashing techniques reportedly used during the Korean War.[3] Yet many prisoners successfully resisted behavior modification and engaged in mutual aid instead of individualism. The state branded these people the "worst of the worst" and "put them away" into deeper storage. Mumia Abu Jamal has recorded the tendency of prison authorities to punish jailhouse lawyers, for instance, by placing them in long-term isolation.[4] Many prisoners in the first modern US supermax, Marion Federal Penitentiary, which went into permanent lockdown in 1983, were sent there for organizing work stoppages.

This raises a question that we often hear when presenting the case that prisoners are exiles. How is prison "living at the edge of capitalism"? Are not prisons deep in the *heart* of capitalism, as institutions that, in Foucault's words, reproduce delinquency and thereby help contemporary capitalism function by creating a justification for the use of state power against its citizens? The deeper you go into the prison, into higher and higher levels of security, are you not traveling deeper into the heart of capitalism?

While we have taken issue with Foucault on his conception of "the gaze" and its demobilizing effects on prisoners, his analysis of "delinquent society" is compelling.[5] Nonetheless, we defend our conception that prisons, especially isolating "superprisons" like the H-Blocks in Northern Ireland or Pelican Bay in California, are indeed at the edges of capitalism. They are distinctly cut off from normal society by their placement behind walls. More importantly, they represent a form of *structural exile*, where the normal rules of citizenship and market participation are swept aside in favor of alternative rules of provisioning and production of community. Even in the age of prison privatization, prisoners in isolation rarely work; they in no way participate in the market through waged labor. Their basic needs are provided by the state, in an act of redistribution, but they must procure many other things largely outside of the market. The most important of these may be sociability and community, rather than material objects.

Moreover, isolation is a place where prisoners are stored. As a Kurdish prisoner in Turkey told us, it is less a world of "the gaze" than a return to the ancient practice of throwing incorrigibles or political enemies into a well, out of sight, into a state of "temporary death."[6] With respect to capitalism, solitary confinement is an "edge" created in the very middle. Braudel's conception of the "black hole" is perhaps most apt here,[7] where cellular isolation units are a sort of *event horizon* with respect to both the state and capitalism. What happens beyond this event horizon? Do prisoners follow the rules of rational choice theory and the so-called "prisoners' dilemma" to pursue their own interests against those of their fellows? Or do they build societies that are based on mutual aid, in a way that has affinities to Cossack *liberty* or Zapatista *autonomy*?

These questions are directly connected with what we have called "world time." As we discussed in chapter 2, world time refers to cycles of accumulation and their associated divisions of labor and technologies of production and control. This in turn leads to changing hegemonic regimes and strategies for maintaining power, including how local or regional authorities try to impose control over populations. Most studies concentrate on the control of labor, but in the increasingly globalized age following the Second World War, and especially under neoliberalism, the control of huge sectors of the population who are excluded from access to formal work must also be considered.

Social movements and unrest, both in their intensity and their forms, are associated with these changes. Most importantly, connections can be drawn between changing world-systemic conditions and waves of political uprising, most notably in 1848 and 1968.[8] The latter wave of popular unrest, which actually began with the anticolonial and national liberation movements following the Second World War, directly motivated a wave of efforts to contain political movements in prisons. The most extreme reactions to political activism, regimes of isolation, occurred in the H-Blocks in Northern Ireland (which we discuss at length, below) and in responses to European leftist groups such as the Red Army Faction in Germany, whose members were placed in isolation in Stammheim Prison. In the United States, the first policy response to political activism—beginning with the Black Muslims but intensifying after the emergence of the Black Panther Party, the Black Liberation Army, and leftist groups[9]—was behavior modification, followed by mass long-term isolation after 1983.

The 1968 political uprising was associated with the loss of US hegemony (political, economic, and military dominance) across the world. At the systemic level, the reestablishment of stability in the system was attempted through the launch of what we have now come to know as neoliberalism, an important part of which was the elevation of "macroeconomic stability" to the highest priority even among social democrats. Attacks on government spending were and are especially acute with regard to programs for the poor. Thus, not only did the state require programs to fight the new left and national liberation movements, but it also had even greater requirements to deal with millions of (often urban) poor for whom there was no prospect of meaningful work and a disappearing safety net because of fiscal austerity.

The result was mass incarceration or, as Wacquant puts it, "punishing the poor."[10] Prisons became overcrowded, unmanageable, and often dominated by gangs that had been encouraged by the state as a way of (1) drawing support from more explicitly political prison movements and (2) controlling prisoners through a strategy of divide and rule. Long-term isolation became a convenient policy tool in countries like Turkey that still faced political insurgencies and in countries like the US that faced increasing problems of prison control as inmate numbers spiraled after the mid-1970s.[11] At the same time, a state- and media-driven ideology of possessive individualism became rampant.[12]

In this context, one may ask how the changing political economy moved the "event horizon" of structural exilic spaces within the heart of capitalism, in the highest security prisons, which, increasingly, became spaces of long-term isolation and extreme stripping. Central to answering this question is to observe what kind of societies, if any, prisoners build in isolation. Returning to our exilic definition of economy, do they expend their energies on creating community? Are the core relations of such communities based on solidarity and mutual aid rather than possessive individualism?

It is difficult for prisoners in strict isolation to mobilize the resources to build fully developed solidary communities, although perhaps the Irish prisoners we examine below have come closest. This is not to say, however, that prisoners cannot cross the barriers to sociability that states build in their attempts to isolate them. Time and again, prisoners with whom we have communicated have described a process that they variously call "waking up" (those who committed "ordinary crimes" from theft to drug dealing to murder) or "gaining consciousness" (those who committed politically motivated offenses). Whether in street gangs or political movements (or some combination thereof), these captives often lived by a "code" before prison, whereby certain actions such as snitching to gain personal advantage was considered wrong. Yet many were involved in petty actions for personal gain, or their motives for political affiliation were largely personal (they joined the *guerrilla* because of things the state did to *them* or to their loved ones). The process of "waking up" is one of intense consciousness transformation toward a collective ethos. For those involved in political movements, including armed guerrillas, the common story is how the prison experience gave them a political consciousness of *why* they are involved in struggle, a consciousness that is tied to a sense of shared responsibility or solidarity with a community that aims to create "another world," however they define that world and by whatever means they hope to get there. For others, it is an even more profound transformation that often involves a denial of the consumerist goals that motivated their earlier behavior. They often build a conception that they are part of a "prisoner class" that transcends groups such as gangs that are based primarily on ethnicity.[13]

Most political prisons have been open prisons, often of the type seen in old war movies. They encourage communal solidarity because inmates are enclosed in open spaces and left to their own devices, with limited resources that they can use creatively in mutual aid projects to enhance their own conditions; their solidarity is enhanced partly because they face a common enemy. As in Kropotkin's formulation, they are best able to survive a hostile environment by practicing mutual aid. Their propensity to do so is enhanced by their previous association in organizations where mutual aid is a distinguishing feature.

But the more recent exilic experiences in which we are particularly interested are new experiments in cellular confinement, often of prisoners who had previously been kept in open prison camps or at least in a general prison population where they enjoyed substantial freedom of movement and assembly. These solitary cellular regimes are experiences of "bare life," where the minimum of subsistence is guaranteed by the authorities (food, shelter, possibly rudimentary entertainment), and where other forms of exilic "production" (material things like tobacco and reading/writing materials, but especially solidary activities such as music, storytelling, and "education") are done surreptitiously through smuggling and the creation of autonomous "spaces" with the creative use of language and time. Perhaps ironically, cells that are meant to divide the prisoners are used as autonomous exilic spaces, beyond what Foucault refers to as "the gaze." Rather being isolated, prisoners use oral practices (often in their own languages: Irish, Kurdish, Basque) and surreptitious yet ingenious "delivery systems" to tie these autonomous spaces together and create a single solidary territory that is beyond the control of the authorities. As in other cases, governance is directly democratic and decisions are made by long discussions and consensus. Interestingly, if there is a "loyalty bargain," it is less likely to be with the authorities, who are required to provide a minimal subsistence regardless of the prisoners' behavior and who provide extra privileges in exchange for "good behavior" (loss of autonomy). As with the Zapatistas, the loyalty bargain will be made with movement members, family members, and civil society outside of the prison.

The dynamics of this exilic community are determined by internal conditions: first, the nature of the internal prison regime, including the expectations of authorities and the prison architecture; second, the past experiences of prisoners in their movements and in open prisons. And they are determined by external conditions: first, the dynamics of the political struggle between their movements and the state, which is also dependent on world time; second, on the loyalty bargains reached between prisoners and outsiders. An important question about this kind of exilic experience is the impact of "victory": winning better conditions, getting out of prison, and so forth. It may be that the bare-life conditions that encourage solidarity and exilic practices are necessary to sustain them. Once prisoners' conditions improve—for instance, they get access to material items such as televisions or they are released back into a "general population"—the exilic practices may also subside. Moreover, prison authorities (what amounts to "the state" in this context) may introduce privileges and penalties in ways that split the prisoners—they may manipulate their responses to prisoners' demands (often the basis of solidarity and mutual aid) in ways that favor certain prisoners over others.

This raises a disturbing general question about the sustainability of exilic spaces/practices under state and capitalist control: if economic and other conditions improve, for example, through processes we refer to as "development," are exilic (solidary, communalistic) practices likely to fade away? Are class or other divisions likely to reemerge? To what extent may the experiences of organizing life through solidarity and mutual aid carry over into less extreme circumstances?

Now, let us examine real experiences of solitary confinement and exilic formation. In particular, we want to address the nature and consequences of *stripping*, or *bare life*, on the formation of exilic communities of prisoners. Are spatial and other characteristics of prison isolation, including relations between inmates and staff, destructive or reinforcing of solidarity and mutual aid? What are the possibilities and limitations of bare life with regard to exilic formation? What do findings in prison environments mean for other exilic communities?

Over the past thirty to forty years there has been a tendency in some countries to introduce isolation as a way to deal with "recalcitrant" prisoners, especially those who are associated with political movements or (in the US) so-called gangs. A widely renowned example of this policy occurred in Northern Ireland after 1976, when the British government moved Irish Republican Army (IRA) and other political prisoners from open barracks to closed cellular confinement. This was primarily an attempt to criminalize armed insurgents by forcing them to wear prison uniforms and engage in prison work along with "ordinary decent criminals." But when IRA prisoners refused to cooperate, they were put into solitary confinement for twenty-four hours a day, seven days a week. Irish prisoners usually had one cell mate, so isolation was not total. But the prison authorities hoped that by isolating and separating the prisoners they would break them and end their use of imprisonment as a "school for terrorists." A number of countries followed the British example, the most consistent and harshest examples being the US supermax and the Turkish F-type prisons.

In 1983, US authorities placed the federal penitentiary at Marion, Illinois, in "permanent lockdown" for twenty-three years after a violent incident where two guards were killed. Since then, prison authorities have typically used prison uprisings or inmate violence as a pretext for moving prisoners who were identified as "gang leaders" or simply "troublemakers" from open confinement to isolation. Marion was followed by Pelican Bay State Prison in California, where prisoners in the security housing unit (SHU) are isolated for 22½ hours a day in windowless cells, spending the other 1½ hours "exercising" alone in a concrete bunker. By 2010, some eighty to one hundred thousand prisoners were held in isolation units in most states of the US, some of them for decades without contact with other living beings—human, animal, or plant. This form of imprisonment took on an explicitly political character after 2002 with the use of the Guantanamo Bay detention camp and extraordinary rendition as a way to deal with real and imagined enemy combatants. More recently, it spawned a series of protest events, including a work strike in Georgia and hunger strikes at Ohio State Penitentiary, at Pelican Bay in California, and at Menard State Prison in Illinois.

Turkey is the other case where isolation has been used as a primary strategy to fight political insurgence, in this case by leftist and Kurdish organizations. In 1987 the Turkish government introduced a pilot program of isolated imprisonment, but this was terminated after a successful hunger strike against the policy. Political prisoners remained in ward-style open prisons with considerable self-government until December 2000, when the Turkish army stormed twenty prisons in an operation code-named "return to life." The army forcibly removed 524 leftist and PKK prisoners from twenty ward-type prisons and transferred them into three new "F-type" prisons with isolated confinement. The operation was extremely violent; at least thirty prisoners (by official count—over one hundred in prisoners' accounts) died during the transfer, a fact that did not seem to overly disturb European Union human rights bodies, which openly encouraged the Turkish government to move to cellular isolation on the grounds that it would be "safer" for Turkish prisoners.[14] Since then leftist, Kurdish, right-wing Hezbollah, and mafia captives have been held in thirteen F-type prisons, where they live either singly or with two other prisoners. Each prison has 103 cells for three prisoners each and fifty-nine individual cells, with a total capacity of 368 inmates. The split-level three-man cells are 25m2. Each cell has a concrete outdoor yard of 50m2, surrounded by five-meter-high walls that block any contact with other prisoners. Single cells measure 11m2, including a partitioned bathroom of 1.5m2. Until recently, inmates saw only guards—having contact with no other prisoners except their cellmates. While the Turkish authorities repeatedly cite EU bodies that supported the transfers from wards to cellular prisons as being more humane, their admitted purpose in introducing isolation is to break up political prisoners so that they cannot organize or train cadres in prison. The head of the Turkish Prison Service assured a delegation of academics and activists in 2011 that no more F-type prisons would be built "because we know that people are naturally social and they need to be with other people." But when one of his aides was asked whether this meant the F-types might be closed one day, the answer was a firm "No! These are terrorists and if we let them start seeing each other they will start plotting again."[15]

THE IRISH "BLANKET PROTEST"

After a hunger strike by IRA prisoners in 1972, many of whom had been held without trial, the British government granted "special category" status to all internees and prisoners convicted of offenses related to the conflict in the north of Ireland. The prisoners were moved to Long Kesh Prison outside Belfast, where they lived in a series of "compounds," or "cages," that contained Quonset huts and other simple buildings. The prisoners, including now well-known figures such as Gerry Adams and Bobby Sands, self-organized education, work, recreation, food, and escape attempts. They used their relative freedom to raise their collective and individual consciousness about the nature of their struggle and their role in it.

As the IRA rebuilt their organization from within the prison, the British government changed strategy. All prisoners found guilty of offenses committed after March 1976 were stripped of special category status and committed to cellular confinement in the newly built "H-Blocks" of Long Kesh, now renamed "HM Prison, the Maze." Eventually, there were eight cell blocks built in the shape of an H, with twenty-five cells on each wing and an administrative area on the crossbar of the H, otherwise known as "the circle."

Many aspects of the new cellular arrangement closely resemble Goffman's description of the total institution. In degrading "initiation ceremonies," prison guards literally stripped the prisoner of his clothes and other belongings, including his name. After circling naked in front of prison staff, the new inmate was offered a prison uniform and a number. He was informed that he was not a political prisoner but an ordinary criminal. Once in their cells, prisoners were subjected to a structure of punishments and rewards. Rewards for conforming included the right to wear clothing (uniform), access to reading/writing materials and basic luxuries (candy bars, tobacco), association with other prisoners in common areas (including outdoors), access to radios and television, and extra packages and letters. Conforming was also rewarded by 50 percent reduction of sentence.

IRA prisoners who refused to wear the prison uniform were put into a cell without clothing, reading materials (except for a bible and a few religious pamphlets), pens, paper, or any appliances (such as a radio). The eight-by-ten-foot cells included only basic furniture: bunk bed, desk, and locker (all of which were later removed). The only personal items the prisoners were allowed were soap, toothpaste, a toothbrush, a hairbrush, and several packets of tissues a month (all except the tissues were later taken away). Having

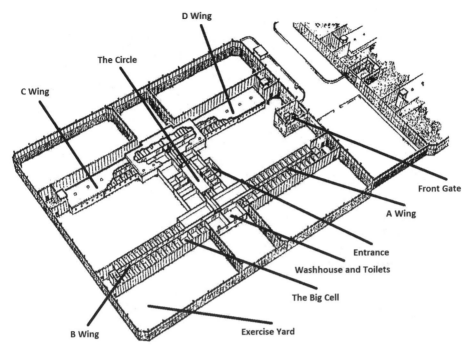

FIGURE 9. Diagram of an H-Block, Long Kesh Prison, Northern Ireland. Beyond the Pale Publications.

no clothing, the prisoners wore their blankets around their shoulders and waists, becoming known as "blanketmen."[16] They were kept in such bare lockup twenty-four hours a day, seven days a week; they were allowed out of their cells only to slop out (fill their water containers) and shower (later this privilege was withdrawn); on Sunday, they were allowed to attend mass in the block cafeteria, but only after they put on prison uniform trousers.

We will not recount in detail the nature of conflict between the prisoners and the prison authorities,[17] but a short summary will indicate how the blanketmen responded to conflict by intensifying and building new practices of mutual aid, very much in the manner Kropotkin describes with respect to communities who face severe environmental threats. From late 1976 until early 1978 the prisoners passively remained in their cells under the assumption that the authorities could not leave prisoners in such horrific conditions for an extended period and would eventually re-confer political prisoner status. Slowly, it began to dawn on them that this regime could go on indefinitely, and they embarked on several years of accelerated collective action.

FIGURE 10. IRA prisoners in an open cage, Long Kesh Prison, about 1975 (Bobby Sands appears on left in checkered sweater). Photograph reproduced with the permission of the Bobby Sands Trust.

FIGURE 11. Blanketmen in H-Block cell, Long Kesh Prison (note excrement smeared on walls). Photograph reproduced with the permission of the Bobby Sands Trust.

First, they began taking their allotted monthly visits, even though they had to wear a uniform to get them. In doing so, they appropriated prison spaces for collective purposes: smuggling communications with the outside movement as well as securing small comforts such as tobacco, ballpoint pen refills, cigarette papers (for writing on), reading materials (tiny writing on cigarette papers or rice paper), and plastic wrap (to keep things protected from bodily fluids when hidden inside the prisoner's body). They even smuggled miniaturized radios and cameras.

Visits and smuggling raised the collective's morale by improving their lives and heightened solidarity because each act of smuggling was a tremendous risk taken on behalf of the community. According to one prisoner, when there was tobacco on the wing, everyone was happy, whether they smoked or not.

Every time they left their cells, the prisoners contested new spaces. The authorities had come to enjoy total control over prison corridors and yards, yet now the blanketmen were appropriating them as routes for procuring things they wanted or needed to turn the wings into letter-writing factories, schools, and sites of cultural production.

Instead of acts of capitulation, visits were raids into enemy territory. Not only did prisoners get material things, they gained collective pride when the prison guards made it obvious that smuggling presented a major threat to their control (thus, "luxuries" were redefined as collective goods rather than as individual consumer items). The corridors became battlegrounds as guards introduced violent new measures such as strip searches to regain control. Some guards made a practice of probing a prisoner's anus with a gloved finger and then sticking the same finger into his mouth to search for contraband.[18]

In spring 1978, as the numbers of blanketmen rose, the battle over the corridors intensified. When the guards refused to let young prisoners out of their cells to shower, all of the blanketmen refused to leave their cells to wash. The guards reacted to the prisoners' refusal to wash by randomly sending prisoners to punishment cells. In a further act of solidarity, all of the prisoners refused to leave their cells to slop out.

Things rapidly deteriorated. After three weeks of escalating protest and punishment, Bobby Sands smuggled out the following account.

We received our dinner cold—it was served half an hour late. Dishes which we left out were used as missiles against us, before being later removed. Another comrade was taken hostage and shipped off to punishment block.

At 8:30 P.M. lock-up there was no point in putting out our water containers. The chamber pots were overflowing: We urinated into the boots, which
are part of the criminal uniform, and then threw the urine out the window.
On top of this the men had to leave excrement lying in a corner of the floor . . .
My own cell is stinking and my body has a sickening smell about it.[19]

Each Monday, the prisoners heightened their protest by introducing a new
action. The guards reacted to each act of intensification with greater punishment. The result was counterintuitive. Each new escalation raised the prisoners' morale because they felt they were winning their struggle against the
authorities. As one prisoner later recalled,

Morale was sky high. We felt that we were winning and for a change that
we, not the screws, had control over our lives because we dictated the pace of
events. The screws for their part were demoralized because they had no control
over what happened next. They dreaded Mondays because that was the day
that we kept upping the tempo of the protest by introducing something new.[20]

As the mess in the cells became unbearable, the guards removed all furniture except the sponge rubber mattresses from the cells. They searched the
cells and took away toothbrushes, toothpaste, combs, and rosary beads.
Eventually, the prison authorities took away all of the prisoners' material
possessions . . . except the rotting food and the human waste.

When the prisoners tried to get rid of *these*, the guards gave them back.
Prisoners emptied their urine under the doors and guards squeegeed it back
at night so the prisoners woke up on sopping wet foam mattresses. The prisoners threw their solid waste out the window but the guards threw it back.
In response, the blanketmen had to smear the excrement on the walls and
ceiling. Ironically, morale heightened once again as they found strength to
endure conditions that would have been unimaginable even a few days
previous.

How could an environment be more stripped? But of *what* were the blanketmen stripped? And what were the results? How did this situation affect
their ability to create institutions and practices of mutual aid?

THE H-BLOCKS AS EXILIC COMMUNITY

A counterintuitive dynamic was occurring where the more the authorities
repressed the prisoners, the more powerful the prisoners seemed to become.

Many ex-blanketmen indicate that their power lay precisely in the degree to which stripping the accoutrements of individual life left them with no other option than to respond collectively. The more they were stripped, the more they discussed, debated, planned, and *carried out* a collective response where they not only confronted the authorities in solidarity but also built remarkable practices that were based primarily on oral communication and that could only succeed if the collective participated as a whole. Bobby Sands told one of his cell mates that it was the closest they would ever come to living in true communism.[21] Extreme trust and sharing is a common element of the stories that ex-prisoners tell of this period.

Three exilic practices of solidary culture stand out: Irish language and other self-education, cultural production, and the "propaganda factory."

Irish language. Learning Irish gave the prisoners a sense of agency because they could communicate with confidence that the guards would not understand them. One of the most important positions among the blanketmen was that of "scorcher" (from the Irish word "*sceart*," "to shout"), a prisoner with fluent Irish and a strong voice who shouted back and forth at nighttime to other H-blocks, sharing news and coordinating the protest. "[Irish] was really a weapon," one prisoner said. "It wasn't just our culture or our language. And we employed it very effectively."[22]

At the end of 1977 only a few prisoners were fluent in Irish. Within eighteen months nearly four hundred blanketmen could speak it. Irish was spoken constantly. Most prisoners learned it by "picking up half-baked sounds from out the door," as one ex-blanketman describes it.[23] There were no blackboards, so teachers introduced new words by shouting their pronunciation and spelling. Prisoners scribbled words on the small clean spaces of their walls, using any writing implement they could secure, such as a zipper tab broken off of uniform trousers during a visit. The language was primarily reproduced orally, as children and communities do but not formal schools and "modern" literate cultures.

Irish lessons involved whole wings and were often followed by political debates or history lessons, all conducted verbally and from memory or bits of smuggled "research." The prisoners developed creative ways to learn through songs, Bible translations, and games. They encouraged each other to write poems, articles, and songs to share with each other and to smuggle out for publication.[24]

This was a different experience from the open "cages" of Long Kesh before the H-Blocks were built. The blanketmen, who enjoyed none of the teaching materials and supports of the cages, nonetheless achieved a much greater level of language fluency, one that could be accurately describe as an alternative, parallel community of Irish speakers. Without doubt, this level of solidarity was encouraged if not *caused* by the authorities' repression and particularly by the severe stripping of the standard commodities of English-speaking life and culture from the prisoners.

Cultural production. The Irish language was related to broader cultural production. The whole range of learning and production in the H-Blocks was largely oral. Poems and articles were shared orally. Bobby Sands memorized and recited his epic poem the "Crime of Castlereagh," more than one hundred verses adapted from Oscar Wilde's *Ballad of Reading Gaol*, before he wrote it down on cigarette papers that he kept hidden up his anus until he smuggled the poem out for publication.

Cultural performance was the highlight of each night. After the guards left, the prisoners distributed cigarettes and messages, shared news, and had political debates.[25] Without watches or clocks, they told the time by the night guard's "bell checks." He came on at nine o'clock, and every hour he pushed the security grille at the bottom of the wing to show that he had checked the cells. Time was measured by the first bell check at nine, the second at ten, and the third at eleven. After the third bell check the last business of the night was entertainment. Early on, this included simple entertainments like collective singing or bingo. As life became more stripped, the blanketmen invented new entertainments that resurrected the Irish oral storytelling tradition of the *shanachie* (or *seanchaí*, Irish for storyteller/historian). Their favorite nighttime activity became the "book at bedtime," where the best storytellers told a story after the guards left the wing. The *shanachie* pulled his mattress up to his cell door and shouted out his tale while the rest of the men lay, listening and sometimes providing a running commentary. All the surfaces in the prison were hard, so noises traveled. When the story was a good one and the storyteller was engaging, everyone got lost in the story as it wound on for nights on end.

Bobby Sands was widely regarded as one of the best storytellers. He told a range of stories about struggles for freedom, from the biography of Geronimo to the tale of a US marine deserter from Vietnam who was on the run from the forces of the US state. To the prisoners, these tales were about *them*, and how they could achieve inner freedom even as they lay isolated in their grim cells surrounded by barbed wire, concrete, and hostile prison guards.

Cultural production was tied to trust and solidarity. A prisoner describes when he first heard Bobby Sands sing a song: he announced that he had written a song and sang it at the top of his lungs, a bit off-key because of the effort he put into it. The prisoner thought about it and decided that Sands's off-key singing enhanced the song because he was in an environment where he would never have to fear embarrassment. The blanketmen trusted each other, and each man knew that anyone else on the wing would do *anything* for him. Sands contributed to the atmosphere of trust by laying himself bare to the others.

This was leading by doing. Sands smuggled out and published his first article within a month of arriving in the H-Blocks, and it was not long before dozens of prisoners were smuggling literally hundreds of stories, poems, and drawings out of the protesting blocks every week. Cultural output was an important way to build on the spaces that the blanketmen appropriated through collective confrontation with the authorities. They were building highly participative alternative structures of governance in their communities that aimed to build "now" the kind of social relations that they envisaged for a revolutionary future.

Propaganda factory. Collective cultural production was soon turned to another purpose in 1979 when a number of "leading" prisoners were moved together into a single H-Block, H-6. In H-6, Bobby Sands organized a writing network, coordinating it with an energetic group of about a dozen women who visited the jail several times a day to smuggle messages in and out and to smuggle in pen refills, cigarette papers, cling wrap, and miniature homemade radios.[26] Prisoners could send out messages in the morning and receive a reply from their movement that afternoon.

The new communications network helped to extend the struggle by getting the prisoners involved in "a production factory for comms." Each prisoner received lists of names and wrote several letters a day, combining boilerplate descriptions of their conditions with a personalized section that was tailored to the recipient. They wrote to hundreds of trade unionists, actors, writers, and musicians in various countries.[27]

Through this stream of communications, the blanketmen provided information for a support campaign outside of prison while they used their propaganda to convince the movement that the prison struggle was crucial to the overall struggle. Once the movement committed itself to supporting the prison protest, communications from the prison provided them with strategies of protest, campaign slogans, and even a utopian analysis of a political way forward where the movement would nominate prisoners for elected office and then use the legitimacy they gained from electoral victories to build parallel government in their communities, much as the prisoners were creating a solidary community within the prison walls.

Eventually, British prime minister Margaret Thatcher's unwillingness to recognize any form of political status led dozens of blanketmen to embark on two hunger strikes, in 1980 and 1981. Ten prisoners died, led by Bobby Sands, seemingly without achieving their objective of political status. Yet they won a clear moral victory, with the world's media overwhelmingly convinced, like the *New York Times*, that Bobby Sands, who won election as a member of the British parliament before he died, had "bested an implacable British prime minister." National parliaments honored the hunger strikers with resolutions and moments of silence.[28]

Most importantly for the history of exilic practice, the blanketmen confronted repression and created a solidary culture within the H-Blocks. It is doubtful that they could have achieved this by withdrawing into safe spaces to avoid confrontation This solidary culture of resistance was not just *built* into the context of a sustained episode of contention, but *fueled* by its very dynamic of confrontation and (repressive) response. The ability of insurgent prisoners to subvert the control of spaces by authorities, to create parallel material and symbolic uses of spaces, and to imperfectly control the pace and direction of contention, was critical. The blanketmen gained significant ground both by initiating confrontation with the authorities (raiding economy) and by building their own exilic community based on solidarity and mutual aid. Mortification, while horrific in many ways, heightened the blanketmen's sensitivity to their environment and to each other, strengthening their resistance beyond what they could have imagined at the outset of the prison conflict. Stripping the prisoners of their "personal identity kits" left the collective aspects of their identities for them to build on. This encouraged the spread of the Irish language and cultural production. Oral communication, learning, and storytelling increased their collective solidarity, morale, mutual trust, and sharing.

Because of their extreme isolation, construction of a loyalty bargain was especially important for the blanketmen to build and maintain an exilic community. In "normal" prison conditions, a loyalty bargain is usually struck with the authorities, whereby minimal subsistence (food, clothing, shelter) and a few luxuries (entertainment, education, recreation) are provided in return for the tacit agreement that the prisoners will obey certain rules set down by the authorities. This may involve wearing uniforms or performing prison work, but more importantly it involves keeping order in the prison. It also means agreeing to adopt an institutional identity that is defined by the authorities.

The usual signs of "exit" from such a bargain are acts of refusal by prisoners, such as work or hunger strikes. Day-to-day forms of exit might involve refusal to act individually by practicing acts of solidarity, such as jailhouse lawyering or organizing forms of self-organized education. The breakdown of a loyalty bargain is considered especially serious by authorities if such actions become collective and not just individual "adjustments" to prison discipline.

With the continued refusal of Irish political prisoners in the open regime to maintain order—prison breaks, military training, even burning down the prison—the British state moved to isolate them so that they could no longer disrupt the prison regime. The authorities proposed a new loyalty bargain: if they wore uniforms, performed prison work, and accepted the status of individualized "common criminals," they would receive rewards, many of which would usually be considered normal prison privileges. If not, they would be punished by placement in complete isolation and literal stripping of material essentials such as clothing, as described above.

With the refusal of the new loyalty bargain offered by the prison authorities, the prisoners had to seek a new one. Like the Zapatistas, once they refused the state they could only acquire things they needed or desired by forming new loyalty bargains with "civil society," including their movement outside of prison but also the wider public and supporters of human rights. This did not come free of charge.

Even as the blanketmen sank into the depths of the no-wash protest, prisoners' rights were surprisingly low on the IRA's agenda. The IRA leadership told them that they could not afford to divert resources from popular struggle into a prison support campaign, especially during a time of extreme repression. Says Gerry Adams:

I would have a view that prisoners should always take second place . . . People were being shot in the streets. People were being arrested on sight . . . and these areas were under very heavy occupation and people were living underground. So there was enough to be getting on with and those of us who wanted to try and build some sort of a popular movement, it was very difficult to do. It's very difficult to build open and democratic politics if you're on the run or if you're not able to meet and debate and have public manifestations and so on and so forth.[29]

The movement supported the prisoners through Sinn Féin's POW department, and the IRA added concrete support by attacking prison officers. But as far as a public campaign was concerned, the blanketmen had to rely largely on their own resources, including connections through their families with broader support movements and human rights activists in civil society.

Things changed somewhat after Adams was arrested on a charge of IRA membership and sent to the H-Blocks to await trial. In prison, he saw the conditions of the blanketmen at first hand. Before, he thought the blanketmen had voluntarily started putting their excrement on the walls to draw attention to themselves. Now, he realized that the horrid conditions in the H-Blocks were forced on them by the actions of the prison guards. When he was released due to lack of evidence, Adams successfully approached the movement's leadership with a proposal to build a full-fledged prisoners' support campaign.

In return for this heightened commitment, of course, the blanketmen were expected to show loyalty to the outside IRA leadership. The new smuggling operation brought materials and information into the H-Blocks but, just as importantly, messages smuggled in the other direction informed the IRA leadership what was going on and sought their approval and support for new initiatives and strategies of prison protest.

A most telling example of the limitations this bargain placed on the prisoners involved a hunger strike. At a critical point in 1979, the blanketmen decided that the best way to move the protest forward was through a hunger strike. They told the movement of their plans and immediately came under severe pressure not just from the IRA but from civil society, including the highest representatives of the Catholic Church, to postpone a hunger strike while political and religious authorities attempted to negotiate a bargain with the Thatcher government in London to grant the prisoners' demands (even though the prisoners had little or no expectation that such negotiations would achieve anything). In an explicit example of the loyalty bargain,

Catholic archbishop (later cardinal) Tomás O Fiaich made a statement that compared the prison conditions in the H-Blocks to the "sewers of Calcutta," giving the prisoners unprecedented moral legitimacy; in return, the prisoners had to accede to joint pressures by the IRA and Catholic leaders to moderate their protest campaign while the archbishop negotiated with Thatcher.

Generally, prisoners acceded to the loyalty arrangement, but the complexities of the communication channels enabled them to "avoid loyalty" in certain circumstances when they were in critical disagreement with outside forces. On one occasion, the IRA instructed young prisoners to "resist" guards if they tried to forcibly and violently wash them with harsh brushes. But commanding officers in the prison decided that such a course of action would draw unacceptable violence against the prisoners and possibly break their resistance; they simply "did not hear" the instruction when it was shouted to them from another H-Block.[30] At another critical moment between the two hunger strikes of 1980 and 1981, the blanketmen sent out word to the IRA leadership that they intended to wreck their cells if the prison authorities refused to let them wear their own clothes. This would be the prelude to launching a second hunger strike. The IRA frantically sent smuggled communications through a priest telling them not to do so. The blanketmen "did not receive the communications in time" and wrecked their cells anyway, a critical move that led to the hunger strike in which ten prisoners died.[31]

The use of priests and family members to smuggle tobacco, writing materials, and messages also involved maintaining careful tacit and explicit rules: certain priests, for instance, would not carry messages that had operational details for the IRA. In wider civil society, care had to be taken to express the prisoners' situation in human rights terms rather than as a part of a liberation struggle. To Irish American supporters, the prisoners had to present themselves as oppressed Irish nationalists without a whiff of Marxism, whereas to supporters elsewhere their message of Marxist national liberation was explicit. This was reflected in the "propaganda factory" of smuggled letters to influential people around the world. One prisoner wrote to a US journalist about how his founding fathers had fought the British for independence and the Irish had as much right to fight for theirs. Then he wrote to Pravda about the working-class struggle against imperialism and called his reader "comrade."

As with the Zapatistas, the blanketmen's loyalty bargain with civil society provided material support and public legitimacy to the exilic space and its campaign for autonomy; but this carried a price that moderated the prisoners' strategic options at key points. Also like the Zapatistas, the blanketmen used remarkable creativity to intensify their exilic autonomy by introducing new forms of community-building activities, mostly through oral sharing, while moderating the degree to which they communicated their real aims to the outside world.

NORTHERN IRELAND: SOME INITIAL CONCLUSIONS

The following propositions follow from our review of exilic practices and prison isolation in Northern Ireland.

First, in certain conditions *stripping can be conducive to a collective culture of resistance* because it removes the distractions of individualized consumer life. "Bare life" conditions create in prisoners a desire to recover what has been lost, and the most effective way to do this may be through building a *collective* culture based on mutual aid.

Second, mutual aid appears to be strengthened by a combination of collective-culture building (an *us* identity) *and* resistance (a shared *us-them* dichotomy) where prisoners appropriate spaces and win victories, thus achieving a sense of *collective* agency that encourages them to face further risks or to expend energy building the exilic community. In certain conditions, both the positive (collective-building) and negative (conflict) activities have a sort of "looping" effect, so that collective life intensifies over time.

Yet the battle of will between imprisoned exiles and state authorities takes place at different levels: prison administration, much less government itself, is hardly a monolith. Thus, while a battle of wills was under way between the blanketmen and the prison administration, conflict emerged in larger contexts: first, the Northern Irish (Protestant) state argued that a loss to the blanketmen would weaken the union with Britain and, thereby, the basis of its power. At key points, when compromise might have been achieved between the blanketmen and liberal sections of the British security apparatus, parties within the Northern Irish state intervened to sabotage any solution that included compromise with the prisoners.[32] At an even higher level, the blanketmen were operating in a context of Prime Minister Thatcher's efforts to launch what would become known as neoliberalism. From 1979 to 1981, the blanket protest and especially the hunger strike led by Bobby Sands became a personal battle between Thatcher and the Irish prisoners.

One reading of that period, suggested by a reviewer of an earlier draft of this volume, is that this battle of wills was a tragic personal loss for Sands and his comrades, including the ten men who died on hunger strike, and a triumph for Thatcher that parallels the more profound triumph of her project of neoliberalism. We disagree. The hunger strike was a moral victory for the blanketmen and especially for Sands, who was elected to the British parliament while he was dying, receiving a larger vote total than Thatcher ever received; it was also the beginning of a revitalization of the IRA that forced the British government into peace compromises in the 1990s. Moreover, it was a step toward the restoration of political status, the main demand of the blanketmen, which was achieved within months of the end of the hunger strike. According to a leading participant, hunger striker, and analyst of prison life during and after the blanket protest, the period following the hunger strikes was one where the exilic community of prisoners developed new practices of self-government that in many ways paralleled the earlier "open" regime of the cages, but with an intensified understanding of mutual aid made possible only by living "on the blanket" and engaging in community-building and radical participative pedagogy.[33]

Centralized party discipline can discourage participation and create a passive or reactive attitude among cadres, who await orders from above. We propose that the success of the blanketmen was partly due to the fact that the movement, especially in prison, had already been reformed to make decision making more participative and horizontal. This reform had taken place during the period of open imprisonment, and it positively affected the ability of isolated prisoners to form solidary collectives based on oral communication. However, if repression is severe enough—or even if the architecture of isolation is different—the collective may simply be defeated and unable to win significant victories on which to build solidarity.

Thus, institutional context is important. The British authorities in the 1970s and 1980s were affected to a reasonable extent by public and especially international opinion. While they publicly ignored or denied allegations of torture by the International Court of Human Rights and Amnesty International, they were unable to introduce severe *enough* repression to defeat the prisoners (or, indeed, the IRA in general). Other regimes (US, Turkey) have had the advantage of learning from the British experience in Ireland and have made important innovations to their regimes of isolation. We now turn to those regimes.

Mass long-term cellular isolation of political captives in Turkey began in December 2000, when more than one thousand political prisoners were transferred from ward-type prisons to new "F-type" prisons in a violent operation in which ten thousand Turkish soldiers invaded forty-eight prisons.[34] The operation, ironically named "Return to Life" by the Turkish government, left at least thirty-one prisoners and two soldiers dead and wounded more than four hundred prisoners.[35] In the new F-type prisons, captives are kept in one-person and three-person cells with no inter-cell contact and extremely limited visits with family and approved contacts.[36]

Political imprisonment in Turkey is basically split between leftists, Kurds, and right-wing Islamists. The Revolutionary Left (RL; formally, the Revolutionary People's Liberation Party-Front, or in Turkish, Devrimci Halk Kurtuluş Partisi-Cephesi [DHKP/C]) was a product of several splits on the Turkish left. The party became very strong in the mid-1990s and as a result was the major target of state repression. Most of its leadership was imprisoned. In prison, RL maintained a highly centralized and disciplined organization. It conducted heavy and open surveillance of its own members even to the extent that when a member had a visit with his family another member of the organization would go along to listen. Education was mandatory; the readings and topics of discussion were mandated by the leadership ("Marx, Lenin, Stalin," says one former prisoner).[37] Prisoners were not encouraged to read outside of the approved canon. While the members appear to have had strong commitment and solidarity, trust was enforced by internal party surveillance and discipline.

The Kurdish Workers' Party (PKK), founded in 1984 to wage armed struggle for an independent Kurdish region, is the largest insurgent group in Turkey. While the PKK is hardly democratic to the degree that the IRA was in Northern Irish prisons, it is less centrally commanded and appeals more to trust among members than the Revolutionary Left. In addition, prisoners never played a very strong role in PKK ideological development or strategy, and the main site of leadership, training, and education was always "up the mountain," in the guerrilla cadre.[38]

Between the two organizations there were clear differences in attitudes toward imprisonment. Before the transfer to isolation in F-type prisons, the RL erected signs in its prison wings, calling them "reclaimed land." They beat up guards who came into the wards, took other guards hostage, and barricaded the main doors to their wings. The PKK, on the other hand, considering themselves to be prisoners of war, claimed that "no land in prison can be free … These are not our houses, so we will not struggle against them here."[39] They talked with prison officers if they thought they could win concessions or gather intelligence from them.

As a result, the two organizations had different perceptions of the threat posed by the transfer to isolation in F-type prisons. For the RL, the transfer was an extreme threat, possibly fatal to the movement, because its leadership was so concentrated in prison. Without free association, it would be impossible to organize training and education and to maintain the degree of communication with the outside that was necessary for the leadership to guide the movement.

The "blanketmen" in the H-Blocks effectively turned the threat of isolation into opportunity through their escalating and creative resistance, through their ability to communicate with their supporters on the outside by smuggling, and especially by their development of an exilic community based on mutual aid, solidarity, and participation. The RL, on the other hand, only saw threat and therefore opposed the new F-type regime without really trying to build a society within it.[40] At first, this entailed physical resistance to the transfer, but the force used by the state was too violent and overwhelming. Once its prisoners were in the F-type prisons, the RL's only real weapon was to embark on a hunger strike ("death fast," in their terminology). Possibly, they expected that the state would be unable to withstand the moral force of multiple deaths in its jails or that the international community would put pressure on the Turkish state to liberalize its prison regime. This did not happen, and by the time the hunger strike ended in 2007, more than 120 RL members and supporters were dead from hunger strikes or associated events. Surviving RL prisoners remain in isolation. Our respondents from the RL view the hunger strike as a total defeat and the introduction of F-type prisons as a complete victory by the state over the left, although many other members would not concede defeat.[41]

The RL's predicament is partly of their own making. They never went through an internal democratization like IRA prisoners in Northern Ireland but remained highly centralized. In this sense they are unlike other prison groups analyzed here, suggesting that exilic groups must have direct democracy to survive and that there are necessary connections between mutual aid institutions/practices and direct democracy. Because of its centralization, once the RL's rank and file were split off from the leadership by cellular

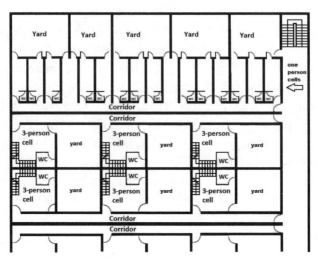

FIGURE 12. Floor plan of F-type prison, Turkey. Denis O'Hearn.

confinement, they could not reproduce collective activities because there was less participation and trust.

Yet their real problem lay in the architecture of the F-type prison. The blanketmen could communicate and celebrate regularly with everyone on a wing (fifty prisoners in twenty-five cells) by oral communication and by sending messages through the walls and under doors. They could communicate directly with prisoners in other wings and even blocks by shouting in Irish. And they built other structures of communication through weekly meetings at mass and through visits and smuggling. In the F-types, each group of three prisoners in a "living area" is almost completely blocked off from other prisoners. They can communicate with difficulty by tapping or shouting through certain pipes and by throwing messages from one exercise yard to another in plastic bottles. But the regular oral interchange that enabled the blanketmen to create a solidary *exilic* community is impossible. This raises the proposition that there must be a minimum population of regularly communicating exiles for an exilic community and solidary culture to be meaningfully developed.

The PKK is more pragmatic than the RL about the F-type prison regime. While they oppose and resist isolation and take actions against abuses by prison authorities, they are more tactical than principled in their actions. They may go on hunger strike but they do not "death fast." They may fight prison guards but are more likely to retreat in order to fight again another day. While RL prisoners physically resisted the "return to life" offensive for two days, to the point of exhaustion and at considerable cost of life and limb, PKK prisoners went quietly to the F-types.[42]

Despite the architecture of isolation, PKK prisoners have over the years achieved some success in improving communications within the F-type prisons and in winning limited association outside of their cells. Yet their day-to-day life is still restricted to at most three prisoners, and communication with others is achieved mainly by throwing notes placed in plastic bottles from one cell's courtyard to the next. This undoubtedly restricts their ability to develop a solidary culture, to organize among themselves in prison, or to coordinate any prison struggle with the PKK campaign outside. The closest thing in F-type to the vibrant cultural life that Irish prisoners reported in the H-Blocks are nightly concerts or dramas, where prisoners go to their upstairs windows and shout or sing revolutionary and Kurdish songs as loudly as they can.

Both organizations successfully resisted the initial "ceremonies of mortification" by which authorities attempted to degrade them in the F-type prisons, but the effects of long-term isolation were harder to resist. The state tried to make them wear uniforms and do prison work, but they refused. The guards tried to force prisoners to go to the bottom floor of their two-story cells for inspections, but they refused. They adamantly protected their autonomy, but only in groups of three. Both groups of prisoners stage regular protests by banging on their cell doors and refusing to cooperate with authorities. The PKK tries to disrupt the regime by writing constant appeals; authorities must respond to each written appeal so the prisoners bombard them with appeals in order to disrupt the system. The RL, by contrast, stands on principle and refuses to engage the authorities through appeals. The most apparent difference is the two organizations' reactions to recent reforms that allow up to ten (usually, nine) prisoners to meet together for up to ten hours a week (but in practice much less). The PKK welcomes this, and its prisoners have used their periods of association to improve communications in the prison, to learn trades and handicrafts, and simply to ease daily life. But RL prisoners refuse to come out of their cells on the principle that to do so would be a capitulation to the prison authorities. Again, this is the opposite stance to that of the blanketmen, who used any opportunity to come out of the cells and broaden the struggle.

Despite very small victories, isolation remains a fact of life for both RL and PKK prisoners. Fear seems to hang in the air. One PKK respondent says that "the most common feature of F-type is the tense air, the expectation of attack." Yet isolation rather than fear appears to be the biggest threat to prison life. Prisoners report that life is very slow in F-type because of the monotony and lack of difference from one day to the next. Prisoners become naturally paranoid. Obviously they distrust the authorities. One PKK prisoner says it seemed that every time they began to like something the authorities would take it away. They started to watch the Discovery Channel on television; when the authorities found out that they liked it, they took it off the prison TV network. Yet most worrying to many prisoners is that they become suspicious or even paranoid of each other. Since there are three in a cell, one man usually gets left out of two-person activities or discussions.[43]

RL prisoner G movingly described to us how his mental health slowly deteriorated under isolation, leading to bouts of depression and severe paranoia. He eventually asked to be moved from a three-man cell to a single cell. "You know this is an effect of isolation but knowing it doesn't help," he recalls. "I wanted to be in the dark and alone. Later they allowed one guy [per cell] to have one musical instrument. It helped."[44]

As in the Irish case, pre-isolation experiences had a strong impact on how prisoners faced isolation. Both Turkish organizations were far less flexible, participative, and horizontally organized than the Irish prisoners and the IRA. The blanketmen had strong cultures of education, training, song, storytelling, and poetry. For the PKK, Kurdish language provided similar benefits to the Irish-language culture among IRA prisoners, but the lack of experience with participative horizontalism ill-prepared Turkish prisoners for the transfer to isolation.

This lack of participative experiences, coupled with severe limitations to collective life caused by the architecture of the F-types, made isolation a very different experience in Turkey than it was in Ireland. With respect to the left, isolation broke the movement. State control was so total that even the minimal communications necessary to create a culture of resistance were absent. To try and win rights to associate and communicate, RL prisoners and supporters embarked on a death fast for six years. They would have come off of the fast had the Turkish state simply knocked down a few walls and opened a few doors, so that eighteen instead of three prisoners could come together. Coupled with some organizational changes, this could have enabled the leftist prisoners to create a solidary exilic community. But the Turkish state held fast, many prisoners died, and strict isolation remains the pattern of their life.

The PKK did not try to break the system of isolation, but did fight to ameliorate it around the edges. The main centers of political and military action remained on the outside. They had limited success (with the help of human rights organizations, intellectual supporters, moderate politicians, etc.) in gaining the right to meet in small groups for a few hours each week. The authorities abuse this system by using a "go-slow" strategy, but such meetings do happen. In Ankara F-type #2 we saw considerable activity in workshops (woodworking, computers, art, metal shops, others), but we were told that political prisoners have less access to these workshops than nonpoliticals.

Prisoners have good access to TVs, stereos, and other consumer products from the prison commissaries (much better than we have observed in US supermax prisons). They also have weekly open visits with a restricted number of family members. Possibly, such access to consumer products demotivates prisoners in communal terms, encouraging individualist adjustments to prison life. In US supermaxes, we have spoken to politically aware prisoners who get rid of their TVs because they distract them from "serious" activities.

Despite these restrictions on exilic life, Turkish and Kurdish prisoners strive to create a collective life. They sing together as much as possible within the constraints of F-type. And one PKK prisoner we know, a political cartoonist, organized a remarkable Kurdish-language magazine (*Golik*) containing political cartoons and humor that is drawn or written by prisoners in isolation throughout Turkey. If the Turkish experience is the opposite of that in the H-Blocks in terms of the lack of production of exilic community and practices, F-type prisoners nonetheless find remarkable ways to produce collective institutions and practice mutual aid, however limited.

SUPERMAX AND THE SHU: ISOLATION AND THE
MAKING OF POLITICAL PRISONERS

The blanketmen in Long Kesh Prison, Northern Ireland, had an affinity for horizontal structures of participation and self-organization, a highly developed political consciousness, and a preexisting affinity for solidarity stemming from participation in political life before prison. To this, add the extreme degree to which prisoners were stripped of modern consumerist things and identities and were thus freed to construct new collective social relations based on mutual aid. The construction of an exilic community then depended on the prisoners' own actions, including their decision to come out of their cells and create an active campaign of prison resistance and smuggling, as well as the loyalty bargain they struck with their outside movement and with groups in civil society.

In Turkey, exilic life was stunted because of the limitations of centralized political ideology and the ability of the Turkish state to produce a prison architecture and prison practices that squelched the development of collective life, including oral communication. The Irish and Turkish cases may represent upper and lower limits of exilic life in prison isolation, the most and least developed. Now we turn our attention to isolated prisoners who face many restrictions but who have nonetheless achieved remarkable practices of mutual aid and solidarity: supermax prisoners in the United States.

Supermax prisons and prisons with internal security housing units (SHUs) are common at both the federal and state levels in the United States.[45] They are designed to hold prisoners in isolation from each other. Inmates in such prisons are held for up to twenty-three hours a day, seven days a week, totally isolated in a bare cell the size of a closet, often without windows. The other hour is spent alone in an exercise yard, usually a concrete bunker with an expanded metal grating or some other form of ceiling. In many cases prisoners can be moved through different areas of the prison by electronic doors so that they have little contact even with guards. There are no group activities or work, few educational opportunities, and generally no contact visits (prisoners sit behind a security-glass window, in chains, and are often strip-searched coming to and from visits even though they have no contact). Phone calls and visitation privileges are limited. While prisoners can have reading and writing materials and entertainment devices (TV, radio, CD player), these are limited and are sometimes granted as privileges or removed as punishment.

The authorities claim that this level of isolation is necessary where prisoners are violent and/or disruptive, although the first supermax in Marion federal prison in the state of Illinois held many prisoners whose main offense against the prison system was that they had gone on work strikes. Supermaxes do house prisoners who commit violent acts either against guards or other prisoners, but many prisoners are placed in isolation for practicing solidarity, for example, jailhouse lawyers who help other prisoners challenge their convictions or prison abuses against them. Many supermax prisoners in states like California are placed in long-term isolation because they have been judged to be "gang leaders." Again, their main "offense" is not that they built criminal enterprises in prisons or engaged in violence, but that they under-mined the stripping process, which is designed above all to individualize prisoners, to place them in competition with each other (for example by snitching to gain special rewards), and to force them to deny former friend-ships and associations in favor of institutionalized ones.

The strategy that led to supermax isolation in the US, *behavior modifica-tion*, was originally intended as an *alternative* to long-term isolation.[46] But since the 1990s isolation has been the US prison system's primary way of enforcing behavior modification or, more to the point, keeping those who *refuse* to modify their behavior in perpetual isolation. Today, most isolation units and supermaxes have "step-down" programs where individual prisoners have to prove that they have conformed or taken on an institutional mental-ity if they are to get back into the general prison population. In California, this has been done through a system called *debriefing*, where prisoners who have been accused by the state of gang affiliations or associations must snitch against other alleged gang members to get out of isolation. As a result, prison-ers who practice solidarity, who refuse to harm other prisoners in order to help themselves by snitching, are kept in perpetual isolation. Many have been in isolation for decades, never touching another living thing.

The rise of isolated imprisonment in the US was rapid and closely paral-leled the rise of mass incarceration. In 1984 only one prison was designated for long-term isolation: USP Marion, Illinois. A dozen years later there were fifty-five supermax units in thirty-five states holding more than seventy thou-sand prisoners in long-term isolation.[47]

We have corresponded with and visited twenty-six prisoners in super-maxes around the US, some of whom have been isolated for more than twenty-five years. While many of them feel stripped of relationships with family and friends, they are unwilling to turn on fellow inmates (even across racial barriers) to get out of isolation. In essence, most of them are in isolation for life or until prison policies change. Their fellow prisoners are their fami-lies. M, a white jailhouse lawyer associated with a prison group called the Latin Kings, is quite frank about his prison "family life": "Since the '70s gangs have taken the place of a prisoner's family while he is in prison. We have our brothers that we will kill or die for, the leaders and old heads serve as father figures, and we are taught one thing above all—your gang is your family."[48] M speculates that this "family unit" may also be applicable to "our ghettos, trailer parks, and Barrios all across America, where the average home life is, at minimum, dysfunctional."

Whether solidarity takes the form of gangs or other groupings, could this be the germ of exilic society? Affinity groups appear in all kinds of prisons. They may compete with other groups and contain both "solid" and untrustworthy members. While there is much mutual aid, there may also be competition and frequent violence. Unlike political prisoners in Turkey or Northern Ireland, these prisoners often have low levels of political consciousness, so group solidarity may rely more on unwritten "prison codes" than on developed political awareness. When we asked long-term supermax prisoners why they decided to practice solidarity, rather than gain personal advantage at the expense of other prisoners, the typical answer was something like, "I was always taught that you look after each other's back, even on the street before I came to prison."

This is not so different from what ex-IRA prisoners told us about their early prison experiences: they had great feelings of solidarity with others who shared their experiences of injustices imposed by state authorities. Then, prison gave them a real consciousness, raising their understanding about building the collective, not just fighting injustice but building an alternative society and practicing mutual aid. In the Northern Irish case, isolation, rather than breaking this exilic experience, intensified it. Stripping prisoners removed habits of individualism and competition, leaving them open to rebuilding an exilic identity based on oral communication and mutual aid. Could supermax life in the US encourage such exilic practices, even if certain of their aspects militate against full-fledged exilic community?

The isolation regime in the US is similar to that in the H-Blocks but there are key differences. The most obvious is that there were two prisoners in most cells in the H-Blocks but only one in the supermax/SHUs. This is important, yet, as we have seen in the Turkish case, placing three prisoners in a living area can cause as many barriers as encouragements to solidarity. A more serious problem is that the pods of SHUs and supermaxes hold men of mixed backgrounds in terms of race, group affiliation, level of education, age, and other key factors. A given pod of eight to sixteen prisoners usually has men who are "bugging out," screaming and even throwing feces or urine out the doors. Others steal things that are lent to them. Even small things like postage stamps or a magazine can cause violent confrontations. They throw trash onto "the range" (the open area between the pods) or the corridors. Since many prisoners are indigent, while others have support from families and friends, practices to "redistribute" resources through gambling on anything from football to chess can cause tensions.

Other features of the supermax may favor exilic formations and practices. We know of several remarkable instances where prisoners used creativity and patience to help each other, often transcending divisions such as race, which the authorities manipulate to keep them at each other's throats. Perhaps the most interesting and sustained example of an exilic formation, which parallels in many ways the H-Block experiences in Northern Ireland, took place in one of the most notorious prisons in the US: Pelican Bay State Prison (PBSP) in California.

The Pelican Bay SHU houses over one thousand men in total solitary confinement.[49] The SHU contains four corridors arranged in the shape of an X, three of which have thirty-six pods that hold eight prisoners each. One has only twenty-four pods: the "short corridor." The cells in the SHU are eight by ten feet and made of smooth, poured concrete. They have no windows; instead, there are fluorescent lights. The fronts of the cells are perforated steel, through which the prisoners look out with difficulty at a concrete wall. Food and mail are delivered through slots in the cell doors. Prisoners remain in their cells for 22½ hours a day, leaving only for visits (which take place only on weekends) or for 1½ hours of exercise, alone, in a concrete bunker about the size of three cells and partly open to the sky.[50]

Each block has a control booth, a tower in the center of six "pods" of cells, which radiate from the control booth like wheel spokes. Each pod has eight cells, four on the ground level and four on the second tier. There are two shower cells per pod and a yard door at the end of each pod that leads into a small concrete yard that is monitored via CCTV. An armed guard in a control booth operates the cell doors, showers, and exercise yard doors.

The SHU, however, is *not* a panopticon. The armed guards can see the tiers and cell doors but not inside the cells. The prisoners have very little contact with staff, who feed them by passing a tray or lunch sack through a slot in the door, pass out mail, and walk by to count. The only extended contact with guards is when a prisoner goes for a medical visit or on weekend visits with those on his approved visitors' list. Periodically, a group of guards runs into the pod, cuffs up the prisoners, and searches their cells. Prisoners are not allowed any phone calls, and some have severe restrictions on who they can correspond with by mail.

Todd Ashker, a prisoner in the short corridor, summarizes the experience terms similar to what we heard from Kurdish prisoners in Turkey: "The idea here is to put us in our little cement tombs and act like we no longer exist— that's it in a nut shell. So, it's not a case of having to report daily activity etc. we're isolated and contained and out of sight, out of mind. HA!"[51]

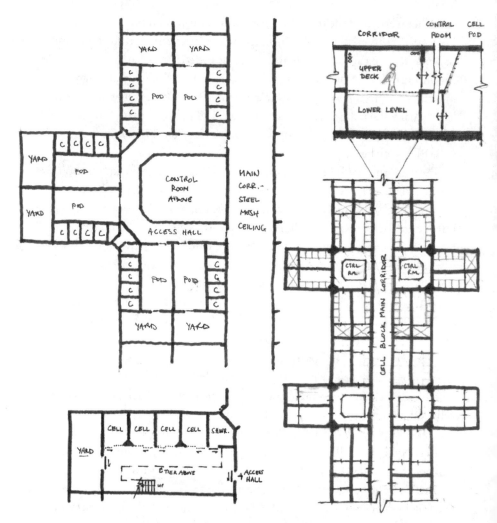

FIGURE 13. Architect's drawings of the "short corridor," Pelican Bay SHU, California. Raphael Sperry, architect, president of Architects/Designers/Planners for Social Responsibility.

In February 2006, Pelican Bay officials decided to isolate nearly two hundred prisoners in the short corridor. These, they branded *"the worst of the worst of the worst"* in the whole California prison system, primarily on information provided by prison informers. Most of the two hundred already knew of each other because they had all been in the SHU for many years, some since it opened in 1989. The state accused them of leading California's best-known prison gangs: the Mexican Mafia, La Nuestra Familia, the Aryan

Brotherhood, and the Black Guerrilla Family. The men themselves simply claim to have influence among Southern and Northern California Latino, white, and Afro-American prisoners.

As with Ohio during and after the 1993 Lucasville uprising,[52] one of the remarkable things about prison under special conditions like long-term solitary is its potential to create an environment in which prisoners build solidary communities that transcend race. As Todd Ashker, one of the main representatives of what would later become known as the Short Corridor Collective, puts it, " We've come to recognize and respect our racial, cultural differences . . . while recognizing that we're all in the same boat when it comes to the prison staff's dehumanizing treatment and abuse—they are our jailers, our torturers, our common adversaries."[53]

The men in one particular pod of the short corridor, D1 block, were highly respected by different prison groups. They were older men, all over forty years of age. In 2009, Ashker described the pod as follows:

> I've been in [this pod] for nearly 4 yrs . . . I am 46 one guy is 43 the rest are 56, 58, 59, 67 and 68, all with 20 to 30 yrs. in SHU all here in PBSP–SHU since 1989-1990. None have been found guilty of committing an illegal gang related act. We're here indefinitely based on confinement informants telling stories (to get out of here).[54]

By putting such men together, the prison authorities clearly intended to isolate them from other prisoners who might come under their influence; they possibly even thought that the men would fight or refuse to communicate with each other because of their alleged gang enmities. This was a mistake. Even in solitary confinement, prisoners communicate by shouting. The men on the short corridor soon began to relate to each other, in spite of racial differences. According to Ashker, their maturity and experiences helped them come together. Yet they still had to overcome hurdles in order to build a *community*.

> Prior to PBSP-SHU [where we've all been since '89–'90] we were very clannish—with little interaction—and quite a bit of conflict . . . we were also much younger and prone to staff manipulation [This was a time period I was at Folsom—'85–'86 were bloodiest in Folsom's entire history!]

Despite their differences, they began the work of building community.

> Here at PBSP—isolated in the small pods and gains in maturity enabled us to see one another in a more human being perspective.

As a jailhouse lawyer, Ashker was poised to become a spokesperson for the group, despite being white and accused by authorities of ties to the Aryan Brotherhood (which he denies). In short, says Ashker, "a bunch of factors all came together—Right Time/Right Place!!!"

The prisoners on D1 were well read although none had much formal education. Placed together in a secure environment without much interference by guards and able to communicate pretty freely, these men began to share and debate reading materials: anything they could get their hands on about history, culture, sociology, politics, philosophy, anthropology, and so on. They soon began to discuss strategies of collective action.

> When the administration came up with their bright idea to place all in even closer proximity to one another it was a given that we'd be communicating amongst ourselves in our pod areas and comparing notes re: treatment, conditions, legal strategies, etc., etc., etc., we socialized as best we could, in the way human beings are prone to.[55]

Ashker and another white man on the pod, Danny Troxell, had been double-celled, or next door to each other, since July 2003. Together, they had mounted a number of legal challenges to prison policies and practices about solitary confinement, lack of parole, lack of medical treatment, and other issues. One of their civil suits evolved into a class-action suit in 2012, arguing that prolonged solitary confinement constitutes cruel and unusual punishment in violation of the Eighth Amendment and that prisoners are placed in the SHU on suspicion of gang affiliation without meaningful review, which violates their due process rights.[56] Ashker led the legal challenges; meanwhile, Troxell introduced him to radical literature: Tom Paine's *Rights of Man*; Naomi Wolf's *The End of America—Letter of Warning to a Young Patriot*; Howard Zinn's *The Zinn Reader on Disobedience and Democracy*; and others. They also began reading about ancient cultures from South America, Africa, Asia, and the Middle East. Mayan cosmology became a special interest.

After Troxell and Ashker were moved to D1 block, their dialogue expanded to eight men and continued to cover history, culture, politics, and law. They applied all of these subjects to their analysis of the punitive conditions of confinement. Others in the pod included Arturo Castellanos and Ronald Dewberry (aka Sitawa Jamaa). At first, the talk was chaotic and unformed, with eight men shouting to one another all day. The Chicanos often spoke in Spanish while others spoke English. Because of the layout of the cells—four in a row on each level facing a blank wall—no one could see the others. But they could pass a few words to each other as they went to shower or exercise. Troxell and Ashker, in particular, shouted to each other about things they were reading.

In 2009, the men read two things that would change their lives and strategies, enabling them to take what was now a small exilic community to higher levels. One was an article by psychiatrists arguing that it was unethical for doctors to assist in interrogations at Guantanamo. In their discussions, the men began to see similarities between what was happening in Guantanamo and the uses of psychiatric evaluations as part of the prisoners' annual reviews in Pelican Bay. According to Ashker, "The common pronouncement /mantra/song of the [California Department of Corrections] has been 'there's no psychiatric reason for not retaining the prisoner in SHU indefinitely . . . until he debriefs.'"[57]

None of the men in the short corridor attended their annual reviews or spoke to psychiatrists. Yet psychiatric reports in their personal files supported their continued solitary confinement. Ashker wrote a three-page memorandum and a formal complaint[58] about the use of psychiatry in the review process. He and his pod mates found ways to distribute the document among prisoners and the public, to educate them about conditions and practices in the SHU.[59]

The document was the beginning of outreach to other prisoners outside of the short corridor and a potential support community outside of prison. But the men in the pod were still not satisfied that their message was reaching enough receptive ears. This is where the second reading came in. As part of a prison course organized at Binghamton University in New York, Troxell and Ashker were reading books and articles written by academic "prison experts." They corresponded with university students who read the same materials and answered the students' questions about how their prison experiences, including solitary, corresponded to what the "experts" had written. The students and prisoners read and discussed a biography of the Irish hunger striker Bobby Sands,[60] which included detailed descriptions of the creation of exilic life in the H-Blocks of Northern Ireland. According to Ashker, reading about the Irish prisoners turned around the whole nature of discussions in the pod. The men began to discuss nonviolent resistance using the one weapon that could not be taken from them: their own bodies.

> Between late 2009 and January 2011, I reread the book about Bobby Sands several times, which together with other reading material, opened my eyes to the power of peaceful action for the purpose of resisting human rights abuse. We watched the Arab Spring on public television news, and the large scale

FIGURE 14. Todd Ashker's cell, short corridor, Pelican Bay SHU. Reproduced with the permission of Todd Ashker.

prisoner work strike in the Georgia system in 2010. Then we heard about the Ohio Supermax prisoners going on hunger strike to protest conditions similar to ours and on top of all this, at that time, just like now after our 2013 Hunger Strike, we had (and have) Pelican Bay SHU staff's ongoing increase in punitive–restrictive actions against us. All of this came together and Danny and I began talking about a hunger strike to peacefully protest decades of solitary confinement here, where we were being tortured, at Pelican Bay.[61]

Troxell and Ashker decided that legal challenges were ineffective because the US Supreme Court directs lower courts mostly to stay out of solitary confinement challenges. They needed additional ways to fight solitary.

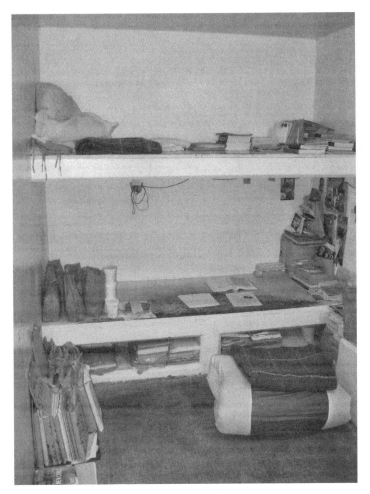

FIGURE 15. Inside Todd Ashker's cell, short corridor, Pelican Bay SHU.
Reproduced with the permission of Todd Ashker.

As their discussions proceeded, the two men noticed something. Most of
the time everyone shouted across each other, but when they started to talk
about Bobby Sands and the Irish experiences in H-Block, the pod went quiet.
They knew the others were listening.[62] In time, everyone read the Bobby Sands
biography and began joining the conversation to add their own ideas. Ashker
argued for the advantages of nonviolent strategies, but he says it was hard to
convince others at first because "they've always done it the other way."[63]

A common discussion that emerged from the study of Mayan cosmology
was about "alignment." The group discussed the idea that there are certain

periods when time seems to speed up, more things are happening, and things come together in a way that allows perceptive people and groups to achieve new things.

"Have you noticed that in the past ten or twelve years things are just getting faster?" Todd asked on a visit.

The men discussed time and decided that if they were aware enough they could harness it, recover ways of learning how to deal with it, and move to a higher plane. They even discussed it as a form of "second coming": "Have you ever thought that this is not about a person but about a spirit?" [64]

The men in the pod agreed to form, or perhaps they realized that they had *already* formed, a multiracial collective. Ashker explains,

> As for the actual forming of the collective————we simply stepped up and took the responsibility for representing the prisoner class.; it was our idea and in my case I knew that I'd be able to competently represent and look out for the interests of those similarly situated based on all of my experience with dealing with prisoncrats in the context of the litigation I'd been involved in!!! It had absolutely [nothing] to do with gangs/gang leadership roles/votes, etc. [65]

Soon, the seed of a tactic of resistance formed.

> A big influence on Danny and I was the Bobby Sands book, which combined with everything else going on at the time, was what helped guide our decision to resist and move for reforms via [hunger strike] protest!!! We initially planned to do so solo! (One a.m. I told him that I was fed up and thinking about going on h.s.; and he immediately said he was thinking of the same thing!!!) And it took off from there . . . it's as simple as that! The reason it's as simple as that is we were all similarly situated and all of us recognized that our prior methods were not effective (e.g., legal challenges in the courts), and something had to be done to expose and put these ppl in check on their continual abuse of power!! [66]

Some others questioned whether a hunger strike would achieve anything, but the more they talked about it the more they realized how effectively it had been used in other parts of the world, including, most recently, at the supermax in Youngstown, Ohio. They agreed that they "were going to die a long, slow death here and were at the point of having nothing to lose!!!" [67] By the end of January 2011, they were firmly decided that the time was right to combine their legal challenges with nonviolent resistance. A hunger strike could gain widespread exposure and support for their struggle to end long-term solitary confinement.

They agreed to begin a hunger strike on July 1, 2011, giving them time to build support within the prison system and outside. Like the Irish blanketmen and the hunger strikers at the Ohio State Penitentiary, they developed a list of five core demands, which they published in a statement of April 3, 2011:

1. End Group Punishment & Administrative Abuse

2. Abolish the Debriefing Policy, and Modify Active/Inactive Gang Status Criteria

3. Comply with the US Commission on Safety and Abuse in America's Prisons 2006 Recommendations Regarding an End to Long-Term Solitary Confinement

4. Provide Adequate and Nutritious Food

5. Expand and Provide Constructive Programming and Privileges for Indefinite SHU Status Inmates.

The statement was signed by "Todd Ashker, Arturo Castellanos, Sitawa N. Jamaa (aka R. N. Dewberry), George Franco, Antonio Guillen, Lewis Powell, Paul Redd, Alfred Sandoval, Danny Troxell, James Williamson, Ronnie Yandell . . . *and all other similarly situated prisoners*" (our emphasis).[68]

This, like other documents developed by the Short Corridor Collective, evolved out of direct discussions and consensus building:

> Each of us were in the mix on the discussion and creation of our documents re: Formal Complaint, and Five Core Demands, etc., and we volunteered for the representative roles we assumed without consulting anyone——— remember, we initially were thinking we might have 50 or so [people] joining in with us.[69]

The collective spread the word to other prisoners and support groups on the outside. They stressed that the movement was a collective one: they had *no leaders*, only representatives. Moreover, joining the hunger strike had to be voluntary. Again as in the Irish example, people with medical problems were discouraged from participating.

While communication within the pod was relatively easy, communications with other pods, prisons, and support groups presented problems. The prisoners could communicate with adjoining pods at the exercise yard, either through steel doors between two yards or through the drainpipe. Word spread further in Pelican Bay through the prison "grapevine." But communications to other prisons were more difficult. To resolve this problem, the collective sought help from an outside support group based in Oakland called Prison Focus. This group, which had opposed solitary confinement from the opening of Pelican Bay, agreed to print the collective's "Formal Complaint" in their newsletter, which they sent free to prisoners across the state of California.

The collective then used Prison Focus to get the word to other prisons that they were planning a mass hunger strike on July 1, 2011. The newsletter containing the article on the planned hunger strike reached many prisoners only a week before the planned action. Normally, this kind of public notice could have been seen as a disadvantage because it would alert the prison authorities and give them time to plan countermeasures. According to Ashker, however, this was not a problem because prison staff viewed their mass hunger strike plans as a joke, openly stating that "they didn't see prisoners joining together for anything." They were wrong. More than sixty-five hundred prisoners across the state of California joined the hunger strike on July 1. Prisoners from other states also joined in solidarity. For Ashker, "It was the beginning of prisoners awakening to the power of unified-collective group action using peaceful methods to educate and expose decades of state-sanctioned torture."[70]

The collective faced hazards similar to those brought on by the loyalty bargain between the Irish blanketmen and the outsiders they depended on to enable communications.[71] The blanketmen transcended this problem by creating a dense network of message smugglers, enabled by contact visits. In California, the "architecture" of visits made communications slower, more perilous, and certainly more public.

Between July 1 and October 14, 2011, after careful planning and difficult communications, California prisoners went on two hunger strikes for a total of thirty-eight days. More than eighteen thousand prisoners from prisons across California eventually participated (substantially more than the collective's earlier hopes of fifty supporters). Finally, they suspended their action in response to a negotiated agreement in which prison officials promised to make changes that met the five core demands.

During the second hunger strike, members of the Short Corridor Collective were moved to the "administrative segregation tier" of the SHU to further isolate them from other prisoners. The move brought them even closer together as a community. For the first time, they exercised in cages rather than concrete bunkers, so they could see each other's faces and speak directly with each other. After twenty days on hunger strike, morale was so high that Sitawa Jamaa told a visitor they could last another sixty days. He invented a slogan for the hunger strikers—"Forty days and forty nights!"—signifying the promised land that hopefully lay at the end of their ordeal.[72]

Conditions in the ad seg unit had other advantages. The men could feel the breeze for the first time in years. There was grass and there were flowers . . . and wildlife, in the form of frogs that jumped into the cages.

Yet the men were still cut off from the outside world and isolated from media reports about their hunger strike. Ashker met with his new attorney, the experienced civil rights lawyer Anne Weills, who told him there was tremendous and growing support for them in other prisons and in the public. That conversation, Ashker says,

hit me very hard because I'd forgotten what it was like to be actually connected to the human race . . . But the biggest thing was when I was escorted, fully shackled, back to the ad seg tier after the visit . . . We were on H-row (hell-row we called it), and it had 12 cells on it, with my cell being on the very end (Cell 12), and as I'm being escorted by all the cells it's quiet as a tomb, and all the men were standing at their doors, looking at [me] with hopeful-ness————that I'd have good news, . . . and what hit me so hard was the eerie ways it resembled the scene when Bobby [Sands] had met with the prison-crats and returned to the tier of men hoping for good news . . . It was as if his spirit was there that day with me . . . .I'll never forget it————nor the highest degree of respect and admiration I'll always hold in my heart (and love!), for him and his comrades!!![73]

Ashker told us that as the hunger strikes continued during 2011 and 2012, "our sense of similarly situated collective unity grew stronger and more wide-spread." The collective began a dialogue about how the California prison authorities manipulated prisoners, particularly how they had for two decades "successfully pit[ted] all the racial groups against each other all across the California prison system to the point where 'lock down' is the common state of affairs at many prisons." The collective developed an analysis that con-nected top security policy to the coal face where, if prisoners are kept in their cells without yard time or programming, "It means higher security and more guards' jobs, and higher security pay. It is in the interest of the guards' union to have violence in the prisons, resulting in more jobs, more dues paying members, more political power in the state." He concluded, "We recognized the *prisoner class* was getting the short end."[74]

On August 12, 2012, the collective published "Agreement to End Racial Group Hostilities." They called on all racial groups in California's prisons to end violence against each other.

> If we really want to bring about substantive meaningful changes to the CDCR system in a manner beneficial to all solid individuals, who have never been broken by CDCR's torture tactics intended to coerce one to become a state informant via debriefing, that now is the time for us to collectively seize this moment in time, and put an end to more than 20–30 years of hostilities between our racial groups ... Therefore, beginning on October 10, 2012, all hostilities between our racial groups ... in SHU, Ad-Seg, General Population, and County Jails, will officially cease ... we must all hold strong to our mutual agreement from this point on and focus our time, attention, and energy on mutual causes beneficial to all of us [i.e., prisoners], and our best interests. We can no longer allow CDCR to use us against each other for their benefit!! Because the reality is that collectively, we are an empowered, mighty force, that can positively change this entire corrupt system into a system that actually benefits prisoners, and thereby, the public as a whole ... and we simply cannot allow CDCR/CCPOA—Prison Guard's Union, IGI, ISU, OCS, and SSU, to continue to get away with their constant form of progressive oppression and warehousing of tens of thousands of prisoners, including the 14,000 (+) plus prisoners held in solitary confinement torture chambers [i.e., SHU/Ad-Seg Units], for decades!!![75]

The call to end violence was taken up by youth gangs in Los Angeles:

> On this day, October 10, 2012, the men in the Security Housing Unit at Pelican Bay are again leading all of us. They have called for "an end to all hostilities" within our state's prisons and jails. After doing so much time, the men in the Pelican Bay SHU have realized that they are being recycled over and over through the same dead-end system ... As young people who have experienced bloodshed on the streets of Los Angeles, and the violence and humiliation within juvenile halls, Probation camps and Division of Juvenile Justice Youth Prisons, we are also calling for an end to the war between the youth.
>
> We are challenging all youth in the streets, schools and lock-ups throughout California, to do the following:
>
> 1. End all the killing and drama between hoods, crews and races. Declare a temporary cease fire and work toward building lasting truces.
>
> 2. Take the same mentality and skills we have used to hustle drugs, bang our hoods and promote our crews to unite in a powerful movement to demand dignity, respect and equality for all our people.
>
> 3. We must also demand an end to police and sheriff violence, an end to the mass incarceration of youth -especially Black and Brown youth, an end to

ICE detention and deportation, living wage jobs, and a quality education that prepares all youth for college and a career.

4. Demand an end to the War on Gangs—including the CalGang Database that labels people (as young as ten) as gang members without their knowledge or right to appeal; gang injunctions that incarcerate people for non-criminal acts; and gang enhancements that turn courtrooms into death chambers.

5. Do not fall victim to traps set by a wicked system that seeks to make us permanent members of the prison industrial complex.

6. Spread the word to unite all hoods, all barrios, all crews and all cliques, all cells, all dorms and all units—from the Nickerson Gardens to Estrada Courts, from the PJs to the Y.A., from TJ to Pelican Bay, to the Bay Area and back down to Sac Town—let everyone know, as youth of California we are NOT DOWN WITH THE LOCK DOWN!!![76]

The state of California's response to these initiatives was negative, despite the hope they provoked in some urban neighborhoods. Under ideal conditions, the Short Corridor Collective's peace initiatives and leadership would be taken as a sign that these men could help ease racial tension in the state's prisons and could thus one day be returned to the general prison population or even to the streets. The state, however, encourages prisoner-on-prisoner violence and gang conflicts because they split prisoners, criminalize their primary identities, enable placement of spies among them, and make them easier to control. When a collective of influential prisoners threatens such a strategy, albeit by taking a position that seems progressive to most observers, it is even *more* critical to isolate them because they are expressing their *humanity*.

By January 2013, prison officials had failed to introduce a satisfactory policy that would give prisoners a way out of isolation short of snitching. Nor had they met the prisoners' other demands. So the prisoners announced a third hunger strike beginning on July 8, 2013, to renew pressure on the authorities to meet their five demands. On that day, more than thirty thousand prisoners joined the strike from all California prisons, possibly the largest mass hunger strike in world history. The action lasted fifty-nine days, with about one hundred men still fasting at the end.

This third hunger strike tested the authorities, but it also tested the exilic community of prisoners on the short corridor. In particular, they suffered again from "loyalty bargains" with both jailors and outside supporters. They remained dependent on their jailors for sustenance and housing. When they acted up, the authorities could punish them in debilitating ways. During the hunger strike, the prison's gang unit ("Security Threat Group") began issuing rule violations for passing communications, artwork, and photos. In July 2013, Todd Ashker was found guilty of "promoting gang activity" categorized as "serious" for having an old photo of Danny Troxell. The charge stated that "based on training & experience," the authorities knew that Ashker would not keep possession of such a photo simply based on friendship but only because of mutual gang affiliation (a statement that we know to be absurd from our knowledge of both men over many years). It was Ashker's first violation for gang activity in thirty-one years and his first "serious" violation of prison rules since January 1994.[77]

Then, on October 25, the sixteen members of the Short Corridor Collective whose names appeared on the 2012 agreement to end hostilities received serious rule violations for "leading a mass disturbance." In a Kafkaesque move, the authorities withheld the incident report that presented evidence on which the charges were based, saying that it contained the numbers (not names) of hunger strike participants from each prison. If the collective got these numbers, they said, they could use them to organize future protests.[78]

Prior to the start of the third hunger strike in 2013, in an apparent attempt to weaken the collective, the authorities moved Ashker to another cell block in the short corridor, away from his comrades. His new cell had polycarbonate (lexan) sheets over the perforated steel door. He had to shout to be heard, and all voices and sounds were muffled. He said it was "like living underwater." He was removed from Danny Troxell, his closest friend and medical aid of many years. The authorities took his address book and said he would not get it back because he had used it to send illicit communications (including with the authors of this volume).

Ashker wrote, "Yesterday, they finished a big ocean/cliffs mural on the wall in front of cells in my pod—it's nice, *but* I'm still in this cell without physical contact with family/friends!!!"[79]

Punishments for hunger strikes, as violations of the "loyalty bargain" with the prison authorities, are to be expected. The loyalty bargain prisoners made with outsiders was even more fraught. Lawyers from the Center for Constitutional Rights and Prison Focus, who assisted the Short Corridor Collective in their class-action suit against the California authorities, were very careful to consult the prisoners before taking any actions on their behalf.[80] According to Ashker, their care in giving the four main representatives of the collective "meaningful input" in all decisions regarding the case was "a critical step toward changing the culture of prisoncrats seeing prisoners as nothing but ... numbers on a spread sheet—it's a step toward them seeing us as human beings—and bringing an end to the 'social death' that is inherent in our prison systems."[81]

Yet other lawyers were not so careful. The 2013 mass hunger strike ended when a lawyer representing California prisoners in a different class action was convinced by state officials to co-sign a request for the federal court to issue an order that enabled prison officials to force-feed the hunger strikers. The resulting issuance of the order made it impossible to maintain the hunger strike past sixty days. The men had to agree to end their hunger strike in exchange for a promise by the state legislature to hold hearings about solitary and possibly to introduce legislation to moderate its use (although there was little hope that effective legislation would pass the legislature).[82] This was similar to a move by Catholic priests in Ireland, who continually pressured families to force the 1981 hunger strikers off of their actions. Often and for various reasons, religious, medical, and "human rights" supporters feel that they have a right to violate prisoners' resolve to die in order to further the cause of the collective.

Lawyers often obstruct prisoner initiatives: settling with states for agreements that fall short of prisoners' demands, failing or refusing to file motions before the courts, and so forth. Support groups who "know better" or have their own agendas change prisoners' documents or alter their demands, or portray them in the media in ways that mislead the public. In a case like California's, where solidary communities are formed in spite of racial group affiliations, trust is always shaky; a supporter's failure to publish a document or even a delayed action may raise suspicions that other prisoners did the tampering. As Ashker put it,

> It is difficult to keep a movement together when we are so isolated and constrained. It is hard to keep everyone in the loop, to adequately explain decisions, to keep our business our own when we are surveilled all the time and everywhere. CDCR counts on our internal disputes, and hopes for us to implode thus their increased pressure on us post hunger strike, with constant rule violations criminalizing innocuous normal human interaction, worse food, more mail delays, lock downs and provocations; we need to stay strong, stick together and stand behind our collective representatives. We all do the best we can.[83]

Soon, California prison authorities introduced a new "step-down" process to further split the collective. The step-down is a five-stage process that involves journaling and interviewing with authorities at different stages. Stages 1–4 are all still strict isolation and may take years to complete. Only in stage 5 does a prisoner reestablish contact with other humans in general population, although even then he is denied privileges such as contact visits. Prisoners in stages 3 and 4 are moved to SHUs at Tehachapi and other prisons, where they have windows (unlike Pelican Bay) but have less outside-of-cell exercise and fewer showers.[84] According to Sitawa Jamaa, the only one of the four prisoner representatives from the short corridor who was transferred to Tehachapi, many aspects of life are worse there than in Pelican Bay, and some things that Pelican Bay prisoners won through the hunger strike (for example, more commissary) have not been implemented elsewhere.[85]

Soon after the new step-down policy was introduced, four main plaintiffs in the 2012 class action against the state of California, including Jamaa and Troxell, were transferred to Tehachapi (supermax prison). Others (including Ashker) were kept in the Pelican Bay SHU on the basis that they "pose the greatest threat to the safety of staff, inmates, and the public."[86] Then, the state of California attempted to argue that those who had been transferred to Tehachapi could no longer be included as plaintiffs in the Eighth Amendment (cruel and unusual punishment) litigation against the state of California because they were no longer in Pelican Bay. US District Judge Claudia Wilken ruled, however, that "prolonged stays in SHU—no matter which SHU—may violate the Eighth Amendment." She kept the transferred prisoners in the class action.[87]

The state's attempt to weaken ongoing litigation by narrowing the definition of cruel and unusual punishment to Pelican Bay SHU was unsuccessful. But it also hoped to divide the prisoners from the short corridor by encouraging them to participate in the step-down in other SHUs. In the H-Blocks of Northern Ireland, the authorities moved all of the leaders into a single block and the result, as with Pelican Bay's Short Corridor Collective, was the creation of a strong leadership that moved the prison collective forward. When the authorities realized their mistake and scattered these "leaders" back into different H-Blocks, the prisoners took their strengthened solidary culture with them and radicalized the collective in all blocks. The same thing happened to a degree in California. Danny Troxell, a founding member of the collective, agreed to test the step-down process for a year, primarily to prove the prisoners' point that it was "a sham." He was transferred to Tehachapi state prison near Los Angeles in May 2014; a year later, Sitawa Jamaa, who was also transferred, announced that the prisoners there would no longer participate in the step-down.

> We shall stop participating Monday, May 11, 2015, indefinitely. We won't be attending any CC hearings directly dealing with Steps 3 and 4, nor shall we go to those group meetings or do any more of those journals. Now there are two groups for each Step 3 and 4, and that's a total of 40 prisoners who would have been attending those group meetings weekly. This [Step-Down-Process] cannot function without prisoners participating.[88]

With former Short Corridor Collective members like Jamaa and Troxell in Tehachapi, the movement that had begun in Pelican Bay expanded. They formed their own Tehachapi Collective and, along with similar new collectives in other prisons, the Short Corridor Collective evolved into a statewide prisoners human rights movement. According to Ashker, "As people are transferred, they simply expand, and promote the agenda re: agreement to end hostilities, etc., wherever they land, creating a local collective group."[89] A lawyer for the SHU prisoners told us that "Sacramento [California's state capital] is trying to contain the contagion of *not participating* in the step-down."[90]

Only time would tell whether the exilic community that had been crafted in the short corridor of Pelican Bay could be spread to other prisons. The agreement to end hostilities significantly reduced racial violence across California's prisons. Could the end of hostility be transformed into a solidary community in a single "prisoner class"?

Our unavoidable conclusion is that prison-based exilic spaces, however remarkable, are fragile and temporally bounded. Yet exilic experiences move across time and space and prisoners learn from each other even across continents and decades. The rewards of solidarity can be great. In Ohio, a twelve-day hunger strike in 2011 led to a victory in which prisoners in long-term solitary, for the first time in more than twenty years, won contact visits where they could hug their families and friends. The Short Corridor Collective built upon the Ohio prisoner successes and provided a means by which its members could regain their humanity by practicing mutual aid. Ashker wrote,

> It is an honor for me to be part of our collective coalition. For the third time in 29 years I have felt a sense of human connectedness ... Our collective energy inside and out, keeps us strong positive, alive, sane; it gives us hope of one day having a glimpse of trees, the warmth of the sun, the hug or kiss

FIGURE 16. Jason Robb, Bomani Shakur, and friends celebrating Bobby Sands's sixtieth birthday in Ohio supermax. Their hunger strike won them the right to have full contact visits and spurred the mass hunger strikes in California. Denis O'Hearn.

of a mother, or father, wife, or girlfriend, brother or grandchild, or a handshake or hug of a friend, a basketball game or checkers, a face to face conversation with a chosen neighbor, a hot meal that has flavor, a bed that is warm. I am thankful for all of us being united together in our righteous struggle for a better tomorrow. I stand strong, united in solidarity with each of you.[91]

On September 1, 2015, Ashker's dream came true. The state of California, pressed between the "contagion of not participating in step-down" on the side of the prisoners and a likely ruling against indeterminate isolation by the federal courts, came to an agreement with the prisoners of the Short Corridor Collective. They agreed to end indeterminate solitary confinement in California. Within two months, about two thousand prisoners would be released to the general population, where they could do all of the things that Ashker dreamed of. It had taken considerably longer than the twelve days in which the Ohio prisoners won their rights, but the stakes were far higher. And the legacy of solidarity that finally got them out of solitary isolation went straight back to Bobby Sands and his comrades "on the blanket" outside of Belfast during 1976–1981.

CONCLUSIONS: PRISON ISOLATION
AND EXILIC FORMATION

We have seen some unexpected outcomes of prison isolation. In particular, the removal of access to the usual accoutrements of capitalist consumerism leaves prisoners the option to create collective solutions and consciousness within prison walls, a process that Carlo Ginzburg has called *prison communism*.[92] As the Irish blanketmen demonstrated, exilic practices can become quite advanced. But we have also seen that their practices can be limited by authoritarianism within prison movements and especially by state practices and architectures that permanently separate prisoners (the Turkish case). Even where such architecture is extreme (US supermaxes), however, some groups of prisoners strive to create exilic communities, a hopeful confirmation of Kropotkin's basic theory of mutual aid.

What of the loyalty bargain? This is a most interesting and potentially instructive area of inquiry into solidary life under prison isolation. Prisoners depend on guards for material subsistence and occasional extra pleasures. The ideal bargain, from the authorities' point of view, is that prisoners exchange good behavior for subsistence, that they become *ideal prisoners* and make the prison workable on the authorities' terms. Yet prisoners have options, including simply ignoring the authority of the guards. The authorities will likely retaliate by providing bare subsistence and imposing punishments.[93]

Strategies against such punishment regimes include (1) refusing to come out of one's cell and engage the authorities, on the principle that doing so would amount to capitulation; and (2) coming out of one's cell whenever possible to confront the authorities and appropriate prison spaces. The latter is dangerous, as in the extreme case of the Irish blanketmen. Coming out, appropriating, and confronting evoked punishments that were previously unthinkable. Yet such confrontation may be necessary for the collective to move forward. The blanketmen and the Short Corridor Collective support this hypothesis. Alternatively, confrontation may threaten the collective as the authorities will always be on the lookout for (often violent) ways to quash resistant prisoners.

To succeed, confrontation requires what Goldstone calls "process tracing,"[94] the ability on the part of the exilic community to effectively read changing circumstances and create new and successful ways of adapting to them. Confrontation may result in punishment, yet, as the Ohio hunger strikers demonstrated in 2011, it *can* force authorities to grant prisoners' demands. Moreover, if we see coming out of cells as a form of raids, as the blanketmen effectively did in Northern Ireland, is this not akin to the exilic economic strategy of the Cossacks? (Of course, the blanketmen forced their way through enemy lines to obtain things from supporters, like a community under siege, while the Cossacks forcibly took things that belonged to others.)

A further comparison can be made with the Zapatistas, who faced similar choices about looking inward to build the collective versus moving outward to make Zapatismo more widespread. The 2003-4 reforms that created *juntas de buen gobierno* were an inward movement, a retreat from the loyalty bargain with outside supporters such as the Mexican population. These reforms strengthened the communities internally, but also restricted the influence of the movement in Mexico and worldwide. A few years later, the Other Campaign was an explicit attempt to move Zapatismo outward, to appropriate new spaces and communities in Mexico and beyond.

The US prison experience, while hopeful, reveals clear limitations of building exilic spaces in prisons. Todd Ashker, for one, thought a lot about how the Irish blanketmen built a solidary community. He concludes that this never happened to the same extent in Pelican Bay:

> I don't see it—too many different dynamics, each with their own agenda, etc ... the men in Erin were all pretty much kin, in heart and spirit, subject to the same upbringing, experiences, history, politics, etc., which made it easier in some ways for them to come together the way they did; they also had the discipline stemming from what they stood for and were a part of ... [in Pelican Bay] you have a mixed stew of dynamics—and it's all the more amazing that we've accomplished what we have to date ... Our coming together is based largely on the fact of having the right combination of [people] in the right place at the right time, coupled with/related to having the experience and maturity to recognize the wisdom of coming together collectively for the benefit of all those similarly situated.

And is that not the definition of *mutual aid* presented by Kropotkin? What remains is the work of *building community*, which clearly happened to a remarkable extent in the short corridor but never achieved its full potential.

Indeed, Ashker points to building a pluri-ethnic community as the missing factor:

> Until such time as people ... come together ... putting color to the side, and act in concert with a collective of similarly situated people—the work-

ing class poor, proletariat, lumpen, etc., there will be division amongst the classes and as long as such division persists there will be no major change!!!

Yet he adds, hopefully,

> But you never know, I continue to push the idea of [people] getting an awareness/recognition that it's to our benefit to focus on working class-poor collectivism efforts—rather than the separatist race-based focus.[95]

Finally, there is an elephant in the room that cannot be ignored. Prisoners are generally held for limited terms. Conflicts that create political imprisonment are resolved. Prisoners are moved and even released to the streets. What happens then, when the bare life conditions that encouraged the development of exilic communities are lifted, when *homo sacer* is returned, once again, to the status of *homo economicus*? We have observed encouraging and discouraging answers. In Northern Ireland, groups of prisoners continued to form collectivities for purposes ranging from teaching and speaking the Irish language to communal homebuilding. In neighborhoods of Istanbul and cities and regions of Kurdistan, insurgents strive to achieve political autonomy by creating cooperative institutions. In the United States, outcomes are often less positive, but even in ghettoes and trailer parks some prisoners who have experienced solidary life in prison try to practice and preach aspects of what they have learned. We cannot say that this is enough, not nearly; but such practices remain as sparks, seeds beneath the snow.

SIX

Conclusions

BEGINNINGS

IN THE PRECEDING CHAPTERS we analyzed a long experience of exilic life through its historical sweep (Don Cossacks); a fragile but tenacious contemporary exilic society (Zapatistas); and an example of forced exit and exilic life (solitary prisoners). We distinguished between nonstate spaces before capitalism (with state-repelling structures as well as a residual hierarchical legacy of the state and of indigenous society); changes to exilic spaces during and after world-systemic incorporation (especially, the consequences of the "loyalty bargain"); and restructured exilic spaces, conditioned by the transformation of the world-economy (Zapatistas and prisoners, but also Cossacks who were privatized, as it were, by the state). So what have we learned from our explorations of the Cossack steppe, Zapatista territories, and solitary prisons? Our guiding principle was to see exilic spaces from the perspective of the world-economy and to try to understand the world-economy from the perspective of the exilic space.

We have presented three distinct instances that illustrate a singular world-systemic process. We do not pretend to nor would we agree with the usual Millian case method (methods of agreement and difference, concomitant variation), nor do we want to "predict." Yet, while our studies are not exhaustive, we think that they provide indicative results. Where do these three instances leave us?

WHY ESCAPE? FORCED AND VOLUNTARY EXILE

An initial set of questions are about why people escape and whether the reasons for escape may have differential effects on outcomes. Cossack exile was voluntary (escape from Muscovy, from the emerging regulations of the state, and especially from emerging serfdom); Zapatista exile was mixed (some of the inhabitants of the Lacandon were expelled from their lands and forcibly resettled, some moved there because ejidal lands were opened up and were not available elsewhere, while others joined exilic communities in order to escape "bad government" and build a new society); and solitary imprisonment is clearly forced exile (prisoners are first expelled from mainstream society and then expelled from the prison system's general population). Of course, things are not quite so simple. Cossacks "chose" exile because emergent Russian society was so repugnant and, thus, they were also "forced" to leave if they desired liberty. Many prisoners "chose" to live a lifestyle that was likely to result in their imprisonment; in prison, they "chose" to engage in practices of solidarity that would likely provoke the authorities to isolate them. Still, the extremes of forced and voluntary exile serve well as a first approximation.

DID IT MAKE A DIFFERENCE?

A possible difference between voluntary and forced exiles comes from the motivations or dispositions of the exilic population, or what Goffman calls the "presenting culture."[1] Because voluntary exiles are escaping the state, one might expect that they would have ideas about good government (autonomy), some form of unalienated economy, perhaps a more social or communal life, and greater equality if not a class-free society. Forced exiles come into the community with a more differentiated and perhaps less specified identity and interests. Although they may be driven by opposition or antipathy toward the forces that sent them into exile, what they make of exilic life and society is less defined.

The foregoing seems to be borne out by our studies. The Cossacks appear to have valued liberty, community (high participation in decision making), and equality, including sharing the wealth of the community (by household although *not* by gender, on which see the discussion below). There is ample evidence that mutual aid was a driving principle of Cossack society. "Liberty" was their reason to escape.

These features of Cossack life persisted for some time, although they were eventually worn away by world-systemic processes and successive bargains made with the Russian state, so that *exit-with-autonomy* became *exit-*

without-autonomy. But the founding principles of exile were about autonomy and mutual aid, and new exiles who entered the Don were clearly seeking the same.

The exilic experience of the Zapatistas differs somewhat. Undoubtedly, the mestizo exiles from the north, who were forcibly expelled from urban areas by government security forces, went to Chiapas in the 1980s in hopes of building a revolutionary movement and a classless society. There, they met exiles who had ideas that were in many ways similar but that included (1) indigenous, customary forms of justice and communal democracy that had been built over decades of alienation from Mexican state institutions; and (2) communal land relations that were both indigenous and developed in the wake of the Mexican Revolution. Whether these indigenous exiles came to the jungle to find ejidal lands or were expelled when their lands were taken away (i.e., whether they were voluntary or forced exiles), all were escaping bad government, bossism, and degrading economic conditions and relations on the land (including having no land). The result was a group of communities that, with the help of ejidal unions and indigenous customs, developed *asambleas* based on consensus through open discussion within communities and careful consensus making among them. The Zapatista *asamblea* resembles the Don Cossack *krug* but with a stronger reliance on indigenous communal principles than one found in the Don.

Despite the remoteness of the jungle, its proximity to state-dominated areas and the availability to the Mexican state of "friction-reducing" technologies made exile incomplete in two ways. First, many communities were mixed: Zapatistas lived beside compañeros with loyalties to the traditional state parties, including the PRI. Second, poor as they were, communities still had access to state-provided services. For these and other reasons, exilic formation was incomplete and staged: first, the exiles depended on some state resources but later, in the period of *la resistencia*, they eschewed them. Doing so required a strong act of will and was a challenge to consensual governance.

The Zapatista experience was therefore one that moved toward greater autonomy, where the Don Cossacks moved in the other direction over time (admittedly, we are talking decades in one case and centuries in the other). This mixed experience was a result of both the forced/voluntary mix of migrants in the exilic spaces and the effects of world time, which we discuss in greater detail below.

Finally, the completely forced examples of isolated prisoners present different results. Here, the "presenting culture" of the exiles is very important, and thus the disposition of Irish and Turkish prisoners was immediately and unsurprisingly toward communalism, democracy, and mutual aid. As guerrillas, they were already exiles before prison, even those who lived in cities (much like the original guerrillas who helped form the Zapatistas). Yet the stripped nature of prison isolation intensified their communalism to greater lengths, most clearly in the case of the Irish blanketmen. This again has parallels with the stripped nature of jungle life, as told in Subcomandante Marcos's writings.[2] Without material things and means of communicating directly with the non-exilic world, they built a solidary culture that had all of the features we have identified with exilic societies.

A more interesting example in many ways is the forced exile of prisoners in the US, for these men had a presenting culture that was, at best, formed by the solidarity of gangs and at worst was highly informed by the competitive and violent drug culture of post-1980 US society. Not only did they often lack formal education but they had little experience of communal solidarity and mutual aid, apart from following "street codes" that forbade certain individualistic activities such as snitching on other gang members. They were forced out of this culture into maximum-security prisons, where they began to learn the competitive solidary culture of the gang, and then were forced into complete isolation, where they were stripped of many of the things that made their cultures competitive and individualistic—and often overtly racist. Forced exile, which is defined among other things by extreme stripping, also stripped these men of almost everything from their presenting culture *except* their experiences of solidarity. Left in a situation where they had only each other to depend on—that is, in a heightened them-and-us situation—differences of ethnicity receded in favor of, as Ohio inmates called it, "prison race." Left with orality and time, the forced exiles began together to try and explain their situation, how to deal with it, and how to transcend it. They read, discussed, and built a solidary exilic society. In the economic terms we have proposed, they worked hard at building community. Cultural production and sharing was not as broad as in the H-Blocks, and differences remained, especially between African American prisoners and others. Yet exilic participatory education aimed at solidary practice, eventually culminating in hunger strikes and joint moves against interracial violence, became the main product of their exilic economy.

The classic sociologist of prison society, Gresham Sykes, puts an interesting spin on Kropotkin's explanation of the relationship between the difficulties of living in harsh nature and the development of practices of mutual aid:

Unlike a community living in a harsh physical environment where no effort can overcome the stinginess of nature, the prisoners live in an environment made harsh by man-made decrees and only officialdom stands interposed between the inmates and many of the amenities of life as represented by institutional supplies.[3]

Sykes presents this problem in a mainstream way to probe the ways that prisoners may try to get at material goods that are available in the prison but considered contraband to prisoners. One outcome is that prisoners will make what we have called a *loyalty bargain* with certain guards, who will deliver goods from the prison "state." Yet there is another possibility: unable to get at these amenities or even to enjoy the basic amenity of daylight, the prisoners in the short corridor of Pelican Bay's SHU constructed a very different and at least somewhat exilic economy where the highest value was placed on building community.

EXIT, VOICE, AND LOYALTY

The interaction of a changing world-capitalism with the ongoing infrapolitics of the world-system forces groups of exiles to combine strategies of exit, voice, and loyalty. While exit, of course, is the basis of our study, we have added some conditions that we have woven into our three studies:

- Exit can be forced, voluntary, or take a combination of these forms.
- Exit may be *territorial*, that is, it may involve escaping from the territories controlled by forces of state and capital and setting up life at the territorial edges of capitalism; yet it may also be *structural*, that is, groups of people may continue to live within the territories over which states claim authority yet set up practices and institutions that give them autonomy within those spaces.
- Exit requires the use of complementary protective strategies such as *voice* (open rebellion, threat of rebellion, insubordination, threat of dispersal, and a variety of other strategies exiles use to actively oppose the structures of capital and state), and *loyalty* (strategic dependence on the state or extra-state actors).
- Exit may, therefore, likely require some kind of *loyalty bargain*; to keep states and capital at bay, exilic societies may have to give something in return, especially if they are haunted by the chronic problems of material

subsistence and must obtain some needed resources from outside of the exilic zones.

This last point raises additional propositions:

- Loyalty bargains are likely to change over time, and their renegotiation may impose special challenges on exilic societies, especially as the development of the capitalist world-system (what we have called "world time") reinforces the power of states and capital relative to that of exiles and populations. In Scott's terms, for example, states introduce *friction-reducing technologies*.[4]
- Renegotiating loyalty bargains in the context of changing access to material resources and specificities tied to world time may produce patterns of change in exit/recapture and autonomy/incorporation.
- Exilic societies may choose to make loyalty bargains with entities other than the states that claim or threaten to claim authority over their territories; at certain times such strategies may protect autonomy.

The central problem from a strategic perspective is the problem of subsistence. In order to avoid the exit-without-resources trap, exilic spaces lend themselves to the following classification:

1. *Exit-with-autonomy*: cooperative exilic practices of politics, economy, and membership
2. *Exit-without-autonomy*: hierarchical exilic practices of politics, economy, and membership
3. *Autonomy-without-exit*: ethnic and cultural exilic practices within an empire or nation-state

AUTONOMY, WORLD TIME, AND THE LOYALTY BARGAIN

Let us return to the original basis of our problem. We proposed that Polanyi's model of a *double movement*—whereby the development of world-capitalism imposes limits on material life but also where popular classes (sometimes through states and sometimes on their own) try to regain well-being and liberties—could be reinterpreted through the lens of Kropotkin's proposals about mutual aid. In particular, as the practices and institutions of possessive individualism and "free-market" capitalism are imposed by state and capitalist formations, people react by trying to strengthen or even reinvent institutions and practices of sociability and mutual aid. One characteristic way that they may do so, we propose, is by creating *exilic spaces and practices*. We have defined these as areas of social and economic life where people and groups attempt to escape from state authority and capitalist economic processes, whether by territorial escape or by attempting to build structures that are autonomous of capitalist processes of accumulation and social control.

Much of the literature on autonomy, a concept that we have extended as *exilic constitution and practice*, is rather sanguine, as is much utopian literature. There may be a tendency to elide the objectionable practices of indigenous or precapitalist communities (such as gender oppression or ethnic subjugation); exilic communities may also do objectionable things in order to maintain subsistence. Cossack raiding is an obvious example of a practice that reinforced communal solidarity by helping the community overcome subsistence crises, yet that was clearly bloody and horrific to the "external" people who were raided. Thus, even if a community practices mutual aid internally, it may do rather unpleasant things to people outside of the community. Our study of Don Cossacks over some centuries raises the possibility that such external practices, which are in many ways the antithesis of mutual aid, can become part of the culture of the exilic group and may therefore, under certain conditions, become internalized into hierarchies and practices of subjugation within the exilic community. Clastres,[5] for instance, identified external violence as a state-avoiding mechanism, a deliberate means of achieving territorial decentralization and avoiding state formation. We see the influence of this proposition in Scott's descriptions of dispersal as a strategy in *Zomia*.[6] If this is indeed the case, the history of the Cossacks shows such a state-resisting device to be ineffective. The works that we have built upon—specifically, those by James Scott and Raul Zibechi—have paid far less attention to internal forms of inequality and oppression, to the ways that exilic communities maintain themselves by oppressing others, or to the impact of external practices on internal society.

A critical part of our analysis, therefore, is to distinguish negative aspects *imposed by the advances of states and capitalism* (which often result from the working out of a loyalty bargain) from the negative aspects that *already existed* in pre-state/capitalist societies or that were re-created or introduced as exilic practice. Ideally, exilic practices are those of mutual aid, but many of the hardships faced by exilic societies, particularly subsistence crises but also pressures of loyalty bargains, may encourage or force hierarchical practice. While we propose that exilic societies are the home of mutual aid to the degree that their people escaped state regulation and exploitative economy in the first place, can we be certain that exilic life will undermine cultural/gendered and other hierarchies that preceded the expansion of states and capital? Or, as de Sousa Santos put it, does the formation of exilic society and practice avoid the problem whereby social movements that overthrow or replace an existing form of oppressive regulation tend to impose new forms of oppressive regulation?[7]

Time was particularly important to the development of autonomy in all three exilic instances we have presented, including what we have called *world time*, that is, the position and development of the capitalist world-system as it interacts with local regions and actors. In secular terms, the capitalist world-economy, states, and the interstate system expand and deepen their control over populations across time. This may make it difficult for exilic societies to reproduce themselves if world capitalist control becomes greater. But the cyclical movements of the world-system provide opportunities for exilic formation. Cyclical downturns are often associated with the reorganization of global power structures, commodity chains, and divisions of labor, all of which can provide space for social movement voice and exile. Moreover, as we saw in the case of the Zapatistas, the imposition of new trading and productive regimes such as NAFTA can mobilize forces of opposition and influence the production of exilic spaces.

An important question that arises from our consideration of world time is whether there are tendencies for hierarchies to reemerge in the form of classes, castes, gender divisions, and so forth. A common hypothesis from the mainstream (Hobbes, Locke, and contemporary adherents to the ideology of possessive individualism) is that hierarchy is "natural" and thus it will inevitably reemerge as individuals follow their interests and as differences in access to resources such as land emerge or reemerge. One possible hypothesis from this perspective is that early migrants will likely have favorable access to the best land while later migrants have inferior access. As the best land becomes scarcer, private property will reemerge so that early migrants can protect their advantages to the detriment of later ones. Forms of private property and class will reappear, and direct democracy will be curtailed to the advantage of officeholders from the early migrants. At first glance, Cossack history appears to provide evidence in favor of this hypothesis. While early Cossack communities tenaciously avoided private property, agriculture, and thus agrarian hierarchies in favor of equality and liberty, the "natural" pressures of possessive individualism eventually caught up with them and they instituted a land-based class hierarchy as they were integrated into normal Russian society. We referred to this as a movement from exit-with-autonomy to exit-without-autonomy and, eventually, to (cultural) autonomy-without-exit.

Such a reading of Cossack exilic history, however, is ahistorical. Possessive individualism is hardly "natural" but is historically and socially constructed. As we have shown, what propelled the Cossacks into agrarian-based class society was the expansion of the Russian state and, especially, the expansion of the Europe-centered capitalist world-system, with its seemingly insatiable appetite for grain. This compelled Cossacks, after long resistance, to re-create private property and class, to abandon state-resisting practices such as the right to refuge, and to undermine the institutions of direct democracy such as the *krug* (assembly). Along with the renegotiation of the "loyalty bargain" under terms that were consistently to the greater advantage of the Russian state, strengthening world-systemic forces were irresistible and the Cossacks lost autonomy. Cossack private property was not "natural" but was a product of world time: pressures of state expansion in the context of world-systemic change.

How does our understanding of Cossack history inform what we have seen among the Zapatistas? There, the exilic community (like that of the early Cossacks) fought to preserve autonomy, one basis of which was communal rights to the land as promised in the Mexican institution of the *ejido*. Forced exiles in the Lacandon jungle were joined by other migrants, some of whom identified with the exilic project while others maintained relations with the state and, especially, its political parties, who could provide patronage in the form of metal roofs, access to fresh water, and so on. The debt crisis and restructuring of the world-economy left the Mexican state weak and provided a space for exilic consolidation, while the subsequent introduction of NAFTA helped to mobilize campesinos behind the exilic project because of the threatened breakup of the *ejido* and also the possible flooding of Mexican markets by US and Canadian commodities.

The biggest threat to exilic solidarity, together with horrendous paramilitary violence, was the way the Mexican state responded to subsistence crises by providing patronage in the form of material goods. The Zapatistas could have bought into this by negotiating a loyalty bargain with the Mexican state, and this would have secured building materials, health care, education, and so on, *but on the terms of the state and not as autonomous indigenous resources and services.* Instead, unlike the Cossacks, they took advantage of the solidarity that was made available by world time, by fissures in the national and international capitalist regime, and they reached out to negotiate an alternative loyalty bargain with civil society. The Zapatistas, in contrast to pluri-autonomous regions in Chiapas, have refused cultural autonomy-without-exit. As we saw, this was not a smooth process, and especially after 2003 the Zapatistas had to act creatively to take control even of this loyalty bargain so that it acted more in Zapatista interests and less in the interest of international donors and supporters. Yet this strategy enabled the Zapatistas to strengthen autonomy by creating explicitly exilic forms of education and health care, all at a time when liberation movements around the world were becoming increasingly integrated into mainstream economy and polity by peace processes and other integrative moves within the world-system.

Of course, the struggle is not over for the Zapatistas. The Cossacks also succeeded in avoiding Russian state moves to end their autonomy at key points of history, only to be eventually swallowed up by that state and in the context of world-systemic change. The history of Zapatismo is a short one and, creative as they have been in clinging to autonomy, pressures of integration and exilic disintegration still abound.

The prison exiles studied here faced a different set of problems from either of our preceding two instances. The rise of mass incarceration and widespread solitary confinement was undoubtedly produced by world time, as a strategy against insurgencies, whether liberation movements like the IRA and the PKK or internal insurgencies like the Black Panthers and the Red Army Faction. Imprisonment was a strategy used by core states like the US and Britain to stem the domestic rise of insurgencies that accompanied the Cold War. It was extended into the post–Cold War era and used against Islamic insurgents, gangs, and other groups that often came to prominence as a byproduct of the anti-leftist strategies of Western states in the Cold War.[8] In the US, in particular, prison authorities explicitly encouraged the rise of prison gangs as a counterweight to politically insurgent groups. Then, mass incarceration was imposed against large poor populations in an age when insurgent prison groups were largely defeated or transformed into gangs, which were in turn replenished by a flood of new young prisoners who joined out of identification or simple self-protection. Our older respondents tell us that prisons today are less "political" than they were in the 1960s and 1970s, and that young prisoners today are less interested in political conversation.

Perhaps this is the common complaint of grumpy old men. Yet, even as "gangs" populated by less inquisitive prisoners, the new prison groups retain the potential to become politically aware and thus insurgent.

The form of autonomy in prisons and its connection with loyalty bargains, however, is quite distinct. As we have seen, states have a moral obligation to provide prisoners a minimal subsistence, particularly food and shelter but not necessarily clothing, education, or entertainment. To gain "extras," prisoners maintain formal or informal loyalty bargains with the authorities in a reward/punishment structure. The agreement is relatively simple: maintain a certain level of discipline or obeisance and do not threaten prison order by engaging in disruptive individual or collective behavior, including acts of mutual aid such as prison lawyering. In return, the authorities provide privileges such as more and better visits, access to material things, freedom within prison spaces, and even the turn of a blind eye when prisoners smuggle items such as drugs or cell phones.

For certain prisoners, however, such a loyalty bargain is not acceptable. Prisoners who are forced into semi-exile in the general prison population have the least problem: material subsistence and a loyalty bargain are relatively unproblematic. Once a choice is made to refuse this bargain and go into complete exile, stripping is total. The loyalty bargain with the authorities is either not available or too unattractive, and this leaves open many new possibilities for the construction of a new kind of society. As in the case of Zapatistas, the dynamic is from partial autonomy, with a loyalty bargain that makes the inmate more and more dependent on authorities, to refusal of the bargain and the opening of a more complete autonomy with stronger collective ties and practices of mutual aid.

OTHER HIERARCHIES

To what extent does the practice of mutual aid and collective solidarity affect other social hierarchies that are produced and reproduced by forces other than states and capital? Does exilic life necessarily mean equality? We have recognized that indigenous and renegade cultures have hierarchies that are based, for example, on gender and ethnicity. Some of these hierarchies predate conquest while others might be introduced, strengthened, or modified in new forms in reaction to the pressures of incorporation by states and capital.

Ethnicity. A striking feature of Cossack society is its ethnic diversity or, rather, lack of ethnic definition. As we have argued, this inverted *insurgent ethnicity* served as an effective state-avoiding practice. Early Cossack "citizenship" was simply defined by escape, and there are known examples of Cossacks of different ethnic origins. Cossack economy, though, is defined largely by raiding, and therefore by attacks on communities that *are* ethnically defined, such as Tatars and Persians. As is often the case, solidarity is internal, and this may be strengthened if external forces are seen as "the enemy."

One might surmise that a dynamic could emerge whereby the *state*, from whom the exilic society has escaped, might replace other external peoples as the main enemy of exilic society (which it *is* in *objective* terms). In the case of the Cossacks, however, this was impossible because their loyalty bargain with the Russian state was all about attacking external forces on behalf of Muscovy. Thus, Cossack "glories" are about defeats of armies who were at war with Rus. The Cossacks were eventually homogenized into an ethnicity, a people with a common culture and history, which was eventually privatized by the state: a state-resisting practice was transformed into a state-supporting mechanism ("tradition"). As the loyalty bargain was renegotiated over and over, the ethnic character of Cossack military action increased until they were in the despicable position of attacking Jewish communities and striking workers and peasants on behalf of the tsar. Finally, contemporary *ethnic* Cossacks are known to patrol the Moscow subway disciplining non-Russians or to serve as the government's informal police at events such as the Olympic Games.

Could things have worked out differently? Perhaps the case of the Zapatistas provides some clues. Although indigenous based, the Zapatistas are multilingual and also cofounded by Mestizo exiles from the north. It is, thus, multi-ethnic although indigenous. Given the changes in "world time" since the public emergence of the Zapatistas in 1994, we can imagine such an exilic group being used, through a loyalty bargain with the Mexican state, as a buffer against migrants attempting to cross the frontier with Guatemala on their way to the United States.

Instead, this was an exilic space that made an explicit choice against a loyalty bargain with the Mexican state, its exilic "other." Instead, its bargain was with national and external civil society of all ethnicities. Rather than replacing the state- and capital-avoiding institution of "insurgent ethnicity," the Zapatistas embraced and extended it. Visitors to Zapatista communities are often met by a virtual United Nations of visitors and volunteers. While the EZLN actively seeks to block smugglers from turning the Lacandon into a drugs corridor, it is friendly toward migrants on the move for economic or other reasons. And La Otra, the "Other Campaign," for all of its shortcomings, was explicitly inclusive of all ethnicities; it also sought to attract people of all sexual orientations.

Perhaps the most interesting exilic experience from the point of view of ethnic hierarchies is that of solitary prisoners. In the US, state authorities often encourage ethnic divisions in prisons as a way of controlling inmates. It has been persuasively argued that in states like California gangs were encouraged to explicitly break down political resistance by groups such as the Black Panthers and La Raza. Yet gangs are only semi-exilic: their relationship with the authorities is often one by which they maintain a certain level of order, or even cause intergang warfare, in return for favors from the authorities. Many members are snitches who work as agents for the authorities, passing information on other prisoners or even provoking interracial trouble when asked to do so. This conforms somewhat to the Cossack pattern of behavior, where exiles are free to "raid" in return for certain acts of loyalty to the state from which they have been exiled.

Long-term solitary, it seems, can turn this around. We have argued that long-term solitary life in places such as Pelican Bay, particularly in the "short corridor" of the SHU, provides conditions for the encouragement of exilic society and practices. Inmates are forcibly removed not only from external US communities but also from the prison general population. Once in solitary, stripped of the amenities and many of the material commodities and aspirations of contemporary capitalist life, prisoners not only become exilic by developing an oral community with remarkable practices of mutual aid, but also *can* break down racial barriers and hierarchies. It is not irrelevant that almost all prisoners come from similar class backgrounds; class solidarity, along with a sort of mechanical solidarity as exiles in the same structural and material condition ("convict race"), provides a basis for overcoming ethnic divisions, particularly if they become identified as a state strategy of dividing exilic prisoners.

This appears to be the process that emerged in the short corridor. Prisoners who had been divided by differential identities and affiliations with ethnically and geographically defined groups were closely confined in a similar situation. There, they discussed the political nature of their situation, who *is* the enemy, and strategies for living in and overcoming their isolation. Interestingly, they were influenced by texts that crossed ethnic boundaries. Two white prisoners introduced into the conversation the example of Bobby Sands and the strategy of the hunger strike as a nonviolent weapon for those who have been stripped of other weapons. This was a history that was already familiar to African American prisoners from organizations such as the Black Guerrilla Family and, before that, the Black Panthers. Others discovered writings on Mayan cosmology, and together the group talked about what we have called world time and its connection to exilic strategies and tactics. Their political practices were solidly those of direct democracy, consultation, and consensus (we could almost refer to the Pelican Bay *krug* or *asamblea*). As the men got to know each other they formed a collective that largely transcended race. Perhaps more accurately put, they instituted a variation of what we have called *insurgent citizenship*: a deliberate state-resisting strategy to push away the authorities and protect the exilic content of the reappropriated space. In time, they not only constructed a difficult process of communicating/consulting with prisoners all around California (borrowing again from the Irish example) but also profoundly extended the hunger strike strategy with a series of statements and communiqués that called on *all* prisoners in California to transcend racial differences, stop prisoner-on-prisoner violence, and to recognize the state as the true enemy. It is worth noting that this experience of exilic prisoners forming solidarity across race is not unique: Lynd shows how a similar process emerged among prisoners involved in the 1993 Lucasville uprising,[9] and this cross-racial solidarity and mutual aid has strengthened among the death-sentenced, long-term solitary veterans of that conflict, who were at the center of a legal battle that went to the US Supreme Court (*Austin v. Wilkinson*) and a 2011 hunger strike, as well as other campaigns.

The popular press cites prisoners and prison gangs as intrinsically racist, violent, and cliquish. Undoubtedly there are instances where prisoners and prison gangs recruit along racial lines and practice violence against each other. This makes experiences like Lucasville/Youngstown and Pelican Bay all the more remarkable and a testament to the *possibilities* of exilic society as a force against hierarchy.

Gender. One of the most problematically enduring hierarchies across societies has been gender inequality. Clearly, exilic formation did little to improve the lot of women in Cossack society, apart from the improvements that all Cossacks realized from escaping the Russian state. Cossack life was highly male dominated and gender roles were strictly defined. There is little evidence that women were brought more into the democratic life of the community, had greater responsibilities in the *krug* or other exilic institutions, or had more equal relations in the home or the community. If anything, the degree to which Cossack glory is macho and raiding stories are about the subjugation of women and women captives indicates that the subjugation of women increased in certain ways as Cossack communities developed. This indicates that there is little or no *necessary* connection between the liberties that are gained by exile and the liberty of subjugated groups such as women within the community.

Does this mean that exilic life is inevitably sexist? We believe the answer to this is firmly "no," and that once again the example of the Zapatistas tells a lot about the possibilities of connections between exilic practice and the destruction of gender hierarchies and inequalities. As we have seen, life for Mayan women is far from ideal, not only because of the impacts of the state on health and other issues facing indigenous women but also because of gendered hierarchies that preexisted conquest and became deeper as Mexico developed before and after colonialism. Yet the Zapatistas emerged at a time of "new social movements," when there was more emphasis than before on issues of equality and identity as well as more information about them. Their movement included greater numbers of women in positions of leadership, and their decision to refuse a bargain with the Mexican state in favor of international civil society, as well as their constant daily interaction with activists from all over the world, made them more familiar with and sympathetic to issues of gender equality. Mayan women observed how other women lived and sought many of their relative freedoms. Participation of women had become one of the most cohesive elements of the Zapatista autonomy, with incredibly powerful capital- and state-resisting effect. The result was that the Zapatistas themselves launched a number of initiatives to increase gender equality, including affirmative action to raise the quality of life of women and girls in particular.

Combined with the negative experiences of Cossack women, the Zapatista experience indicates that exilic life *can* but does not necessarily improve the lot of women or ease gender inequalities. It can free the society from capitalist and state relations of domination that may exacerbate or deepen gender inequalities. But exilic societies must themselves create internal dynamics that destroy hierarchies such as those of gender and race. Their willingness to address them will depend on a number of factors, including the nature of the exilic loyalty bargain and the effects of world time. What our studies show is that the extent of mutual aid within an exilic space is directly proportional to the success of capital- and state-resisting practices. Where practices of mutual aid are more developed, the society is more resilient and successful in avoiding recapture.

Obviously, the exilic experiences of isolated prisoners does not speak directly to the issue of gender hierarchy because prisoners are generally segregated by gender. But one finding of our study is important for this question. We have argued that the severe stripping of prisoners from commodities and other elements of modern consumer culture/identity leaves them open to re-create an exilic society based on mutual aid and sociability. One result is a heightened sense of identity: prisoners as "us" and authorities as "them." We saw how this encouraged prisoners to share experiences and to debate and discuss possible futures and strategies. This led them to invent new forms of (insurgent) identity that served an important state-repelling function. Such sharing encouraged them to transcend ethnic and other group differences, which faded considerably, if not completely. One could hypothesize that a similar combination of stripping and sharing could help create the preconditions for the removal of all kinds of hierarchies if they, (1) remove aspects of identity that reinforce hierarchy and (2) encourage forms of solidarity that help exiles to emphasize their similarities and overcome differences. Once again, we are brought to the conclusion that mutual aid practices are more conducive to building effective capital- and state-avoiding capacity.

WORLD-SYSTEMS ANALYSIS REEXAMINED

Let us now go back to the second question we used to organize our study. How does our study of exilic spaces influence our understanding of the world-economy? Once exilic spaces and practices, parts of what Braudel has called *material life*,[10] are recognized as an essential component of the capitalist world-system, we are forced to face a new set of problems. First, the study of exilic spaces and practices forces us to reconsider *economy* to include, at its core, the production of relations between people rather than merely the production of commodities. If so, we must also recover a definition of *work* that includes the real effort and sweat involved in the production of communities and practices of mutual aid, including even the work of collective dancing and singing. Second, rather than insisting on the notion of antisystemic movements, we have studied the *infrapolitics* of the world-system (we prefer this to the more "vocal" term "resistance"), whereby often practically invisible or unnamed forms of creation continue to be practiced on a massive scale.[11] If ignored, these practices and the spaces where they are done have the potential to threaten capitalism. But this is why states and institutions of capitalism do not ignore them but crush, attack, or bargain with them in the ways that we have examined in this book. On the basis of our studies, we suggest the following conceptualization of exilic spaces:

1. Pre-incorporative exilic space (before incorporation into the capitalist world-economy)

2. Post-incorporative exilic space (during and after incorporation into the capitalist world-economy)

3. Restructured exilic space (as a result of successive stages of reintegration into the restructured world-economy, with new hegemonic power hierarchies, leading economic sectors, and global and regional divisions of labor)

The Don Cossacks are an example of the pre-incorporative type, while the Zapatistas and solitary prisoners are examples of post-incorporative, restructured exilic spaces. We have found considerable differences between these pre- and the post-incorporation exilic spaces. Pre-incorporative exilic spaces relate to dynamic forces that threaten their external character, while post-incorporative exilic spaces and practices relate to world-systemic processes at different levels of the world-economy (local, regional, global). To put it in a different way, the exilic space during and after incorporation is a zone of refuge, or a protective organization of communal resistance and survival. During periods of incorporation and relative systemic stability, the state strives to manipulate that space to the benefit of capital accumulation. This was the case with the Don Cossack communities as well as with the "institutionalized" indigenous communities of postrevolutionary (pre-1980s) Chiapas.

However, in moments of systemic crisis and hegemonic transition, the *restructured* exilic space is both protective and transformative. The Zapatistas used space as a strategic resource not only for defense but also for the reconstruction of bonds of mutual aid and solidarity. The Zapatista exilic space, which emerged during and as a result of hegemonic change, is another "black hole in the world-economy"; without being (completely) outside of the world system, the exiles are adept at escaping incorporative pressures, constituting an important obstacle for capital accumulation strategies in the region. Their refusal of the left developmentalist strategy of taking state power resonated far beyond Mexico and inspired a "movement of movements" against neoliberalism. This way of thinking points to a particular and peculiar characteristic of the incorporation process and to a somewhat impoverished understanding of politics in much of world-systems analysis. Rather than an "in or out process," whereby more and more new zones are hooked into the capitalist world-system in a way that they can "virtually no longer escape,"[12] incorporation is "both in and out"; many places are never completely incorporated. In contrast to much world-systems literature, we see the process of incorporation as relational, gradual, ongoing, uneven, and reversible. Equally important, the incorporative process is defined not only by the integration of new territories into a worldwide division of labor but also by the elimination of exilic spaces. The effects of "black holes" in the world-economy and, consequently, of infrapolitics, or territorialization of exit, is a neglected feature in the world-systems literature and in contemporary conversations on de-territorialization. As our Cossacks example has shown, the exilic space was crucial to the process of "co-territorialization" and the subsequent emergence and incorporation of Moscow state space. The Zapatistas have emerged as a result of the incomplete incorporation and restructuring of the world-economy. As a reinvented and restructured exilic society, they have assumed an important, if not a leading, role in the resistance to both the violence of Mexican state space and the accumulation processes of the world-economy.

"ECONOMY," MUTUAL AID, WORLD TIME, AND INFRAPOLITICS

Let us conclude with some comments about our central questions: exilic society as the home of mutual aid, where the *work* of building community is both mutual and collective; the relations between such societies/practices and the capitalist world-system. We believe we can say some things now about possible futures, and point the way toward what could be important areas of future research.

We believe we have demonstrated that it is impossible to study nonstate spaces without a reference to what we have called world time, or the contradictory totality of the temporal and spatial scales that comprise the world-economy. World time was crucial for the demise, or transformation, of the Cossack exilic space. Likewise, it was crucial for the emergence, or rather, restructuring, of exilic self-activity in Chiapas. The reappropriation of space in Chiapas was predicated on changes in world time.

A related point concerns the exilic relationship with the state. We have shown that the world-economy imposes incorporative pressures that make the reliance of exilic spaces on the state unsustainable in the long term. The Zapatistas made a strategically productive choice by avoiding a bargain with the Mexican state, an avoidance that was itself made possible only by the changes in the organization of the world-system. And in the "laboratory" conditions of isolated imprisonment, the Irish and US cases demonstrate a clear positive relationship between avoiding a loyalty bargain with the authorities and building a solidary community based on mutual aid.

Another result of our study was that exilic spaces place limits on incorporation. One reason why incorporation is incomplete, partial, and reversible is precisely the existence of exilic spaces that predated capitalist incorporation. While we do not claim that this is the only reason processes of incorporation are delayed or shaped in a particular way, we do believe that we made a case that former nonstate spaces can have a decisive influence on the patterns of expansion of the world-economy. This was certainly the case in relation to the Don Cossacks and the semiperipheral incorporation of the Russian state. In the case of Mexico, the partial nature of incorporation of eastern Chiapas along with changes effected by world time allowed for the reappropriation of spaces that have now become an important obstacle to regional capitalist processes of reincorporation. As for prisoners, the case is more provocative. Is the exilic space inscribed in the *soul*, in the sense Foucault uses the word, so that humanity is hardwired to seek sociability and relations of mutual aid? Are we as humans in a constant war between our competitive individualistic sides and our communal sides, so that once the commodities and relations of possessive individualism are stripped, we strive to reconnect with each other, to be sociable, to engage in relations of mutual aid?

We have shown that mutual aid has been unduly neglected as an explanatory and conceptual tool in historical social sciences. We extended the meaning of mutual aid to include cooperative habits and practices in economy, politics, and membership. This conceptualization of mutual aid puts into question the conventional classification of politics, membership, and economics as separate and distinct levels of society and, especially, of exilic society. We have suggested that exilic economy is best understood as the *production* of communal bonds, and this includes the *work* of politics and membership as practices carefully organized to nourish communal cohesion and protect the community from the intrusion of states and capital.

We have found that the process of exile and exilic society-building encourages collective relations of mutual aid and direct democracy. We have also discovered that mutual aid encourages exile. A central finding of our study has been that societies that practice mutual aid in the form of cooperative exilic practices are much more likely to prevent recapture. The Zapatistas, for example, who even extended mutual aid to include such practices as sending economic help to Latin American countries like Cuba, demonstrated much greater cohesion and resilience than the Cossack exiles in the eighteenth century (one is reminded of the impoverished Choctaw community sending $170 to the starving Irish during the famine in 1847, just sixteen years after they suffered involuntary exile along the first "Trail of Tears"[13]). The same could be said of isolated prisoners, whose insurgent identity and solidary cultures protected the integrity of the recovered space.

But this is not enough. There are considerable forces of state-building and capital accumulation that either pull exilic spaces back into world-capitalism or insert possessive individualism and hierarchy back into the exilic space. Moreover, the "purest" examples of exilic society, such as isolated prisons, are temporally bound, by definition: prisoners are released, achieve their objectives, or are moved around; the result is the disruption of the exilic community. The poorest, most stripped communities, such as those in the Lacandon, understandably seek a more comfortable life, and the ways to achieve this involve forays into the world of capital, as migrant labor to get goods or money to send back to the exilic space. Often, these forays are longer, even permanent, and the loss of youth to migration can seriously disrupt the exilic community. As communities raise their standards of living and wealth, the pressures of mainstream agents, including political parties and businesses, may also increase. Even successful exilic "enterprises" such as coffee cooperatives, which are originally established to provide material resources for the community, can come under the pressure to privatize or to become more capital-like.

Another conclusion we draw from our study is that the politics of the world-system cannot be reduced to the relationship between states or even to the exercise of voice by "antisystemic" social movements.[14] We should extend the scope of politics to include the hidden transcript of rebellious territoriality, the infrapolitics of state- and capital-resisting spaces and practices.

While we have proposed that exilic spaces and practices do not have to involve separate territories, but may be built within the interstices of mainstream societies—in tenement yards, ghettos and favelas, suburbs, or cultural groups—our studies in this volume have been about communities that have been separated, voluntarily or forcibly, from territories controlled or dominated by the state and capital. Much research is yet to be done about what we have called structural exile. Is a group of people who come together to sing exilic? After all, they are working at the job of building community, practicing mutual aid, and engaging in direct democracy as an alternative to the usual individualized and commodified activities of capitalist life.

What of the role of states? Are they always inimical to exile or do they sometimes encourage exilic spaces and practices? Was Yugoslav self-management conducive to, or tolerant of, exilic practices? Can cooperative projects (including farming communities) encouraged by the Bolivarian movement in Venezuela be considered exilic and, if so, in what ways? What is the relationship between an exilic space and a state-space influenced by exilic practices?

Finally, a most important area of research is exile as movement and strategy. After the experiences of the antiglobalization and occupy movement, the prefigurative path of changing the world by *living* the life you would like to live and creating the kinds of community structures and practices that would envelop such a life has become popular in many circles.[15]

But how effective is this form of politics? The studies in this book have without doubt contributed to this question and raised new problems for such interstitial prescriptions for change. Caffentzis, for instance, proposes that the way to begin transforming capitalism is *not* by imagining possible futures but by finding "necessary conditions" of capitalism, negating one or more of them, and moving on from there.[16] He proposes that the annihilation of the commons is such a necessary condition for the existence of capitalism and, therefore, the way forward is to build and protect the commons. While embracing the idea of the commons, we believe our studies point to the need to complement this strategy of *negation*. In particular, we do not believe that the annihilation of what we have termed exilic spaces and practices (of which the commons are but one element) is a necessary condition of capitalism. One of the strengths of capitalism is its ability to deal with and contain exilic spaces and commons, primarily through the loyalty bargain and through the imposition of subsistence crises. One of the most important tasks ahead of us is rigorously empirical research of spaces of escape and the protective strategies they employ.

Such analytical effort is particularly important in moments of hegemonic shift and structural transition of the capitalist world-economy. It has been argued that in the long period of uncertainty that began in the 1980s, the power of states has been changed and even undermined by forces such as the so-called financialization of the world-economy. Yet states and coalitions of states have also become more aggressive at war-making and the direct exercise of power. In such a situation, there is an undoubted rise of new territories in competition with nation-states. Some of them are ungoverned spaces, characterized by an escalation of religious and ethnic violence, or by the rise of an urban subproletariat. In such times, there is no way to predict what form the territorialization of exit will take.

What of reactionary exile? Analysts like Craib[17] have begun to study libertarian capitalists who establish communities on the sea or in remote jungles to evade state regulation and taxation. Of course, these could be considered to be *anti-exilic* to the extent that they are based on extreme individualism, competition, and hierarchical subjugation. They also fundamentally depend on capitalist markets and therefore on the regulations of the interstate system. Sometimes they directly depend on state protection of their territories. Nonetheless, they have certain structural affinities with the kinds of communities we have studied herein, and it is worth exploring whether they have anything to tell us about the dynamics of exile.

There are also violent societies that compete with nation-states *and* exhibit high internal solidarity, albeit a reactionary solidarity that is often based on religious or other fundamentalisms and that allows no democratic *asambleas* or *krugs*. The so-called war on terror that the US launched in the wake of the Cold War spawned a slew of such groups, the most notorious of which include the Islamic State (IS) and Boko Haram. In a stark but brutal irony, the same process that enabled the Islamic State also produced a society that has many of the characteristics we have called exilic: Rojava. In 1911 one could sit atop a laundry in El Paso, Texas, and watch the exilic forces of Pancho Villa in a shooting war with the Mexican *federales*; one hundred years later, one could sit across the Turkish border from Kobane and watch an exilic society in armed conflict with a fundamentalist group that shared many of its characteristics, *except* direct democracy and the desire to obliterate hierarchies based on gender, ethnicity, and religion. The temptation is to say that one society comprised the *good* exiles and the other the *bad* ones. But such a simple explanation avoids many of the important issues we have tried to raise in our comparisons of three exilic societies. The Islamic State, as its name indicates, is a would-be state-in-the-making. In this instance, one can observe two distinct and very different forms of territorialization: one of rule (IS) and one of exit (Rojava). In other words, the weakening of the interstate system can go either way: to state-like territorial fragments, and nonstate (exilic) spaces.

It is an urgent task for emancipatory scholarship to analytically comprehend and conceptualize the infrapolitics of escape. We believe it is crucial to put the struggle between mutual aid and possessive individualism back at the center of the study of the historical social sciences. We hope the studies we have presented are the beginning.

We have studied exilic spaces because we have hope. We have hope that another society is possible, where social relations of mutual aid predominate and where the *work* of building community and producing joy is recognized as a central part (perhaps *the* central part) of *economy*, at least as much as the work of producing commodities and services. We think that another approach to *politics* is both useful and necessary, where production and circulation of exilic spaces and practices are recognized as a central part of the politics of the world-economy. It is not just the noise of the dominant system, and the antisystemic voice of the resisting movements, that produces dissonant notes in the world-system; the struggle is also expressed in silences and refusals that are sometimes less vocal but certainly not less confrontational. Such silence and refusals used to travel on ships and live in jungles, steppes, and mountains; today, they still live in jungles and mountains, in Zapatista and Aymara regions, but also in the urban exilic spaces of Kingston, autonomous Kurdish regions, supermax prisons, and occupied town squares.

An infrapolitics of self-organized exilic sites where resistance can germinate is a structural underpinning for more visible political action—not its substitute, but its condition. The frictionless world, like the free market utopia of capitalist civilization, remains as elusive today as it was in the sixteenth century. In this partial and reversible triumph of capitalist expansion, and in the accompanying stubborn refusal (sometimes uttered in silence and at high altitude), one should find reasons for optimism even—or especially—today.

NOTES

PREFACE

1. Grubačić, "A Conversation with Dennis O'Hearn."
2. Lynd and Grubačić, *Wobblies and Zapatistas.*
3. O'Hearn, "The Second Economy in Consumer Goods and Services"; O'Hearn, "The Consumer Second Economy."
4. Grubačić, *Don't Mourn, Balkanize.*
5. Hirschman, *Exit, Voice, and Loyalty.*
6. See Lynd, *Doing History from the Bottom Up.*

CHAPTER ONE. INTRODUCTION

1. On Cossacks, see Boeck, *Imperial Boundaries*; on pirates, see Linebaugh and Rediker, *The Many-Headed Hydra,* and Rediker, *Villains of All Nations*; on escaped slaves, or maroons, see Price, *Maroon Societies.*
2. On Zapatistas see, among many others, Earle Simonelli, *Uprising of Hope*; on land occupations, see Wolford, *This Land Is Ours Now*; and on political prisoners, see O'Hearn, "Repression and Solidary Cultures of Resistance."
3. On Jamaica, see Gray, *Demeaned but Empowered*; on shack-dwellers, see Pithouse, "Struggle Is a School"; on South American suburbs, see Zibechi, *Territories in Resistance.*
4. Braudel, *The Perspective of the World*, 229–30.
5. Marx, *Capital*, 451.
6. Luxemburg, *The Accumulation of Capital;* Lenin, *Imperialism;* Baran and Sweezy, *Monopoly Capital*; on world-systems analysis, see Wallerstein, *The Modern World-System I.*
7. Linebaugh and Rediker, *The Many-Headed Hydra*; Boeck, *Imperial Boundaries.*
8. De Sousa Santos, "Public Sphere and Epistemologies of the South," 57.

9. It is important to note that the notion of exilic space should not be confused with that of "exile" or "flight"; see Deleuze and Guatari, *A Thousand Plateaus*; Hardt and Negri, *Empire*, 206; Papadopolous, Stephenson, and Tsianos, *Escape Routes*. The notion of exit used in this study comes from Hirschman, *Exit, Voice, and Loyalty*, and Gray, *Demeaned but Empowered*. Gray introduced the concept of *exilic spaces*; our use of the concept may differ in certain ways from his, particularly in its breadth (exile is economic and social, as well as political and cutural) and its historical range (beyond urban Jamaica). We conceive of space as a dynamic social product and as a constitutive dimension of (always temporal) social relations, not as a physical location emptied of time and movement.

10. Wright, *Envisioning Real Utopias*; Sober and Wilson, *Unto Others*; Bowles and Gintis, *A Cooperative Species*.

11. Wallerstein, *Geopolitics and Geoculture*, 230.

12. See, e.g., Federici, *Revolution at Point Zero*.

13. Kropotkin, *Mutual Aid*.

14. Scott, *The Art of Not Being Governed*; Zibechi, *Territories in Resistance*.

15. Wright, *Class, Crisis and the State*.

16. Polanyi, Karl 1957. "The Economy as Instituted Process"; Hopkins, "Sociology and the Substantive View of the Economy"; Mauss, *The Gift*; Graeber, *Toward an Anthropological Theory of Value*.

17. Hirschman, *Exit, Voice, and Loyalty*.

18. Quoted in Todes, "Darwin's Malthusian Metaphor and Russian Evolutionary Thought, 1859–1917," 546.

19. Kropotkin, *Mutual Aid*, 6.

20. For instance, Sober and Wilson, *Unto Others*.

21. Clastres, *Society against the State*.

22. Scott, *The Art of not Being Governed*, 3.

23. Ibid., 8.

24. Abram, *The Spell of the Sensuous*; Bunker, *The Snake with Golden Braids*; see also Basso, *Wisdom Sits in Places*.

25. O'Hearn, "Repression and Solidary Cultures of Resistance."

26. Scott, *The Art of not Being Governed*, 132.

27. Ibid., 38.

28. Ibid., 15.

29. Ibid., 5.

30. Ibid., xii.

31. See Holloway, *Crack Capitalism*.

32. Zibechi, *Territories in Resistance,* 67.

33. Ibid., 71.

34. Ibid., 76.

35. Ibid., 74.

36. Ibid., 16.

37. Braudel, *The Perspective of the World*, 40.

38. Ibid., 42.

39. Scott, *Domination and the Arts of Resistance*, 38, 183.

40. Ibid., 58.

41. Gray, *Demeaned but Empowered*.

42. Ibid., 118.

CHAPTER TWO. THINKING ABOUT AND RESEARCHING
EXIT AND RECAPTURE

1. Hopkins and Wallerstein, "Capitalism and the Incorporation of New Zones into the World-Economy"; Wallerstein, *The Modern World-System III*.

2. For Wallerstein, luxuries are "socially low-valued items" that may be exported "at prices far higher than those obtainable from their alternative usages." This concept only applies to trade between two separate historical systems, which therefore can have different measures of social value. "Hence, the concepts 'luxury' and 'external arena' go hand in hand." Wallerstein, *The Modern World-System III*, 132.

3. Hopkins and Wallerstein, "Capitalism and the Incorporation of New Zones into the World-Economy," 765.

4. Wallerstein, *The Modern World-System III*, 131.

5. McMichael, "Incorporating Comparison within a World-Historical Perspective."

6. On abstraction in Marx see Sayer, *The Violence of Abstraction*.

7. Tomich, *Through the Prism of Slavery*, 29.

8. Ibid., 55.

9. Tomich, *Through the Prism of Slavery*.

10. Kaye, "The Second Slavery." Apart from its efforts to capture and utilize different forms of labor, capital also defines and redefines what constitutes work, so that human efforts that do not produce exchange values are no longer considered "work." We discuss the importance of this definitional process in the section on value and production, below.

11. Tilly, "War Making and State Making as Organized Crime," 173.

12. Wallerstein, *The Modern World-System III,* 778.

13. Hirschman, *Exit, Voice, and Loyalty,* 18.

14. Ibid., 96, 97.

15. Ibid., 17.

16. Ibid., 76.

17. Price, *Maroon Societies*; Boeck, *Imperial Boundaries*.

18. Rediker, *Villains of All Nations*.

19. Hall, *Social Change in the Southwest, 1350–1880*.

20. Goffman, *Asylums*.

21. Foucault, *Security, Territory, Population*, 1.

22. Foucault, *Discipline and Punish*.

23. Actually, Aristotle distinguishes three forms of *bios*, or life, beyond bare life: contemplative life (*bios theōrētikos*), pleasure (*bios apolaustikos*), and political life

(*bios politikos*). Yet Arendt, Foucault, and Agamben for some reason focus solely on political life as that which distinguishes humans from the bare life of animals. This severely restricts their understandings of the meaning of life and, thus, of the effects of power upon it and the potentialities of human self-emancipation. For an excellent critique of Agamben's and Arendt's uses of Aristotle, see Finlayson, "'Bare Life' and Politics in Agamben's Reading of Aristotle."

24. Agamben, *Homo Sacer*, 9. Notice the common mistake of naturalizing the division between "home" and "society." As Kropotkin and other anthropologists emphasize, the clan preceded the household/family, which is a premodern invention that developed into modernity as the nuclear family. In clan societies the distinction between home life and social life either did not exist or was much less clear.

25. Ibid., 10.

26. Ibid., 171.

27. Ibid., 12.

28. Ibid., 14.

29. Foucault, *Discipline and Punish*, 143.

30. Quoted in Agamben, *Homo Sacer*, 11.

31. See Alexander, *The New Jim Crow*. This is also the basis of Wacquant's analysis of the use of mass imprisonment to "punish the poor." See Wacquant, *Punishing the Poor*.

32. Laclau, "Bare Life or Social Indeterminacy"; Ziarek, "Bare Life."

33. Polanyi, *The Great Transformation*.

34. Polanyi, "The Economy as Instituted Process"; Hopkins, "Sociology and the Substantive View of the Economy"; Polanyi, "The Economy as Instituted Process."

35. See Graeber, *Toward an Anthropological Theory of Value*; Graeber, *The Democracy Project*.

36. See Bowles and Gintis, *A Cooperative Species,* and Sober and Wilson, *Unto Others*.

37. Turner, "Production, Exploitation and Social Consciousness in the 'Peripheral Situation,'" 100.

38. Graeber, *Toward an Anthropological Theory;* see also Mauss, *The Gift*.

39. Komlosy says the association of work with pain is reflected at least in the German usage by the replacement of *werk* (creative autonomous vocation, leading to *opus*) by *arbeit* (painful, hard labor). Komlosy, *Arbeit*. Of course, the absurd yet obvious end of this dissociation was seen in the signs above the entrances to German concentration camps: "*Arbeit macht frei.*"

40. Ehrenreich, *Dancing in the Streets*.

41. Freeman, W. J., "A Neurobiological Role of Music in Social Bonding," 411.

42. Ehrenreich, *Dancing*, 99.

43. Elias, *The Civilizing Process*.

44. Ehrenreich, *Dancing in the Streets*, 129–31.

45. Crary, *24/7*.

46. Hopkins and Wallerstein, "Capitalism and the Incorporation of New Zones into the World-Economy," 777.

47. Federici, *Revolution at Point Zero*, 99.

48. Ibid., 101.

49. Staples, *No Place like Home.*

50. Zibechi, *Territories in Resistance*, 22.

51. Zibechi, *Territories in Resistance*. See also Rojas and Guaygua, "El empleo en tiempos de crisis."

52. Poveda, "Trabajo, informalidad y acumulación," 17, 22ff.

53. García Linera, Alvaro, *Reproletarización*, 201.

54. Steiner, *The Threefold Commonwealth*; Preparata, Guido 2006. "Perishable Money in a Threefold Commonwealth."

55. On "new forms of investment" and the shift from post-WWII US hegemony to Japanese economic ascendance, see Bunker and O'Hearn, "Strategies of Economic Ascendants for Access to Raw Materials."

56. Each type of governance has multiple variants. Research into exilic spaces will also ask questions about whether and how these variants make a difference in the workings and sustainability of a given exilic space.

57. Scott, *The Art of not Being Governed.*

58. Zibechi, *Territories in Resistance*, 23.

59. Gray, *Demeaned but Empowered.*

CHAPTER THREE. COSSACKS

1. Wallerstein is worth quoting extensively:

And where was this European world-economy? . . . Atlantic islands and perhaps a few enclaves on the African coast might also be included in it, but not the Indian Ocean areas; not the Far East, except perhaps, for a time, part of the Philippines; not the Ottoman Empire; and not Russia, or at most Russia was marginally included briefly. There are no clear and easy lines to draw, but I think it most fruitful to think of the sixteenth century European world as being constructed out of the linkage of two formerly more separate systems, the Christian Mediterranean system centering on the Northern Italian cities and the Flanders-Hanseatic trade network of north and northwest Europe, and the attachment to this new complex on the one hand of East Elbia, Poland, and some other areas of Eastern Europe, and on the other hand of the Atlantic islands and parts of the New World. (Wallerstein, *Modern World-System III*, 68)

2. In Wallerstein's view,

We shall denote this distinction as one between the periphery of a world economy and its external arena. The periphery of a world-economy is that geographical sector of it wherein production is primarily of lower ranking goods (that is, goods whose labor is less well rewarded) but which is an integral part of the overall system of the division of labor, because the commodities involved are essential for daily use. The external arena of a world-economy consists of those other world-systems with which a given world-economy has some kind of trade relationship, based primarily on the exchange of luxury items, what was sometimes called the "rich trades." (301–2).

One of the most comprehensive and lucid analyses of the concept of the periphery can be found in Derlugian, "The Social Cohesion of the States."

3. "Perhaps, alternatively, we could think of it as a gigantic success. Russia was *not* pulled into the European world-economy. Her bourgeoisie and her monarch were spared, at least for the moment, the fate of their Polish counterparts." Ivan aimed to create a Russian Empire, not to gain "a piece of the European pie." That would become the objective some years later under Peter the Great. Wallerstein, *Modern World-System I*, 136.

4. Nolte, "The Netherlands and Russia in the Seventeenth Century."

5. Pokrovsky was a Bolshevik economic historian who was much admired by Lenin but whose books were later banned by Stalin, purportedly because they repudiated "great man" theories of Russian history, focusing instead on economic explanations of change. Among his influential works were *Russian History from the Most Ancient Times* (1910–13) and *Brief History of Russia* (1920).

6. Russia was a colony of Western powers as early as the sixteenth century, supplying the world market with grain. A pivotal element of Pokrovsky's analysis is the development of merchant capital. The form that class alliance took in Russia resulted in the integration of Russia into the world-economy, which was "accompanied not by a weakening of autocracy, but by its strengthening, and not by a transition to capitalist agriculture, but by a strengthening of serfdom." Kagarlitsky, *Empire of the Periphery*, 122.

7. Kagarlitsky, *Empire of the Periphery*, 108. It is easy to establish that each new phase in the development of the European economy, and later of the global economy as well, coincided with crucial events for Russia—and there was nothing accidental about it. In the Muscovite state, the great transformations that took place in sixteenth- and seventeenth-century Europe were paralleled by the repressions of Ivan the Terrible and the Time of Troubles. The economic boom of the eighteenth century became the golden age of the Russian nobility, an era of grandeur and enlightenment based on merciless exploitation of the peasants. In the 1860s and 1870s, a new revolutionary transformation of the world-system was under way. In Russia, the era of reforms was beginning. The crisis of world capitalism in the years from 1914 to 1918 manifested itself not only in the First World War but also in the Russian Revolution. The Great Depression of 1929 to 1932 was accompanied by Stalin's collectivization, and so forth (Kagarlitsky, *Empire of the Periphery*).

8. Ibid., 156.

9. Ibid., 149.

10. Quoted in ibid., 45.

11. In European economic history, Russia is still considered a classic example of "backwardness" by many (Gerschenkron, *Economic Backwardness in Historical Perspective*; Chirot, *The Origins of Backwardness in Eastern Europe*; Hroch, Miroslav, and Luda Klusâková, *Criteria and Indicators of Backwardness*). We, however, interpret "backwardness" as a result of the incorporation of Russian territory

into the capitalist world-economy, as a result of processes of *underdevelopment* rather than lack of development. *Incorporation* into the capitalist world-system refers to the process of integrating the Russian economy into its production networks or commodity chains, as well as integrating the Russian state-space into the interstate system of the capitalist world-economy (Wallerstein, *Modern World-System I*). In the process, key changes are effected in Russian class structure—crucially, the rise of serfdom and the division of lord and serf throughout the countryside.

12. Kagarlitsky, *Empire of the Periphery*, 63. On the emergence of Moscow and the formation of the Russian state, see Kollmann, *Kinship and Politics*.

13. Kagarlitsky, *Empire of the Periphery*, 63. The so-called "Novgorodian alternative" is hardly convincing. Novgorod was losing its place in the new epoch. "The brutal and unforgiving autocracy in Moscow" does not appear to be any more brutal or unforgiving than contemporary Western states. On this issue, see Martin, "Muscovite Frontier Policy."

14. Lieberman, *Strange Parallels*, 215.

15. Quoted in ibid., 216. Ostrowski, Lieberman, and Hellie all emphasize the mid-1400s as a crucial period. Ostrowski, *Muscovy and the Mongols*; Hellie, "The Expanding Role of the State in Russia." Further, Ostrowski and Lieberman both offer a very similar periodization of Russian history: 1304–1448 (first period), 1448–1589 (second period), and 1589–1722 (last period). For Wallerstein and Romanello the turning point is the conquest of the Volga khanate of Kazan and the city of Astrakhan in 1552 and 1556. Wallerstein, *Modern World-System I*, and Romaniello, "Controlling the Frontier."

16. Kolchin, *Unfree Labor*, 5.

17. Wallerstein, *Modern World-System I*, 314.

18. "While the local bourgeoisie was encouraged by the degree of protection afforded to the local market, most notably by Custom Statutes (1653) and New Trade Statutes (1667), the main centers of accumulation were in the core countries of the capitalist world-system. This relationship accounted not only for technological innovation, but also for serf labor assigned to the factories in the emerging industrial production. It was thus 'civilized' Western investors who laid the basis for what was later considered the barbaric, and peculiarly Russian form of organization of production" (Kagarlitsky, *Empire of the Periphery*, 112–13). At the same time, "Russian elites, the first in world history, self-consciously began to define themselves as leaders of a 'backward' realm that had to 'catch up' with central and western Europe militarily and, by extension, economically" (Lieberman, *Strange Parallels*, 289).

19. According to Wallerstein, Ivan succeeded in protecting the autonomy of Russia from the encroaching European world-economy (Wallerstein, *Modern World-System I*, 315). His defeat in the Livonian war (1558–83) delayed the incorporation of Russia, which would be absorbed only later, as a semiperipheral state (like Spain) rather than a peripheral one (like Poland). For Kagarlitsky, too, the Livonian war was a pivotal moment, but as part of a desperate struggle to be included in the world-economy (Kagarlitsky, *Empire of the Periphery*). The alternative to peripheral

incorporation and ensuing backwardness was isolation, and isolation is what Ivan tried desperately to avoid.

20. Nonetheless, between 1565 and 1572, the *oprichnina* took the form of a massacre in much of the countryside because slaughter and damage induced by the 1571 Crimean Tatar raid left more than eight hundred thousand people dead.

21. See Avrich, *Russian Rebels, 1600–1800*. For a slightly different explanation of Bolotnikov, see Lieberman, *Strange Parallels*; Lieberman sees the rebellion as one of a frontier region least well integrated into the new state, in parallel with Southeast Asia.

22. Lieberman thinks that the troubles were "more purgative than toxic." *Strange Parallels*, 277. See also Blum, *Lord and Peasant in Russia from the Ninth to the Nineteenth Century*. On 1580–1613, see especially Pavlov and Prerie 2003, *Ivan the Terrible*, and Platonov, *The Time of Troubles*.

23. Kolchin, *Unfree Labor*, 30.

24. On the evolution of sixteenth- to seventeenth-century social controls and center-provincial relations, see Hellie, "The Expanding Role of the State in Russia"; Kivelson, "The Devil Stole His Mind"; Kivelson, *Autocracy in the Province*; Stevens, *Soldiers on the Steppe*; Kollmann, *By Honor Bound*. On boyar roles from the late 1500s to the mid-1600s, see Crummey, *Formation of Muscovy*; Crummey, "Muscovy and the 'General Crisis of the Seventeenth Century.'" On the mir's (village commune's) communal functions, see Hoch, *Serfdom and Social Control in Russia*.

25. Kolchin argues persuasively that the delay in codifying serfdom between 1603 and 1649 resulted from class discrepancy between frontier authorities and landed nobility on one side, and smaller landholders on the other. The code of 1649 reflected a new alliance between Russian aristocrats and merchants in Moscow. The new class, known as "the gentry," emerged around 1682. The new class deal was founded on the exclusion of peasants and the lower orders from the political process. Kolchin, *Unfree Labor*.

26. Kagarlitsky, *Empire of the Periphery*. For a synthesis of the role of cartography and mapmaking in the process of Russian state-building, see Biggs, "Putting the State on the Map." For incisive comments on the topic of mapmaking and sovereignty in modern Europe, see Sahlins, *Boundaries*, and Anderson, *Imagined Communities*. For breakthrough research on mapping and Russian local history, see Kivelson's work on Russian cartography and Sunderland's synthesis on "taming the wild field." Kivelson, *Cartographies of Tsardom*; Sunderland, *Taming the Wild Field*.

27. Kolchin, *Unfree Labor*, 12.

28. Boeck, *Imperial Boundaries*.

29. Ibid., 24.

30. Menning, "The Socialization of the Don Cossack Host Prior to the Reign of Nicholas I," 58–59.

31. Boeck, *Imperial Boundaries*, 26.

32. Boeck observes that

the early Cossacks represented a mix of nomads, fugitives, and entrepreneurs. Their numbers were no more than a few thousand. Their weapons and dress adhered to no common standards and can best be described as multicolored and multicultural: integrating elements from the steppe nomads and populations of North Caucasus. They combined steppe skills of horsemanship with expertise in sea, river, and portage navigation that can be traced to Rus.' Their hybrid raiding culture conducted amphibious operations in both the river basins and prairies of the southern steppes. (*Imperial Boundaries*, 19–20)

This description resembles the experience of improvised "ethnic" creation in maroon and pirate societies (see Linebaugh and Rediker, *The Many-Headed Hydra*; Bilby, *True Born Maroons*).

33. Menning, "The Socialization of the Don Cossack Host Prior to the Reign of Nicholas I," vii, 61.

34. Boeck, *Imperial Boundaries*, 14–15. To McNeil, the exilic space of the early Cossacks represented one of the many interstitial polities which "flourished in the interstices of civilized political power during the 16th-17th centuries" and "constituted remoter instances of the same phenomenon." McNeill, *Europe's Steppe Frontier, 1500–1800*, 115. McNeil included the Barbary Coast and communities of Caribbean pirates in this list.

35. Longworth, *The Cossacks*.

36. Hrushevsky, *History of Ukraine-Rus'*.

37. Boeck, *Imperial Boundaries*, 41–42.

38. Avrich, *Russian Rebels, 1600–1800*, 61.

39. Boeck, *Imperial Boundaries*, 55.

40. Menning, "The Socialization of the Don Cossack Host Prior to the Reign of Nicholas I."

41. Stevens, *Soldiers on the Steppe*.

42. Menning, "The Socialization of the Don Cossack Host Prior to the Reign of Nicholas I," 140.

43. This relationship between the state and the Don Host would change fundamentally during the course of the eighteenth century. Menning refers to this process as the "socialization" of the Host, which lasted for about 250 years: a process during which the Don Host changed from "an independent interstitial polity of free Cossack warriors" into "an obedient and pliant military organization designed to meet the needs of the Imperial Russian state." Socialization is a "historical process through which the Cossack Host became part of Imperial Russian society" (vi). The Russian state followed a policy of subordination and perpetuation: imperial interference had the dual purpose of subordinating and perpetuating the Don Cossack Host with its "mercurial instability." The process of socialization ended with Cossacks being transformed into a military class and granted, in return, the common ownership of all land within the territory of the Host. Menning, "The Socialization of the Don Cossack Host Prior to the Reign of Nicholas I," iii.

44. When, on June 3, 1793, General Dmitri Ilovaiskii and Colonel Ivan Ivanov received from Catherine II a map defining Cossack lands, the process of the territorialization of rule was accomplished with the disintegration of the exilic sovereignty

of the Don Host. The situation in the sixteenth and seventeenth centuries was quite different.

45. Anderson, *Imagined Communities*; Sahlins, *Boundaries*.

46. Biggs, "Putting the State on the Map."

47. Boeck, *Imperial Boundaries*, 134.

48. If Boeck's claim that Russia has one of the oldest continuous histories of boundary maintenance is correct, and if the territorialization of Moscow state power along the Belgorod line predated by nearly two centuries Britain's efforts in North America, it is indeed strange that this process has escaped the attention of historians (Boeck, *Imperial Boundaries*). According to Sahlins and Biggs, the rulership and ground were fused into a territorial state only in the nineteenth century (Sahlins, *Boundaries*; Biggs, "Putting the State on the Map"). What is missing from Boeck's innovative and original account is the other aspect of territorialization—exit. While it is true that many scholars take for granted the picture of the world as a jigsaw of states, it is not enough to understand how a state was put on the map. The same atlas that shows a world composed of states (delimited, homogenous territories) also conceals a world of autonomous fragments existing outside of the linear boundaries and homogenous space.

49. Stevens, *Soldiers on the Steppe*.

50. Sunderland, *Taming the Wild Field*.

51. Lefebvre draws an important distinction between *savoir* (abstract knowledge concerned with facts and figures) and *connaissance* (place-based knowledge informed by action against the state) that is relevant in distinguishing between two opposing forms of place-based knowledge (Lefebvre, *The Production of Space*). The relationship between Muscovy and the Don Host can be seen as an earlier instance of the "clash of spatialization" proposed by Hasketh, "Clash of Spatializations."

52. Biggs suggests that territorialization of rule has two aspects: cartographic symbolization of the state as territory, where cartography becomes the object of the state, and imposition of state territory on the ground so they inhere in geographical reality, with the state constituting the object of cartography (Biggs, "Putting the State on the Map"). We could say that territorialization of exit requires the same kind of relationship between political authority and territory, but it is predicated on being unrecorded, unsurveyed, and nonlegible by the political authority of the state. It is interesting that, in Boeck's view, this alternative form of sovereignty in the lower reaches of the Don did not come close to "clearly expressing territoriality in its modern sense" (*Imperial Boundaries*, 55). This comment reveals a statist bias, unusual for a historian so attentive to the nature of the nonstate space. On concept of "territorialization of sovereignty" see Sahlins, *Boundaries*.

53. Menning, "The Socialization of the Don Cossack Host Prior to the Reign of Nicholas I," 15.

54. Ibid., 5.

55. Boeck, *Imperial Boundaries*, 124.

56. Ibid., 82.

57. Menning, "The Socialization of the Don Cossack Host Prior to the Reign of Nicholas I"; Boeck, *Imperial Boundaries*; Prohnstein, *Zemlia Donskaia v XVIII veke*.

58. Quoted in Boeck, *Imperial Boundaries,* 82.

59. Boeck, *Imperial Boundaries,* 82.

60. Menning, "The Socialization of the Don Cossack Host Prior to the Reign of Nicholas I," 23.

61. The Cossack historian Prohnstein distinguishes between "negative" and "positive" factors in immigration, negative being serfdom and positive being the pacification of the Don after Peter the Great, which served as a necessary precondition for increased immigration (Prohnstein, *Zemlia Donskaia v XVIII veke*).

62. Boeck, *Imperial Boundaries*; Stevens, *Soldiers on the Steppe*.

63. Boeck, *Imperial Boundaries*.

64. Stepan (or Stenka) Razin was a Cossack leader who attempted to spread autonomy to new areas and who eventually led an uprising against the Russian state in 1670.

65. Boeck, *Imperial Boundaries,* 61.

66. The Old Believers were a sect of traditionalists who split from the Russian Orthodox Church in 1666 over reforms introduced by the Patriarch Nikon.

67. Menning, "The Socialization of the Don Cossack Host Prior to the Reign of Nicholas I."

68. Prohnstein, *Zemlia Donskaia v XVIII veke*.

69. Svatikov, *Rossiia I Don*.

70. Longworth, *The Cossacks*; O'Rourke, *The Cossacks*.

71. Menning, "The Socialization of the Don Cossack Host Prior to the Reign of Nicholas I," 16.

72. Boeck, *Imperial Boundaries,* 39.

73. Svatikov, *Rossiia I Don*.

74. Menning, "The Socialization of the Don Cossack Host Prior to the Reign of Nicholas I," 61.

75. Avrich, *Russian Rebels, 1600–1800*, 60; see also Boeck, *Imperial Boundaries*.

76. Menning, "The Socialization of the Don Cossack Host Prior to the Reign of Nicholas I," 137.

77. Menning, "The Socialization of the Don Cossack Host Prior to the Reign of Nicholas I"; Svatikov, *Rossiia I Don*; O'Rourke, *The Cossacks*; Longworth, *The Cossacks*.

78. Svatikov, *Rossiia I Don*.

79. Boeck, *Imperial Boundaries,* 36.

80. Svatikov, *Rossiia I Don*.

81. Boeck, *Imperial Boundaries*.

82. Ibid., 37.

83. Avrich, *Russian Rebels, 1600–1800*, 69, 88.

84. Boeck, *Imperial Boundaries*.

85. Menning, "The Socialization of the Don Cossack Host Prior to the Reign of Nicholas I," 61; see also Svatikov, *Rossiia I Don*.

86. Menning, "The Socialization of the Don Cossack Host Prior to the Reign of Nicholas I," 139.

87. Boeck, *Imperial Boundaries*, 38–39.

88. Ibid., 40.

89. Avrich, *Russian Rebels, 1600–1800*, 61.

90. Clastres, *Society against the State*, 207.

91. Lefebvre, *State, Space, World*, 135.

92. Lefebvre, "Space and State," 98.

93. Lefebvre, *The Production of Space*, 190.

94. Menning, "The Socialization of the Don Cossack Host Prior to the Reign of Nicholas I"; Longworth, *The Cossacks*.

95. O'Rourke, *The Cossacks*.

96. Svatikov, *Rossiia I Don*.

97. Quoted in Boeck, *Imperial Boundaries*, 89–90.

98. Lunin, *K Istorii donskoga kazachestva*; and Menning, "The Socialization of the Don Cossack Host Prior to the Reign of Nicholas I."

99. Longworth, *The Cossacks*.

100. Menning, "The Socialization of the Don Cossack Host Prior to the Reign of Nicholas I."

101. Boeck, *Imperial Boundaries*, 40.

102. Avrich, *Russian Rebels, 1600–1800*, 20.

103. Ibid., 64.

104. Ibid.

105. Svatikov, *Rossiia I Don*.

106. Boeck, *Imperial Boundaries*.

107. Ibid., 50.

108. Longworth, *The Cossacks*.

109. Avrich, *Russian Rebels, 1600–1800*, 61.

110. Menning, "The Socialization of the Don Cossack Host Prior to the Reign of Nicholas I."

111. Ibid., 53.

112. Ibid., 54.

113. Boeck, *Imperial Boundaries*, 26.

114. Quoted in Boeck, *Imperial Boundaries*, 32.

115. All quotes are from Boeck, *Imperial Boundaries*, 32.

116. O'Rourke, *The Cossacks*.

117. Plokhy, *The Origins of the Slavic Nations*; Kornblatt, *The Cossack Hero in Russian Literature*.

118. Boeck, *Imperial Boundaries*.

119. Quoted in ibid., 82.

120. Avrich, *Russian Rebels, 1600–1800*, 5.

121. Ibid., 60.

122. Yaresh, "The 'Peasant Wars' in Soviet Historiography," 241–59.

123. Quoted in Kolchin, *Unfree Labor*, 250.

124. Menning, "The Socialization of the Don Cossack Host Prior to the Reign of Nicholas I," 136; see also Longworth, *The Cossacks*; Longworth, "Reply"; Prohnstein, *Zemlia Donskaia v XVIII veke*; Riabov, *Donskaia zemlia v XVII veke*; and Svatikov, *Rossiia I Don*.

125. Menning, "The Socialization of the Don Cossack Host Prior to the Reign of Nicholas I," 72.

126. Riabov, *Donskaia zemlia v XVII veke*.

127. Svatikov, *Rossiia I Don*.

128. Boeck, *Imperial Boundaries*, 117, 121, 146.

129. Tambiah, "Presidential Address," 750.

130. Menning, "The Socialization of the Don Cossack Host Prior to the Reign of Nicholas I," 66.

131. Quoted in Boeck, *Imperial Boundaries*, 29.

132. Quoted in ibid., 88.

133. Menning, "The Socialization of the Don Cossack Host Prior to the Reign of Nicholas I," 71.

134. Ibid., 66–67.

135. Prohnstein, *Zemlia Donskaia v XVIII veke*; Lunin, *K Istorii donskoga kazachestva*.

136. Longworth, *The Cossacks*; Avrich, *Russian Rebels, 1600–1800*.

137. Boeck, *Imperial Boundaries*, 79.

138. Ibid., 100.

139. Ibid.

140. Menning, "The Socialization of the Don Cossack Host Prior to the Reign of Nicholas I," 67; Svatikov, *Rossiia I Don*.

141. Boeck, *Imperial Boundaries*.

142. Ibid.; Menning, "The Socialization of the Don Cossack Host Prior to the Reign of Nicholas I."

143. Boeck, *Imperial Boundaries*, 107.

144. Ibid., 109, 110.

145. Ibid., 115.

146. Menning, "The Socialization of the Don Cossack Host Prior to the Reign of Nicholas I."

147. Boeck, *Imperial Boundaries*.

148. Menning, "The Socialization of the Don Cossack Host Prior to the Reign of Nicholas I"; Longworth, *The Cossacks*; O'Rourke, *The Cossacks*.

149. Menning, "The Socialization of the Don Cossack Host Prior to the Reign of Nicholas I," 85, 86.

150. This last right is no longer in force. When the authors of this volume were initiated into the Cossack Host, it was done with a colorful ceremony involving whips and the drinking of moonshine from a sword. To get the moonshine, our host had to travel to a private house at the instructions of the ataman, where she purchased it illicitly from a private vendor.

151. Menning, "The Socialization of the Don Cossack Host Prior to the Reign of Nicholas I," 74.

152. Nolte, "The Position of Eastern Europe," 37.

153. Attman, "The Russian Market in the World Trade, 1500–1869."

154. Kagarlitsky, *Empire of the Periphery*.

155. Ibid., 83.

156. Attman, "The Russian Market in the World Trade, 1500–1869," 179.

157. Kagarlitsky, *Empire of the Periphery*, 117.

158. Nolte, "The Netherlands and Russia in the Seventeenth Century," 233.

159. Kagarlitsky, *Empire of the Periphery*, 105.

160. Wallerstein, *The Modern World-System III*.

161. Attman, "The Russian Market in the World Trade, 1500–1869," 186.

162. Kagarlitsky, *Empire of the Periphery*, 157.

163. Kolchin, *Unfree Labor*, 17.

164. Ibid., 41.

165. Wallerstein, *The Modern World-System III*.

166. Blum, *Lord and Peasant in Russia from the Ninth to the Nineteenth Century*.

167. Lieberman, *Strange Parallels*.

168. Wallerstein, *The Modern World-System III*.

169. Blum, *Lord and Peasant in Russia from the Ninth to the Nineteenth Century*; Wallerstein, *The Modern World-System III*.

170. Wallerstein, *The Modern World-System III*. Some economic historians, including Tugan-Baronovskii and Lenin, proposed that this was Russia's prerevolutionary period of industrial capitalism, but there is much debate about this. Tugan-Baranovskii, *The Russian Factory in the 19th Century*; Lenin, *The Development of Capitalism in Russia*.

171. Lieberman, *Strange Parallels*, 298.

172. Kagarlitsky, *Empire of the Periphery*, 170, 179; also Wallerstein, *The Modern World-System III*, 172.

173. Wallerstein, *The Modern World-System III*, 161.

174. Kolchin, *Unfree Labor*, 257.

175. Boeck, *Imperial Boundaries*, 210.

176. Ibid., 197, 243.

177. Ibid.; Sunderland, *Taming the Wild Field*.

178. Lefebvre, "Space and State," 86.

179. Quoted in Boeck, *Imperial Boundaries*, 243.

180. Plokhy, *The Cossacks and Religion in Early Modern Ukraine*, 169.

181. Svatikov, *Rossiia I Don*.

182. Menning, "The Socialization of the Don Cossack Host Prior to the Reign of Nicholas I," 106.

183. Ibid., 146–47.

184. Svatikov, *Rossiia I Don*.

185. Menning, "The Socialization of the Don Cossack Host Prior to the Reign of Nicholas I."

186. Svatikov, *Rossiia I Don*.

187. Quoted in Boeck, *Imperial Boundaries*, 191.

188. Boeck, *Imperial Boundaries*, 199.

189. Ibid., 207.

190. Menning, "The Socialization of the Don Cossack Host Prior to the Reign of Nicholas I," 103–44.

191. Svatikov, *Rossiia I Don*; Menning, "The Socialization of the Don Cossack Host," 152.

192. Quoted in Menning, "The Socialization of the Don Cossack Host Prior to the Reign of Nicholas I," 156.

193. Menning, "The Socialization of the Don Cossack Host Prior to the Reign of Nicholas I," 153.

194. Ibid., 167; see also Svatikov, *Rossiia I Don*.

195. Menning, "The Socialization of the Don Cossack Host Prior to the Reign of Nicholas I," 200.

196. Ibid., 130.

197. Boeck, *Imperial Boundaries*, 34.

198. Boeck, *Imperial Boundaries*; also Sunderland, *Taming the Wild Field*.

199. Boeck, *Imperial Boundaries*, 35; Svatikov, *Rossiia I Don*; Prohnstein, *Zemlia Donskaia v XVIII veke*; Menning, "The Socialization of the Don Cossack Host Prior to the Reign of Nicholas I."

200. Quoted in Boeck, *Imperial Boundaries*, 35.

201. Svatikov, *Rossiia I Don*; Menning, "The Socialization of the Don Cossack Host."

202. Boeck, *Imperial Boundaries*.

203. Prohnstein, *Zemlia Donskaia v XVIII veke*.

204. Svatikov, *Rossiia I Don*; Menning, "The Socialization of the Don Cossack Host Prior to the Reign of Nicholas I"; Longworth, *The Cossacks*; O'Rourke, *The Cossacks*.

205. Menning, "The Socialization of the Don Cossack Host Prior to the Reign of Nicholas I."

206. Ibid.

207. Ibid.

208. Ibid.; Longworth, *The Cossacks*; O'Rourke, *The Cossacks*.

209. Menning, "The Socialization of the Don Cossack Host Prior to the Reign of Nicholas I"; Longworth, *The Cossacks*; O'Rourke, *The Cossacks*.

210. O'Rourke, *The Cossacks*.

211. Menning, "The Socialization of the Don Cossack Host Prior to the Reign of Nicholas I."

212. Svatikov, *Rossiia I Don*; Prohnstein, *Zemlia Donskaia v XVIII veke*; Menning, "The Socialization of the Don Cossack Host Prior to the Reign of Nicholas I."

213. Menning, "The Socialization of the Don Cossack Host Prior to the Reign of Nicholas I," 128.

214. Ibid., 102.

215. Ibid., 103.

216. Ibid., 84.

217. Boeck, *Imperial Boundaries.*

218. Menning, "The Socialization of the Don Cossack Host Prior to the Reign of Nicholas I," 151.

CHAPTER FOUR. ZAPATISTAS

1. Pozas, *Juan the Chamula.*

2. A *promotore* at the Zapatista secondary school in Oventic quotes Mariátegui: "The problem of the Indian is the problem of land." Mariátegui, *Seven Interpretive Essays on Peruvian Reality.*

3. There is a division of thought among scholars about the ideological character of this revolution. Cockroft contends that Mexico's was a bourgeois revolution, led by segments of the industrial bourgeoisie. Cockroft, *Mexico's Hope.* This is disputed by scholars who claim that no nationally oriented bourgeoisie existed at the time. See Hamilton, *The Limits of State Autonomy*; Hansen, *The Politics of Mexican Development*; Knight, "The Mexican Revolution; and Hasketh, "Clash of Spatializations.".

4. Womack, "The Mexican Economy during the Revolution, 1910–1920."

5. Warman, "We Come to Object"; Gilly, "Chiapas and the Rebellion of the Enchanted World."

6. Khasnabish, *Zapatistas*; Stephen, *Zapata Lives!*; Bonfil Batalla, *Mexico Profundo.*

7. Gilly, *The Mexican Revolution*, 73.

8. Khasnabish, *Zapatistas*; Gilly, "Chiapas and the Rebellion of the Enchanted World."

9. Khasnabish, *Zapatistas.*

10. Cockroft, *Mexico's Hope.*

11. "The occupation of Mexico City by the peasant armies is one of the finest episodes of the entire revolution—an early, impetuous yet orderly show of strength that has left its mark on the country; one of the foundations that, unshaken by setbacks, treachery, and conflict, uphold the pride and self-respect of the Mexican peasantry." Gilly, *The Mexican Revolution*, 149.

12. Stephen, *Zapata Lives!*. Without a doubt, the most enduring legacy of the Mexican Revolution was the agrarian reform constituted under article 27 of the constitution, which allowed for the formation of *ejidos* as collective entities with legal stature, specific territorial limits, and representative bodies of governance. The formation of *ejidos* since the Mexican Revolution has involved the transference of over seventy million hectares from large estates to slightly more than three million peasant beneficiaries (Kaufman, "We Are from Before, Yes, but We Are New"; Stephen, *Zapata Lives!*; Craib, *Cartographic Mexico*).

The term "*ejido*" refers to a specific area of land; *ejidatarios* are people who have land rights in the *ejido* and voting rights in its governing body. Some of the areas granted as *ejidos* have a rich history, like in Oaxaca. Others, such as those in the Lacandon jungle of eastern Chiapas, where the Zapatista rebellion took place, were the result of recent colonization and have no long historical tie to the *ejidal* land.

13. Khasnabish, *Zapatistas*, 44; see also Gilly, "Chiapas and the Rebellion of the Enchanted World."

14. Womack, "The Mexican Economy," 102.

15. For regional variations, on Chihuahua, see Nugent and Alonso, "Multiple Selective Traditions in Agrarian Reform and Agrarian Struggle." On Chiapas, see Bobrow-Strain, *Intimate Enemies*.

16. Stephen, *Zapata Lives!*; Khasnabish, *Zapatistas*.

17. Stephen, *Zapata Lives!*, 38.

18. Vaughn, *The State, Education, and Social Class in Mexico, 1880–1928*.

19. Stephen, *Zapata Lives!*

20. Vasconcelos, *La raza cósmica*.

21. Lewis, "Revolution and the Rural Schoolhouse"; see also Stephen, *Zapata Lives!*

22. Scott, *Domination and the Arts of Resistance*.

23. Khasnabish, *Zapatistas*; Vaughn, *Cultural Politics in Revolution*; Knight, "Popular Culture and the Revolutionary State in Mexico, 1910–1940."

24. Khasnabish, *Zapatistas*.

25. Stephen, *Zapata Lives!*, 42.

26. Khasnabish, *Zapatistas*, 54.

27. Craib, *Cartographic Mexico*; Hamilton, *The Limits of State Autonomy*.

28. Stephen, *Zapata Lives!*

29. Khasnabish, *Zapatistas*.

30. Ibid., 107.

31. Washbrook, "The Chiapas Uprising of 1994"; see also Harvey, *The Chiapas Rebellion*.

32. Washbrook, "The Chiapas Uprising of 1994."

33. Harvey, *The Chiapas Rebellion*, 66–67.

34. Benjamin, *A Rich Land, a Poor People*; Benjamin, "A Time of Reconquest"; Rus, "Local Adaption to Global Change"; Rus, Hernández Castillo, and Mattiace, *Mayan Lives, Mayan Utopias*.

35. Hasketh, "Clash of Spatializations," 227. There are more than one million *indígenas* in Chiapas, but they are quite diverse. The indigenous highlands are divided by intense localism that is promoted by native political bosses in the name of "timeless tradition." They are further divided by language differences: Tzotzil Maya is spoken in the western highlands, Tzeltal in the eastern municipalities and in the lowlands, Chol Maya in the northeast, and Tojolabal Maya in the southeast. Zoque, a non-Mayan language, is mostly spoken in the northwest region of the state. Yet further, these communities are divided by politics, land, wealth, and religion (traditional Catholicism, liberation theology Catholicism, and evangelical Protestantism). However, as Benjamin points out, the exodus from the highlands to the Selva Lacandona (jungle area of eastern Chiapas) in recent decades is breaking down many of these divisions (Benjamin, "A Time of Reconquest").

36. Rus, "The 'Communidad Revolucionaria Instituional,'" 266.

37. Rus, "The 'Communidad Revolucionaria Instituional.'"

38. See ibid., and Washbrook, "The Chiapas Uprising of 1994."

39. Stephen, *Zapata Lives!*

40. Washbrook, "The Chiapas Uprising of 1994"; see also Rus, "The Struggle against Indigenous Caciques in Highland Chiapas."

41. Reyes Ramos, *El reparto de tierras y la política agraria en Chiapas, 1914–1988*; Reyes Ramos, Eugenia, and López Lara, "Una década de programas agrarios en Chiapas"; see also Washbrook, "The Chiapas Uprising of 1994."

42. Reyes Ramos, *El reparto de tierras*; Reyes Ramos et al., "Una década de programas agrarios en Chiapas."

43. Van der Haar, "Land Reform, the State, and the Zapatista Uprising in Chiapas."

44. Benjamin, *A Rich Land, a Poor People*; Harvey, *The Chiapas Rebellion*.

45. Washbrook, "The Chiapas Uprising of 1994"; Van der Haar, "Land Reform, the State, and the Zapatista Uprising in Chiapas"; Reyes Ramos, *El reparto de tierras*; Reyes Ramos et al., "Una década de programas agrarios en Chiapas."

46. Van der Haar, "Land Reform, the State, and the Zapatista Uprising in Chiapas," 498.

47. Ibid., 503.

48. Hasketh, "Clash of Spatializations," 230.

49. In addition to *ejidos*, an important part of the rural land held in social tenancy lies in *comunidades agrarias* (agrarian communities). This communal land constitutes a significant part of the holdings of indigenous communities and is based on historical claims, usually dating to colonial or precolonial times. The main difference between this and ejidal land, after the changes made to article 27 of the constitution, is that communal lands cannot be privatized. However, if an agrarian community converts to an *ejido*, then its land can be privatized. Exact statistics are hard to locate, but the total number of beneficiaries could be as high as two to three hundred thousand.

50. Barmeyer, *Developing Zapatista Autonomy*; Harvey, *The Chiapas Rebellion*; Benjamin, *A Rich Land, a Poor People*; Benjamin, "A Time of Reconquest."

51. Barmeyer, *Developing Zapatista Autonomy*; Benjamin, *A Rich Land, a Poor People*; Benjamin, "A Time of Reconquest"; Harvey, "Rebellion in Chiapas"; Harvey, *The Chiapas Rebellion*; Van der Haar, "Land Reform, the State, and the Zapatista Uprising in Chiapas."

52. Harvey, *The Chiapas Rebellion*.

53. Stephen, *Zapata Lives!*, 66.

54. Reyes Ramos, *El reparto de tierras*. At the same time, individual smallholdings and private cattle ranches were also established in the region. Harvey, *The Chiapas Rebellion*; Washbrook, "The Chiapas Uprising of 1994."

55. Baronnet, "Rebel Youth and Zapatista Autonomous Education."

56. Harvey, "Rebellion in Chiapas," 57; see also Khasnabish, *Zapatistas*.

57. Khasnabish, *Zapatistas*, 19.

58. Barmeyer, *Developing Zapatista Autonomy*, 348–55.

59. Harvey, *The Chiapas Rebellion*.

60. Washbrook, "The Chiapas Uprising of 1994."

61. Stephen, *Zapata Lives!* Barmeyer speculates about reasons for this systemic and, in hindsight, shortsighted neglect. In his estimation, the probable cause for the federal development aid was to gain access to Lacandon resources such as timber, oil, minerals, and patentable genetic material. Barmeyer, *Developing Zapatista Autonomy*.

62. Rus et al., *Mayan Lives, Mayan Utopias*; Harvey, *The Chiapas Rebellion*.

63. Aubry, "Autonomy in the San Andres Accords."

64. Rus, "Local Adaption to Global Change."

65. Barmeyer, *Developing Zapatista Autonomy*, 31. On ARIC, see Harvey, *The Chiapas Rebellion*.

66. Van der Haar, "Land Reform, the State, and the Zapatista Uprising in Chiapas," 495.

67. Van der Haar, "Land Reform, the State, and the Zapatista Uprising in Chiapas"; Barmeyer, *Developing Zapatista Autonomy*.

68. Barmeyer, *Developing Zapatista Autonomy*, 37; see also Harvey, *The Chiapas Rebellion*.

69. Washbrook, "The Chiapas Uprising of 1994."

70. Womack, *Rebellion in Chiapas*, 32, 47. Tuxtla Gutiérrez is the state capital of Chiapas, but San Cristóbal de las Casas is generally considered to be the de facto capital of indigenous Chiapas.

71. Harvey, "Rebellion in Chiapas."

72. Benjamin, "A Time of Reconquest," 427.

73. Ibid., 428.

74. Harvey, *The Chiapas Rebellion*.

75. Collier and Quaratiello, *Basta!*

76. Collier and Quaratiello, *Basta!*; Harvey, *The Chiapas Rebellion*.

77. Kaufman, "We Are from Before, Yes, but We Are New."

78. Forbis, "Never Again a Mexico without Us"; Khasnabish, *Zapatistas*.

79. Van der Haar, "Land Reform, the State, and the Zapatista Uprising in Chiapas," 496.

80. Forbis, "Never Again a Mexico without Us," 117.

81. Kaufman, "We Are from Before, Yes, but We Are New," 44.

82. Barmeyer, *Developing Zapatista Autonomy*; Harvey, *The Chiapas Rebellion*; Collier and Quaratiello, *Basta!*; Higgins, *Understanding the Chiapas Rebellion*.

83. Harvey, *The Chiapas Rebellion*, 167.

84. Stephen, *Zapata Lives!*, 149. According to most sources, the origins of the EZLN can be traced to two earlier guerrilla forces: the Ejército Insurgente Mexicano (Mexican Insurgent Army), or EIM, secretly organized in the 1960s and disbanded after unreported action in Chiapas in 1968 and 1969; and the Fuerzas de Liberación Nacional (Forces of National Liberation), or FLN, organized in Monterrey in 1969 (Womack, *Rebellion in Chiapas*; Stephen, *Zapata Lives!*).

85. Stephen, *Zapata Lives!*

86. Cited in ibid., 149.

87. Barmeyer, *Developing Zapatista Autonomy*.

88. Benjamin, "A Time of Reconquest," 114.

89. Ibid., 449.

90. On the history of the founding of the EZLN, see Benjamin, *A Rich Land, a Poor People*; Collier and Quaratiello, *Basta!*; Harvey, *The Chiapas Rebellion*; Le Bot, *Subcomandante Marcos*; Legorreta, *Religión, política y guerrilla en las cañadas de la Selva Lacandona*; Muñoz Ramírez, *The Fire and the Word*; Ross, *The War against Oblivion*; Weinberg, *Homage to Chiapas*.

91. See Horton and Freire, *We Make the Road by Walking*.

92. Nash, *Mayan Visions*.

93. Mattiace, "Regional Renegotiations of Space."

94. Collier and Quaratiello, *Basta!*

95. Stahler-Sholk, "Resisting Neoliberal Homogenization"; Barmeyer, *Developing Zapatista Autonomy*; Esteva, "The Meaning and Scope of the Struggle for Autonomy"; Nash, *Mayan Visions*; Mattiace, "Regional Renegotiations of Spaces."

96. Stahler-Sholk, "Resisting Neoliberal Homogenization"; Barmeyer, *Developing Zapatista Autonomy;* Kaufman, "We Are from Before, Yes, but We Are New."

97. As stated by the EZLN, "For us, theoretical reflection on theory is called meta-theory. Our meta-theory is our practice." Quoted in Kaufman, "We Are from Before, Yes, but We Are New," 20. As EZLN Commander Sandra explained to the Second Encounter of Zapatista Peoples and Peoples of the World in July 2007, "Compañeros, we did not have a manual to do this!" Kaufman, "We Are from Before, Yes, but We Are New," 163.

98. Barmeyer, *Developing Zapatista Autonomy*, 64.

99. Personal conversation, 2004.

100. Mora, "The Zapatista Anticapitalist Politics and the 'Other Campaign,'" 73.

101. Quoted in Hasketh, "Clash of Spatializations," 226.

102. Muñoz Ramírez, *The Fire and the Word*; Zibechi, *Territories in Resistance*.

103. Hasketh, "Clash of Spatializations," 27.

104. The Ley Revolucionaria Agraria started as follows (in the translation by Womack): "The struggle of poor peasants in Mexico continues to claim land for those who work it. After Emiliano Zapata and against the reforms to article 27 of the Mexican Constitution, the EZLN takes up the just struggle of rural Mexico for land and liberty. With the purpose of establishing a general rule for the new agrarian redistribution of land that the revolution brings to the Mexican countryside, the following revolutionary agrarian law is issued." Womack, *Rebellion in Chiapas*, 253. The Zapatista revolutionary land law was of obvious importance in providing formal justification for the occupations that the Zapatistas carried out after January 1994. Interestingly, the law itself echoed official land reform legislation and even incorporated some of its central elements. There were over 1,700 occupations, affecting nearly 148,000 hectares. Villafuerte, *La Tierra en Chiapas*.

105. Quoted in Kaufman, "We Are from Before, Yes, but We Are New," 150.

106. Muñoz Ramirez, *The Fire and the Word*; Kaufman, "We Are from Before, Yes, but We Are New."

107. Comandanta Esther quoted in Speed, *Rights in Rebellion*, 41.

108. Barmeyer, *Developing Zapatista Autonomy*, 61.

109. Ibid.

110. Zibechi, *Territories in Resistance*.

111. Hale, "Does Multiculturalism Menace?"

112. Leyva Solano, "Indigenismo, indianismo and 'ethnic citizenship' in Chiapas"; Olesen, *International Zapatismo*. See also Khasnabish, *Zapatistas*.

113. Barmeyer, *Developing Zapatista Autonomy*, 78.

114. Quoted in Forbis, "Never Again a Mexico without Us," 170.

115. Ibid., 189.

116. An excellent example of internal education of women in Zapatista territory is provided in Klein, *Compañeras*. Klein, a San Francisco–born solidarity activist, worked with Zapatistas in Morelia and Garrucha between 1997 and 2003 to develop a project called Women and Collectivism. The stated goal of the project was to "support women's economic cooperatives, women's organizing at the regional level, and women's participation in the Zapatista movement. The project included leadership development, facilitating training workshops, developing popular education materials, helping with regional women's gatherings, and setting up a revolving loan fund to form new women's cooperatives" (xxi). In addition to this ambitious project, Klein has produced an extensive internal document that was used primarily for the education and organizing of women within Zapatista villages. This collection of interviews and testimonies, titled *Long Live our History! A History Book of the "Compañera Lucha" Zapatista Women Organization,* was the basis of *Companeras*. It is important to note that Klein had to ask Zapatista authorities in Morelia for permission to use the collected testimonies in her book.

117. Yet things are far from perfect. Subcomandante Marcos estimates that the percentage of women in the Clandestine Revolutionary Indigenous Committee (CCRI) is between 30 and 40 percent, but women's representation on *juntas de buen gobierno* is under 1 percent on average. Olivera, "Subordination and Rebellion."

118. Forbis, "Never Again a Mexico without Us," 142.

119. Barmeyer, *Developing Zapatista Autonomy*, 117. For interviews with Zapatista women, see Klein, *Compañeras*; Stephen, *Zapata Lives!*; and Mora, "Decolonizing Politics."

120. Mora, "Decolonizing Politics"; Forbis, "Never Again a Mexico without Us."

121. Barmeyer, *Developing Zapatista Autonomy*.

122. Forbis, "Never Again a Mexico without Us," 215.

123. Mora, "Decolonizing Politics."

124. Barmeyer, *Developing Zapatista Autonomy*.

125. Kaufman, "We Are from Before, Yes, but We Are New."

126. Barmeyer, *Developing Zapatista Autonomy*.

127. E.g., Stephen, *Zapata Lives!*; Forbis, "Never Again a Mexico without Us"; Khasnabish, *Zapatistas*.

128. Barmeyer, *Developing Zapatista Autonomy*, 95.

129. Leyva Solano, "Indigenismo, indianismo and 'ethnic citizenship' in Chiapas."

130. Good Government Council of La Realidad, quoted in Kaufman, "We Are from Before, Yes, but We Are New," 89.

131. Ibid., 91.

132. Alcohol is banned within the communities, and this should be seen in its historical context. Alcohol was used (or forced onto) indigenous communities as payment instead of money and was one of the chief means by which *caciques* enriched themselves. This so-called Dry Law has also been instituted due to the insistence of women concerned with domestic violence. See Hasketh, "Clash of Spatializations."

133. Barmeyer, *Developing Zapatista Autonomy*; Speed and Collier, "Limiting Indigenous Autonomy in Chiapas, Mexico."

134. The campaign for community schools is inspired more than anything else by the illiteracy in the exilic territory. Chiapas has one of the highest rates of illiteracy in the nation for those over fifteen years old: 28.9 percent of women and 16.6 percent of men (the average in Mexico is 11.3 percent and 7.4 percent, respectively). Baronnet, "Rebel Youth and Zapatista Autonomous Education."

135. Zibechi, *Dispersing Power*, 144.

136. The Zapatista communication system serves an important educational role. Radio Insurgente, the EZLN mobile radio station, presents programs in indigenous languages on a variety of topics ranging from indigenous history and the history of agrarian struggles, to contemporary mobilizations and political campaigns.

137. Baronnet, "Rebel Youth and Zapatista Autonomous Education."

138. Two medical kits are used in community health centers, one with herbs and the other with pharmaceuticals. According to Zibechi, "This practice of combining 'the two medicines' is a result of experience within the communities and is tied to the indigenous cosmology and culture that promotes the use of traditional medicines." *Territories in Resistance*, 134.

139. Muñoz Ramírez, *The Fire and the Word*; Barmeyer, *Developing Zapatista Autonomy*; Zibechi, *Territories in Resistance*; Kaufman, "We Are from Before, Yes, but We Are New"; Hasketh, "Clash of Spatializations."

140. Kaufman, "We Are from Before, Yes, but We Are New"; Barmeyer, *Developing Zapatista Autonomy*.

141. Earle and Simonelli, *Uprising of Hope*; Barmeyer, *Developing Zapatista Autonomy*; Kaufman, "We Are from Before, Yes, but We Are New"; Hasketh, "Clash of Spatializations."

142. Barmeyer, *Developing Zapatista Autonomy*; Earle and Simonelli, *Uprising of Hope*.

143. Hasketh, "Clash of Spatializations."

144. Earle and Simonelli, *Uprising of Hope*; Barmeyer, *Developing Zapatista Autonomy*.

145. Kaufman, "We Are from Before, Yes, but We Are New."

146. O'Brien, *Sacrificing the Forest*; Barmeyer, *Developing Zapatista Autonomy*. This process had already begun in the 1930s with the settling of the Selva Lacandona: "Settling in the jungle also required an intensive process of clearing lands, which often brought with it environmental degradation as the traditional practice of Milpa cultivation was inappropriate to the soil of the jungle and thus the biodiversity was threatened." Hasketh, "Clash of Spatializations," 237.

147. Barmeyer, *Developing Zapatista Autonomy*.

148. Earle and Simonelli, *Uprising of Hope*; Barmeyer, *Developing Zapatista Autonomy*; Kaufman, "We Are from Before, Yes, but We Are New."

149. Barmeyer, *Developing Zapatista Autonomy*. Recognizing the economic hardships faced in communities, Zapatistas can ask their community and the organization for permission to work outside of Chiapas for a period of three months. Forbis, "Never Again a Mexico without Us."

150. Quoted in Khasnabish, *Zapatistas*, 216–17.

151. Forbis, "Never Again a Mexico without Us," 165.

152. Earle and Simonelli, *Uprising of Hope*; Barmeyer, *Developing Zapatista Autonomy*; Kaufman, "We Are from Before, Yes, but We Are New."

153. Kaufman, "We Are from Before, Yes, but We Are New"; Barmeyer, *Developing Zapatista Autonomy*.

154. Aquino Moreschi, "Entre el 'sueño zapatista' y el 'sueño americano.'" In chapter 2 we discussed "economy" as social production, or the production of communities. Production in the Zapatista territory is also production of people and "other" social relationships. Federici contends that producing "self-reproducing" communities is the most significant challenge of autonomy (Federici, *Revolution at Point Zero*). This crucial aspect is missed by observers such as Brass, who label the Zapatistas "petty small holders." Brass, "Neoliberalism and the Rise of (Peasant) Nations within the Nation," 665.

155. Kaufman, "We Are from Before, Yes, but We Are New," 53.

156. Ibid., 116. Forbis writes, "I am not trying to argue here that the Zapatista struggle has not engaged with or made demands on the state. I am arguing, however, that the state arena was never the sole focus of attention and has become less so each year of the struggle." "Never Again a Mexico without Us," 150.

157. Muñoz Ramírez, *The Fire and the Word*, 80.

158. Barmeyer, *Developing Zapatista Autonomy*, 227.

159. Stephen thinks that this was a local rebellion unexpectedly transformed into a global event: "Thus, ironically, while the Zapatistas have provided Mexico with a reworked nationalism built on the traditional symbols of the Mexican Revolution, they have used the same symbols to promote a global discourse. The media and the Internet are what have made what would have been a local rebellion into a global event." Stephen, *Zapata Lives!*, 175; see also Harvey, *The Chiapas Rebellion*;

Midnight Notes Collective, *Auroras of the Zapatistas*; Cleaver, "Zapatistas and the Electronic Fabric of Struggle"; Hasketh, "Clash of Spatializations."

160. Barmeyer, *Developing Zapatista Autonomy*; Khasnabish, *Zapatistas*; Collier and Quaratiello, *Basta!*; Harvey, *The Chiapas Rebellion*; Otero, *Farewell to the Peasantry?*; Gilberth and Otero, "Democratization in Mexico."

161. Esteva, "The Meaning and Scope of the Struggle for Autonomy."

162. Observers believe this was one of the most brilliant propaganda moments in the history of the EZLN. Zapatista Comandante David introduced himself to government negotiators as "David, Tzotzil, one-hundred percent Chiapanecan, one-hundred percent Mexican" (quoted in Gilberth and Otero, "Democratization in Mexico," 21). David, together with other delegates, unrolled the Mexican flag in front of the completely befuddled government commissioner, Manuel Camacho Solís. The commissioner felt obliged to join them by holding up a corner. The message could have not been clearer: the fight was not against, but for, Mexico, the country of Emiliano Zapata and of dignified indigenous peoples.

163. Barmeyer, *Developing Zapatista Autonomy*, 45.

164. The CNI was created in 1996 for the indigenous movement of Mexico to seek new relationships with the Mexican state and civil society. See http://www .laneta.apc.org/cni/.

165. According to recent scholarship by antiglobalization movement scholars, this event marked the official beginning of the "antiglobalization movement"; see Graeber, *The Democracy Project*; Notes from Nowhere, *We Are Everywhere*.

166. For an explanation of the CDI infrastructure projects, see http://www.cdi .gob.mx/index.php?id_seccion = 192.

167. Barmeyer, *Developing Zapatista Autonomy*.

168. Ibid., 50.

169. Collier and Quaratiello, *Basta!*

170. Washbrook, "The Chiapas Uprising of 1994"; Ross, *The War against Oblivion*; Kaufman, "We Are from Before, Yes, but We Are New."

171. Kaufman, "We Are from Before, Yes, but We Are New," 81.

172. From this point on, the Zapatistas committed themselves to strengthening escape mechanisms by way of a policy of building autonomous municipalities outside the purview of the national state. Washbrook, "The Chiapas Uprising of 1994."

173. Barmeyer, *Developing Zapatista Autonomy*.

174. Olivera, "Subordination and Rebellion"; Forbis, "Never Again a Mexico without Us"; see also Mora, "Decolonizing Politics." Of the beneficiaries in 2004, 86 percent lived in rural areas. Forbis sees this program as a spatial strategy of diffusing the exilic project by transforming self-governed spaces into "governable spaces." To put this in perspective, however, *Fortune* magazine estimated Mexico's richest person, Carlos Slim, to be worth US$58 billion (about 630 billion pesos) in 2007.

175. Wilson, "The Urbanization of the Countryside," 223.

176. Ibid., 235.

177. Hasketh, "Clash of Spatializations."

178. Wilson, "The Urbanization of the Countryside."

179. Stahler-Sholk, "Resisting Neoliberal Homogenization," 59.

180. Forbis, "Never Again a Mexico without Us"; Centro de Derechos Humanos Fray Bartolomé de las Casas, *Camino a la Masacre*.

181. Stephen, *Zapata Lives!*, 173.

182. Mora, "Decolonizing Politics."

183. Stephen, *Zapata Lives!*

184. De Leon, "From Revolution to Transition." This "refashioning of government-claimed nationalist symbols" (Stephen, *Zapata Lives!*, 150) was especially successful in transforming Emiliano Zapata into Votán Zapata (a hybrid Tzeltal/nationalist figure created by Marcos and the EZLN) and in projecting the local struggle represented by Votán Zapata back to the rest of the nation. Stephen refers to this process of "transvaluation" as the hybridity of local Zapatismo (Stephen, *Zapata Lives!*, 164). As we have seen in the case of the Cossacks, this is an important part of what we call exilic communication.

185. Stephen, *Zapata Lives!*, 70. "The EZLN established a cultural strategy that called into question the PRI's hegemony by reinterpreting national symbols and discourses in favor of an alternative transformative project." Gilberth and Otero, "Democratization in Mexico," 9.

186. Stephen, *Zapata Lives!*, 71.

187. Quoted in ibid., 338.

188. Stephen, *Zapata Lives!*; Mattiace, "Zapata Vive!"; Mattiace, "Peasant and Indian"; Mattiace, "Regional Renegotiations of Spaces."

189. Barmeyer, *Developing Zapatista Autonomy*, 216.

190. Stephen, *Zapata Lives!* As Forbis argues, it is precisely the creativity and open-ended nature of the Zapatista indigenous identity that offers a challenge to reinscription in the Mexican nation as ethnic citizens. Forbis, "Never Again a Mexico without Us."

191. Hale, "Does Multiculturalism Menace?"

192. Stahler-Sholk, "Resisting Neoliberal Homogenization."

193. Tsing is worth quoting in full: "Indigenous rhetoric familiarized activists with internationally powerful genres that became useful in the early 1990s with the loss of potency of peasant idioms. When Mexico accepted structural adjustment and, most drastically, rewrote the constitution to exclude commitments to peasants, the rhetoric of peasant struggle became ineffective. Peasant activists became indigenous activists to utilize the international cachet of indigenous politics. The conflation of indigenous and peasant demands allowed the indigenous struggle to build directly on the peasant struggle without having to use discredited keywords. EZLN militancy won wide support because it brought together familiar peasant social justice demands and the language of indigenous rights." Tsing, "Indigenous Voice," 47.

194. Speed and Collier, "Limiting Indigenous Autonomy in Chiapas, Mexico," 877.

195. Speed and Collier, "Limiting Indigenous Autonomy in Chiapas, Mexico"; Speed, *Rights in Rebellion*.

196. Barmeyer, *Developing Zapatista Autonomy*.

197. Quoted in Khasnabish, *Zapatistas*, 197.

198. From the beginning of the conflict, the most important role played by the internationals in Zapatista communities was to counter the threat of annihilation and repression by the army, paramilitaries, and special police units, which remains to this day. The so-called peace camps were very important in this respect.

199. Barmeyer, *Developing Zapatista Autonomy*, 214.

200. "In any case, loyalty to outsiders was driven by the sheer need of the Zapatistas to survive as a broad-based and largely civilian movement." Barmeyer, *Developing Zapatista Autonomy*, 12.

201. Speed and Reyes, "In Our Own Defense."

202. Barmeyer, *Developing Zapatista Autonomy*.

203. Mora, "Decolonizing Politics"; Kaufman,"We Are from Before, Yes, but We Are New."

204. Barmeyer, *Developing Zapatista Autonomy*; Khasnabish, *Zapatistas*; Kaufman, "We Are from Before, Yes, but We Are New"; Hasketh, "Clash of Spatializations."

205. Notes from Nowhere, *We Are Everywhere*.

206. Mora, "Decolonizing Politics."

207. Barmeyer, *Developing Zapatista Autonomy*, 137.

208. Ibid., 137, 143.

209. For a humorous account of international volunteer projects, see Ryan, *Zapatista Spring*.

210. Barmeyer, *Developing Zapatista Autonomy*, 146, 150.

211. Ibid., 151.

212. One northern donor, SEVA, funded pro-Zapatista NGOs in San Cristóbal. The activities included workshops in herbal medicine and building infrastructure in Zapatista villages. According to Barmayer, the funding amounted to US$10,000 annually.

213. EZLN, "Sixth Declaration of the Lacandona, pt. 3."

214. Ibid.

215. Kaufman, "We Are from Before, Yes, but We Are New," 200.

216. Stahler-Sholk, "Resisting Neoliberal Homogenization"; Stahler-Sholk, "The Zapatista Social Movement."

217. Zibechi, *Territories in Resistance*, 149–50.

218. Quoted in ibid., 151.

219. Mora, "Decolonizing Politics"; Hasketh, "Clash of Spatializations"; Zibechi, *Territories in Resistance*.

220. Harvey, *The Chiapas Rebellion*.

221. EZLN, "Sixth Declaration of the Lacandona, pt. 3."

222. Ibid.

223. Castells, *The Power of Identity*, 9.

224. Hasketh, "Clash of Spatializations."

225. Barmeyer, *Developing Zapatista Autonomy*.

226. Ibid., 118.

227. We disagree with Barmeyer's assertion that the overwhelming majority of Zapatista strategic decisions were made on the basis of "public image." This statement contains an important element of truth but it denies the complexity of the exilic challenge. It seems more likely that the EZLN assumed (in our view quite correctly) that dependency on the state was far more costly than depending on (inter)national civil society. Simply put, the Zapatistas were looking for nonstate partners, more than certainly aware of the negative historical balance sheet of state-dependent exilic loyalty. Like any other exilic bargain, this strategic dependency arrived with certain costs. Barmeyer, *Developing Zapatista Autonomy*.

228. Stahler-Sholk, "Resisting Neoliberal Homogenization"; Barmeyer, *Developing Zapatista Autonomy*.

229. Legorreta, *Religión, política y guerrilla en las cañadas de la Selva Lacandona*; Barmeyer, *Developing Zapatista Autonomy*.

230. Barmeyer, *Developing Zapatista Autonomy*.

231. Quoted in Zibechi, *Territories in Resistance*, 141.

232. Forbis, "Never Again a Mexico without Us."

233. Villafuerte and Carmen García, "Crisis rural y migraciones en Chiapas."

234. Sixty-year-old Don José, a María Trinidad Zapatista, muses: "Life! ... We fought to free ourselves from bosses and our children go north looking for them, even paying to do so." Or, consider this attitude from a member of the government council: "The change is temporary: they come back with caps, big hats, northern boots and, six months later, this is worn out and they have to buy the same things we do, and we all go back to being dressed the same way, with what is available in the area. They come back all stuck up, fat, they want to kill a chicken every day, but their money runs out some time later and they're back to eating beans and pozol every day, just like us. This is how it goes, what comes from the north runs out, stops working, and a bit later we are all back being the same. So, what good was leaving?" Aquino Moreschi, "Entre el 'sueño zapatista' y el 'sueño americano,'" 79, 80.

235. Aquino Moreschi, "Entre el 'sueño zapatista' y el 'sueño americano.'"

236. Villafuerte and García, "Crisis rural y migraciones en Chiapas."

237. By the first six months of 2004, Chiapas—now the recipient of US$229 million in remittances—had overtaken the state of Zacatecas. If this growth trend continues, Chiapas will soon pass the US$500 million mark, a figure comparable to the value of basic grains and the three principal export commodities (coffee, bananas, and mangoes) combined.

238. Olivera, "Subordination and Rebellion." See also Klein, *Compañeras*; Barmeyer, *Developing Zapatista Autonomy*; and Washbrook, "The Chiapas Uprising of 1994."

239. "On the very day that the Revolutionary Women's Law was adopted, an indigenous man was heard saying: 'The good thing is that my wife doesn't understand Spanish, because if she did. . . .' A female Tzotzil insurgent with the rank of major in the infantry started in at him: 'You're screwed, because we're going to

translate it into all of our dialects.' The impertinent man could only lower his gaze."
Poniatowska, "Women's Battle for Respect Inch by Inch," 56.

240. Olivera, "Subordination and Rebellion," 608–28.

241. Olivera, "Subordination and Rebellion."

242. Earle and Simonelli, *Uprising of Hope*.

243. Barmeyer, *Developing Zapatista Autonomy*; O'Brien, *Sacrificing the Forest*.

244. O'Brien, *Sacrificing the Forest*.

245. Rus, "Local Adaption to Global Change."

246. Baronnet, "Rebel Youth and Zapatista Autonomous Education"; Barmeyer, *Developing Zapatista Autonomy*.

247. Earle and Simonelli, *Uprising of Hope*, 16.

248. Barmeyer, *Developing Zapatista Autonomy*, 232.

249. Barmeyer, *Developing Zapatista Autonomy*.

250. Authors' observations; see also Ryan, *Zapatista Spring*, and Forbis, "Never Again a Mexico without Us."

251. Barmeyer, *Developing Zapatista Autonomy*.

252. Ibid.

253. See, for instance, Kaufman: "NGOs thus become in one sense a place for civil society organization, purportedly in opposition to neoliberalism but fulfilling exactly its mandate for social services outside the public realm, while keeping those initiatives contained to organizations that as a rule operate at a distance from any representational relationship to the base with whom they work . . . . It is a controversial but necessary task to question to what extent they thus undermine and in some cases openly subvert movements or practices of autonomy." Kaufman, "We Are from Before, Yes, but We Are New," 114.

254. Barmeyer, *Developing Zapatista Autonomy*.

255. Ibid., 206.

256. Barmeyer, *Developing Zapatista Autonomy*; Benjamin, *A Rich Land, a Poor People*.

257. Barmeyer, *Developing Zapatista Autonomy*, 193.

258. Kaufman, "We Are from Before, Yes, but We Are New"; Barmeyer, *Developing Zapatista Autonomy*.

259. Barmeyer, *Developing Zapatista Autonomy*, 212.

260. EZLN (2003d), "Chiapas."

CHAPTER FIVE. FORCED EXILE

1. Goffman, *Asylums*.

2. Agamben, *Homo Sacer*.

3. Schein, "Man against Man." Schein proposes disorganizing prisoners by cutting off their ties to previous relationships, including family; undermining emotional supports; creating division by sowing seeds of distrust among prisoners; putting prisoners into a new and ambiguous situation where standards of behavior

are unclear; and then putting pressure on individual prisoners to conform to new standards of behavior. This is meant to demonstrate to prisoners that collective behavior is untrustworthy, thus undercutting any aspiration to practice mutual aid; they are then expected to forge relations of individualism within accepted rules of prison behavior.

4. Abu Jamal, *Jailhouse Lawyers.*

5. Foucault, *Discipline and Punish.*

6. T's letter is worth quoting at length. "Prison has always and everywhere been a center for temporary killing. The reason why I call it a center for temporary killing is related to the roles that you are expected to play . . . Places like dungeons in prison have been places for many years where one is put to spend time until the actual punishment becomes clear. In other words, to be thrown into a well replaces the image of death in stories. Inanna of the Samarians experienced such a time of captivity. That Gilgemesh's drum fell into the well, that Yusef was thrown into a well by his brothers and then came out . . . these are the states of temporary death . . . There is the story of Memu Zin among Kurds in which Mem too dies in a well. In essence these stories demonstrate that it is not widespread punishment to keep someone in an enclosed area. The punishments that are more common are the killing, maiming or torturing, confiscation of property and money, or dispelling and exclusion. The laws of Hammurabi in Egypt are like this. So are those of Judaism, Christianity or Mohammedanism." Letter from T, Kurdish prisoner in F-type prison, June 18, 2012.

7. Braudel, *The Perspective of the World.*

8. See, for example, Wallerstein and Zukin, "1968, Revolution in the World-System."

9. For a review of these groups, see Berger, *The Struggle Within.*

10. Wacquant, *Punishing the Poor.*

11. For a statistical analysis of the rise of mass imprisonment in US states after 1975, see Wagner, "Tracking State Prison Growth in 50 States."

12. See McChesney, "Global Media, Neoliberalism, and Imperialism."

13. Rodriguez argues that prisons today have been transformed into primary sites of radical discourse and organization. Rodriguez, *Forced Passages.* We go a step further and argue that they are, potentially, broader sites of production of exilic society.

14. O'Hearn, "Hücre tecridi ve mahpus direnişi."

15. O'Hearn, "Diaspora of Practice."

16. For data sources on the Irish blanket protest, see O'Hearn, *Nothing but an Unfinished Song.* Several books contain general accounts of the structure, history, and daily life of the H-Blocks, including Coogan, *On the Blanket*; Campbell, McKeown, and O'Hagan, *Nor Meekly Serve My Time*; Ryder, *Inside the Maze*; McKeown, *Out of Time*; and McEvoy, *Paramilitary Imprisonment in Northern Ireland.* On the hunger strikes of 1980 and 1981, see Beresford, *Ten Men Dead.*

17. Coogan, *On the Blanket*; O'Hearn, *Nothing but an Unfinished Song*; O'Hearn, "Repression and Solidary Cultures of Resistance."

18. Publicly, authorities claimed that prisoners' accounts of violence were fabricated or exaggerated (Northern Ireland Office, *H-Blocks*). However, their accuracy is confirmed by the consistency of prisoners' accounts and by interviews with others. A governor of the whole prison admitted to O'Hearn that "you can believe everything the prisoners tell you about the violence in the H-Blocks" ("Repression and Solidary Cultures," 508). Priests who visited the prison also witnessed violence and its aftermath. On the violent nature of relations between prisoners and authorities see McEvoy, *Paramilitary Imprisonment*.

19. PRO, H-Block [Bobby Sands], "H-Block Protest Intensifies." Interestingly, after just three weeks of intensified protest, Sands (in discussion with Brendan Hughes) described the no-wash as "our long protest."

20. Jaz McCann, ex-blanketman, quoted from unpublished manuscripts written by prisoners and eventually published as Campbell et al., *Nor Meekly Serve My Time*.

21. O'Hearn, "Repression and Solidary Cultures," 510.

22. Ibid., 511.

23. Ibid.

24. Ibid., 512.

25. The prisoners developed astonishing methods of communicating and distributing food, tobacco, writing materials, and communications through minute spaces in the cell walls; by "shooting" strings with messages attached to them across corridors under the cell doors; and by swinging strings or ropes made from their blankets out of the cell windows (for further details, see Campbell et al., *Nor Meekly Serve My Time*, and O'Hearn, *Nothing but an Unfinished Song*). Also astonishing was their ability to coordinate debates, games, and political discussions from isolated cells, without visual cues.

26. On the ordeal women went through to smuggle things to and from the prisoners, see O'Hearn, *Nothing but an Unfinished Song*, 241–44.

27. O'Hearn, "Repression and Solidary Cultures," 515.

28. For an account of the global reaction to Bobby Sands's death, see O'Hearn, *Nothing but an Unfinished Song*, chap. 23.

29. Quoted in O'Hearn, *Nothing but an Unfinished Song*, 179.

30. O'Hearn, *Nothing but an Unfinished Song*, 204–5.

31. This story is confirmed by various interviews with ex-blanketmen and by communications between Bobby Sands and the IRA. See O'Hearn, *Nothing but an Unfinished Song*, 318–19.

32. Beresford, *Ten Men Dead*.

33. McKeown, *Out of Time*. We suggest that Thatcher's main triumph was not tragic deaths during the Irish hunger strikes but victory over striking miners in 1984–85.

34. For data sources on Turkish prisons see O'Hearn, "Diaspora of Practice."

35. Paker, "Turkey's Operation Return to Life."

36. The most thorough history of Turkish prisons, including F-type prisons, is Eren, *Kapatılmanın Patolojisi*. For personal descriptions of life in F-type prisons, see Kurnaz, *Tecrit Yaşayanlar Anlatıyor*.

37. Interview with M, former leftist prisoner and hunger striker.

38. O'Hearn, "Diaspora of Practice." The notable exception is PKK leader Abdullah Öcalan, who has been held as the only inmate on a prison island in the Sea of Marmara since 1999 yet still has a strong leadership role in the movement.

39. Interview with C, former PKK prisoner.

40. RL prisoners showed remarkable resourcefulness in their efforts to establish communications with each other in the F-types, but creation of a real exilic community was defeated by the architecture of the F-type prisons. The RL's uncompromising attitude toward the authorities kept them from exploiting changes in the prison regime, such as a court ruling that prisoners had to be given ten hours a week association in groups up to ten.

41. According to M, a former prisoner: "Obviously that policy worked"; and G: "It did work on the left ... Fasting in prisons is no longer a viable tool. 122 people died, unique in the world. Despite the fact that casualties are so extensive, if the end result is that there is no material gain, then that action is no longer tenable." Quoted in O'Hearn, "Diaspora of Practice."

42. A former PKK prisoner says: "We had over 10,000 people in jail, why put them at risk? It is more important to protect them. 125 were killed in 'return to life' but if PKK had joined more than 1,000 would have been killed. At the end of the day the Turkish government is the most racist and fascist on earth so they would never break off." Quoted in O'Hearn, "Diaspora of Practice."

43. Ex-PKK prisoner H says: "Isolation makes you forget your humanness. You get bored and snap at your friends ... Getting to know each other lasts about a month, then you become predictable. You look for a different cell. You start self-isolation. You create your own prison within your soul."

44. When he was finally released in 2005, G couldn't walk down the street. He could not concentrate when talking. He didn't want visitors. He couldn't stand noise. He had problems focusing mentally. G says that simple long-term imprisonment might have caused a "walking problem," but isolation caused his focus problem.

45. On the history and use of supermax prisons and SHUs see, Shalev, *Supermax*; Guenther, *Solitary Confinement*; and Richards, *The Marion Experiment*. On life in supermax prisons, see Rhodes, *Total Confinement*. On the spread of prison isolation through the world, see O'Hearn, "Diaspora of Practice"; and Ross, *The Globalization of Supermax Prisons*.

46. Comptroller General of the United States, *Behavior Modification Programs*.

47. Long-term isolation began as a political project against selected members of the Black Panther Party but became general prison policy following the lockdown at Marion. There is evidence that states such as California encouraged group-on-group prison violence in the 1980s through policies of "integrated yards," as a way of making supermaxes and SHUs "inevitable" or "necessary." See Shakur, Duguma, Jamaa, and Ganda, "The Pelikkkan Bay Factor"; and Muntaqim, "The Deadly 'Integrated Yard Policy.'" On the connection between racism and imprisonment, see

Childs, *Slaves of the State*; and Davis, *Are Prisons Obsolete?* For a popular argument about mass imprisonment as an extension of "Jim Crow" racism, see Alexander, *The New Jim Crow*. On the connections between race, mass imprisonment, and prison activism in the United States, see Berger, *Captive Nation*; and Rodriguez, *Forced Passages*.

48. Correspondence with M, supermax prisoner in Illinois, October 7, 2013.

49. Lawyers who work with SHU prisoners in California tell us that the authorities insist that no prisoners are in isolation there because they can shout to each other from their cells and speak to three other prisoners on their way to showers (even though they may be punished if they talk for more than ten seconds).

50. A haunting twenty-five-minute film of a SHU prisoner exercising alone can be seen at https://www.youtube.com/watch?v = Fc3OoYYp96s.

51. Letter from Todd Ashker, November 3, 2009. Ashker provides the following description of conditions in the pod: "Most of us are single celled. We have the opportunity for 1½ hour yard by ourselves each day and 3 showers and shave per week—in cell we're allowed 6 cubic feet of property—5 books/mags. (not including legal books, 40 photos, legal paperwork etc). You can have a TV if you can afford to buy one—state issue clothes—mattress, pillow, blankets—$45.00 canteen once a month to buy cosmetics, paper, envelopes some food and drink at a 60–90% markup cost so it doesn't amount to much."

52. See Lynd, *Lucasville*; Lamar, *Condemned*.

53. Ashker, *A Prisoner's Story from Pelican Bay's SHU*.

54. Letter from Todd Ashker, November 3, 2009. Ashker continues: "Here is an example of how twisted it is. A guy here, paroled from here in 1980, he did a few violations and discharged his parole in '81. He stayed out 5 yrs and then got a drunk driving .01% over legal limit for which he received 25 yrs to life under California 3 strikes law. He has returned to prison and immediately placed back here based on the old [gang] label."

55. Letter from Todd Ashker, December 10, 2014.

56. *Ashker v. Brown*; see https://ccrjustice.org/home/what-we-do/our-cases/ashker-v-brown. Accessed July 13, 2015.

57. Ashker, *A Prisoner's Story from Pelican Bay's SHU*. The noted psychologist Craig Haney disagrees. In his testimony to a 2012 hearing on solitary confinement by the US Senate Judiciary Subcommittee on the Constitution, Civil Rights, and Human Rights, Haney detailed numerous psychological and social pathologies that are experienced by practically all prisoners in long-term solitary confinement. See "Testimony of Professor Craig Haney, Senate Judiciary Subcommittee on the Constitution, Civil Rights, and Human Rights Hearing on Solitary Confinement, June 19, 2012," http://www.judiciary.senate.gov/download/testimony-of-craig-haney-pdf. Accessed July 6, 2015.

58. "Complaint on Human Rights Violations and Request for Action to End 20+ Years of State Sanctioned Torture to Extract Information From (Or Cause Mental Illness to) California's PBSP-SHU Inmates," http://prisonerhungerstrikesolidarity.wordpress.com/the-prisoners-demands-2/.

59. In a similar effort Jason Robb, an artist in Ohio's supermax, drew a "zine" on behavior modification in 2013 and distributed it to prisoners through outside supporters.

60. O'Hearn, *Nothing but an Unfinished Song*.

61. Ashker, *A Prisoner's Story*.

62. Wallace-Wells, "The Plot from Solitary."

63. Personal conversation, November 11, 2012.

64. Personal conversation, November 11, 2012. Would it be overstating things to say that these men had a profound perception of world time? Without doubt, they were expressing in their own way something that is widespread in the social sciences literature: the idea (as in Marx, or Schumpeter) that social change and innovation agglomerates, that there are periods of rapid social change, and that perceptive social movements should be able to harness change for progressive purposes.

65. Letter from Todd Ashker, December 10, 2014.

66. Ibid.

67. Ibid.

68. "Prisoners' Demands," http://prisonerhungerstrikesolidarity.wordpress .com/the-prisoners-demands-2. Accessed July 11, 2014.

69. Letter from Todd Ashker, December 10, 2014.

70. Letter from Todd Ashker, September 7, 2015.

71. This indicates that the state is not the only entity that requires "friction-reducing technologies" with regard to space.

72. Wells-Wallace, "The Plot from Solitary."

73. Letter from Todd Ashker, December 10, 2014.

74. Ashker *A Prisoner's Story*, our emphasis.

75. "Agreement to End Racial Group Hostilities, August 12, 2012," http:// prisonerhungerstrikesolidarity.wordpress.com/2012/09/11/short-corridor-collective-calls-for-statewide-end-to-hostilities/.

76. Youth Justice Coalition, "Statement to the Streets and All Youth Lock-ups," https://prisonerhungerstrikesolidarity.files.wordpress.com/2015/03/agreement-statement-to-youth.pdf. Accessed July 14, 2015.

77. Letter from Todd Ashker, October 30, 2013. From our association with Ashker and Troxell over many years we are fully aware of their deep friendship, including the mentoring role Troxell played by introducing Ashker to key works of literature. The gang allegation, based on mere possession of a photograph, is patently ludicrous and it raises a basic question of this study: when is "gang" activity actually collective behavior and mutual aid, which is punished by the authorities because it is a form of resistance to their goal of stripping prisoners of their former identities and replacing them not with collective but individualist identities that reflect the goals of the capitalist state?

78. Letter from Todd Ashker, October 30, 2013.

79. Ibid. Ashker remained in the lexan-covered cell until UN Rapporteur on Torture Juan Méndez came to Pelican Bay and was scheduled to meet him. Just before Mendez arrived, Ashker was moved back to a "normal" short corridor cell. A

similar tactic was used against the perceived leaders of a mass hunger strike later in 2013 in Menard Prison in the state of Illinois. Not only were they isolated in administrative segregation, they were punished by means such as placing metal plates over their windows to block any outside view. Then, they were split up entirely by transfers to federal prisons in West Virginia, New Mexico, California, and elsewhere.

80. The Center for Constitutional Rights (CCR) were the lead attorneys for the Short Corridor Collective, along with local attorneys from Prison Focus, in *Ashker v. Governor of California*, a federal class-action lawsuit on behalf of prisoners held in solitary for more than a decade in the Pelican Bay SHU. The case charges that prolonged solitary confinement "violates the Eighth Amendment's prohibition against cruel and unusual punishment" and that the absence of meaningful review for SHU placement "violates the prisoners' rights to due process." CCR, "Ashker v. Governor of California," https://ccrjustice.org/home/what-we-do/our-cases /ashker-v-brown. Accessed September 28, 2015.

81. Letter from Todd Ashker, September 7, 2015.

82. Ashker puts the matter as follows: "Thus, when these lawmakers made supportive, public statements, requesting our co-operation in order to enable them some time to do their best to enact legislation ending California's long term solitary confinement (torture) practices, we strongly believed it would be a bad move to snub them. Especially when they publically supported us, in spite of the prison officials' vicious propaganda campaign, where they targeted the four principal prisoner representatives. They portrayed us as 'violent, murderous gang leaders, making a power play to regain control of the prison system by forcing prisoners to hunger strike.'" Ashker, *A Prisoner's Story*.

83. Ibid.

84. Ruling by Claudia Wilken, United States district judge, in *Todd Ashker et al. v. Governor of the State of California et al.*, Order Granting Motion for Leave to File a Supplemental Complaint (Docket No. 345), United States District Court for the Northern District of California, Case 4:09-cv-05796-CW Document 387, March 9, 2015.

85. Jamaa, "Worse than Pelican Bay."

86. Three of the four prisoner representatives from the short corridor—Ashker, Arturo Castellanos, and George Franco—remained in Pelican Bay SHU at the time this book was written. Profoundly, about 70 percent of SHU prisoners who were evaluated under the new step-down procedure were transferred directly into general population, which speaks volumes about the lack of need for the SHU in the first place. Wilken, *Todd Ashker et al. v. Governor of the State of California et al.*

87. Ibid.

88. Jamaa, "CCI Step Down Program Is Bogus." Despite nonparticipation, a lawyer for the prisoners in *Ashker v. Brown* told us that the prison administration was advancing them through the step-down *as if* they *were* participating. She speculated that the state might reduce the time it took to proceed through each stage so

that the number of plaintiffs remaining in the SHU, to contest the lawsuit on eighth amendment (cruel and unusual punishment) grounds, would be reduced to a mere few. Personal conversation, July 13, 2015.

89. Letter from Todd Ashker, September 7, 2015.

90. Personal conversation, July 13, 2015.

91. Ashker, *A Prisoner's Story.*

92. Ginzburg, "Comunismo di carcere."

93. A documentary on supermax isolation in the state of Maine shows a form of looping where isolated prisoners who cut themselves are given time in punishment cells; when the cuts are healed, they are placed back in isolation, whereupon they cut themselves again and the cycle repeats, over and over again. NPR, "Solitary Nation," *Frontline,* April 22, 2014, http://www.pbs.org/wgbh/pages/frontline/locked-up-in -america/#solitary-nation. Accessed December 30, 2014.

94. Goldstone, *Revolution and Rebellion in the Early Modern World.*

95. Letter from Todd Ashker, February 12, 2015.

CHAPTER SIX. CONCLUSIONS

1. Goffman, *Asylums.*

2. Marcos, *Our Word Is Our Weapon.*

3. Sykes, *Society of Captives,* 27–28.

4. Scott, *The Art of not Being Governed.*

5. Clastres, *Archeology of Violence.*

6. Scott, *The Art of not Being Governed.*

7. De Sousa Santos, *Toward a New Common Sense.*

8. It is commonly known that the Taliban and other Islamist insurgencies were sponsored by the US government as enemies of the Soviet Union and its affiliated regimes. US prison gangs and street gangs emerged directly out of governmental strategies to suppress insurgent prison groups. And the influx of drugs into American cities that became the excuse for mass incarceration after 1980 was in large part tied to the contra war against Sandinismo amidst fears of general insurgencies in Central and South America.

9. Lynd, *Lucasville.*

10. Braudel, *The Perspective of the World.*

11. Scott, *The Art of not Being Governed.*

12. Wallerstein, *The Modern World-System III,* 130.

13. See the Choctaws' own version of this story at http://www.choctawnation .com/history/choctaw-nation-history/choctaws-helped-starving-irish-in-1847-this- act-shaped-tribal-culture/. Accessed June 2, 2015.

14. Arrighi, Hopkins, and Wallerstein, *Antisystemic Movements.*

15. Graeber, *The Democracy Project*; Holloway, *Crack Capitalism.*

16. Caffentzis, *In Letters of Blood and Fire.*

17. Craib, "Anarcho-Capitalist Archipelagoes."

REFERENCES

Abram, David. 1996. *The Spell of the Sensuous: Perception and Language in a More-Than-Human World*. New York: Vintage.

Abu Jamal, Mumia. 2009. *Jailhouse Lawyers: Prisoners Defending Prisoners v. the USA*. San Francisco: City Lights.

Agamben, Giorgio. 1998. *Homo Sacer: Sovereign Power and Bare Life*. Palo Alto, CA: Stanford University Press.

Alef, Gustav. 1983. *Rulers and Nobles in Fifteenth-Century Moscow*. San Francisco: Valerium Reprints.

Alexander, Michelle. 2012. *The New Jim Crow: Mass Incarceration in the Age of Colorblindness*. New York: New Press.

Anderson, Benedict. 1991. *Imagined Communities*. London: Verso.

Aquino Moreschi, Alejandra. 2009. "Entre el 'sueño zapatista' y el 'sueño americano.'" *Migración y Desarollo* 13: 69–84.

Arrighi, Giovanni, Terence K. Hopkins, and Immanuel Wallerstein. 1989. *Antisystemic Movements*. London: Verso.

Ashker, Todd. 2013. "A Prisoner's Story from Pelican Bay's SHU: Concrete Windowless Isolation Cells, a California Tale of Evolving Resistance." Unpublished manuscript.

Attman, Artur. 1981. "The Russian Market in the World Trade, 1500–1869." *Scandinavian Economic History Review* 29(3): 177–202.

Aubry, Andrés. 2003. "Autonomy in the San Andres Accords." In *Mayan Lives, Mayan Utopias*. Edited by Jan Rus, Rosalva Hernández Castillo, and Shannon L. Mattiace, 219–41. Lanham, MD: Rowman & Littlefield.

Avrich, Paul. 1976. *Russian Rebels, 1600–1800*. New York: Norton.

Baran, Paul, and Paul Sweezy. 1966. *Monopoly Capital*. New York: Monthly Review Press.

Barkin, David. 1990. *Distorted Development: Mexico in the World Economy*. Boulder, CO: Westview Press.

———. 2002. "The Construction of a Modern Mexican Peasantry." *Journal of Peasant Studies* 30: 73–90.

Barmeyer, Niels. 2009. *Developing Zapatista Autonomy: Conflict and NGO Involvement in Rebel Chiapas.* Albuquerque: University of New Mexico Press.

Baronnet, Bruno. 2008. "Rebel Youth and Zapatista Autonomous Education." *Latin American Perspectives* 35(4), 112–24.

Basso, Keith. 1996. *Wisdom Sits in Places: Landscape and Language among the Western Apache.* Albuquerque: University of New Mexico Press.

Benjamin, Thomas. 1996. *A Rich Land, a Poor People: Politics and Society in Modern Chiapas.* Albuquerque: University of New Mexico Press.

———. 2000. "A Time of Reconquest: History, the Maya Revival, and the Zapatista Rebellion in Chiapas." *American Historical Review* 105 (2): 417–50.

Beresford, David. 1987. *Ten Men Dead: The Story of the 1981 Irish Hunger Strike.* London: Harper Collins.

Berger, Dan. 2014a. *Captive Nation: Black Prison Organizing in the Civil Rights Era.* Chapel Hill: University of North Carolina Press.

———. 2014b. *The Struggle Within: Prisons, Political Prisoners, and Mass Movements in the United States.* Oakland, CA: PM Press.

Biggs, Michael. 1999. "Putting the State on the Map: Cartography, Territory, and European State Formation." *Comparative Studies in Society and History,* 41(2), 374–411.

Bilby, Kenneth. 2008. *True Born Maroons.* Gainesville: University Press of Florida.

Blum, Jerome. 1961. *Lord and Peasant in Russia from the Ninth to the Nineteenth Century.* Princeton, NJ: Princeton University Press.

Bobrow-Strain, Aaron. 2007. *Intimate Enemies: Landowners, Power and Violence in Chiapas.* Durham, NC: Duke University Press.

Boeck, Brian. 2009. *Imperial Boundaries: Cossack Communities and Empire-Building in the Age of Peter the Great.* Cambridge: Cambridge University Press.

Bonfil Batalla, Guillermo. 1996. *Mexico Profundo: Reclaiming a Civilization.* Austin: University of Texas Press.

Bowles, Samuel, and Herbert Gintis. 2011. *A Cooperative Species: Human Reciprocity and Its Evolution.* Princeton, NJ: Princeton University Press.

Brass, Tom. 2005. "Neoliberalism and the Rise of (Peasant) Nations within the Nation: Chiapas in Comparative and Theoretical Perspectives." *Journal of Peasant Studies* 32(3–4): 651–91.

Braudel, Fernand. 1979. *The Perspective of the World: Civilization and Capitalism, 15th–18th Century.* Vol. 3. Berkeley: University of California Press.

Bunker, Stephen. 2006. *The Snake with Golden Braids: Society, Nature, and Technology in Andean Irrigation.* Lanham, MD: Lexington Books.

Bunker, Stephen, and Denis O'Hearn. 1993. "Strategies of Economic Ascendants for Access to Raw Materials: A Comparison of the U.S. and Japan." In *Pacific-Asia and the Future of the World-System.* Edited by Ravi Palat, 83–102. Westport, CT: Greenwood Press.

Caffentzis, George. 2013. *In Letters of Blood and Fire.* Oakland, CA: PM Press.

Campbell, Brian, Laurence McKeown, and Feilim O'Hagan. 1994. *Nor Meekly Serve My Time: The H-Block Struggle, 1976–1981*. Belfast: Beyond the Pale.

Castells, Manuel. 1997. *The Power of Identity*. London: Blackwell.

Centro de Derechos Humanos Fray Bartolomé de las Casas (CDHFC). 1997. *Camino a la Masacre: Informe especial sobre chenalhó*. San Cristóbal de las Casas: Frayba.

Chandler, Alfred. 1990. *Scale and Scope*. Cambridge, MA: Belknap Press of Harvard University Press.

Childs, Dennis. 2015. *Slaves of the State: Black Incarceration from the Chain Gang to the Penitentiary*. Minneapolis: University of Minnesota Press.

Chirot, Daniel. 1989. *The Origins of Backwardness in Eastern Europe: Economics and Politics from the Middle Ages until the Early Twentieth Century*. Berkeley: University of California Press.

Clastres, Pierre. 1987. *Society against the State: Essays in Political Anthropology*. Cambridge, MA: MIT Press.

———. 2010. *Archeology of Violence*. New York: Zone Books.

Cleaver, Harry. 1998. "Zapatistas and the Electronic Fabric of Struggle." In *Zapatista! Reinventing Revolution in Mexico*. Edited by John Holloway and Eloína Peláez, 81–103. London: Pluto Press.

Cockroft, James. 1998. *Mexico's Hope: An Encounter with Politics and History*. New York: Monthly Review Press.

Collier, George, and Jane Quaratiello. 1994. *Basta! Land and the Zapatista Rebellion in Chiapas*. Oakland, CA: Food First Books.

Commander Esther. 2003. *Speech by Commander Esther*. Oventic, Chiapas.

Comptroller General of the United States. 1975. *Behavior Modification Programs: The Bureau of Prisons' Alternative to Long-Term Segregation*. Washington, DC: US Department of Justice.

Coogan, Tim Pat. 1980. *On the Blanket: The Inside Story of the IRA Prisoners' "Dirty" Protest*. New York: Palgrave Macmillan.

Craib, Raymond. 2004. *Cartographic Mexico: A History of State Fixations and Fugitive Landscapes*. Durham, NC: Duke University Press.

———. 2014. "Anarcho-Capitalist Archipelagoes: Ocean, Island, and Beach." Lecture delivered at Fernand Braudel Center, Binghamton University, April 9.

Crary, Jonathan. 2013. *24/7: Late Capitalism and the Ends of Sleep*. London: Verso.

Cresson, W. P. 1919. *The Cossacks: Their History and Country*. New York: Bretano's.

Crummey, Robert. 1987. *Formation of Muscovy*. London: Routledge.

———. 1998. "Muscovy and the 'General Crisis of the Seventeenth Century.'" *Journal of Early Modern History* 2: 156–80.

Davies, Brian. 1983. *The Role of the Town Governors in the Defense and Military Colonization of Muscovy's Southern Frontier: The Case of Kozlov, 1635–1638*. Vol. 1. Chicago: University of Chicago Press.

Davis, Angela. 2003. *Are Prisons Obsolete?* New York: Seven Stories Press.

De Leon, Garcia. 2005. "From Revolution to Transition: The Chiapas Rebellion and the Path to Democracy in Mexico." *Journal of Peasant Studies* 32(3–4): 508–27.

Deleuze, Gilles, and Félix Guatari. 1988. *A Thousand Plateaus: Capitalism and Schizophrenia*. London: Athlone Press.

Derlugian, Georgi. 1996. "The Social Cohesion of the States." In *The Age of Transition: Trajectory of the World-System, 1945–2025*. Edited by T. Hopkins and I. Wallerstein, 120–210. London: Zed Books.

de Sousa Santos, Boaventura. 1995. *Toward a New Common Sense: Law, Science and Politics in the Paradigmatic Transition*. New York: Routledge.

———. 2012. "Public Sphere and Epistemologies of the South." *Africa Development* 37(1): 43–67.

De Vos, Jan. 1995. "El Lacandón: Una introducción histórica." In *Chiapas: Los rumbos de otra historia*. Edited by Juan Pedro Viqueria and Mario Humberto Ruz, 150–212. Mexico City: Universidad Nacional Autónoma de México.

Earle, Duncan, and Jeanne Simonelli. 2005. *Uprising of Hope: Sharing the Zapatista Journey to Alternative Development*. Lanham, MD: Altamira Press.

Ehrenreich, Barbara. 2007. *Dancing in the Streets: A History of Collective Joy*. New York: Metropolitan Books.

Elias, Norbert. 2000 (originally published 1939). *The Civilizing Process: Sociogenetic and Psychogenetic Investigations*. Oxford: Blackwell.

Eren, Mustafa. 2014. *Kapatılmanın Patolojisi: Osmanlı'dan Günümüze Hapishanenin Tarihi*. Istanbul: Kalkedon Yayıncılık.

Esteva, Gustavo. 2001. "The Meaning and Scope of the Struggle for Autonomy." *Latin American Perspectives* 28(2): 120–48.

Evans, Sara. 1979. *Personal Politics*. New York: Vintage Books.

EZLN (Ejército Zapatista de Liberación Nacional). 1993. "Women's Revolutionary Law." http://flag.blackened.net/re-volt/mexico/ezln/womlaw.html.

———. 1994. *EZLN: Documentos y Comunicados, Tomo 1*. Mexico City: Ediciones Era.

———. 1995. *EZLN: Documentos y Comunicados, Tomo 2*. Mexico City: Ediciones Era.

———. 1996. "First Declaration of La Realidad for Humanity and against Neoliberalism." http://flag.blackened.net/revolt/mexico/ezln/ccri_1st_ dec_real .html.

———. 1997. *EZLN: Documentos y Comunicados, Tomo 3*. Mexico City: Ediciones Era.

———. 2001a. "Second Declaration of the Lacandón Jungle." In *Our Word Is Our Weapon*. Edited by Subcomandante Insurgente Marcos, 25–78. New York: Seven Stories Press.

———. 2001b. "Second Declaration of La Realidad for Humanity and against Neoliberalism." In *Our Word Is Our Weapon*. Edited by Subcomandante Insurgente Marcos, 21–46. New York: Seven Stories Press.

———. 2001c. "Opening Remarks at the First Intercontinental Encuentro for Humanity and against Neoliberalism." In *Our Word Is Our Weapon*. Edited by Subcomandante Insurgente Marcos, 110–45. New York: Seven Stories Press.

———. 2001d. "First Declaration of the Lacandón Jungle." In *Our Word Is Our Weapon.* Edited by Subcomandante Insurgente Marcos, 170–210. New York: Seven Stories Press.

———. 2002. "The People of the Color of the Earth." In *The Zapatista Reader.* Edited by Tom Hayden, 106–14. Emeryville, CA: Thunder's Mouth Press.

———. 2003a. "Chiapas: La treceava estela. Quinta parte: Una historia." http://palabra.ezln.org.mx/comunicados/2003/2003_07_e.htm.

———. 2003b. "Chiapas: La treceava estela. Segunda parte: Una muerte." http://palabra.ezln.org.mx/comunicados/2003/2003_07_b.htm.

———. 2003c. "Chiapas: La treceava estela. Septima y ultima parte: Una posdata." http://palabra.ezln.org.mx/comunicados/2003/2003_07_g.htm.

———. 2003d. "Chiapas: La treceava estela. Sexta parte: Un buen gobierno." http://palabra.ezln.org.mx/comunicados/2003/2003_07_f.htm.

———. 2003e. "Chiapas: La treceava estela. Tercera parte: Un nombre." http://palabra.ezln.org.mx/comunicados/2003/2003_07_c.htm.

———. 2003f. *EZLN: Documentos y Comunicados, Tomo 4.* Mexico City: Ediciones Era.

———. 2004. "Third Declaration of the Lacandón Jungle." In *¡Ya Basta! Ten Years of the Zapatista Uprising.* Edited by Žiga Vodovnik, 20–45. Oakland, CA: AK Press.

———. 2004b. "Fourth Declaration of the Lacandón Jungle." In *¡Ya Basta! Ten Years of the Zapatista Uprising.* Edited by Žiga Vodovnik, 45–90. Oakland, CA: AK Press.

———. 2004c. "Fifth Declaration of the Lacandón Jungle." In *¡Ya Basta! Ten Years of the Zapatista Uprising.* Edited by Žiga Vodovnik, 90–123. Oakland, CA: AK Press.

———. 2005. "Sixth Declaration of the Lacandona, pt. 3." Translated by Irlandesa. Available from chiapas95-english@eco.utexas.edu.

Federici, Sylvia. 2012. *Revolution at Point Zero: Housework, Reproduction, and Feminist Struggle.* Oakland, CA: PM Press.

Finlayson, James. 2010. "'Bare Life' and Politics in Agamben's Reading of Aristotle." *Review of Politics* 72(1): 97–126.

Forbis, Melissa. 2006. "Autonomy and a Handful of Herbs: Contesting Gender and Ethnic Identities through Healing." In *Dissident Women: Gender and Cultural Politics in Chiapas.* Edited by Shannon Speed, Rosalía Aída Hernández Castillo, and Lynn Stephen, 176–99. Austin: University of Texas Press.

———. 2008. "Never Again a Mexico without Us: Gender, Indigenous Autonomy, and Multiculturalism in Neoliberal Mexico." PhD diss., University of Texas at Austin.

Foucault, Michel. 1979. *Discipline and Punish.* New York: Vintage.

———. 2009. *Security, Territory, Population: Lectures at the Collège de France, 1977–1978.* New York: Picador.

Freeman, W. J. 2000. "A Neurobiological Role of Music in Social Bonding." In *The Origins of Music.* Edited by N. Wallin, B. Merkur, and S. Brown, 411–24. Cambridge, MA: MIT Press.

García Linera, Alvaro. 1999. *Reproletarización: Nueva clase obrera y desarrollo del capital industrial en Bolivia (1952–1998)*. La Paz: Muela del Diablo.

Gerschenkron, Alexander. 1962. *Economic Backwardness in Historical Perspective*. Cambridge, MA: Belknap Press.

———. 1972. "Wirtschaftliche Rückständigkeit in historischer Perspektive, German." In *Industrielle Revolution, Wirtschaftliche Aspekt*. Edited by R. Braun, 59–78. Cologne: Kiepenheuer & Witsch.

Gilberth, C., and G. Otero. 2001. "Democratization in Mexico: The Zapatista Uprising and Civil Society." *Latin American Perspectives* 28(4): 7–29.

Gilly, Adolfo. 1998. "Chiapas and the Rebellion of the Enchanted World." In *Rural Revolt in Mexico: US Intervention and the Domain of Subaltern Politics*, edited by Daniel Nugent, 261–335. Durham, NC: Duke University Press.

———. 2005. *The Mexican Revolution*. New York: New Press.

Ginzburg, Carlo. 1994. "Comunismo di carcere." In *Il registro: Carcere politico di Civitavecchia (1941–1943)*. Edited by Aldo Natoli, Vittorio Foa, and Carlo Ginzburg, 45–50. Rome: Editori Riuniti.

Goffman, Erving. 1961. *Asylums: Essays on the Social Situation of Mental Patients and Other Inmates*. New York: Doubleday.

Goldstone, Jack. 1991. *Revolution and Rebellion in the Early Modern World*. Berkeley: University of California Press.

Gould, Roger. 1995. *Insurgent Identities: Class, Community, and Protest in Paris from 1848 to the Commune*. Chicago: University of Chicago Press.

Graeber, David. 2001. *Toward an Anthropological Theory of Value: The False Coin of Our Own Dreams*. New York: Palgrave Macmillan.

———. 2013. *The Democracy Project: An Idea, a Crisis, a Movement*. New York: Spiegel & Grau.

Gray, Obika. 2004. *Demeaned but Empowered: The Social Power of the Urban Poor in Jamaica*. Mona: University of West Indies Press.

Grubačić, Andrej. 2007. "A Conversation with Denis O'Hearn: Reflections of Prefigurative Politics, the IRA and the Zapatistas," *ZNet*, March 5.

———. 2010. *Don't Mourn, Balkanize: Essays after Yugoslavia*. Oakland, CA: PM Press.

Guenther, Lisa. 2013. *Solitary Confinement: Social Death and Its Afterlives*. Minneapolis: University of Minnesota Press.

Hale, Charles R. 2002. "Does Multiculturalism Menace? Governance, Cultural Rights and the Politics of Identity in Guatemala." *Journal of Latin American Studies* 4: 485–524.

Hall, Thomas. 1989. *Social Change in the Southwest, 1350–1880*. Lawrence: University Press of Kansas.

Hamilton, Nora. 1982. *The Limits of State Autonomy: Post-Revolutionary Mexico*. Princeton, NJ: Princeton University Press.

Hansen, R. 1971. *The Politics of Mexican Development*. Baltimore: John Hopkins University Press.

Hardt, Michael, and Antonio Negri. 2000. *Empire*. Cambridge, MA: Harvard University Press.

Harvey, Neil. 1995. "Rebellion in Chiapas: Rural Reforms and Popular Struggle." *Third World Quarterly* 16(1): 39–73.

———. 1996. "Rural Reforms and the Zapatista Rebellion: Chiapas, 1988–1995." In *Neoliberalism Revisited: Economic Restructuring and Mexico's Political Future*. Edited by Gerardo Otero, 187–208. Boulder, CO: Westview Press.

———. 1998. *The Chiapas Rebellion: The Struggle for Land and Democracy*. Durham, NC: Duke University Press.

Hasketh, Chris. 2010. "Clash of Spatializations." PhD diss., University of Nottingham.

———. 2013. "Social Movements in Oaxaca and Chiapas." In *Marxism and Social Movements*. edited by Colin Barker, Laurence Cox, John Krinsky, and Alf Gunvald Nilsen, 209–233. Leiden: Brill.

Hellie, Richard. 1987. "What Happened? How Did He Get Away with It? Ivan Groznyi's Paranoia and the Problem of Institutional Restraints." *Russian History* 14: 199–224.

———. 2004. "The Expanding Role of the State in Russia." In *Modernizing Muscovy*. Edited by Jarmo Kotilaine and Marshall Poe, 29–55. London: Routledge.

Higgins, Nicholas. 2004. *Understanding the Chiapas Rebellion: Modernist Visions and the Invisible Indian*. Austin: University of Texas Press.

Hirschman, Albert. 1970. *Exit, Voice, and Loyalty: Responses to Decline in Firms, Organizations, and States*. Harvard University Press.

Hoch, Steven. 1986. *Serfdom and Social Control in Russia*. Chicago: University of Chicago Press.

Holloway, John 2002. *Change the World without Taking Power*. London: Pluto Press.

———. 2010. *Crack Capitalism*. London: Pluto.

Hopkins, Terence. 1957. "Sociology and the Substantive View of the Economy." In *Trade and Market in the Early Empires. Edited by* Karl Polanyi, Conrad Arensberg, and Harry Pearson, 270–306. New York: Free Press.

Hopkins, Terence, and Immanuel Wallerstein 1987. "Capitalism and the Incorporation of New Zones into the World-Economy." *Review* 10(5–6, Supplement): 763–80.

Horton, Myles, and Paulo Freire. 1990. *We Make the Road by Walking: Conversations on Education and Social Change*. Philadelphia: Temple University Press.

Hroch, Miroslav, and Luda Klusâkovâ, eds. 1996. *Criteria and Indicators of Backwardness: Essays on Uneven Development in European History*. Prague: Faculty of Arts.

Hrushevsky, Mykhailo. 2005. *History of Ukraine-Rus'*. Vol. 8. Edmonton: Canadian Institute of Ukrainian Studies Press.

Jamaa, Sitawa. 2014. "Worse than Pelican Bay." *San Francisco Bay View*, August 29.

———. 2015. "CCI Step Down Program Is Bogus." *San Francisco Bay View*, June 27. http://sfbayview.com/2015/06/cci-step-down-program-is-bogus/. Accessed July 13, 2015.

Kagarlitsky, Boris. 2008. *Empire of the Periphery: Russia and the World System*. London: Pluto Press.

Kaufman, Mara. 2010. "We Are from Before, Yes, but We Are New: Autonomy, Territory, and the Production of New Subjects of Self-government in Zapatismo." PhD diss., Duke University. UMI no. 3433944.

Kaye, Anthony. 2009. "The Second Slavery: Modernity in the Nineteenth-Century South and the Atlantic World." *Journal of Southern History* 75(3): 627–50.

Khasnabish, Alex 2010. *Zapatistas: Rebellion from the Grassroots to the Global*. London: Zed Books.

Kivelson, Valerie. 1993. "The Devil Stole His Mind: The Tsar and the 1648 Moscow Uprising." *American Historical Review* 98: 733–56.

———. 1997. *Autocracy in the Provinces: Russian Political Culture and Gentry in the Seventeenth Century*. Palo Alto, CA: Stanford University Press.

———. 2006. *Cartographies of Tsardom: The Land and Its Meanings in Seventeenth-Century Russia*. Ithaca, NY, Cornell University Press.

Klein, Hillary. 2015. *Compañeras: Zapatista Women's Stories*. New York: Seven Stories Press.

Knight, Allan. 1985. "The Mexican Revolution: Bourgeois? Nationalist? Or Just a 'Great Rebellion?'" *Bulletin of Latin America Research* 4(2): 1–37.

———. 1994. "Popular Culture and the Revolutionary State in Mexico, 1910–1940." *Hispanic American Historical Review* 74(3): 393–443.

Knudson, Jerry. 1998. "Rebellion in Chiapas: Insurrection by Internet and Public Relations." *Media, Culture, and Society* 20: 507–18.

Kolchin, Peter. 1990. *Unfree Labor: American Slavery and Russian Serfdom*. Cambridge, MA: Belknap Press of Harvard University Press.

Kollmann, N. S. 1987. *Kinship and Politics: The Making of the Muscovite Political System, 1345–1547*. Palo Alto, CA: Stanford University Press.

———. 1999. *By Honor Bound*. Ithaca, NY: Cornell University Press.

———. 2004. "Society, Identity, Modernity in Seventeenth-Century Russia." In *Modernizing Muscovy: Reform and Social Change in Seventeenth-Century Russia*. Edited by Jarmo Kotilaine and Marshall Poe, 417–32. London: Routledge.

Komlosy, Andrea. 2014. *Arbeit: Eine globalhistorische Perspektive*. Vienna: Promedia.

Kornblatt, J. D. 1992. *The Cossack Hero in Russian Literature: A Study in Cultural Mythology*. Madison: University of Wisconsin Press.

Kotoshikhin, Grigorii. 1906. *O Rosii v tsarstvovanie Alekseia Mikhailovicha*. 4th ed. Moscow: Tipografiia Glavnogo Upravlenia Udelov.

Kropotkin, Petr. 2012 (originally published 1902). *Mutual Aid: A Factor of Evolution*. www.forgottenbooks.com.

Kurnaz, Selami. 2005, *Tecrit Yaşayanlar Anlatıyor*. Istanbul: Boran Yayınevi.

Laclau, Ernesto. 2007. "Bare Life or Social Indeterminacy." In *Giorgio Agamben: Sovereignty and Life*. Edited by Matthew Calarco and Steven DeCaroli, 11–22. Stanford, CA: Stanford University Press.

Lamar, Keith. 2014. *Condemned: The Whole Story*. www.createspace.com.

Le Bot, Yvon. 1997. *Subcomandante Marcos: El sueño zapatista*. Mexico City: Plaza & Janés Editores.

LeDonne, John. 2004. *The Grand Strategy of the Russian Empire, 1650–1831*. Oxford: Oxford University Press.

Lefebvre, Henri. 1991. *The Production of Space*. London: Blackwell.

———. 2003. "Space and State." In *State/Space: A Reader*. Edited by Neil Brenner, Bob Jessop, M. Jones, and Gavin MacLeod, 223–89. London: Blackwell.

———. 2009. *State, Space, World: Selected Essays*. Edited by N. Brenner and S. Elden. Minneapolis: University of Minnesota Press.

Legorreta, Carmen. 1998. *Religión, política y guerrilla en las cañadas de la Selva Lacandona*. Mexico City: Cal y Arena.

Lenin, Vladimir. 1899. *The Development of Capitalism in Russia: The Process of the Formation of a Home Market for Large-Scale Industry*. https://www.marxists.org /archive/lenin/works/1899/devel/index.htm.

———. 1917. *Imperialism: The Highest Stage of Capitalism*. Petrograd.

Lewis, Stephen. 1997. "Revolution and the Rural Schoolhouse: Forging State and Nation in Chiapas, Mexico, 1913–48." PhD diss., University of California, San Diego.

Leyva Solano, Xóchitl. 2005. "Indigenismo, indianismo and 'ethnic citizenship' in Chiapas." *Journal of Peasant Studies* 32(3–4): 555–83.

Lieberman, Victor. 2009. *Strange Parallels: Southeast Asia in Global Context, c. 800–1830*. Vol. 2. Cambridge: Cambridge University Press.

Linebaugh, Peter, and Marcus Rediker. 2000. *The Many-Headed Hydra: Sailors, Slaves, Commoners, and the Hidden History of the Revolutionary Atlantic*. Boston: Beacon Press.

Longworth, Philip. 1970. *The Cossacks*. London: Holt, Rinehart and Winston.

———. 1974. "Reply." *Slavic Review* 33(2): 411–14.

Luccisano, Luisa. 2004. "Mexico's Progresa: An Example of Neoliberal Poverty Alleviation Programs Concerned with Gender, Human Capital Development, Responsibility, and Choice." In *Maternal Health Policy and the Politics of Scale in Mexico*, 31–57. Oxford: Oxford University Press.

Lunin, B. V. 1939. *K Istorii donskoga kazachestva*. Rostov-on-Don, Russia: Rostovskoe oblastnoe knigoizdatel'stvo.

Luxemburg, Rosa. 1913. *The Accumulation of Capital*. London: Routledge and Kegan Paul.

Lynd, Staughton. 2004. *Lucasville: The Untold Story of a Prison Uprising*. Philadelphia: Temple University Press.

———. 2012. *Accompanying: Pathways to Change*. Oakland, CA: PM Press.

———. 2014. *Doing History from the Bottom Up: On E.P. Thompson, Howard Zinn, and Rebuilding the Labor Movement from Below*. Chicago: Haymarket.

Lynd, Staughton, and Grubačić, Andrej. 2008. *Wobblies and Zapatistas: Conversations on Anarchism, Marxism, and Radical History*. Oakland, CA: PM Press.

Mangini, Shirley. 1995. *Memories of Resistance: Women's Voices from the Spanish Civil War*. New Haven, CT: Yale University Press.

Marcos, Subcomandante. 1994. "Communiqué about the End of the Consultations." In *Zapatistas! Documents of the New Mexican Revolution.* Edited by the EZLN Editorial Collective, 309–14. New York: Autonomedia.

———. 2002. *Our Word Is Our Weapon.* New York: Seven Stories Press.

———. 2004. "Three Shoulders." http://flag.blackened.net/revolt/mexico/ezln/2004/marcos/shouldersAUG.html.

Mariátegui, José. 1988. *Seven Interpretive Essays on Peruvian Reality.* Translated by Marjory Urquidi. Austin: University of Texas Press.

Martin, Janet. 1992. "Muscovite Frontier Policy." *Russian History* 19: 169–80.

Marx, Karl. 1992. *Capital.* Vol. 1. New York: Penguin.

Mattiace, Shannan. 1997. "Zapata Vive! The EZLN, Indian Politics, and the Autonomy Movement in Mexico." *Journal of Latin American Anthropology* 3(1): 32–71.

———. 1998. "Peasant and Indian: Political Identity and Indian Autonomy in Chiapas, Mexico, 1970–90." PhD diss., University of Texas, Austin. UMI no. 9905795.

———. 2001. "Regional Renegotiations of Spaces: Tojolabal Ethnic Identity in Las Margaritas, Chiapas." *Latin American Perspectives* 28(2): 73–97.

———. 2003. "Regional Renegotiations of Space: Tojolabal Ethnic Identity in Las Margaritas, Chiapas." In *Mayan Lives, Mayan Utopias: The Indigenous Peoples of Chiapas and the Zapatista Rebellion.* Edited by Jan Rus, Rosalía Aída Hernández Castillo, and Shannan L. Mattiace, 109–33. Lanham, MD: Rowman & Littlefield.

Mauss, Marcel. 1954. *The Gift.* New York: W. W. Norton.

McChesney, Robert. 2001. "Global Media, Neoliberalism, and Imperialism." *Monthly Review* 52: 10.

McEvoy, Kieran. 2001. *Paramilitary Imprisonment in Northern Ireland: Resistance, Management and Release.* Oxford: Oxford University Press.

McKeown, Laurence. 2001. *Out of Time: Irish Republican Prisoners, Long Kesh, 1972–2000.* Belfast: Beyond the Pale.

McMichael, Philip. 1990. "Incorporating Comparison within a World-Historical Perspective: An Alternative Comparative Method." *American Sociological Review* 55(3): 385–97.

McNeill, William H. 1964. *Europe's Steppe Frontier, 1500–1800.* Chicago: University of Chicago Press.

Menning, Bruce W. 1972. "The Socialization of the Don Cossack Host Prior to the Reign of Nicholas I." PhD diss., Duke University. UMI no. 7223245.

Midnight Notes Collective. 2001. *Auroras of the Zapatistas: Local and Global Struggles of the Fourth World War.* New York: Autonomedia.

Mora, Marianna. 2007. "The Zapatista Anticapitalist Politics and the 'Other Campaign': Learning from the Struggle for Indigenous Rights and Autonomy." *Latin American Perspectives* 34(2): 64–77.

———. 2008. "Decolonizing Politics: Zapatista Indigenous Autonomy in an Era of Neoliberal Governance and Low Intensity Warfare." PhD diss., University of Texas, Austin. UMI no. 3341951.

Muñoz Ramírez, Gloria. 2008. *The Fire and the Word: A History of the Zapatista Movement*. San Francisco: City Lights Books.

Muntaqim, Haazim W. (Jeffrey Milo Burks) 2013. "The Deadly 'Integrated Yard Policy': Commentary on 'The Pelikkkan Bay Factor: An Indictable Offense.'" *San Franciso Bay View,* November 20.

Mutersbaught, Tad. 2002. "Migration, Common Property, and Communal Labor: Cultural Politics and Agency in a Mexican Village." *Political Geography* 21: 43–94.

Nash, June. 2001. *Mayan Visions: The Quest for Autonomy in an Age of Globalization.* New York: Routledge.

Nieboer, H.J. 1900. *Slavery as an Industrial System: Ethnological Resources.* The Hague: Martinus Nijhoff.

Nolte, Hans-Heinrich. 1982. "The Position of Eastern Europe in the International System in Early Modern Times." *Review* 6(1): 25–84.

———. 1986. "The Netherlands and Russia in the Seventeenth Century: Economic and Social Relations." *Review* 10(2): 230–44.

Northern Ireland Office. 1980. *H-Blocks: The Facts.* Belfast: Northern Ireland Office.

Notes from Nowhere. 2004. *We Are Everywhere: The Irresistible Rise of Global Anticapitalism.* London: Verso.

Nugent, Daniel, and Ana María Alonso. 1994. "Multiple Selective Traditions in Agrarian Reform and Agrarian Struggle: Popular Culture and State Formation in the Ejido of Namiquipa." In *Everyday Forms of State Formation: Revolution and the Negotiation of Rule in Modern Mexico.* Edited by Gilbert Joseph and Daniel Nugent, 23–45. Durham, NC: Duke University Press.

O'Brien, Karen. 1998. *Sacrificing the Forest: Environmental and Social Struggles in Chiapas.* Boulder, CO: Westview Press.

O'Hearn, Denis. 1980. "The Consumer Second Economy: Size and Effects." *Soviet Studies* 32(2): 218–34.

———. 1981. "The Second Economy in Consumer Goods and Services." *Critique* 15: 93–109.

———. 2006. *Nothing but an Unfinished Song: Bobby Sands, the Irish Hunger Striker Who Ignited a Generation.* New York: Nation Books.

———. 2009. "Repression and Solidary Cultures of Resistance: Irish Political Prisoners on Protest." *American Journal of Sociology* 15:2: 491–526.

———. 2013. "Diaspora of Practice: Northern Irish Imprisonment and the Transnational Rise of Cellular Isolation." *Breac* 1. https://breac.nd.edu /articles/36998-diaspora-of-practice-northern-irish-imprisonment-and-the-transnational-rise-of-cellular-isolation/.

———. 2014. "Hücre tecridi ve mahpus direnişi." *Teorik Bakış* 4: 85–106.

Olesen, T. 2005. *International Zapatismo: The Construction of Solidarity in the Age of Globalization.* London: Zed Books.

Olivera, Mercedes. 2005. "Subordination and Rebellion: Indigenous Peasant Women in Chiapas Ten Years after the Zapatista Uprising." *Journal of Peasant Studies* 32(3–4): 608–28.

Olivier, Johan. 1990. "Causes of Ethnic Collective Action in the Pretoria Witwatersrand and Triangle, 1970 to 1984." *South African Sociological Review* 2: 89–108.

O'Rourke, Shane. 2007. *The Cossacks*. Manchester: Manchester University Press.

Ostrowski, Donald. 1998. *Muscovy and the Mongols: Cross-Cultural Influences on the Steppe Frontier, 1304–1589.* Cambridge: Harvard University Press.

Otero, G. 1999. *Farewell to the Peasantry? Political Class Formation in Rural Mexico.* Boulder, CO: Westview Press.

Paker, Murat. 2000, "Turkey's Operation Return to Life." *MERIP* (The Middle East Research and Information Project). Press Information Note 42, December 29.

Papadopolous, Dimitris, Niamh Stephenson, and Vassilis Tsianos. 2008. *Escape Routes: Control and Subversion in the Twenty-First Century.* London, Pluto Press.

Pavlov, Andrei, and Maureen Prerie. 2003. *Ivan the Terrible.* London: Routledge.

Pithouse, Richard. 2006. "Struggle Is a School: The Rise of a Shack Dwellers' Movement in Durban, South Africa." *Monthly Review* 57: 9.

Platonov, S. F. 1986. *The Time of Troubles: Historical Study of the Internal Crisis and Social Struggles in Sixteenth- and Seventeenth-Century Muscovy.* Lawrence: University Press of Kansas.

Plokhy, Serhii. 2001. *The Cossacks and Religion in Early Modern Ukraine.* Oxford: Oxford University Press.

———. 2006. *The Origins of the Slavic Nations: Premodern Identities in Russia, Ukraine, and Belarus.* Cambridge: Cambridge University Press.

Polanyi, Karl. 1957. "The Economy as Instituted Process." In *Trade and Market in the Early Empires.* Edited by Karl Polanyi, Conrad Arensberg, and Harry Pearson, 243–70. New York: Free Press.

———. 2001 (Originally published 1944). *The Great Transformation: The Political and Economic Origins of Our Time.* Boston: Beacon Press.

Poniatowska, Elena. 2002. "Women's Battle for Respect Inch by Inch." In *The Zapatista Reader.* Edited by Tom Hayden, 55–57. Emeryville, CA: Thunder's Mouth Press.

Poveda, Pablo. 2003. "Trabajo, informalidad y acumulación: Formas de producción y transferencia de excedentes de la industria manufacturera boliviana." Serie Documentos de trabajo, no. 30. La Paz: CEDLA.

Pozas, Ricardo. 1962. *Juan the Chamula: An Ethnological Re-creation of the Life of a Mexican Indian.* Berkeley: University of California Press.

Preparata, Guido. 2006. "Perishable Money in a Threefold Commonwealth: Rudolf Steiner and the Social Economics of an Anarchist Utopia." *Review of Radical Political Economics* 38(4): 619–48.

PRO, H-Block [Bobby Sands]. "H-Block Protest Intensifies." *Republican News,* April 8, 1978, 6.

Price, Richard. 1996. *Maroon Societies: Rebel Slave Communities in the Americas.* Baltimore: Johns Hopkins University Press.

Prohnstein, A. P. 1961. *Zemlia Donskaia v XVIII veke.* Rostov-on-Don, Russia: Izdatel'stvo Rostovskoga Universiteta.

Quijano, Anibal. 2000. "Coloniality of Power, Eurocentrism, and Latin America." *Nepantla: Views from South* 1(3): 533–80.

Rasler, Karen. 1996. "Concessions, Repression, and Political Protest in the Iranian Revolution." *American Sociological Review* 61(1): 132–52.

Rediker, Marcus. 2004. *Villains of All Nations: Atlantic Pirates in the Golden Age.* Boston: Beacon Press.

Reyes Ramos, María Eugenia. 1992. *El reparto de tierras y la política agraria en Chiapas, 1914–1988.* Mexico City: Universidad Nacional Autónoma de México.

Reyes Ramos, María Eugenia, and Álvaro F. López Lara. 1994. "Una década de programas agrarios en Chiapas." *Cuadernos Agrarios* 4(8–9): 10–19.

Rhodes, Lorna. 2004. *Total Confinement: Madness and Reason in the Maximum Security Prison.* Berkeley: University of California Press.

Riabov, S. I. 1992. *Donskaia zemlia v XVII veke.* Moscow: Peremena.

Richards, Stephen, ed. 2015. *The Marion Experiment: Long-Term Solitary Confinement and the Supermax Movement.* Carbondale: Southern Illinois University Press.

Rieber, Alfred. 1982. *Merchants and Entrepreneurs in Imperial Russia.* Chapel Hill: University of North Carolina Press.

———. 1993. "Persistent Factors in Russian Foreign Policy: An Interpretive Essay." In *Imperial Russian Foreign Policy.* Edited by Hugh Ragsdale, 315–59. Cambridge, MA: Harvard University Press.

Rigel'man, A. I. 1846. *Istoria ili povestvovanie o donskiih kazakakh.* Moscow: Izdatel'stvo Obschestva istorii I drevostei rossiiskikh.

Rodriguez, Dylan. 2006. *Forced Passages: Imprisoned Radical Intellectuals and the U.S. Prison Regime.* Minneapolis: University of Minnesota Press.

Rojas, Bruno, and German Guaygua. 2003. "El empleo en tiempos de crisis." Avances de Investigación, no. 24. La Paz: CEDLA.

Romaniello, Mathew. 2000. "Controlling the Frontier: Monasteries and Infrastructure in the Volga Region, 1552–1682." *Central Asian Survey* 19(3–4): 429–43.

Ross, Jeffrey. 2013. *The Globalization of Supermax Prisons.* New Brunswick, NJ: Rutgers University Press.

Ross, John. 2000. *The War against Oblivion: The Zapatista Chronicles.* Monroe, ME: Common Courage Press.

———. 2006. *¡Zapatistas! Making Another World Possible—Chronicles of Resistance, 2000–2006.* New York: Nation Books.

Rus, Jan. 1994. "The 'Communidad Revolucionaria Instituional': The Subversion of Native Government in Highland Chiapas, 1936–1968." In *Everyday Forms of State Formation: Revolution and the Negotiation of Rule in Modern Mexico.* Edited by G. Joesph and D. Nugent, 265–300. Durham, NC: Duke University Press.

———. 1995. "Local Adaption to Global Change: The Reordering of Native Society in Highland Chiapas, Mexico." *European Review of Latin America and Caribbean Studies* 58: 71–89.

———. 2005. "The Struggle against Indigenous Caciques in Highland Chiapas: Dissent, Religion and Exile in Chamula, 1965–1977." In *Caciquismo in*

Twentieth-Century Mexico. Edited by A. Knight and W. Pansters, 169–200. London: Institute for the Study of the Americas.

Rus, Jan, Rosalía Aída Hernández Castillo, and Shannan L. Mattiace, eds. 2003. *Mayan Lives, Mayan Utopias: The Indigenous Peoples of Chiapas and the Zapatista Rebellion.* Lanham, MD: Rowman & Littlefield.

Ryan, Ramor. 2011. *Zapatista Spring: Anatomy of a Rebel Water Project and the Lessons of International Solidarity.* Oakland, CA: AK Press.

Ryder, Chris. 2000. *Inside the Maze: The Inside Story of the Northern Ireland Prison Service.* London: Methuen.

Sahlins, Peter. 1989. *Boundaries: The Making of France and Spain in the Pyrenees.* Berkeley: University of California Press.

Sands, Bobby. 1982. *Skylark, Sing Your Lonely Song.* Dublin: Mercier Press.

Sayer, Derek. 1987. *The Violence of Abstraction: The Analytic Foundations of Historical Materialism.* London: Basil Blackwell.

Schein, Edgar. 1962. "Man against Man: Brainwashing." *Corrective Psychiatry and Journal of Social Therapy* 8(2): 90–97.

Schumpeter, Joseph. 1964. Business Cycles: A Theoretical, Historical, and Statistical Analysis of the Capitalist Process. New York: McGraw-Hill.

Scott, James. 1990. *Domination and the Arts of Resistance.* New Haven, CT: Yale University Press.

———. 1998. *Seeing like a State: How Certain Schemes to Improve the Human Condition Have Failed.* New Haven, CT: Yale University Press.

———. 2009. *The Art of not Being Governed: An Anarchist History of Upland Southeast Asia.* New Haven, CT: Yale University Press.

Shakur, Abdul Olugbala, Mutope Duguma, Sitawa Nantambu Jamaa, and Abasi Ganda. 2013. "The Pelikkkan Bay Factor: An Indictable Offense." *San Francisco Bay View,* January 17.

Shalev, Sharon. 2009. *Supermax: Controlling Risk through Solitary Confinement.* Cullompton, Devon: Willan.

Sober, Elliott, and David Wilson. 1999. *Unto Others: The Evolution and Psychology of Unselfish Behavior.* Cambridge MA, Harvard University Press.

Speed, Shannon. 2008. *Rights in Rebellion: Indigenous Struggle and Human Rights in Chiapas.* Palo Alto, CA: Stanford University Press.

Speed, Shannon, and Jane Collier. 2000. "Limiting Indigenous Autonomy in Chiapas, Mexico: The State Government's Use of Human Rights." *Human Rights Quarterly* 22(4): 877–905.

Speed, Shannon, and Álvaro Reyes. 2002. "In Our Own Defense: Rights and Resistance in Chiapas." *POLAR* 25(1): 69–79.

Stahler-Sholk, Richard. 2007. "Resisting Neoliberal Homogenization: The Zapatista Autonomy Movement." *Latin American Perspectives* 34(2): 48–63.

———. 2010. "The Zapatista Social Movement: Innovation and Sustainability." *Alternatives: Global, Local, Political* 35: 269–90.

Stanford, L. 1994. "The Privatization of Mexico's Ejidal Sector: Examining Local Impact, Strategies, and Ideologies." *Urban Anthropology* 23(2–3): 97–119.

Staples, David. 2006. *No Place like Home: Organizing Home-Based Labor in the Era of Structural Adjustment*. New York: Routledge.

Steiner, Rudolf. 1923. *The Threefold Commonwealth*. London: Anthroposophical Publishing.

Stephen, Lynn. 2002. *Zapata Lives! Histories and Cultural Politics in Southern Mexico*. Berkeley: University of California Press.

Stevens, Carol. 1995. *Soldiers on the Steppe: Army Reform and Social Change in Early Modern Russia*. DeKalb: Northern Illinois University Press.

Sunderland, William. 2004. *Taming the Wild Field: Colonization and Empire on the Russian Steppe*. Ithaca, NY: Cornell University Press.

Svatikov, S. G. 1924. *Rossiia I Don*. Belgrade.

Sykes, Gresham. 1958. *Society of Captives: A Study of a Maximum Security Prison*. Princeton, NJ: Princeton University Press.

Tambiah, Stanley J. 1990. "Presidential Address: Reflections on Communal Violence in South Asia." *Journal of Asian Studies* 40(4): 741–60.

Tilly, Charles. 1985. "War Making and State Making as Organized Crime." In *Bringing the State Back In*. Edited by Peter Evans, Dietrich Rueschemeyer, and Theda Skocpol, 169–91. Cambridge: Cambridge University Press.

Todes, Daniel. 1987. "Darwin's Malthusian Metaphor and Russian Evolutionary Thought, 1859–1917." *Isis* 78(4): 537–51.

Tomich, Dale. 2003. *Through the Prism of Slavery: Labor, Capital, and World Economy*. Lanham, MD: Rowman & Littlefield.

Tsing, Anna. 2007, "Indigenous Voice." In *Indigenous Experience Today*. Edited by Marisol de la Cadena and Orin Starn, 33–67. New York: Berg.

Tugan-Baranovskii, M. I. 1970 (originally published 1898). *The Russian Factory in the 19th Century*. Homwood, IL: R. D. Irwin.

Turner, Terence. 1986. "Production, Exploitation and Social Consciousness in the 'Peripheral Situation,'" *Social Analysis* 19: 91–115.

Van der Haar, Gemma. 2005. "Land Reform, the State, and the Zapatista Uprising in Chiapas." *Journal of Peasant Studies* 32(3–4): 484–507.

Vasconcelos, José. 1966. *La raza cósmica*. 3rd ed. Mexico City: Espasa-Calpe Mexicana.

Vaughn, Mary Kay. 1982. *The State, Education, and Social Class in Mexico, 1880–1928*. DeKalb: Northern Illinois University Press.

———. 1997. *Cultural Politics in Revolution: Teachers, Peasants, and Schools in Mexico, 1930–1940*. Tucson: University of Arizona Press.

Veltmayer, Henry. 1997. "Latin America in the New World Order." *Canadian Journal of Sociology* 22(2): 207–42.

Villafuerte Solís, Daniel. 1999. *La Tierra en Chiapas: Viejos problemas nuevos*. Mexico City: Plaza y Valdez.

Villafuerte, Daniel, and María del Carmen García. 2006. "Crisis rural y migraciones en Chiapas." *Migración y Desarrollo* 1: 102–30.

Wacquant, Loic. 2009. *Punishing the Poor: The Neoliberal Government of Social Insecurity*. Durham, NC: Duke University Press.

Wagner, Peter. 2014. "Tracking State Prison Growth in 50 States." *Prison Policy Initiative,* May 28. http://www.prisonpolicy.org/reports/overtime.html. Accessed July 3, 2015.

Wallace-Wells, Benjamin. 2014. "The Plot from Solitary." *New York Magazine,* February 26.

Wallerstein, Immanuel. 1974. *The Modern World-System I: Capitalist Agriculture and the Origins of the European World-Economy in the Sixteenth Century.* New York: Academic Press.

———. 1989. *The Modern World-System III: The Second Era of Great Expansion of the Capitalist World-Economy, 1730–1840s.* New York: Academic Press.

———. 1991. *Geopolitics and Geoculture: Essays on the Changing World-System.* Cambridge: Cambridge University Press.

Wallerstein, Immanuel, and Sharon Zukin. 1989. "1968, Revolution in the World-System." *Theory and Society* 18(4): 431–49.

Warman, Arturo. 1976. *"We Come to Object": The Peasants of Morelos and the National State.* Baltimore: Johns Hopkins University Press.

Washbrook, Sarah. 2005. "The Chiapas Uprising of 1994: Historical Antecedents and Political Consequences." *Journal of Peasant Studies* 32(3–4): 417–49.

Weinberg, Bill. 2000. *Homage to Chiapas: The New Indigenous Struggles in Mexico.* London: Verso.

Wickham-Crowley, Timothy. 1989. "Winners, Losers, and Also-Rans: Toward a Comparative Sociology of Latin American Guerrilla Movements." In *Power and Popular Protest: Latin American Social Movements.* Edited by Susan Eckstein, 132–81. Berkeley: University of California Press.

Wilson, Japhy. 2013. "The Urbanization of the Countryside: Depoliticization and the Production of Space in Chiapas." *Latin American Perspectives* 40(2), 218–36.

Wolford, Wendy. 2010. *This Land Is Ours Now: Social Mobilization and the Meanings of Land in Brazil.* Durham, NC: Duke University Press.

Womack, John, Jr. 1978. "The Mexican Economy during the Revolution, 1910–1920: Historiography and Analysis." *Marxist Perspectives* 1(4): 80–123.

———. 1999. *Rebellion in Chiapas: An Historical Reader.* New York: New Press.

Wright, Erik. 1978. *Class, Crisis and the State.* London: Verso.

———. 2010. *Envisioning Real Utopias.* London: Verso.

Yaresh, Leo. 1957. "The 'Peasant Wars' in Soviet Historiography." *American Slavic and East European Review* 16: 241–59.

Ziarek, Ewa Plonowska. 2012. "Bare Life." In *Impasses of the Post-Global: Theory in the Era of Climate Change.* Vol. 2. Edited by Henry Sussman. Ann Arbor, MI: Open Humanities Press and University of Michigan Library, http://dx.doi.org/10.3998/ohp.10803281.0001.001.

Zibechi, Raul. 2011. *Dispersing Power.* Oakland, CA: AK Press.

———. 2012a. "Subterranean Echos: Resistance and Politics 'desde el Sótano.'" *Socialism and Democracy* 19(3): 13–39.

———. 2012b. *Territories in Resistance.* Oakland, CA: AK Press.

ACKNOWLEDGMENTS

This work could not have happened without the mutual aid of the following people.

Georgi Derluguian, Richard Robinson, Olga Rvachiova, Slava Yashchenko; the staff of the Volgograd public library; the people of Ust'-Medveditskaya, especially Maria Ivanovna and family and Andrey Goncharov, Yurtovoy Ataman of the Serafimovich Cossacks' Yurt; the staff of the Ust'-Medveditskoe Cossack State History Museum and A.S. Serafimovich House-Museum; the students and staff of the Buerak-Popovskii Comprehensive School; Yan Prusskii and staff of the Dmitrov Museum.

Michael McCaughan, Henry McLaughlin, Ramor Ryan, Emma Shaw Crane; the people of Oventic; the promotores and alumni of Escuela Secundaria Rebelde Autónoma Zapatista "primero de enero."

Todd Ashker, Mehmet Boğatikin, Carlito Cabana, Flair Campbell, Taylan Çintay, Secil Doğuc, Julie Duchatel, Mustafa Eren, Derya Firat, Paul and Amy Gordiejew, Arda Ibikoğlu, Jake Jackson, Zafer Kiraç, Jules Lobel, Staughton and Alice Lynd, Brian McAteer, Lawrence McKeown, Danny Morrison, Mary Ratcliffe, Jason Robb, Baris Sannan, Bomani Shakur, Danny Troxell, Anne Weills, Aytekin Yilmaz.

Maja Izquierdo, Sara Maria Acevedo, Walden Bello, Herb Bix, Chris Carlsson, Fernando Castrillon, Christopher Chase-Dunn, Noam Chomsky, Ray Craib, David Escobar, Silvia Federici, Michelle Glowa, David Graeber, Obika Gray, Raquel Guttierez, John Holloway, Brandon Jourdan, Ramsey Kanaan, J.R. Karlin, Femke Kaulingfreks, Cem Kursonoglu, Richard Lee, Claudia Lodia, Sasha Lilley, Peter Linebaugh, Marianne Maeckelbergh, David Martinez, Targol Mesbah, Jason Moore, Tim Moynihan, Mutombo Mpanya, Rallie Murray, Raj Patel, Claudia Lodia, Richard Pithouse, Dylan

Rodriguez, James Scott, Anne Teich, Dale Tomich, Judie Wexler, Gerardo Lopez Amaro, Talia Mole, Lisa Hunter, Isha Lucas, Lucia de la Fuente, Nyki Duda, Dale Johnson, Austin Lawhead; members of the Retort Collective; members of the research working group on exilic spaces and practices at the Fernand Braudel Center for the Study of Economies, Historical Systems, and Civilizations, Binghamton University; graduate students in sociology at Binghamton University and at the Anthropology and Social Change Department at the California Institute for Integral Studies.

Our friends at University of California Press, especially Niels Hooper, Ryan Furtkamp, Bradley Depew, and Cindy Fulton; copy editor Sue Carter; indexer Ruth Elwell.

Friends from Ireland, Turkey, Kurdistan, Russia, and Chiapas.

Special mention and love to Beka, Sloba, Gega, Mari, Hana, Vesna, Bella, Chupa, Charna, Nina, Sinéad, Caitríona, Pat, Charlotte, and Bilge.

And to all our fellow members of the Yeti Cossack Host.

INDEX

absences, sociology of, 4, 17
Abu Ghraib, 31
Abu Jamal, Mumia, xi, 178, 179, 184–85,
  200–205, 281n6
accumulation, capitalist. *See* capitalist
  world-system
Acteal massacre, 152
Adams, Gerry, 186, 195–96
Africa, 1, 11, 212, 257n1; armed insurgencies
  in, 44; highland, 9
African Americans, 211, 233, 243; Jim Crow
  segregation of, 32
Against Neoliberalism and for Humanity,
  147
Agamben, Giorgio, 29–32, 178, 256n23
Agrarian Law, Mexican (1915), 113
agrarian reform. *See* land reform
agriculture, 9–11, 14, 33, 39, 44, 250; Cossack attitudes toward, 43, 60, 62, 71–72,
  75, 80, 101, 107, 111, 237–38; Russian, 28,
  90, 92, 94–95, 105, 258n6; subsistence,
  110, 143, 168, 170; Zapatista, 131, 140–
  41, 152, 168–70. *See also* cattle ranching;
  land reform
Alexander I, Tsar, 102
Alexei I, Tsar, 84
Algeria, 8
Alianza Campesina Independiente Emiliano Zapata (ANCIENZ), 125
Alianza Nacional Campesina Independiente Emiliano Zapata (ACIENZ),
  125–26
Amazonia, 9

Americas: colonization of, 93, 125–26. *See
  also* Latin America; South America;
  United States
Amnesty International, 199
Amsterdam, 91, 92
anarchism, xi–xii, xiv, 1, 5
Ankara F-type #2, 205
Aquino Moreschi, Alejandra, 167
Arabs, 8, 58
Arab Spring, 213–14
Arendt, Hannah, 30, 256n23
Argentina, 13
Aristotle, 30, 31, 255–56n23
Aryan Brotherhood, 210–12
Ashker, Todd, xiv, 211–19, 222–26, 284n54,
  286nn82,86; cell of, 214*fig,* 284n51,
  285n79; class action lawsuit brought by,
  286nn80,88; found guilty of "promot-
  ing gang activity," 222, 285n77; hunger
  strike of, 214, 218, 219; influenced by
  Irish prisoners' experiences, xv, 213,
  215–17, 219, 226, 228
Asia, 212; Southeast, 8, 9. *See also specific
  countries and regions*
Asociación Rural de Interés Colectivo
  (ARIC), 121
Assembly Code of 1649, 52
Astrakhan, 59, 68, 84, 87, 91, 106, 259n15
Attman, Arthur, 91, 92
Austin v. Wilkinson (2005), 243
Australia, 8
authoritarianism, 44, 134, 156, 166, 169,
  227

F-type prisons, 178, 184–85, 200–205, 281n6, 283n40
Fuerzas de Liberación Nacional (FLN), 271n84
Fyodor I, Tsar, 90–91

gangs, 16, 104, 182, 220–21, 239, 242, 287n8; prison, xiv, 181, 184, 206–8, 210–12, 222, 233, 239–40, 243, 287n8
García Linera, Alvaro, 39–40
Garrucha, 273n16
gender issues, 38, 131, 237, 240, 243–45, 252; Cossack, 46, 76, 169, 244. *See also under* Zapatistas
geographic escape, 12, 25, 42–43, 63, 128, 163, 177
Georgia (Caucasus region), 88
Georgia (United States), prison work strike in, 185, 214
German Ideology, The (Marx and Engels), 34–35
Germany, 36, 91, 180, 256n39
Geronimo, 192
Gilly, Adolfo, 113
Ginzburg, Carlo, 227
gladiatorial Darwinism, 7–8
globalization, 5, 38, 180; movement against, 157, 250, 276n165. *See also* capitalist world-system
Goffman, Erving, 29, 31, 178, 186, 231
Goldstone, Jack, 227
Golik (Kurdish language magazine), 205
Golitsyn, Prince Vasilii Vasilievich, 67, 85
Gorchakov, Prince, 102
Gordon, Patrick, 67, 71, 76–77
governance, 21, 41, 44, 45, 58, 134–35, 158, 257n56; autonomous, 61, 119, 132, 163; communal, 169, 193; consensual, 232. *See also* representative governance; self-government
Graeber, David, 35
Gray, Obika, 16, 46, 254n9
Great Depression, 258n7
Greeks, 76; ancient, 30
Guantanamo Bay detention facility, 31, 185, 213
Guatemala, 40
Guerrero, state of, 110, 176

guerrillas, xiii, 113, 124, 200, 233, 271n84. *See also* Irish Republican Army; Zapatistas
Guillen, Antonio, 217

Hammurabi, 281n6
Han Chinese, 8
Haney, Craig, 284n57
Hapsburgs, 8
Harvey, Neil, 120, 128, 160–61
Hasketh, Chris, 117, 151, 163, 262n51
H-Blocks, xv, 179, 180, 213, 282nn18,19; isolation regimes in US compared to, 208, 209, 224, 233. *See also* blanketmen
health care, 3, 38, 74, 111, 123–26, 128, 239; community, 121, 123, 125, 126, 138–40, 139*fig*, 175, 274n138; impact of state on, 38, 148, 150, 238, 244; NGO support for, 158; regional systems of, 131, 139–40; unpaid labor in, xiii, 40
hegemony, 20, 91–92, 160, 166, 181, 277n185; regional, 17, 27, 95, 106
Hellie, Richard, 52, 259n15
herding, 28, 43, 40, 44, 71, 105, 107, 177
Hezbollah, 185
Hirschman, Albert, xii, 7, 25–27, 32, 254n9
HM Prison, the Maze. *See* Long Kesh Prison
Hobbes, Thomas, 237
Holland, 20, 28, 43, 49, 91–92, 105
homo sacer (banished person), 30–32, 229
Hopkins, T.K., 6, 19, 33n34, 37–38
Hrushevsky, Mykhailo, 58
Hughes, Brendan, 282n19
Hugo, Victor, xi
humanism, 7, 158
hunger strikes, prisoner, 32; Irish, xi, 186, 194–98, 213, 282n33; Turkish, 185, 201, 202; in US, xiv, 185, 214, 216–19, 221–28, 233, 243, 286n79,82
Huxley, Thomas, 7

Illinois, prisons in, 286n79; federal, 179, 184, 206, 207, 283n47
illiteracy, 10, 274n134
Ilovaiskii, General Dmitri, 261n44
imperialism, 8, 20–21, 197, 235. *See also* Britain, colonialism of; Ottoman Empire; Russian Empire

Independent Confederation of Agricultural Workers and Indians (CIOAC), 123

India, 91, 92

indigenous peoples, 8, 35–36, 90, 142, 145–49, 230, 232, 240, 277n193; autonomy of, 129, 148, 153–54, 161, 163, 236, 239; congresses of, 122–23, 127, 149, 154; institutionalized communities of, 246; loyalty bargain and, 155–58, 161, 171–72; Maoist activists and, 136; Mexican government and, 114–19, 121, 127, 132, 137, 146, 148–49, 154–55, 169, 178, 270n49, 276n162,164; migration of, 166–67; revolts of, 146, 153; women, 132, 134, 141, 159, 167–68, 173, 273n117, 274n132, 279–80n239. See also ethnicity; Mayans

individualism, 10, 29, 179, 205, 208, 281n3, 285n77; competitive, 233, 248, 251. See also possessive individualism

infrapolitics, 15–16, 105, 161–64, 234, 246, 247, 250, 252

infrastructures, 21, 28, 40, 43–45, 105; Zapatista, 40, 44, 128, 149, 151, 156, 158, 175–76, 278n212

innovations, 155, 174, 199; technological, 3, 5, 20, 259n18; social, 8, 285n64

Institute for Mayan Language, 158

Institutional Revolutionary Party (PRI), 115–17, 129, 148, 152, 165, 169, 171, 232

Inter-American Development Bank, 151

Intergalactic Meeting against Neoliberalism and for Humanity, 147

International Court of Human Rights, 199

Ireland, xi–xii, xv, 18, 178; potato famine in, 250. See also Northern Ireland

Irish language, 183, 191–94, 204, 229

Irish Republican Army (IRA), 186–87, 188*fig*, 195–97, 199, 200, 204, 208, 239. See also Northern Ireland, prisoners in

Islam. See Muslims

Islamic State (IS), 251, 252

Islamists, 200, 287n8

isolation, long-term. See F-type prisons; H-blocks; security housing units (SHUs); supermax prisons

Istanbul (Constantinople), xiv, 72

Italy, 155, 257n1

Iusuf, Prince of Nogai Tatars, 57

Ivan III, Tsar, 52

Ivan IV (the Terrible), Tsar, 49, 52, 53, 57, 59, 60, 91, 258n3,7, 259n19

Ivanov, Colonel Ivan, 261n44

Jamaa, Sitawa, 212, 217, 219, 224–25

Jamaica, 1, 16, 17, 21, 27, 46; urban, 252, 254n9

Jaramillo, Rubén, 153

Japan, 43

Jews, 98, 241, 281n6

Jim Crow segregation, 32

joy. See collective joy

Kagarlitsky, Boris, 49, 52, 91, 92, 259n19

Kalmyks, 58, 86

Kaufman, Mara, 126, 141, 145, 159, 164, 174, 280n253

Kazan, 58, 68, 259n15

Kessler, Karl, 7

Khasnabish, Alex, 115

Kingston (Jamaica,), 252

Klein, Hillary, 273n116

Kobane, 251

Kolchin, Peter, 54, 92–94, 260n25

Komlosy, Andrea, 35, 256n39

Korean War, 179

Ko'soi, Kuz'ma, 85–86

Kotoshikhin, Grigorii, 62, 64, 76

Kropotkin, Peter, xii, xiii, 5, 15, 34, 47, 174, 187, 227, 228, 235–36; anarchism of, xiv; on clan societies, 256n24; on cooperation and voluntary association, 5; evolutionary views of, 7–8, 14, 41–42, 182, 233; possessive individualism contradicted by, xv, 36, 108

krug. See Don Cossack Host, governance of

Kuban, 87

Kurdish Workers Party (PKK), 185, 200–205, 239, 283nn38,42,43

Kurds, 18, 162, 178, 183, 200, 252, 281n6. See also F-type prisons

Lacandón Jungle, 110, 116–23, 125, 136, 147, 242; advocates of exploitation of, 175, 271n61; community territory of, 151;

170–74, 273n116; in prisons, 18, 29–30, 181–84, 189–95, 199–201, 205–8, 218, 225–26, 231, 233; reactionary, 251
solitary confinement. *See* F-type prisons; H-blocks; security housing units (SHUs); supermax prisons
South Africa, 8
South America, 1, 39, 125, 212, 287n8
sovereignty, 30–31, 250n26, 129–31, 138, 166; of Don Cossack Host, 54, 56, 60–62, 65–66, 69, 83–89, 97–98, 106, 261n44, 262n52
Soviet Union, xii, 258n5,n7, 287n8
Spain, 155, 259n19
Spanish Succession, War of, 92
Speed, Shannon, 154
Stalin, Joseph, 200, 258nn5,7
Stammheim Prison, 180
State Human Rights Commission (CEDH), 154
Stephen, Lynn, 152, 275n159
Stroganov family, 90
structural escape, 1, 10–11, 25, 43–45, 111, 127, 131, 137, 162, 163
subsistence, 2, 3, 34–42, 44, 234–38, 251; of Don Cossacks, 60, 72, 78, 236–38; of prisoners, 182–83, 195, 227, 240; of Zapatistas, 40, 121, 141, 143–44, 168, 170, 172, 237, 238
supermax prisons, xiv, 18, 28, 178, 205–8, 252, 287n93; behavior modification in, 179, 181, 207, 285n59; federal, 179, 184, 206, 207, 283n47; gangs in, 184, 206, 207. *See also* Ohio State Penitentiary
Suvorov, Aleksandr, 88
Svatikov, S. G., 80
Sweden, 53, 88, 91, 92
Sweezy, Paul A., 3
Sykes, Gresham, 233–34

Tabasco, 141
Taliban, 287n8
Tambiah, Stanley, 80
Tatars, 52, 63, 76, 86–87, 108, 241; Don Host as protection from, 56, 60, 87, 106; Nogai, 57–58; raiding by, 72–73, 80, 260n20

technology, 3, 5, 20, 235, 259n18
Tehachapi Prison, 224–25
TENAZAS, 158
territorial escape, 1, 2, 42, 236
territorialization, 59, 65, 104, 251; of rule and exit, 56, 61–62, 81, 106, 252, 261–62n44, 262n52
Territories in Resistance (Zibechi), 161
Thatcher, Margaret, 194, 196–99, 282n33
Thirty Years War, 53
Tilly, Charles, 23
Time of Troubles, 53, 258n7
Tlatelolco massacre, 116
Tomich, Dale, xii, 22
Tomsk, 77
Trail of Tears, 249
Transcaucasia, 88
trans-ethnic spaces, xi, xiii, xiv
transvaluation, 81, 277n184
Troxell, Danny, xiv, 212–14, 216, 217, 222, 224, 225, 285n77
Tsaritsyn, 68, 69*fig*
Tsing, Anna, 154, 277n193
Tugan-Baronovskii, M. I., 266n170
Turks/Turkey, 18, 56, 58, 65, 72–73, 76, 91, 92, 178, 251; prisoners of, 180, 181, 199, 227, 233, 283nn38,42,43; in war with Russia, 88, 100, 106. *See also* F-type prisons
Turner, Terence, 34
Tuxtla Gutiérrez, 271n70

Ukraine, 58, 60, 64–66, 74, 76, 108
Union of Indigenous Workers, 117
Union of Unions (UU), 122
United Nations: International Covenant on Economic, Social, and Cultural Rights, 154; Rapporteur on Torture, 285–86n79
United States, 16, 33, 138, 155, 199, 229, 233, 248, 287n8; Commission on Safety and Abuse in America's Prisons, 217; Constitution, Eighth Amendment to, 212, 224, 286n80; frontier of, 27, 75; genocide of Guatemalan Mayans sponsored by, 163; hegemony of, 43, 181; imperialism of, 20, 21; Irish Americans in, 197; migration from Mexico to, 166; military

United States *(continued)*
intervention in Mexico by, 113; policy response to political activism in, 180–81, 184, 239; Senate Subcommittee on the Constitution, Civil Rights, and Human Rights, 284n57; subjugation of indigenous peoples in, 8, 249; Supreme Court, 214, 243; in Vietnam War, 192–93; war on terror launched by, 251; Zapatista support in, 158, 170, 173. *See also* NAFTA; security housing units (SHUs); supermax prisons
Urals, 93
Ust'-Medveditskaya, xii, 103, 108

Van der Haar, Gemma, 118–19, 124
Vasiliev, Naum, 68
Velaso Suárez, Manuel, 122–23
Venezuela, 250
Vietnam War, 192–93
Villa, Pancho, 113, 251
voice, xii, xv, 7, 13–14, 24, 25–27, 30–32, 36, 234; antisystemic, 250, 252; of prisoners, 183, 191–94, 197, 204, 217–18, 220–23, 229. *See also under* Don Cossack Host; Zapatistas
Volga region, 52, 60, 259n15
Volgograd, xii, 96
Voronezh, 61, 87

Wacquant, Loic, 181, 256n31
Wallace, Alfred Russell, 7
Wallerstein, Immanuel, xiv, 2, 5, 19, 21, 24, 37–38, 48–49, 94, 255n2, 257nn1,2, 259nn15,19
Weills, Anne, 219
West Virginia, 286n79
Wilde, Oscar, 192
Wilken, Claudia, 224
Williamson, James, 217
Wobblies and Zapatistas (Grubačić and Lynd), xii
Wolf, Naomi, 212
Womack, John, 272n104
Women's Revolutionary Law, (1993), 132, 167
work ethic, 35

World Bank, 171
world-economy. *See* capitalist world-system
world time, 43–44, 235, 237, 239, 243, 247–52, 285n64; black holes outside of, 15–17, 19, 105, 163, 180, 247; exilic spaces in, 24–25, 47, 105, 163, 183, 232, 241, 245
World Wars, 180, 258n7
Wright, Erik Olin, 6

Ya Basta! network, 150*fig*
Yandell, Ronnie, 217
Yashchenko, Slava, xii
Youngstown State University, xiv
Yugoslavia, xii–xiv, 250

Zacatecas, 279n237
Zapata, Emiliano, 113–15, 272n104, 276n162, 277n184
Zapatistas (EZLN), xv, xvi, 2, 47, 48, 109–79, 230, 233, 237, 249, 252, 272n97, 275n156, 276n172, 277n184; autonomy of, 78, 111, 126–28, 144, 156, 161, 165, 176, 180, 198, 238; civil society of, 155–61, 275n154; communication system of, 274n136; economy of, 4, 18, 40, 140–44, 170–74, 246–47, 275n149; education system of, xiii, 40, 111, 121, 131, 133, 137–40, 158, 169–70, 175, 349; ethnicity of, xiii–xiv, 277n190; exilic formation of, 119–24; gender issues of, 131–34, 141, 143, 159, 167–68, 172–73, 244–45, 273nn116,117, 274n132, 279–80n239; governance of, 4, 17–18, 134–37, 169; health care provided by, 139*fig*, 139–40, 274n138; impact of changing world-economy on, 161–64; international supporters of, 278n198; loyalty bargains of, 18, 111, 142, 144–57, 160–67, 172, 175, 191, 195, 228, 238–40, 248, 277n193, 278n200, 279n227; membership of, 131–34, 164–69; Mexican Revolution and origins of, 113–16; Other Campaign (La Otra) of, 79, 128, 159–61, 176, 228, 242; territorial escape of, 1, 12, 17, 28, 128–31, 164–69, 231, 272n104; voice of, 81, 113, 128, 138,